CW00555837

Such Sweet Thunder

Also by Dominic Green

Benny Green: Words and Music

Such Sweet Thunder

Benny Green on Jazz

∾

Edited by Dominic Green

Foreword by Elvis Costello

First published in Great Britain by Scribner, 2001
An imprint of Simon & Schuster UK Ltd
A Viacom Company

1 3 5 7 9 10 8 6 4 2

Simon & Schuster UK Ltd
Africa House
64–78 Kingsway
London WC2B 6AH

Simon & Schuster Australia
Sydney

A CIP catalogue record for this book is available
from the British Library

ISBN 0-7432-0835-8

Typeset in Sabon by Palimpsest Book Production Limited
Polmont, Stirlingshire

Printed and bound in Great Britain by
The Bath Press, Bath

Contents

'. . . I never heard
So musical a discord, such sweet thunder'.

Shakespeare, *A Midsummer Night's Dream*

FOREWORD

Elvis Costello

One Sunday afternoon in the early 1980s, I was making a guest appearance on a Radio One music show. We were playing an 'exclusive preview' of tracks from my latest album. My attitude to the media in those days was not famously co-operative. Nevertheless, the DJ was attempting some matey small talk. He had willingly played one or two of my records in the past, so we were not actually enemies or anything.

The programme stumbled on through another of our new, not very Radio One-friendly cuts. As the music faded away, my host began a new line of enquiry in his still youthful and confidential Canadian delivery, 'So, Elvis,' . . . always an unlikely opening for a conversation . . . 'If this were a regular Sunday afternoon at home, what would you be doing?' Without hesitation, I answered truthfully if with careless disregard for his feelings: 'Listening to Benny Green.'

Benny, I should remind you, was broadcasting on Radio Two at the very same moment. I was just being honest. At that time, I hardly ever turned on the radio to hear the pop music of the day. I had a shelf full of records to play and I could talk rubbish all by myself. However, Sunday afternoon was completely different.

Over on Radio Two, Benny might take one song and present us with its history, tales of the writers and performers, then play several recorded versions that would turn the tune inside out and reveal all its charm and beauty. He seemed to revel in playing the Ella Fitzgerald version of 'Bewitched, Bothered And Bewildered', the one with all of the vaguely risqué verses. Perhaps it was also here that I first heard Louis Armstrong's rendition of 'Let's Do It' – a nine-minute virtuoso lesson in delivering a punch line. It was the kind of show that took the time and had the pace and the place to appreciate riches. When it came to the art of Coleman Hawkins or the debt that the Benny Goodman Orchestra owed to the genius of Fletcher Henderson, Benny Green could take a theme, sustain it and embellish it delightfully.

The result of these Sunday masterclasses in jazz and vocal music appreciation was that I could nearly always be found in Potter's Music Shop at the foot of Richmond Hill on a Monday afternoon hunting for something played on the Benny Green show the day before. I had bought my first serious guitar in this shop when I was thirteen; my mother had worked there for a while in the 1960s, so I had been as regular a customer as pocket money allowed. Now, the owner, Gerry Southard and his wife Ann must have wondered about me coming with my new pop star cash to burn, seeking rare Lee Wiley records. Gerry and I would discuss the merits of Benny's selections and I would sometimes be directed to yet another valuable interpretation of the tune in question. More often than not I went home with a selection of titles first heard on Sunday afternoon. I should have a Benny Green shelf for all those discs. It's either that or we'll have to burn some of the furniture to make room for all this music.

This book is a wonderful collection of Benny Green's writings. The musical appreciation and anecdotes are sometimes founded in the experience of a working musician. Other times, obscure quotations, pieces of background detail or the vivid descriptions of people and places are teased out until the glorious main point emerges. That dry and laconic radio manner can also be detected in print.

You may find compassionate estimation more than combative criticism in these pages. Everybody has an opinion but when it is surrounded and supported by history, humour and the telling of a wonderful tale you are more gently persuaded. Most of all, this is a voice that likes to celebrate more than to break down. There is nothing quite like it in the brittle and trite cacophony of modern critical posturing. At the risk of sounding like an old fool who longs for days that I can barely remember, I shall be diving into these writings from time to time to remind myself of a voice, in every sense, to which I shall always be grateful. In the end, it all leads back to the music.

INTRODUCTION

Dominic Green

Jazz, as Benny Green observed, is the Reluctant Art. America's only indigenous art form was born in the stews of New Orleans in the early years of the twentieth century, having been conceived in 'such cultural innocence that it never even knew it was a form of artistic expression at all'.* Over the following decades, jazz grew so vigorously that within the lifespan of a reasonably tenacious founding father, such as Louis Armstrong (1900–71), it progressed from ginmill to concert hall and from primitivism to post-modernism. In the process, it became a fully-fledged art form whether it had wanted to or not.

Taking as its tools the basics of blues improvisation, jazz discovered the ideal vehicle in the 'standard', the thirty-two bar popular song from Tin Pan Alley whose discreetly complex chords were fecund soil for progressively more and more elaborate improvising. The early and middle decades of the twentieth century were blessed with an almost improbable succession of songwriting talent, the Gershwins, Kerns and Berlins of legend. Through their cross-fertilization with cinema, the sons of Tin Pan Alley were party to that most entertaining of mongrel spectaculars, the Hollywood Musical. By hijacking the songs of these composers and stripping them down to the essentials of rhythm and harmony, jazz created some of the most exciting and dynamic music ever to reach the human ear. And if jazz is now to be considered a finite form, to be consigned to the history of the American Century, then it is only because its creative impulse has been so triumphantly shared among its many-hued pop progeny, who despite their own crudity cannot help but show

---

* *The Reluctant Art*, p. 15 (1962).

their immense debt to jazz and its less articulate cousin, the Blues.

In retrospect, the pace of jazz's growth from its raucous infancy in the brothels of Storyville to its dignified frequenting of the concert hall is as staggering as the notion that Louis Armstrong, born in a time when 'powered flight' suggested a man strapping on a pair of homemade wings, should by the time of his death have seen a man land on the moon. The aesthetic rattle bag that produced jazz was mainly composed of fragments from the nineteenth century: vestigial West African rhythms, the work songs and spirituals of recently-emancipated slaves, the instrumentation of a marching band, vaudeville hoofing, and a smattering of popular song. Because of the jazz musician's constant search for new harmonies on which to experiment, the equally variegated influences of the standard soon became part of the blend: light opera from Vienna, folk songs from Eastern Europe, a dash of Gilbert & Sullivan, and a pinch of Classical music. Yet with all those elements now seeming archly distant, the fruit of their synthesis has been durable enough for jazz to become the grand old man of popular music, even engaging in vigorous debate with electronic dance music as we enter the twenty-first century.

Indeed, jazz's prodigious growth was often thoroughly disorientating at the time, for practitioners and audience alike. When that quixotic tenorist Coleman Hawkins first picked up the saxophone as a teenager, the instrument was 'little more than a vaudeville joke'.* In 1929, he announced himself as its first great stylist with 'One Hour', dragging the jazz saxophone into adulthood, and in the process giving Adolphe Sax the first of many posthumous revolutions. By 1939, although now challenged for his crown by Lester Young, the staggering fluency and poetry of Hawkins's extemporizations on 'Body And Soul' represented the apogee of the Swing Era solo, an event which seemed to many syncopated Hegelians to be roughly equivalent to the End of History. But by 1949, Hawkins, though still universally admired, was considered to have been superannuated by the Modern jazz of Lester's acolyte Charlie Parker, and 'Body And Soul' now seemed one distant occluded peak among many. By 1959, the stylistic fine tunings Hawkins had made in the wake of Parker's

---

**Drums in my Ears*, p. 149 (1973).

innovations led many commentators to decide that Hawkins had now caught up with the Bebop generation, although this may seem an eccentric way of looking at things, given that most of them were yet to catch up with the Hawkins of 'Body And Soul'. And by the time of his death in 1969, with the avant garde and electric rock in full spate, Hawkins's appearances in jazz clubs were exciting the sort of historical interest and totemic reverence that would barely have been surpassed had he ceded the stage to a freshly defrosted woolly mammoth.

Entangled with jazz's hysterical growth from innocent simplicity to debauched sophistication was a similar journey from gimmick to art form, with all the self-consciousness, refinement and flummery that comes with that exalted status. And as with all art forms, with self-consciousness there came self-reference: the chorus of comment and analysis, gossip and fantasy, generally euphemized as Criticism. Flaubert might have been prophesying jazz writing when he remarked that 'the explanation of one artistic form by another is a monstrosity'. As a punctiliously democratic art, jazz has no minimum requirements of its would-be Boswells, other than effrontery. And as the history of jazz's attendant literature has shown, it is entirely possible to earn a living from it while still being under the misapprehension that a cornet is only a receptacle for ice cream. Every drama needs its comedians; in jazz, they have as often been offstage as on, and sometimes both.

For the critic, there were three problems. There was the music itself, which, relying heavily on instrumental improvisation and the rhythmic elixir of swing, has succeeded in reducing the most competent of rocket scientists to raving gibberish. There were also the musicians themselves. They were usually less concerned with aesthetics than with the more immediate pressures of making a living in an unpredictable and distant satrapy of show business, and they had developed a mistrust of jazz writing through bitter experience as the subjects of their interlocutors' fantastical projections. And there was the rate of the music's growth, whose sheer speed made all judgement relative and most criticism merely partisan. How was a critic to keep his professional feet in, say, the early 1960s, when, with Miles Davis and John Coltrane leading jazz into new and exotic territory, many among the younger jazz audience were agitating for a Trad Revival, a studiously gormless nostalgia that was the equivalent of turning on a halogen bulb in order to study plans for returning to the Stone Age? Perhaps the only way of attempting an informed judgement was by a blend of personal experience and perceptive analysis.

Although I must confess a filial bias in the matter, jazz has had few more erudite and able critics than Benny Green, a man who combined a player's feel for the music and its makers with an aesthetic informed as equally by Gershwin, George, as by Shaw, George Bernard. Uniquely among critics, before becoming a writer, Benny was a successful jazz saxophonist, running the musical gamut from the Galtymore Irish Country Dance Band to the orchestras of Ronnie Scott and Stan Kenton. It was this personal experience of jazz that was to be the bedrock of his critical faculty, the practical seedbed to which he referred constantly in his criticism. The years spent wrestling with the harmonies of the standards and the keys of the saxophone had given Benny the privilege of the insider, an intimate understanding of jazz and of the people behind its instruments. To this, he added a passion for literature that was to make him a self-made man of letters, an autodidact whose education had mostly been acquired on the long coach journeys that punctuated a touring band's gigs in 1950s Britain. Benny was surprised to find out that 'among the several inconsistencies about that charming but doomed young man [Bix Beiderbecke] was his ability to quote whole pages verbatim from the works of P. G. Wodehouse'.* This from a saxophonist who, apart from his work as a jazz writer, was also a biographer of Wodehouse, and wrote on subjects as varied as George Bernard Shaw, boxing, the Music Hall, seaside postcards, Alan Jay Lerner, and cricket, not forgetting two novels, the libretti for various musicals, and the scripts for over a thousand radio shows.

From the late 1950s to the late 1990s, Benny wrote on every aspect of jazz, on its players, its songwriters, and its audience. He wrote reviews, sleevenotes and articles on dozens of musicians, and books about the great songwriters. His style alternately

***The Reluctant Art*, p. 9 (1962).

pedagogic and comedic, he wrote about jazz with the affection of a lifelong friend and the passion of a disciple. In the process, and only a little less consciously than the Reluctant Artists he wrote about, he wrote an episodic history of their Reluctant Art, from George Lewis and Louis Armstrong to John Coltrane and Roland Kirk. The collection of Benny's writing in this volume is not an official history; it is far too committed in its beliefs and too honest in its responses for that. It is more like the snapshots that fill a photo album after a peculiarly interesting life, a personal take from the perspective of one who lived it. It may well be that our snapshots are a truer record of our lives than any number of staged portraits.

Benny Green was born in 1927, on the day that Louis Armstrong and The Hot Five recorded 'Struttin' With Some Barbecue', and died in 1998, a few weeks after Frank Sinatra began his residency in the Great Saloon In The Sky. It is difficult not to derive symbolic satisfaction from such coincidences, as Benny's life was constantly and intimately bound up with jazz. Raised in a predominantly Jewish area of the West End by a hard-working mother and an indolent saxophonist father who had been one of the pioneers of British jazz in the 1920s, Benny's earliest memories were of the popular songs that his large extended family would play on the radio and gramophone. While being 'uneducated' at Marylebone Grammar School and enduring the Blitz, the thirteen-year-old Benny began to learn to the rudiments of the tenor saxophone from his father, who by now had thrown over musicianship for the greater challenge of escrying whatever intentions lurked in the pinhead minds of greyhounds, and then speculating on them with his wife's earnings.

By the time he had fallen in love with Lester Young's playing and had begun to emulate it studiously, Benny was receiving advanced tuition from one of Britain's leading dance band saxophonists, his father's old bandmate Harry Hayes. After a long and often comic teenage apprenticeship playing with small groups in the youth club and Jewish wedding circuits of London, Benny went on the road in 1948, at the age of twenty-one. It was the beginning of over a decade spent trawling around the long-since vanished world of Britain's *palais de danse*, the touring life that Sinatra memorably characterized as 'a cross-country college'.

Over the next five years, Benny gravitated through numerous dance bands and innumerable boarding houses, lugging with him either a tenor or baritone sax, a bag of dirty laundry, and a typewriter. He passed through the employ of Freddie Randall, Bertie King, Ralph Sharon, Lew Stone and Roy Fox, before being spotted by Ronnie Scott in late 1952. Scott was in the process of forming the famous nine-piece orchestra that more than any other was to bring Modern jazz into the dance halls of Britain, and the years 1953–5 passed in a whirl that, while its routine may have become grimly familiar in previous years, was musically the most thrilling of Benny's career.

A few days after the Manchester debut of the orchestra, Benny was back in London to make his debut as a jazz critic. The occasion was a historic one for British jazz. In a self-defeating attempt to protect its own interests, if not those of its members, the Musicians' Union had for many years imposed a virtual embargo on visiting American musicians, by insisting that as the appearance of Americans on British stages deprived the local players of work, it should be reciprocated in kind by American promoters. Although the theory may have been sound, in practice this ruling meant that British players and fans were cut off from direct contact with the American sources of their inspiration, as any potential British export to America would be in the invidious position of taking low-grade coal to Newcastle. Thus, the Musicians' Union handicapped the development of its own membership and starved the potential audience for jazz of its best players.

Given this antediluvian farce, it was appropriate that the opportunity to end it came with the severe floods of the winter of 1952–3, and the emergency fundraising they engendered. The mercurial American promoter Norman Granz offered the services of his star-studded 'Jazz at the Philharmonic' touring package for a charity concert, on condition that the embargo was temporarily lifted. The concert duly proceeded at the Gaumont State, Kilburn, on 8 March 1953. To preserve the dignity of the Musicians' Union, the first half of the show was composed of British musicians: Harry Hayes's group, with Benny on baritone, and then the Ronnie Scott Sextet. The second half was for Granz's stars. By now sitting in the stalls with his critical hat on, Benny was as dazzled as the rest of the audience by the opener, when

Oscar Peterson tore into a Protean reading of 'C Jam Blues', as he was by the performances of Ella Fitzgerald and his hero Lester Young, whose burnished, metallic tone was intact, despite using a plastic mouthpiece and an instrument held together with plastic bands. The embargo had been broken, although Granz was never to receive the knighthood he deserved for this service to British culture. Musically sobering for the qualitative gulf it exposed between the British and American players, the night was inspiring for a critic, especially one whose current employer, the *New Musical Express*, would try to wedge him into the role of court jester, with bylines such as 'The Musician with a Sense of Humour', 'The Damon of Dance', 'The Runyon of Rhythm', and perhaps most excruciatingly, 'The Saxophonist with a Twinkle in his Typewriter'.

In 1956, after Ronnie's nine-piece had briefly expanded into a full-scale big band and then promptly deflated, Benny found himself working with the Stan Kenton Orchestra during their British tour, after Kenton had sent home his regular baritonist for a narcotic indiscretion. It was probably the apogee of Benny's career, but such was his growing preoccupation with writing and his equally fervid dislike of the touring life that instead of capitalizing on this success, Benny went to ground almost immediately afterwards. He took a job in a holiday camp orchestra on the Isle of Wight, correctly supposing that there was little else to do but read when he wasn't discharging his light orchestral duties. After all, it had worked for Lord Tennyson, who had perpetrated *The Charge of The Light Brigade* just down the road. A year later, a change of editors at the *NME* deposited Benny at *Record Mirror*, a publication whose brow was marginally higher – 'Modernists! Benny Green is the man for you!' – but it was not until 1958, by which time Benny was moonlighting in the rock'n'roll band Lord Rockingham's XI on the dubiously pioneering TV show *Oh Boy!*, that he found a niche as a writer, when the legendary critic Kenneth Tynan hired him as jazz critic for the *Observer*. Only months later, a chance encounter with Norman Granz led to Benny becoming first choice as sleevenote writer for Granz's labels, first with Verve, and then with Pablo.

Granz had a fan's love of the music. In Benny's writing, he had found an ideal literary complement. Over the next decades,

Benny wrote dozens of notes for Granz, including his Grammy-nominated set for *The Tatum Solo Masterpieces*, and an acclaimed essay for the reissue of *The Ella Fitzgerald Songbooks*, in which Granz had preserved for posterity one of the leading exponents of the American popular song at the peak of her powers, often with Nelson Riddle's arrangements as a setting. With changes in technology and taste, the art of the sleevenote has gone the way of the daguerreotype, the silent movie pianist, and that literary form which is the sleevenote's highbrow parent, the essay. As Norman Granz realized with his *Tatum* and *Songbook* projects, it is the peculiar fate of the popular arts that their greatest moments can be a hit one year, and totally obscure the next. Jazz, as an art reliant upon the most fleeting of inspirations (popular hits of the day) and the most challenging of remits (spontaneous improvisation of new melodies), is more susceptible than most to this cultural amnesia. As Benny put it, with apologies to the Bard, 'Now is the winter of our discotheque.'

It is hard to imagine, in these days when Jazz Studies flourish in the leafier groves of Academe, that in 1958 serious and informed writing on jazz was as rare as a Dave Brubeck joke. Indeed, the general tone was still creakingly arch. It was best exemplified by the autobiographical self-promotions of a sociable rogue, raconteur and trumpeter named Mezz Mezzrow, whose style was heavy on hip witticisms and coy reefers, and light on musical analysis. His *Really the Blues* (1946) retailed luridly prurient tales of the Prohibition-era antics of Mezzrow, Bix Beiderbecke, and Louis Armstrong, but mainly Mezzrow, in a tone more fantastical than musicological. Despite the cloud of reefer smoke in which he seems to have spent his entire adult life, Mezzrow had intuited at least one of the fundamental truths about the relationship between artist and audience in this most misunderstood of art forms. In a relationship that historically had consisted of mutual incomprehension, Mezzrow knew that what the public wanted to hear about was not how a small but passionate group of young black musicians were developing the harmonic frontiers of their music at an astonishing rate in adverse social conditions, but rather the irresistible combination of hot music, illicit substances, fast women and slow horses that the popular imagination suspected (or hoped) were the staff of the jazz musician's life.

Judging from the advertising industry's remorseless annexation of jazz's imagery in the 1980s, it probably still is.

What non-sensationalist writing was available to the discerning 1950s punter was dominated by a small but perfectly formed coterie of American critics, at whose pointed head sat the professorial Leonard Feather. These writers, though admirable for their willingness to recognise great jazz as great art, made the mistake that Brubeck, the Modern Jazz Quartet, and many of the post-Coltrane Sixties avant garde were to make: in their pious efforts to confer intellectual gravitas on the music, they took most of the life and all of the fun out of it. Feather may have compiled a pioneering *Encyclopaedia of Jazz*, but many of his acolytes wrote like men compiling a telephone directory.

Among the British, a people in whose consciousness jazz had traditionally come second to morris dancing, jazz criticism had taken an improbable turn from the start. Of course, back in the hedonistic 1920s, Jazz Age jollity had excited the British literati as much as it did any flapper at one of Jay Gatsby's celebrated parties, where the guests danced to 'the stiff, tinny drip of the banjos' and the syncopated tourism of Vladimir Tostoff's *Jazz History of the World*.* Even the capacious cerebellum of a squinting wallflower like Aldous Huxley could be stirred to tap a well-read toe to the gramophone at Lady Ottoline Morrell's bashes, finding the 'primitive' energy of jazz to be the ideal antidote to post-war ennui, and too much Bach.

> *Dancing, dancing . . . Oh if only, thought Helen, one could go on dancing forever! If only one didn't have to spend all that time doing other things! Wrong things, mostly, stupid things, things one was sorry for after they were done . . .*
>
> *'Yes, sir, she's my baby! No, sir . . .' Gerry broke off his humming. 'I won sixty pounds at poker last night,' he said. 'Pretty good, eh?'*†

But these inter-war writers used jazz as a kind of cultural shorthand. It wasn't jazz writing as such, only writing with jazz in it.

*F. Scott Fitzgerald, *The Great Gatsby* (1925), Everyman edn, p. 39 (1991).
†Aldous Huxley, *Eyeless in Gaza*, p. 159 (1936).

Jazz was deployed as a literary strategy. It was a symbol, symptomatic of troubled times, representing deracination or debauchery, enervation or alienation. Very often, it was used to signify a cultural shallowness, thrown about with the same intellectual abandon as the Beat writers were to show twenty years later when they used it to show their cultural profundity. With such weighty matters as the Decline of The West on their minds, no one thought to actually write about the music itself, although Stravinsky was already conducting his own experiments at blending jazz and modern classical forms. And even the great Igor seems to have preferred his jazz in the abstract. When, during his ill-fated Californian sojourn of 1946, Charlie Parker sought an audience with the hero with whom he felt he had so much in common, Stravinsky wouldn't open the door to him. Then again, it was the middle of the night.

No one could have foreseen what would happen in the next generation, not even in a country as notoriously eccentric as Britain. With jazz's growth from 1920s novelty to a solid if derided piece of cultural furniture, a modest documentary literature began to accumulate around it in the 1950s. This was mainly through the efforts of Feather and company, most notably Nat Shapiro and Nat Hentoff's collection of interviews *Hear Me Talkin' To Ya* (1955). (We shall pass discreetly over Jack Kerouac's *On the Road* (1957), in which the author attempts to construct a philosophical system whose twin pillars are Zen Buddhism and Slim Gaillard.) In Britain, where the music had always been a fringe interest, writing about it became the province of eccentrics who funded their habit from other sources. When Benny was hired by Kenneth Tynan in 1958, the company he found himself in was a bizarre blend of aristocrats and eggheads. The peers among whom he now found himself included a real peer (the Honourable Gerald Lascelles), a leading poet (in the curmudgeonly form of Philip Larkin), and the country's foremost Marxist historian, Eric Hobsbawm.

It is a perfect testimony to the ironies of British society that while the Honourable Lascelles felt able to lower himself precipitately from the Second Estate to the Fourth and still use his own name, Professor Hobsbawm's jazz moonlighting took place under the *nom de guerre* 'Francis Newton'. Hobsbawm did not want to undermine his academic credibility by writing about jazz under his own name. He may also have been concerned that his readers might confuse him with Professor Longhair. Either way, it was almost certainly because of his Marxist convictions that Hobsbawm became perhaps the only figure in jazz history who, when he took on a pseudonym, didn't elevate himself to the peerage in the process. Surprisingly for a historian who has occasionally combined his professional and amateur studies into single works,* Hobsbawm is yet to ponder the influence of Karl Marx upon the formation of the Ronnie Scott Orchestra in 1953. This was a unique co-operative whose members shared all profits and losses, an arrangement deemed so radical at the time that one of the 'syncopated Romanovs' who ran a rival dance band of the day was moved to denounce Scott's orchestra as 'musical Communism'. It goes without saying that the influence of the other three Marx Brothers upon that orchestra is better documentated.

As for the other British critics, the Honourable Lascelles wrote with great enthusiasm and little knowledge about a subject he obviously loved greatly but understood not at all, although he could at least feel at home among jazz's veritable shooting party of aristocrats, such as King Oliver, Duke Ellington, Count Basie and the Earls Bostic and Hines, not forgetting the Dukes of Dixieland. Meanwhile, Philip Larkin was, as might be expected, so fanatically Luddite in his preference for pre-Modern jazz that if Jabbo Smith had been playing at the time of the Crimean war, Larkin would no doubt have insisted he was best listened to from inside a wet balaclava, and preferably while suffering from trench foot.

Having passed the best part of fifteen years sitting in the stocks, Benny was well aware of the value of a well-flung tomato. The ripest of these were reserved for what he saw as the hucksters and con-artists that periodically cluttered the public's consciousness, from the 'popinjay' Swing Era bandleaders whose knowledge of musical theory consisted of little more than theatrical arm waving and suave microphone technique, to the earnest mien and constipated fumblings of Dave Brubeck in the 1950s, and, in the following decade, the gleeful iconoclasm with which

*See Francis Newton, *The Jazz Scene* (1959), and parts of Eric Hobsbawm, *Uncommon People* (1998).

Ornette Coleman and the 'nebulous messiahs' of the Free Jazz mob set about the destruction of the fruits of half a century's worth of harmonic and melodic enquiry. As critics are usually the incarnation of Wilde's cynic in their willingness to tout the price of everything while knowing the value of nothing, Benny's writing is exceptional in its belief that the many-splendoured virtues of jazz were, if barely time-hallowed, certainly precious enough to defend.

The twenty-two year period of Benny's tenure at the *Observer* was a fascinating but torrid one for jazz. In 1958, three years after the death of Charlie Parker, many of the music's originators were still at large, and, in the case of Joe Turner, were still larger than most. The great internecine war between Trad and Modern still generated skirmishes in the music press. Two years ahead lay Miles Davis's crucial *Kind of Blue*, which fled Bop's chordal torrent for the airier spaces of modal harmony, and beyond that lay John Coltrane's most radical recordings. By 1980, having passed through the turbulence of the 1960s avant garde and 1970s rock, jazz was, oddly enough, on the verge of a return to its classical values of Swing and standards, as evinced by the rise of Wynton Marsalis and the neo-Bop school of the 1980s. Perhaps it was the sobering rate at which jazz was losing its greatest players that induced the increased historical reflection of that decade.

Having been born in the 1920s, when jazz was still digesting its first exploratory nibbles at the apple of harmonic knowledge, and having learnt to play the saxophone in the 1940s, when the innovations of Parker and Gillespie dragged the form into technical maturity, Benny was keenly aware of the effect that the passage of time had on the music. As each era passes, the thin slices of shellac, vinyl and CD it leaves behind become an important cultural testimony. As his own career progressed, Benny became increasingly involved in the work of interpreting that testimony, and recording the stories behind it. To his surprise, jazz didn't pass into obscurity with virtually everything else he had grown up with. To his great surprise, two of his sons became jazz musicians, although we occasionally confirmed his worst fears about the general downward trend of civilization with our barbarian tendency towards pop music. And to his even greater surprise, when Leo and I stirred him into picking up the saxophone again, he found there was a large audience for his tenor style, even though he found it mildly perturbing that although his style was the same, he had 'regressed from the avant garde to the last ditch without any sensation of movement'.*

The writing in this collection represents a unique and often very personal testimony of the music and musicians of the American Century. As Benny observed in his sleevenote to Pablo's substantial Joe Pass box-set in 1997, 'Posterity is alive and well.'

Dominic Green
London, 2001

**The Reluctant Art*, preface to the Da Capo edition, p. 7 (1991).

I

Drums in my Ears

Criticism 1958–1986

Drums in my Ears (1973)

I was indeed born with drums in my ears, more or less. My first connections with jazz were established on 9 December 1927, when, by performing the act of being born, I acquired among other things a saxophone playing father. Under his benign tutelage I blew a soprano saxophone for the first time in November 1941, and blew it for the first time before an audience not composed exclusively of blood relatives in February 1943. As my repertoire at the time consisted in its entirety of an old jazz standard called 'Whispering' and a tearjerker of the period called 'Whispering Grass', I had no alternative but to keep repeating this oddly *sotto voce* repertoire throughout the evening, but nobody seemed to notice, least of all the dancers, too preoccupied as usual with the fluctuations of their own private dramas to hear the music.

The occasion was an obscure club dance in a church hall somewhere at the back of Marble Arch and was an event of the deepest possible significance for me for two reasons. First, it was my initiation into the terrifying rite of performing before people who, having paid for admission, consider themselves to be finer judges of music than the musicians, who have not only not paid for admission, but have actually turned up expecting to be paid for it; second, it planted in my mind, numbed though it was by a lack of worldliness approaching complete imbecility, the tiny seed of a suspicion destined not to flower for many years yet, that perhaps not all those who strove for technical mastery over an instrument were moved by purely aesthetic motives. Something about the way the drummer kept grumbling about his fee, allied to the persistence with which his friend, the clarinettist, kept checking the findings of the clock on the facing wall with those of his wristwatch, suggested as much to me. The truth of these suspicions, that there might just conceivably be such a thing as a musician who disliked music, or had no real interest in its welfare, was confirmed long after, when I discovered that, of the members of that very first band, one had become a recording executive and the other a successful music publisher.

I, on the other hand, was an apprentice of palpitating sincerity, a fanatic with the lily of aesthetic endeavour clutched so firmly between my teeth that very often there was no room there for my saxophone mouthpiece. This proved true on a Saturday night in June 1947, when, booked to appear for the first time with a band whose members included two real professionals, I was so disturbed by the prospect of my coming ordeal that I was unable to get any sleep the night before, and finally turned up for the engagement minus the mouthpiece of my instrument. The occasion was a dance at the Wilkinson Sword factory in Acton and there was nothing for me to do but leave my colleagues to struggle on without me, while I turned round and went back by public transport to my home in Euston, where I found my mouthpiece in the top drawer of the bureau, wrapped lovingly in a sheet of clean muslin in which condition I was in the habit of leaving it after each day's practice. Grabbing it, I travelled back to Acton, where I arrived just in time to play two choruses of 'Pennies From Heaven' and one of the National Anthem before returning once more to Euston. For this sustained feat of mobility the bandleader paid me the sum of thirty-two shillings, which, representing as it did an increase of nearly 1300 per cent on my Marble Arch church hall debut, left me contented enough.

The first time I played with a band and was then invited to come back and play with it again was on 1 January 1949, and the occasion when, comprising one seventh of a fully professional orchestra, presumably I became fully professional myself, occurred exactly six months later, on 1 July 1949. It was on an afternoon during this engagement that I recognized among the crowd of eight or ten people which comprised our average tea dance attendance, the face of Ronnie Scott, a musician I hero-worshipped so violently at the time that from the moment I spotted him I found myself unable to produce enough saliva to produce a sound from my instrument, and was therefore reduced to the ignominy of pretending to tinker with the mechanism of my saxophone, of whose structure and workings I had, of course, not the remotest conception.

Two years later I was hired to play for the first time in an orchestra not unknown to the general public, and a year later I became a member of a quintet led by the same Ronnie Scott. It was at this time, in December 1952, that a musical performance of mine was analysed in print for the first time ('. . . although a newcomer to these columns . . . already a most accomplished performer . . .'), although by this time, having already seen myself in print twice in the musical press, I was less inclined to take the event with quite the same degree of seriousness I might have done a year or two earlier.

In the spring of 1955 I began contributing a weekly column to one of the musical papers, on any subject I pleased, although there was an unspoken agreement between the editor and myself that I must not poach on the preserves of the 'serious' reviewers on the staff, it being generally thought at that time that a practical knowledge of making jazz was an insuperable barrier to writing about it coherently. In 1957 the editorship of this paper changed hands, which meant that all the new editor's journalistic friends replaced all the old editor's journalistic friends, including myself. A month later I joined a rival musical weekly, where I soon drifted into the duties of film, jazz, drama and literary reviewer and Elian essayist, juggling with so many noms de plume that there were some weeks when the column under my own name consisted in its entirety of bitter debate with other aspects of my splintered journalistic self.

Some time after I began my weekly pieces, but before I changed papers, I met Kenneth Tynan. All I can remember of this meeting is that it occurred in an all-night jazz club in Lisle Street, and that Tynan's debut as the *Observer* drama critic was due in a few hours' time. Two years later he suddenly phoned to ask me if I would be interested in applying for the job of jazz critic on his paper, explaining to me that I should submit a few published pieces for scrutiny. At that time, although still a working jazz musician, with the Dizzy Reece Quintet, I happened to be involved in a very brief but very exotic episode as the figurehead of an enterprise called Jazz City, an institution which must surely have established some kind of record for the amazing rapidity of its decline from opulence to utter pauperdom, there being 1050 paying customers at our opening Saturday night, and twelve at our closing one six weeks later. (On our second night, having booked John Dankworth's Orchestra, we found ourselves so flooded with customers that at one point, while helping a relative of mine to sneak in for nothing through the back entrance, I was locked out of the building, and had the piquant experience of bunking into my own club.)

Tynan agreed to come down to Jazz City one Saturday night to collect my literary samples, and although I have no idea what it was I gave him to read, I do recall quite distinctly that in spite of strict orders to my partners in the box-office that Tynan, being on an errand of mercy so to speak, should be allowed in free, he and his friends were obliged to pay 8s 6d a head for the privilege of collecting a few of my press cuttings. Nevertheless some months later I joined the *Observer*.

I am unable to account for any of the incidents in this odd tale, least of all why Tynan, who hardly knew me, and had almost certainly never read me, should have taken so much trouble to alter the course of my life, which he did beyond any question, in the most benign sense.

On the day my first review appeared, on the Beaulieu Jazz Festival, August Bank Holiday 1958, jazz was in several respects still a comparatively innocent music. It is true that Miles Davis was already committed to the experiments involving the abandonment of the hitherto obligatory frame of harmonic progression from discord to resolution, true also that names like Sonny Rollins and John Coltrane were familiar to all students of the music. On the other hand, both Louis Armstrong and Duke Ellington were still young enough to have produced some of their finest work only a year or two before, Armstrong with *Satch Plays Fats*, Ellington with his Shakespearean vignettes, *Such Sweet Thunder*. Players like Dizzy Gillespie and Jay Jay Johnson, Cannonball Adderley and Oscar Peterson were still regarded as extreme Moderns, and the degree of our innocence may be gauged from the fact that only a year previously, in New York in 1957, Ronnie Scott had advised me to come and see 'the greatest saxophonist in the world', Sonny Stitt, who was appearing across the river in Newark, and that after taking Scott's advice, I saw no reason to argue with his description.

Many of the dominant figures of the pre-war Swing Age were still not only alive but kicking. Lester Young and Billie Holiday, Coleman Hawkins and Johnny Hodges, Sidney Bechet and Billy Strayhorn, Jack Teagarden and Henry Allen – none of these had qualified yet for memorial albums. Art Tatum and Clifford Brown had been dead only two years, Charlie Parker three, Django Reinhardt five. As for the shocking suggestion, accepted in more recent times without the batting of an eye, that jazz might after all turn out to be a finite art, almost nobody had considered the possibility. In 1958 jazz was just emerging from the disastrous internecine wars caused by the Bebop revolution of the mid-1940s, or rather by critical reaction to it. Only now was the heat beginning to go out of the argument. People still listened, and wrote, and thought, however, in terms of the rigid compartments of jazz so obligingly but so misleadingly supplied by critics. Like Caesar's Gaul or the old Victorian novel, jazz was divided into three parts, Traditional, Mainstream and Modern, although as there was nobody who could define any of these terms to anybody else's satisfaction, certain difficulties presented themselves. There was Duke Ellington, for instance. He had recorded 'Black And Tan Fantasy' in 1927, 'Take The "A" Train' in 1940, 'Star-Crossed Lovers' in 1957, so presumably he must be Traditional, Mainstream and Modern at the same time. And a player like, say, Illinois Jacquet although far more derivative than, say, Bix Beiderbecke, must be considered the more modern of the two simply because Bix died in 1931, when Jacquet was only nine years old.

The truth was that Modernism in jazz, and indeed in everything else, was not a style but an attitude, and it was an attitude discernible not only in the reaction of each musician to the harmonic conventions of his era, but in the precise date on which he may have attempted some departure from those conventions. In other arts this presented no difficulty. For a painter to pursue Impressionism in 1958 would require merely a hero-worship of Monet. To have adopted the identical method in 1758 would demand extremes of courage and originality amounting to genius. The problem was that in jazz, where the rate of evolution was so hysterical that in fifty years it had moved from Primitivism to Sentimental Revivalism, the displacement of a year, or even of six months, might mean all the difference between a stroke of true originality and one of mere ingenious imitation. It seemed to me unfair that a player like Lester Young, whose brilliant exposition of the use of the chord of the Minor sixth had been delivered in 'Dickie's Dream' as early as 1937, should be deprived of the credit simply because within a year there were a dozen disciples doing the same thing.

One of the most remarkable things about the jazz fraternity is the speed with which it can assimilate new findings. Indeed this speed is so remarkable that it has always been taken for granted as a fact of life, instead of for the phenomenon it really is. As a working musician I had already seen, and occasionally participated in, the process by which some new phrase arrived on an American recording, was then dissected, examined and reassembled, and finally reproduced in the local jazz clubs, not by one or two players, but by every musician living the jazz life at the time. And so it was in the American jazz world only more so. A performance like Charlie Teagarden's with the Venuti-Lang All Stars in 1932 would always be moving and beautiful; had it been achieved without foreknowledge of Beiderbecke, then Teagarden would have been one of the great figures of jazz history instead of a charming and talented background character. Similarly, the incandescence of Sonny Stitt which so excited Scott and myself in Newark, 1957, would perhaps have unhinged us altogether had we not been at least partly insulated against the effects of such passionate dexterity by knowledge over the previous ten years of Charlie Parker. My problem was, how to codify the harmonic life of such musicians without reducing the actual writing, at least so far as the layman was concerned, to technical gibberish.

One other factor was of extreme importance in Britain in 1958. Only two years before, a crude and imperceptive union ban on visiting American jazz musicians had been lifted. This ban had obtained for twenty-five years, which meant that a whole generation of jazz fanciers had grown up who had literally never heard the real thing in the flesh. In 1958 we were still a little overwhelmed by imports, and the visits of Americans, steadily increasing in frequency as they declined in effect, comprised a large slice of every reviewer's life. There were thriving at this time two bloated reputations which I did my best to deflate, those of John Lewis and Dave Brubeck. Eventually they arrived within weeks of each other at the tail-end of 1959, and I suppose I was as relentless in my pursuit of them as they were in pursuit of British audiences. The reader may find it difficult to comprehend quite how vast the Modern Jazz Quartet and Brubeck bulked in

1958. It seemed to me that their exalted positions were not only false but usurped, for there were many jazz musicians more gifted than they whose neglect was as scandalous as it was pathetic. In time the reputations of both Lewis and Brubeck were to subside, particularly Brubeck's. Indeed, his almost total retirement from the jazz life, as sudden as it was gratifying, had so disastrous an effect on his reputation that he may be said to have performed the Byronic exercise backwards, by awaking one morning to find himself obscure.

The jazz life has changed beyond recognition since the day I first went to the Beaulieu Festival on Tynan's suggestion. As for my own, having begun it with the purchase of Frank Trumbauer's 'Singing the Blues', having continued it by playing the sedulous ape, first to Benny Goodman and then to Lester Young, having moved from the sentimental jollities of Jewish wedding repertoires in 1948 to the Chicago-style jollities of Freddie Randall's band in 1950 to the avant garde jollities of Ronnie Scott's band two years later, I had, by the time I began composing the pieces which follow, a great many axes to grind. I have been grinding them ever since, whenever the opportunity has presented itself, and sometimes even when it hasn't.

Louis Armstrong (1963)

If there really is anything unique about jazz, it is the ferocious pace of its evolution, from the delicate bloom of its ignorance fifty years ago to its current scrambled pursuit of the techniques of the conservatoire. It has all happened so quickly that it is still possible, in the era of Miles Davis and John Lewis, to witness the performances of Louis Armstrong, a musician whose formative years are inextricably tangled up with the distant legend of the New Orleans heyday.

Armstrong, currently conducting the third British tour of his All-Stars, is now in his sixties, and at least partially inhibited, it would seem, by the aftermath of last year's heart attack. His programme panders quite frankly to that popular market which discovered him, belatedly, about twenty-five years ago, and yet beneath the dross lies a certain incorruptible residue of jazz that will no doubt stay with its owner till his death.

The object lesson of Armstrong's performances is that jazz music does not rely for its eloquence on tortuous harmonic ingenuities, that it remains a music of personal nuance and inflection, of purely individual interpretation. Whether singing or playing the trumpet, Armstrong bends a note here, syncopates a phrase there, recasts a melody in the shape of the most elementary arpeggios, weaving a spell so potent that it can disarm criticism completely.

To pretend he is still the colossus of the old days would be an insult to some of the greatest jazz performances ever recorded, but even now he is capable of that sudden flash of insight reminiscent of his old mastery. He has been written off so many times that it would be foolhardy to do so again. As recently as 1956 he recorded one of his finest albums, and those who may be disappointed by his choice of material will do well to remember that Armstrong in the studio is a different proposition from Armstrong on the concert stage.

The rest of the All-Stars are in a far less enviable position. Little more than stooges for their leader's whims, their playing rarely rises above the mediocre, with the sole exception of pianist Billy Kyle, who succeeds in remaining smilingly aloof from the dated vulgarities going on around him. Kyle alone plays as though this were a musical recital instead of a knockabout variety act, and produces that fire in the right hand which is one of the glories of the old Earl Hines piano style.

The final testimony to Armstrong's stagecraft is to be found in the faces of those leaving the auditorium. If the audience leaves a Miles Davis concert with a distant look in its eye, and a John Lewis recital on tiptoe, it departs from an evening with Louis Armstrong with a broad smile and the happiest of dispositions, like a small boy after watching a Western, which is logical enough.

For Armstrong is the embodiment and the propagator-in-chief of a myth just as potent as the myth of the prairie. His is the myth of the bayou, where the plunking of banjos under a watermelon moon accompanies the saga of mammies and piccaninnies. The expression of this myth is often trite to the point of imbecility, but Armstrong's apparent belief in its depth renders it somehow moving. He opens and closes his concerts with 'When It's Sleepy Time Down South', a song he has recorded several times. The 'South' referred to is, of course, an imaginary South that never existed outside the swampy terrain of the professional lyric writer, but the melody is well-shaped and beguiling.

Armstrong, croaking away like a retired bullfrog, manages to evoke a mood which sounds like the very soul of jazz. And that is exactly what it is.

Dizzy Gillespie's Big 4 (1975)

Back in the days when Modern jazz was still new enough and strange enough for all kinds of opportunists and charlatans to take advantage of it, somebody published a volume, pirated I think, of jazz themes of the new school. These themes on paper looked reassuring enough, especially the first composition in the book, a piece in G Minor whose melody rose in the kind of neat geometric progression which an instrumental student might associate with the formal exercises of Klosé or Lazarus. I soon learned to play this piece at roughly the regulation quickstep tempo and privately wondered to myself what was supposed to be so revolutionary about it. The piece was called 'Be Bop', and was a source of considerable disappointment to me. I had expected it to reveal the secrets of the new jazz to me and it had revealed nothing at all.

Some months later I heard 'Be Bop' played on a recording and realized that like all jazz themes 'Be Bop' had its own ideal tempo and that I had been playing it at roughly quarter speed, which meant that my version bore about as much resemblance to the real thing as a painting-by-numbers version of *The Leaping Horse* would bear to an authentic Constable. Only rarely have I heard 'Be Bop' played since, no doubt because of the prohibitive nature of that ideal tempo, and its reappearance now on this album may serve as a timely reminder of one aspect of early modernism which, in the rush of the Gadarene swine towards the precipice of formlessness, is usually overlooked, the amazing standard of musicianship among the breakers of new ground of the 1940s.

When Dizzy Gillespie plays 'Be Bop' at the pace he originally had in mind when he wrote it, the listener realizes that there comes a point where the tempo becomes so fast as hardly to be a tempo at all so much as a constant stream of sound. This is a dangerous illusion which the musician himself cannot afford, for unless he retains complete control over the pulse of his performance the result is chaos and anarchy. That the effort required is physical as well as mental and musical is a point well known to anybody who has observed the movements of fingers and feet of musicians operating at this pace.

'Be Bop' was manufactured specifically for the new era and has never strayed beyond the specialist fold for which it was conceived. But similar pyrotechnics may be exhibited on the frame of far more conventional melodies. 'Russian Lullaby' is a venerable (1927) waltz whose sentimental cadences contain, according to their composer Irving Berlin, an anti-Tsarist tract. In this version the time signature has been changed to four-in-a-bar and the tempo stepped up to a point not far removed from the whizzing measures of 'Be Bop'. It would be interesting to compute the odds against the composer of 'Marie From Sunny Italy' and the composer of 'Birks Works' sharing credits on the same album, but then Berlin is an altogether phenomenal composer whose work seems to suit all kinds of musical situations for which it was never remotely intended; the Dizzy version of 'Russian Lullaby' reveals how well-suited to jazz improvisation is the song's constant shifting from Minor to Major and back to Minor. Kurt Weill's 'September Song', on the other hand, retains much of its original personality, and has its place on the album as a variant of mood and tempo, being comparatively brief and embodying a quiet gravity which shows an aspect of Dizzy perhaps too often upstaged by his other selves.

The quartet is an interesting blend of those, like Dizzy and Ray Brown, who pioneered the kind of precepts which 'Be Bop' and 'Birks Works' represent, and musicians like Joe Pass and Mickey Roker who appeared later. The challenge presented to Pass in 'Be Bop' appears terrifying, at least to the listener, who can hardly comprehend the implications of such a tempo. In the early days of modernism there used to be a guitarist called Bill d'Arango who specialized in keeping pace with hair-raising tempos, but even he would have blanched at the prospect facing Pass in 'Be Bop'. It is surely a tribute to the precociousness of Dizzy's magnificent technical awareness and agility when he first arrived that so long afterwards an outcome of his youthful exuberance like 'Be Bop' is still stretching the very best contemporary players to their limits.

On the other hand, perhaps after all nothing has changed very much in the art of making jazz since Dizzy first emerged and scandalized so many conservative spirits. The standard small-group formula remains very much what it was then, a handful of musicians relying on the speed of their reflexes to produce some personal expression of their own. Dizzy himself is recognizably very much the same trumpeter he once was. The canons of his style have remained largely intact. There is clearly still the same deep affection for, and complete sympathy with, Latin American rhythms, the same amazing double-tempo passages where the speed at which the thought is expressed is matched only by the clarity of the thought itself.

What is also worth noting is that, as always, there is something serenely classical, I very nearly said traditional, about the rock-solid base of Dizzy's harmonic method. Unlike some modern lions whose names only my good nature and the laws of libel prevent me from naming, Dizzy has always abided by the logic of discord and resolution, knowing instinctively that without chord progressions there can be no formal logic to any improvisation. So far as harmony is concerned, Dizzy has always played the game, a truth which becomes a truism when you hear how he tackles a standard like 'Hurry Home'. Here is a song which is an example of the best that the commercial market has been known to turn out, with an appealing melody and a few interesting changes to keep the soloist – and the listener – on his toes. When Dizzy improvises on 'Hurry Home', giving a beautiful exposition of its harmonies, he makes you wonder about what were once thought to be the outrageous unorthodoxies of his playing. I suppose what has happened is that after twenty-five years we are all beginning to catch up with him.

∾

ERROLL GARNER (1967)

When a jazz pianist commits himself indefinitely to a concert career, as Erroll Garner has done, and undertakes that career virtually unaccompanied, several of the rules of the game are bound in time to be displaced by new ones. At the Royal Festival Hall last Saturday it was clear that this is exactly what has happened to Garner over the last ten years.

Whether the mangling that jazz has endured in the process is worth it is another question, and the fact that right from the beginning Garner has been a freak, in the very best sense of the term, only makes the question more difficult to answer.

Garner is one of the great natural musicians of our time, a man with so intuitive a grasp of the mechanics of piano playing that he became a virtuoso without ever learning to read a note of music. He is also a prime example of the born jazzman, the instrumentalist to whom rhythmical improvisation comes so easily that it is no more vexing a problem than breathing or sleeping. The giant strength of his left hand makes the presence on the current tour of an accompanying drummer and strong bassist superfluous.

His choice of material reflects the reverence he feels for the very best popular composers. There are times when it is not Garner but Kern or Porter or Rodgers who seems to be topping the bill. Indeed, at one stage, during a marvellous Gershwin fantasia, Garner plays with such extraordinary bravura as to obliterate himself completely in favour of his material.

But what of the jazz world, which is too short of great musicians to be able to laugh it off when one of them absconds? Garner can still produce blinding jazz, and did so in London last weekend. But his concert career has tempted him into some dubious devices, none more suspect than his introductions. Before each song, instead of the normal rhythmic prelude to the melody, comes a strange fantasia of sound totally unrelated either to the pace or the mood of the piece to come. It all sounds like a wild pastiche of 'Dream of Olwen', the whole-tone scale and the collected works of Ravel and Debussy, and could easily pass for a lampoon of the 'conshoito' that James Cagney's kid brother was always composing in pre-war gangster melodramas.

If this were mere sentimental indulgence on Garner's part it would be irritating enough, but it is something much more calculated. These introductions, being supine, create a tension which is suddenly released when the piano leaps without warning into the theme. The audience, spellbound by the hypnotic keyboard ramblings, is jerked rudely out of its rose-coloured reverie, realizes that it is listening to 'Night And Day' or 'Where Or When', and is so overcome with the shock of recognition that it ruins the whole of the first chorus by applauding its own perceptiveness.

Garner is far too gifted to need such tomfoolery. The incisiveness of his touch and his ability to invent endless melodic variations should be enough for any audience, specialist or otherwise. Last Saturday he played a version of 'The Man I Love' so magnificent, that it explains why the jazz musician is sometimes obliged to coin new words and phrases to express his admiration for a fellow performer.

George Lewis (1959)

The British tour of George Lewis's New Orleans Band, lasting throughout January, is one of those events which underline the breathless haste of jazz evolution. While the rest of the arts have been cooking over a slow fire for a few thousand years, jazz has been thrust into the pressure cooker of contemporary life, so that it has moved from primitivism to neoclassicism in fifty years.

To the modernist George Lewis's clarinet playing presents the same problems that a buffalo might to Sitting Bull's grandson. Lewis is an authentic New Orleans antique whose experience stretches back into the semi-mythology of street parades, band contests and the Storyville red-light district. And yet there he was last Sunday, almost as large as life on the stage of the Odeon Theatre, Tottenham Court Road, taking over where the Wyatt Earp entourage had left off the day before.

The ages of the six members of the Lewis band are sometimes

disputed, but it is generally accepted that the string bassist Alcide 'Slow Drag' Pavageau was born in 1888. Lewis himself is a callow youth of fifty-nine, while the extreme youth of trumpeter Avery Howard, born in 1908, is underlined by his professional name 'Kid'.

Lewis plays in an uncorrupted turn-of-the-century manner, recalling the days when jazz was the do-it-yourself music of an oppressed minority dumped in an alien society. It is here, on the fringes of the sociologist's world, that the value of Lewis's performance really lies. By strict musical standards his band is abysmal. Intonation is hopelessly at sea. Technical limitations cripple the soloists, and the lead given by Kid Howard is so weak as to be at times literally inaudible. Melodic conceptions are rudimentary and the triad of the tonic major appears again and again in the improvisations of Lewis himself, the most articulate of the six.

The appeal lies elsewhere, in the miraculously preserved artistic naiveté of musicians who were active before their music had begun to travel up-river to St Louis and Chicago, artists whose repertoire of over 500 themes creates echoes of a vanished past in classics like 'Dallas Blues', 'Canal Street Blues', 'Georgia Camp Meeting' and 'Corrina Corrina'.

The mystique which envelops this kind of revivalism in jazz has created audiences hungrier for the legends than for the music which inspired them, audiences unaware either of the serious limitations of the Lewis method or of the place this kind of jazz style has in the history of the music. The sentimental cultist following of Lewis in this country is tremendous, and the explanation lies in the very shortcomings of the music. The jazz past is receding swiftly. Soon there will be none of the New Orleans originals left, hence the craving to examine the unspoilt article while it still exists.

The power of the cult was most effectively demonstrated by the supporting band of British musicians, Ken Colyer and his Band, bearded men in their twenties who have aped the mannerisms of men like Lewis with an unhealthy fanaticism. Indeed, part of Colyer's appeal lies in the fact that as a merchant seaman he was once incarcerated in a New Orleans prison.

The comment I heard on Lewis's performance while leaving the theatre, that it was an assault on the ears, may have had some relevance, but I feel it was unfair. One does not expect a milestone to start walking along the road. Lewis's band is simply a perfect embalming job, and one must learn to approach it with that fact very much in mind. Apart from all else, it is a form of musical expression which will make the fingers of every self-respecting musicologist twitch with fascination.

Oscar Peterson: *Night Train* (1962)

'The past is hidden somewhere outside the realm, beyond the reach of the intellect,' wrote Proust, 'in some material object which we do not suspect.' One of the most potent of all these material objects is a sheet of printed music and the sounds it conveys, as Proust and countless other writers have acknowledged. That is why it is a brave man indeed who would make an album composed of material which he knows belongs in the past consciousness of those likely to listen to it. The musician who does this will be grappling with all kinds of extra-musical intangibles, because when it comes to the past, we are all conservatives at heart.

Oscar Peterson's programme in this album deliberately challenges the russet glow of fond reminiscence and, it seems to me, challenges it triumphantly. Each of the themes he plays has its aura in the jazz past, and, more significant still, has upon it the indelible stamp of previous definitive versions. No matter. Peterson overcomes this terrifying handicap because the force of his own personality is as strong, sometimes stronger, than the originals. Even when he takes a piece like 'Night Train', tailored for the concerted ensemble of a big band, he gives the impression that the trio is the best conceivable setting for the tune. Indeed, there are more overtones of orchestral richness in his 'Night Train' than in most of the big band versions I can remember.

If the dominant emotion of the album is Pastness, its dominant form is the Blues in all its shades of intensity, from the leisurely ease of 'Things Ain't What They Used To Be' to the brilliant sustained pace of 'Honey Dripper'. The sources are varied but the underlying roots identical, the earthy candour of a form that has served all periods and styles of jazz with equal loyalty. In a way, the Blues separates the men from the boys in jazz, for no amount of technical trickery or experimental precosity can shield an inadequate talent from its demands. The first time I ever saw Peterson perform, in London in 1953, he opened with a medium-tempo blues, and I have never forgotten the impact he made, an impact repeated time and again in this collection.

There is a virility about the greatest jazz which is immediately recognizable, and it is this quality in his work which contributes so vastly to Peterson's position as the outstanding pianist of his generation. It asserts itself at the crucial moments with unfailing constancy. After the theme statement of 'Band Call', when Peterson moves into his improvisation, his relaxation is quite sublime. There are hints of limitless untapped power and dazzling melodic invention, and as the solo gathers impetus, it becomes clear that the player is a mature master of his art.

In 'Honey Dripper', at the point where Ed Thigpen increases the rhythmic pressure, and above all at that moment in 'Moten Swing' where, having stated the theme, Peterson takes a two-bar break into his solo, the same effect is created, of power wedded to relaxation, of the curious duality of mood that jazz creates, the serenity and the intensity, with the evident enjoyment of the musician serving as the emotional springboard for the entire performance.

The Blues in its starkest form utilizes a minimal harmonic vocabulary, which is why to leaven a blues set with one or two more elaborately constructed pieces is often an excellent idea. In the choice of one ballad in particular, Peterson flies yet again in the face of convention, of tradition, of nostalgia and the sensibilities of jazz lovers with long memories. It is hardly possible to hear the first few bars of 'I Got It Bad And That Ain't Good' without plunging back twenty years and savouring in the mind once again the lilting grace of Ivie Anderson and the fragility of Johnny Hodges' alto playing on the original Ellington recording. Peterson of course makes no attempt to echo Hodges or Ivie

Anderson or anybody else, and achieves a version which already numbers among its admirers Duke Ellington himself.

With Ray Brown and Ed Thigpen, Peterson has now arrived at what is probably the best musical setting for his gifts that he has ever enjoyed. That break in 'Moten Swing' which typifies the whole album, is a telling demonstration of the importance to musicians of group thinking and feeling. Brown and Thigpen await poised, for the short break to end. When it does, they both re-enter with perfect timing and an exact reading of the mood of that precise moment. It is this kind of expertise which makes the Peterson Trio one of the most enlightening experiences that jazz today has to offer.

Thelonious Monk (1969)

After the shocks and surprises of the past year or two, it comes as a positive relief to discover that Thelonious Monk is still playing like Thelonious Monk instead of trying unsuccessfully to imitate much younger players. Monk's piano style becomes him. It has the same gentle eccentricities of his own nature, the same quiet confidence, the same inability to be false to itself.

The quartet Monk is leading for the rest of this month at Ronnie Scott's is not the most animated of groups. Its members do not excite one another very often, and the drumming is not as subtle as it might be. But in its leader and its tenor saxophonist, Charlie Rouse, it possesses two gifted musicians who have played together long enough to have achieved a rare telepathic communication.

Rouse is now in his twelfth year of unravelling the intricacies of Monk's harmonies, and is a past master at resolving them into something poised and tuneful. He has an excellent technique and a clear light tone which provides the ideal counterweight to the heavy dissonances in Monk's left hand. But what is most striking about this interplay is the discipline lying behind it. Monk and Rouse are proving nightly that it is still possible to work within the accepted rules of the game and find enough freedom of movement to build interesting structures.

Monk himself remains one of the curiosities of jazz, one of its very few pianists who can make the instrument produce a personal sound. He belongs in no pigeon-hole and yet is an unmistakable part of the evolving tradition of jazz piano. Possibly the originality was forced on him by the limited technique of earlier years, but the important thing today is that he can do all he needs to. The key to his playing is the great tension between the deep inverted chords in the bass and the stark angular shapes in the treble. Monk's right-hand phrases are more remote from his bass fingers than the jazz ear is accustomed to, and they repeatedly stride across intervals we never quite expect. There is also a percussiveness about his touch which gives the end product great strength and resilience.

This is most noticeable when the group uses themes which ought to sound tired from over use. 'Sweet And Lovely' has that hint of diffidence which is usually an indication that the players have not been improvising on the theme together for very long. But it works because 'Sweet And Lovely' is made to take on quite a new personality. Here lies the justification for Monk's whole career. Not one of the great piano virtuosos, he has still contrived to make everything he plays sound like himself, which ought to be the aim of every jazz musician worthy of the name.

Jazz Goes To College (1973)

The section which follows deals with one of the most extraordinary episodes in jazz history, and one which perhaps marks a watershed, not only of the music, but of public attitudes towards it. One of jazz's great compensations for being a music too esoteric for marketing on a mass scale was that it had usually been left unattended by the makers of fashion, who had found their sensibilities, if that is the word, more easily attuned to hit parades, dance bands and nightclub cabaret. But by the sheer law of averages, it was perhaps inevitable that one day the trendsetters should batten on to jazz as a new diversion, distort its values, upset its criteria, smother it with wet kisses before leaving it to die of confusion. The makers of fashion took a long time to make their move, and it was laughably predictable that when they did, the objects of their affection should be a pair of extremely astute piano-playing publicists whose musical effects ranged from excessive politeness to the playful roar of a paper tiger.

Twenty years after the event it is difficult to convey the intensity of the furore of devotion for the Modern Jazz Quartet and the Dave Brubeck Quartet displayed by tremulous acolytes who had, until that very moment, mysteriously managed to control their passion for jazz to the extent of not bothering with it at all. Tens of thousands of people who all their lives had believed Bix to be some kind of breakfast food and Ellington the victor of Waterloo suddenly discovered that overnight the grace of art had been bestowed upon them.

I do not question the sincerity of their devotionals, even though at the time many of them questioned the sincerity of mine. Such miraculous conversions as took place at the jazz concerts of the period have been known to occur periodically throughout recorded history, usually in an atmosphere whose religious ecstasy has discouraged the exercise of dispassionate thought, and it was precisely such an atmosphere, compounded in equal parts of piety and adoration, which prevailed the moment either Brubeck or John Lewis, the leader of the Modern Jazz Quartet, so much as poked his nose round a safety curtain. What I was questioning then, and still question now, is whether anyone can hope to arrive at valid conclusions about an artistic performance without having first acquired its historical frame of reference. How could a man be confident that what Brubeck and Lewis were playing broke new ground when he had never been taken over the old? What could they know of Brubeck, these new zealots, who only Brubeck knew? It really was extremely clever of them.

My predicament at the time was complicated by the fact that never once did I attend any of the performances reviewed below without ensuring the companionship of a few friends better informed as to the jazz art than I was. I suppose after all these years it does no harm to confess that I attended the Brubeck and Lewis recitals insulated from errors of judgement in this way, and that many of the opinions I later expressed in print were not mine, or at least had come to be mine at second hand. Probably it was professionally unethical of me, but frankly I had no choice. Each time I sat down to attend to the religious ceremonies conducted by Brubeck and Lewis I was surrounded by a whole battalion of emissaries who had been my boon companions for so long that I would have known of no way to detach myself from them even had I wanted to, which I most certainly did not. In retrospect I suppose it was grossly unfair of me to have taken with me to these concerts the shades of Bix and Louis, Hawkins and Lester, Bechet and Tatum, but there was nothing unusual in this. Every working musician I knew was in the identical predicament, of not being able to help relating what he was hearing with what he had once heard. And what I was now hearing seemed so trivial that the moment the music began and the zealots to genuflect, the invisible host at my side began first to laugh, then to scratch itself, and finally to drift off in search of the nearest bar.

Brubeck was a new phenomenon in jazz, a perennial student who had never worked in anybody's group but his own. This in itself was no disqualification, although it was silly to pretend it was much help. It seemed to me that he played the piano so clumsily, and with such consistent clumsiness, that from the day I first attended one of his performances, my impatience was tempered by a touch of that compassion which one usually feels at the spectacle of a fellow musician flung by circumstances into a hopelessly false position. For either Brubeck chose to accept the myth of his own infallibility, or he did not, each of the options being worse than the other, either to accept the reality of a genius he did not in fact possess, or be obliged to strive hopelessly for it every time he confronted a keyboard. At first I was surprised that such footling juvenilia should be taken even halfway seriously by those who knew of Art Tatum and Bud Powell. Slowly my surprise was replaced by wry acceptance of the fact that possibly those who knew of Tatum and Powell and still took Brubeck seriously did not know of Tatum and Powell after all. When Big Ben strikes thirteen, it has been pointed out, we are informed by the conviction, not only that Big Ben is hopelessly wrong now, but that it must also have been hopelessly wrong in all the years we accepted its findings in good faith.

Attendance at Brubeck concerts for me became a nightmare

which I would not have missed for worlds. The images were too rich to pass over, of Brubeck falling deeper and deeper into the rut of some wretched cross-rhythm, digging a pit for himself with such relentless determination that soon he falls into it and disappears from view; Brubeck climbing out again and arriving at the same juncture of a song for six or seven successive choruses, 'improvising' the same phrase each time; Brubeck shyly telling us that what he is now about to play is more or less impossible, but that he is going to be very gallant and play it anyway.

We met only once, long after the Brubeck era was over, when he emerged from semi-retirement to appear in a BBC television series for which I had been hired as the compère. An hour before filming was due to begin, I was led down the dining room of the auditorium and introduced to him at his table, where, until my arrival, he had been enjoying a light meal. He seemed a mild-mannered man, and as he caught my name he visibly, if only momentarily, flinched. As he did so, the recollection sprang to mind of what a mutual friend had once told me, that Brubeck, having suffered a few of my reviews in silence, had arrived finally at the conclusion that my detestation for his playing must have some obscure personal motivation, which seemed to me to imply an artistic vanity of truly comic proportions. To put it another way, he simply could not accept the possibility that anyone could dislike his music so violently as I appeared to do. I sat down facing him, remarking 'I come in peace', and spent the next ten minutes in pleasant discussion of how I might reconcile my critical instinct to batter him with my temporary obligation to flatter him, although as my announcement at the opening of his recital was limited to one minute, the problem virtually solved itself. A few days later the auditorium burnt to the ground, but I have no reason to believe that this tragedy was connected in any way with our meeting. Today, without the physical presence of his studious personality to buttress it, Brubeck's legend is already disappearing into the middle distance. Posterity may well wonder how such a legend should have come about in the first place.

John Lewis and the Modern Jazz Quartet were an altogether different proposition. I have always felt that Brubeck played the way he did because he could not help himself. The heart of the matter was simply not in him. Appearances suggest that it was not in John Lewis either, but for once, and for an extremely interesting reason, it may just be that appearances are deceptive. Normally in jazz they never are. What a man plays is the sole accurate barometer, and what he believes, or says he believes, remains an irrelevance. He may belittle other musicians, as Benny Goodman and Louis Armstrong once belittled the new modernists; he may question the purity of their artistic souls, as Gary Burton once did Stan Getz's; he may draw ridiculous analogies between their playing and Gabriel's, as Muggsy Spanier once did in reference to Tommy Ladnier. None of it matters. Nothing a musician says, no attitude he strikes, no philosophy to which he subscribes, can invalidate the truth to nature of what he plays. But John Lewis may just possibly be the one exception, the sole example in jazz history of a man who thought himself and talked himself and attitudinized himself out of mastery. I do not believe it myself, but I offer it as a possibility if only in deference to Lewis's position. The case he represents is a very odd one.

As far as I have been able to deduce, from his general behaviour as well as from his playing, Lewis believes jazz to be vulgar. More than one mutual acquaintance over the years has quoted remarks by Lewis to this effect, but I would not be inclined to attach much weight to them were it not for the striking consistency with which they substantiate the evidence of the music. Lewis's dream has been to purge jazz of all indecencies, all coarser overtones, all unfortunate Rabelaisian gestures, which is certainly a thoroughly praiseworthy ambition, always provided that in cleansing her soul you do not make the same mistake as Othello and fracture her windpipe at the same time. There can be no argument that in a strictly limited sense, Lewis's bowdlerizing campaign has flourished famously. No music by the Modern Jazz Quartet has even been tainted by even the faintest hint of vulgarity. Its mannerisms of dress and its stage deportment may have been garish, but of vulgarity in the music itself there has never been so much as a faint suspicion. Indeed, that is the trouble with it. For in his attempts to distil the decorous essence, Lewis has refined jazz out of existence, which raises the question, vulgar in comparison to what? And once we find the answer it seems plain that Lewis is yet another victim of a common American cultural complaint, familiar enough in the arts generally but unprecedented in jazz. From somewhere, perhaps in his studies in anthropology at the University of New Mexico, Lewis has caught a chronic case of Jamesian obsession with Europe.

From its beginning the MJQ paraded titles whose foreign overtones were presumably intended to make them appear more significant. The first two sides by the group I ever heard, purchased from the meagre funds of a co-operative jazz band of which I was a serving member, were titled 'The Queen's Fancy' and 'Delauney's Dilemma'. The dynasty of the queen was unspecified, but it was clear that her postures were vaguely English, vaguely medieval and vaguely Tennysonian, and therefore, presumably, vaguely spurious. Delauney was a French jazz critic. I found the sides very pleasant, but representative of nothing more than a charming little backwater, certainly not of the brave new world of syncopation. But things got much worse after that. At least those first two titles had been in English. It was not always to be so; 'Milano', 'Versailles', 'Fontessa', 'La Ronde', 'Vendôme', 'Baden-Baden', 'Cortège', 'La Cantatrice'. Sometimes the music created a mood which approximated to the implications of its title. Sometimes it did not. The interesting thing was that by annexing a few venerable titles, Lewis won for his music the same polite respect that the titles themselves had earned over the centuries, although why he should find the decrepitude of Venice more congenial than the decrepitude of New Orleans remains a mystery. The MJQ has been playing this game for nearly twenty years now and has evidently still not tired of it. While revising this volume for the printers, I attended a performance by the group in which there was included a piece which was supposed to have parallels with the *Commedia dell'arte*, because both contained an element of improvisation. So does a football match, but Lewis is unlikely to give us a composition describing one.

Lewis's tactics earned the MJQ a prestige so prodigious that in its heyday many people considered even mild criticism to be verging on the sacrilegious. Nor was all of this adulation due to mere cultural snobbery. A great deal of it was, but not all of it. For not only were the titles of the MJQ's repertoire attractive in the way they struck exactly the right balance between the familiar and the inscrutable, but the music itself was reassuring in a way that much of the best work of a Charlie Parker or a Duke Ellington was not. Musicians like Parker and Ellington might well tempt you into deep waters and then leave you to drown, but the worst that could happen to you at the hands of the MJQ was that your feet might get a bit wet. Like all abstract art forms, jazz can present a forbidding face to the uninitiated. It offers no convenient toeholds, no extra-musical points of reference. But here was a group which often gave you a broad hint as to what the music was supposed to be describing. In which case, why had Ellington who, with his suites and his thumbnail sketches, had been doing precisely this for years, and doing it infinitely better, never been accorded the same reverence from audiences? I don't know why.

It used to be said in defence of the MJQ that even if its jazz bona fides were suspect, at least it was drawing into the jazz fold thousands of don't-knows who might otherwise have been lost to the cause, and who might, now that Lewis had initiated them, graduate to better things. This may well have been so, but there was just as much to be said for the opposite case, which is that for those weaned on the liquorice water of the MJQ, a sip of anything stronger might easily kill them stone dead. And as I sat there each time, with my invisible friends at my side, the group's pretensions never failed to appear idiotic.

Perhaps the most predictable price to be paid for this reaction of mine was the breaking off of diplomatic relations. Once my sentiments on the group appeared in print, Lewis wanted no part of me, professionally or otherwise. The night before my first review appeared, we met for the first and, as it proved, the last time, at one of those Saturday night parties where the identity of the host and the purpose of the event are mysteries so inscrutable that nobody bothers to try solving them. Lewis, quietly euphoric after his rapturous reception earlier that evening, stood chatting over a table of salad, cheeses and loaves of bread. (Knowing his predilection for things European, I was happy for him that they were loaves of French bread.) We were introduced by Chris Barber, and I was still naive enough in those days not to feel any fraudulence in the heartiness of my handshake. The knowledge that in an hour or two my review would be on sale did not inhibit my enjoyment of the food or the small talk. Why should it inhibit his? I remember doubting to myself whether he even bothered to read reviews, or if he did, to take them with any degree of seriousness. But he did.

On his next visit he was invited to appear on a television arts programme, in which he would be asked some pertinent questions. But not, apparently, too pertinent, because after I had been invited to appear as his inquisitor, the word came back that he insisted on someone else, at which I withdrew with commendable good grace and somebody else was found to knock up a few polite conversational services across the sagging net of Lewis's vanity. That was several years ago, and we have never been in any kind of contact since nor, I suppose, ever will.

Nor do I have much doubt that when we are both pushing up daisies, our respective executors will see to it that we are separated in the execution of that harmless horticultural function by numberless green fields. A sad loss, but perhaps for the best. In any case, I am well used to such situations. Benny Goodman once cheered me up immeasurably by letting it be known he wanted nothing to do with me, and Gary Burton once wrote a letter expressing the impatience with which he anticipated attending my last rites. So be it. On the other hand Stan Getz and I once had an extremely enjoyable and altogether amicable discussion about an unfavourable review of his playing I had recently composed. And once, Duke Ellington, in referring to an essay I had written about him, fed me the back-handed compliment, 'My friends tell me it was well written,' as if to let me know he had no intention of ever reading it for himself. And quite right too. If I could make music half as well as Ellington can, I wouldn't waste my time reading reviews either.

Dave Brubeck (1964)

It is becoming increasingly difficult to remain detached from the hysteria which now accompanies any public appearance of the Dave Brubeck Quartet, but I will try. The entourage of fans has now been augmented by Tin Pan Alley, momentarily embarrassed by the fact that the Brubeck recording success 'Take Five', was so unexpected a conquest that printed copies have been hard to come by.

At the opening concert at the Royal Festival Hall last Saturday, the stage version of 'Take Five' lasted eighteen minutes, ten of which were taken up by a drum solo whose musical pointlessness was matched by the undiscriminating response of an ecstatic audience.

In the face of such acclaim it is strange indeed to sit there and arrive at the same conclusion one reached on the three previous Brubeck tours of this country. That conclusion is depressing. The quartet is so markedly deficient in certain essential jazz qualities that its popularity can hardly be regarded as a success for jazz at all. At its first recital the group revealed these deficiencies from the very opening bars. Had Brubeck opened with one of those devious compositions of his own, he might have tempted me to reserve judgement. On the contrary, his first tune was 'St Louis Blues', which constituted a grave affront to my sensibilities.

Brubeck himself remains apparently unaware of his own shortcomings as a jazz musician. His keyboard touch remains gauche and, what is much more alarming, apparently uncontrollable. He began 'St Louis Blues' with a pastiche of Count Basie's mannerisms of understatement, but within two or three choruses he had been swept along by the impetus of his own headstrong muse into the routine crashing and bashing of block chords, studiously ignoring the bar lines as he did so. In his next piece, an original called 'Raggy Waltz', he blinded everyone with the science of playing a solo in common time against a rhythmic background of waltz time, an aspect of rhythmic virtuosity having not the remotest connection with the genuine rhythmic vitality of jazz.

His partner Paul Desmond, the most musical member of the quartet, is, it seems, being worn down at last by the sameness of his musical experiences. This is his tenth year with the quartet, and he seems now to have adopted a policy of mere passive resistance. The once girlish laughter of his alto saxophone has now become an effete whimper. He remains a technician of truly marvellous assurance, but the invertebrate nature of his solos suggests not so much an inability for playing jazz as a distaste for the whole idiom.

Audiences continue to be duped by Brubeck's subtle flattery. When they applaud the trick of playing four beats a bar against a background of only three, they are applauding not only Brubeck's cleverness but their own percipience in noticing it. They enjoy being offered titles like 'Blue Rondo À La Turk', because the implication is there that they understand blues, rondos and even Turks. Brubeck appeals to the culture vulture that resides in us all, the beast in the attic of so many jazz fanciers. His quartet produces the warm glow which comes with the assurance that the better artistic things in life are after all within our scope. But to judge Brubeck's music by the highest jazz standards is to marvel at the comparative neglect of so many more musical groups.

THE MJQ (1963)

It is ten years now since the Modern Jazz Quartet began its march to the New Syncopated Jerusalem. If recently a large proportion of its followers have slunk quietly off in search of more interesting crusades, that is hardly surprising.

Jazz fanciers now realize that the promised land was a mirage conjured up by the MJQ's pianist-leader John Lewis. There can be no great jazz without animation, and Lewis's distaste for dramatics in his music necessarily limits the group's contribution, a fact more evident than ever in the MJQ's current British tour.

The music itself is exactly the same music as on the last tour, and the one before that, subtle to the point of paralysis, a whispered oration in which every phrase sounds like every other phrase. The MJQ's programme consists of about sixteen interpretations of various themes, and were it not for the breaks for applause, it would be difficult to know where one mood was supposed to end and another begin.

In his attempt to drain away the Rabelaisian element in jazz, Lewis has succeeded all too well. Unfortunately he has thrown out the baby with the bathwater, leaving us with a residue of tinkling affection which I find charming after ten minutes, tiresome after twenty and excruciating over the length of a full concert. Not even the splendid presumption of Lewis's titles can hide this. 'Animal Dance' turns out to be precisely the same, in mood if not in harmonic shape, as hoary old themes like 'All Of Me' or 'Please Don't Talk About Me'.

The pity is that the four musicians involved are all highly talented jazzmen. One of them, Milt Jackson, is probably something more, but record buyers learned a long time ago that the best way of savouring Jackson's brilliant vibraharp playing is not with the MJQ at all, but in the albums he occasionally makes under his own name with different musicians. Lewis himself continues to play respectable jazz piano clichés with the air of a brilliant aphorist, but he does it with skill and delicacy, sometimes even with humour.

There was a time when to examine the content of the group's repertoire was like a dash on roller skates through the pantheon of Western art, Versailles and Venice one minute, the *Commedia dell'arte* the next. But that, it seems, is all over. Nearly one third of the MJQ's opening concert last weekend was devoted to the score of *Porgy and Bess*, nearly one third of the remainder to conventional twelve-bar themes. It is all much more bearable musically, but it is a strange ending to the quest for respectability in jazz. Gershwin and the Blues. Where next? Or, as John Lewis would perhaps prefer to put it, *quo vadis?*

DUKE ELLINGTON: *SUCH SWEET THUNDER* (1967)

When Duke Ellington first recorded his series of Shakespearian vignettes, *Such Sweet Thunder*, there was a general feeling that he had tried to pull a cultural fast one, and that the connection between his music and the characters on which they were supposed to be based was tenuous to the point of nothingness. That was ten years ago, and because the album was deleted from the British catalogues with an indecent haste, the point has hardly been raised since, especially as Ellington himself appeared long ago to have lost interest in the work and no longer presents extracts from it on his concert tours.

The reissue of *Such Sweet Thunder*, therefore, is sure to rank as one of the most interesting events of the jazz year, especially as it seems much clearer now than it did ten years ago that in using Shakespeare as a basis for a series of jazz situations, Ellington created one of his masterpieces.

Not that all suspicions are allayed. There must be something seriously wrong with a portrait of the Shrew which makes her sound like one of Ellington's long succession of innocuous dream ladies, while Iago seems such a sympathetic chap that one suspects that perhaps he has been confused in the composer's mind with Othello. But for the rest, Ellington hits remarkably close to his target without once crippling the jazz potential of his musicians.

Yet the most brilliant successes in *Such Sweet Thunder* are the sketches of Juliet and Cleopatra, the more so since Ellington, in describing the two poles of womanhood, has used the same musician on the same instrument, Johnny Hodge on the alto saxophone. 'Star Crossed Lovers' is one of Ellington's richest melodies, and evidently Hodges was held close to its written line.

On the other hand, in 'Half The Fun', a witty evocation of Cleopatra's barge sailing down the Nile, Hodges was simply advised to improvise for all he was worth, which was a sensible thing to do, since Hodges' jazz style is as passionate as anything the Queen of Egypt could have mustered.

After ten years it all sounds more impressive than ever, and is probably the only jazz suite by anybody which does not fall between two stools in its attempt to straddle two worlds.

Cult and Culture (1973)

Mine was the generation which saw jazz grow from a cultural backwater in which the train-spotting tiddlers of the discographies and the matrix numbers sported happily to the edification of each other and the enlightenment of absolutely nobody else, into a great flourishing cultural stock exchange where a Black Friday could result in the dramatic fall in this or that musician's market value, or a buoyant period could see vastly inflated reputations go soaring. An example of both of these phenomena is the fact that for a long period in the 1950s, Lee Konitz was being quoted at a far higher figure than Johnny Hodges, Chet Baker than Clark Terry, Herbie Mann than Coleman Hawkins. Of all these fluctuations and the factors which brought them about, the one sure way for a musician to guarantee the improvement of his own position was to die. The increase in prestige which always followed this event was enormous, but it must be understood that it was a manipulative device which could hardly be used more than once.

The increasing cultural significance of jazz culminated finally in the most remarkable scenes of critical carnage, what with the intervention of Norman Mailer with his Hip-Square league tables, and the amazing discovery of Mr L. P. Hartley who, in a 1970 anthology called *Promise of Greatness*, finally solved the problem which had been puzzling the whole world for the previous fifty years, when he announced that jazz had been the cause of the First World War. These vast advances of jazz on the cultural front meant that many thousands of well-intentioned social climbers were left stranded on the shores of ambition without so much as a cockleshell of knowledge to take them out on to the high seas of pretension. The following two pieces were intended as a kind of consumer guide for all would-be jazzosophers, who, having digested the contents of the two essays which follow, would be relieved of the need to listen to the actual music at all. The absolute success of the two pieces in this regard explains the fall of jazz album sales in the last few years. The backwater looms once more.

The Name-Droppers

So far as the Gentle Art of Name-dropping is concerned, the jazz world turns out, as usual, to be a very special case indeed. The difficulty is a very serious one, and is summed up with admirable precision in an exchange of dialogue in an early Lenny Bruce recording. An interviewer is asking an avant garde horn player how he feels about his music:

> Interviewer: *Now tell me, what do you think about Art?*
> Hippy Hornist: *I think Art blows the most, man.*

Feeble as it may be, Bruce's joke teaches one daunting lesson, which is that inside the jazz world there are no second names. By the very act of mentioning a surname the aspiring name-dropper is rendering his own technique totally ineffective. In jazz the name you drop is usually the baptismal one, often the acquired one, never the real one. So far as the professional hippie is concerned, Bruce's interviewer could conceivably have been referring to Art Tatum, Art Blakey, Art Farmer, Art Hodes, Art Ellefson, or even Artie Shaw, but never by the remotest stretch of the imagination to art itself.

This simple fact explains why, when the outsider eavesdrops on an exchange of opinions between insiders, sanity seems to dissolve at an alarming rate:

> *'Ya dig Zoot?'*
> *'It's Stan for me, baby.'*
> *'But that's all Prez and water.'*
> *'That's cool. But Bean's the father.'*
> *'What's Bean to do with Stan, baby? It's like Bird and Rabbit taking fours.'*
> *'You listen to Paul and then you wouldn't think so.'*

The fact that there is much critical shrewdness in that kind of exchange is beside the point. Critical shrewdness is not the object of the exercise. Our two connoisseurs are demonstrating, not their ability to analyse style, but their long familiarity with the elusive art of latching on to the litany, a litany incidentally, which happens to possess at least as much poetic content as Joyce's *Anna Livia Plurabelle*. The aspiring jazz name-dropper has been trying without success for years to devise a mnemonic to cover Stomp, Chuck, Stump, Chick, Tick, Scrap, Snub, Spoon, Stuff, Shake, Snurps, Tut, Chippie, Smokey, Zutty and Zinkie. Even the most subtle performer can stumble over the fine lines which separate Satchelmouth from Gatemouth, Cleanhead from Fathead, Peewee from Peanuts. Neither is there any skirting these issues, because many of these oddly-named gentlemen are vital figures in the development of the music. Had Shaw's Dubedat been a jazzman instead of a painter, his dying speech might have read, 'I believe in Duke, Pops and Diz, in the might of Cannonball, the mystery of Jelly Roll, the redemption of all things by Cow-Cow everlasting and the message of Artie that has made these hands blessed.' And hearing that speech, every name-dropper in the jazz world would be able to tick off each label as it came, lamenting as he did so the sad omission of Chu, Nosey, Stovepipe, Boots, Buster and Smack.

Culturally of course, this kind of thing has proved disastrous for the sociological standing of jazz. The names sound so undignified that the layman may perhaps be pardoned for assuming that the music does too. There was even a sporadic attempt by the name-droppers of a generation ago to recover a hopeless situation by reverting back to surnames. But one of the most lamentable faults of the name-dropper is his preference for the best-sounding names rather than the best-sounding musicians. Just as the classical name-dropper is always best advised to drop Stockhausen rather than Bach, so his jazz counterpart is far wiser to talk about his acquaintance with Beiderbecke rather than his friendship with Bix, even though the two references apply to the same man. The counter-revolutionary jazz name-droppers of the 1940s could quite easily gather a large crowd of adoring neophytes simply by discussing the relative merits of Teschmaker and Stuhlmaker, neither of which players ever contributed a tenth as much to the jazz art as Fats or Fatha or Little Benny. Fortunately this practice died out from the moment that the long-playing era swept away the train-spotters of jazz whose tastes were influenced less by the merits of the music than by the obscurity of the musician and the unavailability of his recordings.

Because today jazz is the common man's cultural bandwagon, the number of practised name-droppers has become too vast for the comfort of the insiders, who have tried to protect the rarity of their status by altering the name-dropping rules as they go. Thus an ambitious but inexpert name-dropper might refer to Basie, learn the error of his ways and get used to talking about The Count, add the final polish by reducing the name to Count, only to learn to his understandable bewilderment that inside the sanctum sanctorum of jazz Basie is always known as Bill. For those who prefer to drop their names on paper, or critics, as they are often referred to, there are certain knotty textual points to be considered. Anyone who writes 'Bix' instead of Bix is instantly revealed as a Philistine or philly, and as for the man who commits to paper a solecism like J. J. Johnson for Jay Jay

Johnson, he will be beyond the hipster's pale for all time.

When in company the jazz name-dropper has to be very careful to match the names he is dropping with the right accompaniment. It is tragic to say 'Brubeck swings, my friend', better to amend it to 'Dave swings, man', best of all to remark 'Dave swings, baby'. The fact that Dave has never succeeded in swinging in his life has nothing to do with it. Name-dropping and artistic ability have not the remotest connection. As for the creeping advance of the word 'baby', this is the phenomenon of the 1960s and has quickly become a vital trick in the game. It is probably harmless, and only becomes really confusing when the subject under discussion happens to be the technique of the New Orleans veteran drummer Warren 'Baby' Dodds. In this situation remarks are apt to fly like 'Baby plays like a baby, baby', at which point the second party, always assuming he is conversant with the rules of the game, will hedge by plunging into a discussion of the relative plunger-mute techniques of Bubber and Cootie, or the degree to which the repeal of Prohibition affected the styles of Muggsy and Wingy, or which of the three legendary Johnsons, Bunk, Keg or Dink, was the biggest fraud.

This dramatic rise of the Baby Syndrome in jazz has of course played havoc with the position of women, who, so far as jazz is concerned, are among the greatest name-droppers in the business. There is a great deal more petticoat government in the jazz world than the outsider realizes, and when one of the matriarchs hears her man repeatedly addressing other men as 'baby', there is a distinct danger of the entire social fabric falling apart. At the moment, however, the women are just about holding their own, and, being like all other women, continue to show an instinctive grasp of what will and what will not enhance their sex appeal. Jazz's female name-droppers realized many years and hundreds of styles ago that the Bubber-Tick-Zinkie ploy was essentially unfeminine, and soon evolved their own style of name-dropping which might fairly be called the Bourgeois Reaction.

On the lips of women all jazz names worth the dropping take on an innocence so pristine as to be hardly recognizable. Cannonball Adderley becomes Julian, Lockjaw Davis turns magically into an innocuous Edward, while Pee Wee Russell undergoes a complete change of personality by being referred to as Charles Ellsworth. Probably this is a subconscious attempt by women to bowdlerize the men in the jazz world and, if so, there is a great deal of logic in the strategy. Presumably it is much easier to control a man called Ferdinand than it is to live with one called Jelly Roll, especially if the neighbours are aware of the connotations of the nickname.

In Britain the art of dropping illustrious jazz names is sadly limited for obvious reasons, jazz being the one art form where not one name worth the dropping has been produced by this country. In such a world, so insular and so ill-informed, it is actually possible to experience the ultimate at the hands of a name-dropper, which is to have one's own name dropped in casual conversation. A few years ago a man I had never seen before and have never seen since, remarked to me, 'I dig Benny Green's work, don't you?' My confusion was compounded by the fact, which my acquaintance may or may not have known, that there is in America another musician called Bennie Green whose skill as a trombonist really makes our name worth dropping.

The most awkward predicament of all, however, is created, not by the truly gifted name-dropper, but by the aspiring apprentice fired by all the necessary enthusiasm and lacking totally in the required finesse. One evening towards the end of my playing days, at just about the time that 'baby' was taking over from 'man', I became involved in a jazz club conversation with a cluster of instrumentalist friends all well versed in the latest amendments to the hipster's vocabulary. The conversation became a discussion, the discussion a debate, and the debate, inevitably, a fierce argument. Our voices rose. Several paying customers stood listening to the row, whose central issue I can no longer remember. Gradually the dispute resolved itself, the vocabulary reverted back to the bourgeois norm and our group dispersed. As I stood there, one of the eavesdroppers approached holding an autograph book. It was a young girl of that truly delightful shape and poundage the jazz environment has always excelled in producing.

'Excuse me,' she said, 'but would you please put your name in my book, Mr Baby?'

As I wrote 'Mr Baby' in her book, I remember wondering what Duke or T-Bone or Lady or Prez or Crackpot or Stovepipe or Blind Lemon or Bogus Ben would have done. Nothing, probably.

The Culture Cults

In the early 1940s two events occurred which galvanized the world of jazz, until then a sleepy backwater with almost no critical history at all. Somebody discovered that William 'Bunk' Johnson was still alive, at least in the biological sense, and an unknown saxophonist called Charlie Parker realized that chromatic harmony was by no means beyond the scope of the jazz instrumentalist. It was these two discoveries that created for the first time the ideal conditions for fashion and cultism to thrive. Until now, there had simply been jazz. Either you liked it or you didn't, although there had been some critical sniping before this, particularly among those who, for reasons best known to themselves, felt obliged to choose between the two great trumpeters of the 1920s: Bix Beiderbecke and Louis Armstrong. Beiderbecke, being white and dead, held all the aces here, but the only real point at issue was who should be placed first or second in the Greatness Stakes. What followed in the wake of Johnson and Parker was something quite different. The tiny principality of jazz suddenly found itself split clean down the middle. Johnson was a sexagenarian New Orleans trumpeter unheard of for at least twenty years, and the archeologists who dug him up insisted on a new criterion of judging jazzmen which may briefly be summarized as the Age Before Beauty theory. Indeed, the fact that by 1940 Johnson was playing third-rate jazz strictly from memory only seemed to add spice to the wooing that followed. Parker, on the other hand, began to introduce into the jazz context sounds which appeared blasphemous to the New Orleans revivalists, bewildering to critics with no technical armoury and baffling to the layman, still fondly clinging to his dream of jazz as a good-time music synonymous with bootlegging, chorus girls and sexual high jinks. From now on everyone hastily arraigned himself on one side or the other, armed himself with a few dirty adjectives, and started the Ancient versus Modern War, or Trad versus Bebop, as it came to be known inside the business.

Each camp was well-stocked with crackpots determined to impose their own definitions of jazz on all the other crackpots. Some young men tried to reproduce in the flesh the sound which Johnson had produced in the recording studio, reminiscent of a bunch of street musicians playing in the middle of a sandstorm.

Other young men tried to copy the Parker mannerisms with the same relentless lack of logic, and one overzealous British modernist actually went to Charing Cross Hospital in search of an injection which would make him coloured and thus bring him closer to Parker's muse.

But there was still one ingredient missing from the recipe, money. Jazz finances up till now were still small beer, but as the two factions, still locked in deadly combat rolled dusty and bruised into the 1950s, the advent of the long-playing record and a sudden gushing of jazz criticism whipped up so great an interest that profits started to rise and the outside world of culture began to sit up and take notice. Jazz suddenly became invested with overwhelming significance, artistic, psychological, sociological, political. Sometimes even music was brought into the argument, although not very often.

The Beboppers, now dignified by the term Modernists, began to win the war hands down. Johnson slid back into the miasma of jazz legend, his imitators graduated to the music hall stage, where their gaily coloured waistcoats and tuppence-coloured advertising methods assured them a rich bonanza, while the Modernists were left more or less in possession of the field. Now the press agents and advertising managers began to move in. Before very long, a pianist called Dave Brubeck was on the front cover of *Time*, and another pianist, John Lewis, was buying his suits in Savile Row.

Brubeck and Lewis are vitally important in any study of jazz cultism because they were the first men to acquire the aura of a Brand Image. But apart from the fact that both of them realized the desirability of being the inspiration for a myth, their approaches were antipathetic. Lewis is the prototype of the modern egghead jazzman. University studies in Anthropology had led him to the curious conclusion that what jazz needed was Dignity. He was repelled by the old New Orleans bordello tradition, and longed to give the music Respectability, which he did by dubbing his compositions with French titles, dressing his quartet like undertakers and by eliminating the Smile from all public occasions. A typical MJQ album cover of the early days usually showed four men in morning coats looking at the camera with the studied gloom of four Eminent Victorians who have just heard about *The Origin of Species*.

All this was enough to make people stop and look. Lewis's next problem was how to make them listen. This he achieved by respecting one of the oldest rules of human intercourse, which is that people will strain to listen to any old platitude, so long as you utter it quietly enough. Lewis's Modern Jazz Quartet made so little noise that a spectator sitting at the back of a large concert hall might have been forgiven for assuming that it was Lewis who pioneered current miming techniques.

If Lewis's policy was Conquest by Persuasion, Brubeck's was Conquest by Flattery. Brubeck began by flattering himself and then finished the job by extending his approval to the audiences. First he would announce his next piece and underline the difficulties about to be encountered by himself and his musicians, rather like the illusionist who tells his audience his next trick is impossible. Then he would arrive at the ultimate flattery by telling his customers what the trick was called. This was most devious, because with a title like 'Blue Rondo À La Turk', the implication was that you and I were readily familiar, not only with blues, but also with rondos and with Turks. This appeal to the culture vulture proved irresistible and, while Brubeck conducted his triumphal processional around the world, his fans began using Brubeck LP covers as complimentary tickets for entry into the world's cultural pantheon. It was easier than reading *War and Peace* or listening to Brahms symphonies, and it had the extra advantage of being unassailably, indisputably modern.

Since Lewis and Brubeck, nobody has enjoyed quite so loftly an eminence, although the saxophonist Gerry Mulligan has appeared in whiskey ads. Recently, *Time* extended its accolade to that professional eccentric among jazzmen, Thelonious Monk, of whose piano playing it has been remarked, 'On the surface it's deep, but deep down it's shallow,' but it is doubtful whether any future stars will ever recapture the first fine careless rapture of John Lewis's goatee or Brubeck's genial giglamps.

A percentage of jazz fans continue to be guided in the record shops by the pictures on the album covers rather than the music between those covers. There has been a distinct advance in taste here. In the 1950s a Chet Baker album was adorned with a photo of a young lady stripped to the waist, clutching a teddy bear against each breast, precisely the kind of thing that Lewis has always fought against. Today the same album would probably be decorated by a Turner landscape or a Klee abstract. The music, however, would remain the same, a point of little interest to some customers.

For all the journalistic frenzy and the mass hero-worship, true reputations in jazz have fluctuated very little. Duke Ellington, who led the best big band of the late 1920s, still leads the best big band. Charlie Parker who died in 1955 still represents the furthest advance so far by the individual jazz musician. And the record companies remain neither less nor more knowledgeable about the products they are peddling than they were thirty years ago. In the monthly puff issued by one of our major companies there recently appeared the judgement that the two most accomplished string bassists in jazz were Charles Mingus and Oscar Peterson. Oscar Peterson plays the piano.

Fletcher Henderson (1964)

Nobody contributed more to the evolution of the large jazz band than Fletcher Henderson, an indifferent pianist, a poor disciplinarian and an absymal exploiter of his own wares, but a man with much instinctive wisdom in his musical approach. *The Fletcher Henderson Story – A Study in Frustration* is a magnificent production showing that Henderson always subordinated his orchestral ambitions to the ability of his soloists, instead of reversing the procedure – like so many of the leaders who usurped his position in the palmy days of the 1930s.

Henderson led a large orchestra from 1923 to 1934 and the value of this four-volume issue lies in the fact that his progress can be charted almost from month to month.

At first the orchestral methods were crude and clumsy. In volumes one and two are to be found all the indulgence of the period, particularly the simulation of train and animal noises, and that curious obsession of jazz in the 1920s with the depiction of bogus orientalism, resulting in oddities like 'Shanghai Shuffle'. At this stage the orchestra is merely an impediment to the enjoyment of superlative instrumental playing by Louis Armstrong and Coleman Hawkins.

Armstrong in 'How Come You Do Me Like You Do' plays with marvellous restrained power and wit, but he hardly eclipses the lesser-known Joe Smith, who, in 'What Cha Call 'Em Blues', playing a trumpet solo which is all charm and modesty, supports the theory of many musicians that the cornetist Bix Beiderbecke modelled his style closely on Smith's.

By the late 1920s Henderson was learning how to blend scored passages into a succession of solos, and although by this time Armstrong had moved on, the individual talent in the ranks remained undimmed. Musicians like Fats Waller, Benny Carter, Rex Stewart, Jimmie Harrison, Buster Bailey and Tommy Ladnier were eager to work for Henderson, who gradually evolved many of the tricks of style fated to become clichés a few years later in the hands of Benny Goodman and the Dorsey Brothers.

The question-and-answer choruses of saxophone and trumpet sections that later brought into being a nation of jitterbugs, the crisply scored ensembles that were really jazz solos written down and multiplied to the power of three, the orchestral figures cunningly wrought so as to further excite the soloist, Henderson pioneered all these effects without ever winning any kind of financial reward.

Perhaps the saddest volume of the four is the last one, which sees Henderson attempting a comeback in 1936. If anything, the music is better than ever, but by now the white touring bands had relegated Henderson to comparative obscurity.

The solo playing on 'Stealin' Apples', performed by saxophonist Chu Berry and trumpeter Roy Eldridge, surely ranks among the finest jazz of the decade, surpassed orchestrally only by the Ellington and Basie bands of the period. That is why the volume's sub-title, *A Study in Frustration*, is especially apt.

The college-trained son of teaching parents, Henderson was too inhibited by the colour bar to pursue his ambitions to their logical end, and he must have accepted with mixed feelings the overwhelming commercial success of the Benny Goodman Orchestra, many of whose scores he wrote, and whose stylistic father he undoubtedly was. The sixty-four tracks of his memorial album, faultlessly documented, are only a belated tribute to one of the most important pioneers in jazz history.

∾

ZOOT SIMS: . . . *AND THE GERSHWIN BROTHERS* (1975)

During the month of October 1925 both the Sims and Gershwin families were preoccupied with creative projects of rather differing natures. On the 29th of the month one of these projects was brought to fruition with the birth of John Haley to be known as Zoot, by which time George and Ira Gershwin had almost completed their score for a Broadway musical called *Tip Toes*, which is remembered today for 'That Certain Feeling' and perhaps 'Looking for A Boy'. Concurrently the two brothers were contributing one or two items to a curious mock-Slavonic concoction called *Song of the Flame*; both shows opened in the last week of the year. This furious activity of the Gershwins continued throughout Zoot's infancy. In 1926, while working on a show called *Oh Kay*, George realized that a fast and wordless tap-dance routine would serve better if halved in tempo and given the benefit of a lyric, which came to be 'Someone To Watch Over Me'. In 1927 their hit *Funny Face* included one of the most celebrated of all trick-lyrics, ''S Wonderful', and a year later a debacle called *Treasure Girl* included an exquisite love song called 'I've Got A Crush On You', a song so irresistible that it reappeared in 1929 in a more successful show called *Strike Up the Band*. Then in 1930, in a show called *Girl Crazy* two relatively unknown young singers called Ethel Merman and Ginger Rogers introduced 'I Got Rhythm' and 'Embraceable You' respectively; in 1933 a commercial failure called *Pardon My English* threw up one of the most underrated ballads of the period, 'Isn't It A Pity?'; and in 1935, in *Porgy and Bess* there was introduced one of the great songs of the musical theatre, 'Summertime'.

By the time Zoot Sims had become a professional saxophonist, in the early 1940s, the Gershwin alliance was history. George died in 1937, after which Ira collaborated with a succession of distinguished composers. By then the Gershwin repertoire had been seized on by jazz musicians, who found that there was usually something about a Gershwin tune which was conducive to good jazzmaking. At that time writers with a blanket ignorance of what jazz was tended to describe Gershwin as a 'jazz composer', a phrase which, being a contradiction in terms, only confused the real issue, which was that Gershwin was a composer whose shorter pieces were so witty harmonically, so appealing melodically, so resilient rhythmically, that they were perfectly suited to improvisation, there are three examples in particular on this album.

In 1924, predating Zoot, the Gershwin brothers had written their first full Broadway score together, a comedy called *Lady Be Good*, whose title song became a jazz standard. Also in the score was a ballad later described by knowledgeable men as the best American song of the twentieth century, a status which did not prevent it being dropped from the show, it's title was 'The Man I Love'. The third example is 'I Got Rhythm', whose chord sequence is so suited to jazzmaking that it has become one of the two basic sequences for jazz improvisation, the other being the Blues. How did the writing of such material influence jazz? To answer that it is instructive to look at the events of 9 October 1936, when the saxophonist Lester Young, already a genius but still relatively unknown, cut his first ever sides, with a Count Basie small group. One of these sides was 'Lady Be Good', and in three minutes Lester altered the course of jazz history by introducing to record buyers the honking tone and elliptical logic of his style, a style destined to influence a whole generation of younger players. This generation included several brilliant tenor players. One of them was Zoot Sims.

Later, in 1939, Lester recorded 'The Man I Love' with Billie Holiday, and also 'Lester Leaps In' again with Basie, a theme which was no more than a loose disguise for 'I Got Rhythm'. The links between those performances of Lester's and Zoot's playing are unmistakeable. What is also interesting are other relationships between Zoot and Gershwin performances and those of earlier musicians. For instance 'Summertime', usually regarded as a slow ballad, is in fact a most promising up-tempo vehicle, as Zoot and company demonstrate here, having made the same discovery that Billie Holiday, Bunny Berigan and Artie Shaw did back in 1936, when they recorded Gershwin's lullaby as a swinger. Again 'The Man I Love' has been amended here, as it often is in the jazz context, to a sixty-four bar song which each of the original measures doubled in length. Far from being a blasphemy, this kind of rough treatment of his songs was precisely what delighted Gershwin about jazz. He was fascinated by what happened when great improvisers used his pieces as points of departure, and one can picture the raptures he would have gone into had he ever heard the splendid flourish with which Oscar Peterson opens 'I've Got A Crush On You', or the guitar obbligato of Joe Pass which introduces 'Embraceable You'. This track, incidentally, shows how a great song can induce an outstanding performance, for the heat of Zoot's saxophone playing almost visibly rises in intensity as the performance proceeds, beginning quite decorously and reaching positively passionate heights.

And when we come to follow the convolutions of 'The Man I Love' and 'I Got Rhythm' riding on the back of the rhythm section, driven by Grady Tate and George Mraz, we see what it was that Gershwin bequeathed to the jazz world. As the five players swing along the grooves of the harmonies, it is almost as though Gershwin had prepared the way for them by building sequences specifically designed for jazz and nothing else. And yet, as we know so well, none of these themes which Zoot and company play so beautifully, was ever intended for anything more elevated than the stereotypes of the Broadway stage. It is odd that the bulk of the standard jazz repertoire should have happened in this way, purely by accident. Odder still that themes which are so ideally suited to the talents of men like the five gifted musicians who made this album, should belong to a world remote from them all. After all, songs like 'Lady Be Good' were hits before Zoot was even born; the show from which it came had closed for several weeks by the time Oscar Peterson was born. As for what came after, during the month of October 1925, both the Sims and Gershwin families were preoccupied with creative projects of rather differing natures.

The Singer not the Song (1973)

There is no accounting for jazz singers, that is to say, singers who suffer from the dangerous delusion that they are jazz singers. I am not talking now about people like Louis Armstrong and

Jack Teagarden, whose methods of vocal expression are so clearly extensions of their instrumental personalities, but of that curious group of non-playing singers, most of them women, who at most stages in the development of the music, have clung with such tenacity to the myth of their own jazz relevance as to occasionally convince other people. However, it remains sad but true that the number of non-playing singers sincerely respected by practising musicians remains so small as to be very nearly non-existent. The sincerity of these singers is of course unimpeachable, but then so was Genghis Khan's, and they remain a band of brave but deluded pilgrims marching resolutely in the wrong direction.

The reasons for this are obvious enough. The art of making jazz consists of creating melodic patterns based on a given harmonic foundation. It is an elusive and highly demanding art, extremely difficult to perform with any degree of subtlety, and the only known way of mastering even its rudiments is to spend ten or twenty years of instrumental practice, learning by trial and error how to play a game whose rules can never really be formulated. It is noticeable that this process is exclusively a musical one, and that lyrics play no part in it. In any case, if there are to be lyrics, whose must they be? Not those of the original lyricist, because once improvisation takes place, all the note pitches and note values to which the words were matched, are jettisoned and new pitches and values, those of the improvised melody, take their place. The utter impossibility of the situation becomes apparent the moment one tries to wed the words of a song to the improvised solo based on its harmonies, for instance the words of 'Body And Soul' with the new melodic line created by Coleman Hawkins in his monumental recording of that song. There is a further drawback, which is that while the improvised findings of the great jazz musicians are free of the responsibility to make explicit statements, the lyrics of many of their favourite vehicles are often trite to the brink of imbecility.

These are shocking handicaps, and over the years various attempts have been made to overcome them. Some singers have been so dense that the banality of the lyrics has never occurred to them, others so egocentric as to believe that the banality could be relieved by the amazing beauty of their voices. Still others have dropped the lyrics altogether and concentrated instead on making vocal noises which they hope with touching optimism will be construed as approximations of instrumental effects. One or two singers have even attempted to compose their own lyrics to existing fragments of improvisations, although they have usually been undone by the fact that there are in an improvised solo so many notes, and often so many notes within the compass of a single bar, that even the most clearly enunciated lyric tends to disappear in a blur of syllabic frenzy.

The truth of it is that there is no such thing as a jazz singer, which raises the awkward problem of people like Bessie Smith and Billie Holiday, whose jazz credentials are irrefutable. Their advent can only be described as fortuitous, a bonus for which our expectations must always have been nil. These two remarkable ladies represent two quite different lyric, though not jazz, traditions, Bessie Smith the uncompromising realism of the Blues, Billie Holiday the soft-centred escape from that realism so cunningly devised by Tin Pan Alley. In a sense, therefore, Billie Holiday's achievement is the greater of the two, for while Bessie Smith interpreted the poetry of the Blues, Billie contrived somehow to solidify that soft centre of the Moon/June syndrome, creating what poetry she could from a convention which had little regard for it.

Most of the jazz musicians I came to know well spoke to me at some time or another about which particular fragment of recorded jazz first impelled them to try making their own jazz, the first piece of music to offer them the categorical imperative of doing the thing for themselves. In some cases these primal sources might scandalize the purists. Indifferent big bands and inept small ones; three-chord tricksters from New Orleans and semi-commercial warblers who were not only devoid of jazz talent but didn't care. Of course it would all have been much more proper if every apprentice jazz musician had taken up his craft at the instigation of some respectable figure like Armstrong or Ellington or Parker, but the truth is that any old second-rater will do so long as he succeeds, however accidentally, in lighting the fire of ambition.

Billie Holiday was not the first great jazz musician whose work I enjoyed, but she was the first whose work brought home to me the injustice of neglect, and whose career taught me the simple truth that to be magnificently accomplished at something is no guarantee that people will ever realize it. A few girl singers I came across in my own career really did think that Billie Holiday was a man, but as they knew only the name and not the voice, that is hardly surprising. When I think of the vocalist who night after night sang: 'You go to my head/and you linger like a hunting refrain'; when I remember the boy who ended 'Laura' with 'but she's only a fool', and after being told that the correct ending was 'but she's only a dream', compromised with 'but she's only a drool'; when I think of the girl who amended the phrase 'Creole babies with flashing eyes' to 'three old ladies with flashing eyes', was told of her error and then managed 'Creole baby with flashing eyes' and on being told that it was plural, ended up with 'Plural babies with flashing eyes'; when I remember incidents such as these, I am amazed, not that there should have been so few competent jazz singers, but that there should have been any at all. And speaking as a worker who once sang 'Silver Dollar' to a ballroom audience in Dundee which responded by throwing pennies, I feel my competence to discuss the subject is not altogether spurious.

ANITA O'DAY (1960)

The exhibition of vocal dexterity by Miss Anita O'Day on the lawn of the Palace House, Beaulieu, last Sunday afternoon, is apparently the last such exhibition to be given at that charming venue. Lord Montagu, bowing gracefully in the face of the inevitable, which this year took the form of fits of drunkenness and a few bottle-throwing episodes outside the village local, has announced that there will be no Beaulieu Festival next year, or perhaps ever again.

It is fitting that the swansong of the Festival should have been sung by Anita O'Day of all artists, for her whole vocal approach is suffused with the wry sense of humour one needs to accept the gallant failure of his lordship to combat extra-musical vandalism. Her decision to include 'Sweet Georgia Brown' and

'Tea For Two' in her programme was more or less obligatory, for these were the tunes which in the film *Jazz on a Summer's Day*, introduced her to a far wider audience than she had ever previously known. A more eloquent testimony to her technique was her note-perfect 'Four Brothers', a famous saxophone instrumental whose chromatic conception makes it a daunting task indeed for any singer.

In the actual quality of her voice Miss O'Day cannot begin to compare with those whose recognition she shares. It is in its content rather than its vocal form that her style commends itself. As she plays capricious tricks with the time values and the duration of the syllables, it seems hard to believe she will ever succeed in fulfilling the one requirement a musician ever dares hope for from a singer, which is to finish at the same time as the orchestra. But Miss O'Day, who seems crazy, is really crazy like a fox, and achieved dead heat after dead heat with the Johnny Dankworth Orchestra with smiling unconcern.

Even more intriguing than Anita O'Day's mannerisms was the rumour that the scuffles in the village might have been between traditionalist and modern enthusiasts. It is gratifying to hear that there is anybody left in the country willing to fight for his artistic convictions, but the fact remains that the war between trads and mods, whether pugilistic or dialectic, is one in which the difference between the warring factions is quite imaginary. For a traditionalist to punch a modernist on the nose is about as sensible as Genesis declaring war on Leviticus because of its advanced position in the narrative pattern.

The trouble with functions like the Beaulieu Festival is that the social respectability of jazz is too new a phenomenon to be taken in their stride by its younger fringe followers. After the first stage, when jazz was besieged by the hordes of musical prejudice, came the second stage, still with us, of unlimited social freedom, which includes the freedom to commit mild acts of vandalism on the lawns of baronial estates.

One day, not too far distant, the reaction to the reaction will take place, and jazz will adjust its attitudes accordingly, neither tolerated as a novelty nor deified as a new source of musical godhead. Only then will organizers like Lord Montagu, whose heroic struggles to organize the Beaulieu Festival and his enlightened approach to selecting programmes were apparently for nothing, be able to organize their syncopated Salzburgs without fear of broken bottles in the bar parlour.

TONY BENNETT (1969)

In order to assess the value of Tony Bennett as a singer it is necessary to stress one simple fact which ought not to need stressing at all, but which is in serious danger of being overlooked in these mad times. That fact is that words in a song are supposed to convey a meaning. When a lyric writer breaks his head to find some way of making a rhymed message make sense he is not just indulging in a pointless habit. The conveying of a sense is what his job is all about, and when we come to evaluate a singer's art, we have not only to worry about whether he sings in tune, whether he can start and finish at the same time as the orchestra, whether his voice sounds pleasant or unpleasant, but also to what extent he can read English. This might sound too obvious, but it is astonishing how many singers, male and female, with towering reputations, perform in so illiterate a way as to worry about the sounds and let the sense take care of itself.

This is why Tony Bennett stands out from the other male singers of his generation. Not only does he understand the meaning of the lyrics, but he is able to express the mood they convey to him, which is very much harder. In the last reckoning, a vocal performance of a standard song should be a dramatic as well as a musical experience, and when it is, we say that the singer responsible is capable of 'good readings'. Nobody since Sinatra has shown so astute a talent for this reading of a lyric as Tony Bennett. Many of the songs have now come to be associated with him, even though they have been around longer than he has. This is because, by giving them a dramatic as well as a musical frame, Bennett has created the illusion that they were written with him alone in mind, which is indeed one of the hallmarks of the outstanding artist.

At first sight it might seem surprising that Bennett rates an entry in Leonard Feather's *Encyclopaedia of Jazz*, but when one realizes that it is very difficult indeed to become as good a phraser of a melody as Bennett is without having had some contacts with jazz, the surprise fades away. In fact, ever since he became a powerful enough public attraction to demand his own musical backgrounds, Bennett has shown a decided taste for the jazz accompaniment. Those who remember his tour here in which the Dixieland veteran trumpeter Bobby Hackett was given featured billing will surely agree with that claim. More recently Bennett came here with John Bunch on piano, Bunch being one of the musicians who toured Russia with Benny Goodman back in 1962. As for Bunch's predecessor, Ralph Sharon, no British jazz fan with a reasonable memory needs to be convinced of Sharon's jazz talents.

There was a period when it seemed that Bennett's success was to be kept secret so far as British audiences were concerned. He had already advanced a long way in the United States while he was still little more than a rumour over here, but the last ten years have seen a tremendous if belated reception given to him, until today he is one of the most popular musical artists that America is able to send us. Even so, for a long time little was known about his background, and even at this late date it is not unreasonable to assume that there may still be those who are closely familiar with his singing style but who have very few facts to go on.

He was born Anthony Benedetto, in Queens, New York, in 1926, and like many people who later became successful, began giving public performances while still a child. When he was seven years old he took part in a neighbourhood parish minstrel show, but in spite of this early start he appears to have shown no inclination at all for a professional singing career. The truth is that Benedetto had already shown more outstanding talents in another sphere, painting and sketching. Like the great Duke Ellington before him, he got off to a false start by enrolling as a student at a school of design, The High School of Industrial Arts. Possibly he would eventually have become an artist had it not been for the intervention of the last war, which disturbed his studies and had the effect of making him think again.

Bennett, or Benedetto, as he still was at this time, became an infantryman in Germany, serving there for three years. There were several army bands around, and he found himself singing with them more and more frequently. He also found that the reaction from his fellow conscripts was distinctly favourable. He summed up the applause and the enthusiasm for his voice and wondered whether, after all, Commercial Art was such a good idea. When the time came for him to choose his direction after demobilization he went back to a very different seat of learning, the American Theatre Wing's professional school for veterans.

He seems to have found it reasonably easy to get work as a singer right from the start. He began working in night clubs, did the occasional radio show and also appeared once or twice on television. But the really important chance came quite by accident, when he was booked as a supporting singer on a bill for a Greenwich Village club whose big attraction was Pearl Bailey. It is always a useful thing to share a date with somebody like Pearl Bailey, because there is always the chance that somebody influential will come in to hear her and get to hear you as well. This is exactly what happened to Bennett. The influential visitor was Bob Hope, who was at the time presenting his own show at the Paramount Theatre in New York. Hope, who had come in to watch Pearl Bailey work, also saw the unknown Bennett, and was so impressed by what he heard that he made one of those instantaneous decisions which very rarely occur outside the minds of second-rate script writers. Hope decided that Bennett ought to be working for him, and within twenty-four hours he was. Hope pushed him on at the Paramount, and after only one show, the audience reaction being quite enough proof that Hope's hunch had been justified, Benedetto had not only a new career but a new name to go with it. 'He doesn't know it yet,' Hope told the audience after Benedetto's recital, 'but I'm taking him along with me on a tour of the United States. He also doesn't know it, but from now on his name is going to be Tony Bennett.'

After the end of the successful tour with Hope, Bennett made a demonstration record and took it to Mitch Miller, at that time head of Columbia's Popular Artists and Repertoire department. Bennett was instantly signed to an exclusive contract and the demonstration record released. It was called 'Boulevard Of Broken Dreams' and became one of the biggest selling vocal hits of 1951. It was from now on that British followers of popular music first began to hear Bennett's name, although they were always behind the game a little. Bennett's advance through the 1950s was phenomenal and culminated in a one-man show at Carnegie Hall in June 1962, which was sold out two weeks in advance and saw more than two thousand people turned away from the door on the night. Those who have not already acquainted themselves with the music from that night can still do so by acquiring a copy of the two albums, *Tony Bennett At Carnegie Hall.*

It is probably unnecessary to run through the statistics of Bennett's success over the last fifteen years, but, just for the record, he has topped a million sales on several occasions with, among others, 'Because Of You', 'Cold Cold Heart', 'From Rags To Riches' and, of course, his biggest success of all, 'I Left My Heart In San Francisco'. The latter disc won him two awards from the National Academy of Recording Arts, one for Record of the Year and another for Best Solo Vocal Performance. But what is most interesting of all about these great successes is that Bennett himself does not seem interested in possessing any of the evidence. He has said on more than one occasion that he owns none of his own recordings and has also explained why.

'I don't want to imitate the way I sound on another record. Every song is different and you sing it differently. I don't want to get into the habit of singing everything in the same way.' On the other hand, he has so individual a style and tone that there is a sense, the very best sense, in which he does sing everything the same way. At all events, he is one of the most easily recognizable of all male singers of his generation. Two or three bars from him and almost everybody recognizes who it is. The tone of his voice is strongly masculine, his enunciation of the lyrics intelligent and vigorously expressed, and his range is wide enough for him to cope with any songs which come along.

One can deduce from the evidence he is also a very good judge of a song. He has frequently chosen half-forgotten vehicles which deserved more popularity than a slipshod musical generation was willing to give them. I recall particularly his excellent version of one of the best songs of the early 1930s, 'Alone Together', also a deeply affecting recording of the Vincent Youmans classic, 'More Than You Know', in which his reading of the verse is a performance of the very highest class. He is also a master at playing games with the time values of the notes in a song. One of his favourite themes, 'It Had To Be You', usually bears evidence of this simple-sounding but in fact very difficult art, always performed by Bennett with the greatest ease and relaxation. The 1960s will probably go down in social history as the most lunatic interlude of this century so far as popular art is concerned. When the time comes to add up the credit and debit columns, Bennett will stand with the tiny élite who have produced something of genuine quality.

Avant Garde (1973)

In 1947 an uncle of mine, hearing me practising one morning in the attic of my grandfather's house, and becoming convinced by the experience that I was an undiscovered instrumental genius ready for the concert hall circuits of the world, attempted to expedite my progress towards the floral tributes and the standing ovations by arranging an audition for me with a friend of his youth who was now a nationally famous bandleader in a central London ballroom. It being understood that I was some kind of musical phenomenon who could actually play for ten consecutive minutes without falling over, my audition was not to be the usual private kind, but rather a baptism under fire. I was to sit in with this orchestra in the full public glare, at what used laughingly to be known in those quaint days as a tea-dance, taking my place in an unfamiliar ensemble, reading the parts at sight, integrating into the saxophone section by sheer instinct. As my professional expertise was minimal and my ensemble experience nil, I was of course in no position to perform any such feats, but some instinct told me that the fiasco before me was somehow vital to my future prospects, for I saw that only by enduring a long succession of such ordeals was I ever likely to arrive at any kind of professional ability at all.

But my feelings about this unsolicited gesture of nepotism were mixed. Certainly I was eager to play with other, more experienced musicians; certainly I was only too ready to relinquish belatedly my amateur status in a frankly mercenary world (I was now twenty, and the whole thing was getting ridiculous). On the other hand, my critical faculties being far better developed than my instrumental ones, I was well aware that this fortunate bandleader before whom I was to display my tray of musical trinkets was perhaps the most execrable clarinettist still at large in England at that time. As for his band, it bore not the remotest resemblance to Count Basie's and therefore held no interest for me, I being too priggish by far at this time to see the absurdity of the comparison. As if this were not enough, there floated at the back of my mind the uneasy recollection of a remark my uncle had made to the effect that his bandleader friend never washed his feet or changed his socks. And to compound it all the date was 28 August, Middlesex were batting against Northants at Lords, and Denis Compton, with fifteen centuries already to his credit that season, needed only one more to equal Jack Hobbs's records. Under circumstances so trying it is not surprising that on arrival at the ballroom I was too confused to know where to look for the tradesman's entrance, and ended up carrying my instrument case into the front foyer and paying for admission.

Soon I was shown into a tiny bandroom and told to wait till I was sent for. So I assembled my instrument and began warming up, drifting without realizing it into Lester Young's solo from 'Dickie's Dream', which I had only recently succeeded in committing to memory. After I had been playing for a few minutes, revelling in the vicarious glory of Young's brilliant exposition of the use of the chord of the Minor sixth, a small bespectacled man of about forty entered the room and stood nervously watching me. I stopped playing and he said, 'They're nearly ready for you. You'll see my chair, second one in from this side.' Then I noticed the saxophone sling round his neck and the corn on the thumb of his right hand and realized he must be the band's resident tenor saxophonist, the man who must by now be convinced that I coveted his job. I could see that although he was doing his best to muster a little of that professional camaraderie which is supposed to overcome all personal anxieties in such situations, but hardly ever does, he could not help revealing a certain blend of envy and worry in his remark to me, 'I can hear that you play this avant garde stuff.' And that was the first time in my life that I ever heard the phrase in normal conversation.

Modestly pleading guilty to the charge that I had indeed been playing avant garde music, and even more modestly omitting to add that I was incapable of playing anything else, I mumbled a few platitudes, not quite knowing how to convince him that I desired my escape from the premises even more passionately than he desired it. Then I shambled out of the room into the unnerving glare of the bandstand, to begin an audition whose course and eventual outcome drift far beyond the prescribed boundaries of this book. But the point of my story is to show how possible it once was for a trained professional musician to be confronted by the venerable harmonic practices of Lester Young and recoil from them as though from total anarchy. The modern reader may find such a reaction quaint enough to induce a certain complacency, but as he has absolutely no chance of remaining modern for very many years after reading these lines, he would be well advised not to become too complacent. Avant garde is not a style but an attitude towards style; all a man has to do to backslide from the vanguard to the last ditch is to grow older, and so the jazz musician, if only he survives long enough, will find himself, much to his own amusement, having at various stages in his working life played not one but both of the roles in the bathetic little comedy which the bespectacled saxophonist and myself acted out exactly a quarter of a century ago.

But the reader, being happily free of the obligation of ingratiating himself in the eyes of bandleaders who never change their socks or their musical approach, will want to know who was right. Which of the two bigotries on display in that bandroom twenty-five years ago was justified, and what is more to the point, were either of them avoidable? The man whose job I was not after rejected Young's solo not simply because I might be a finer musician than he, but because the system of musical thought which made me better was beyond his experience, and therefore no better than malignant sorcery. Whereas he, no matter how hard he practised, would never sound like anything but a poor imitation of Bud Freeman, I would always sound like a poor imitation of Lester Young. It was the difference between the sensibilities of two eras. Perhaps to him Young's spectral Minor sixths sounded like downright wrong notes, in exactly the same way as I myself was very soon to wonder whether the flattened fifths and ninths of the Beboppers might not be wrong notes. Our respective ears belonged to successive and therefore to warring generations, and so there could be no common ground. With my neologisms he recognized he was being served notice to quit by the rising generation, and although for me it was the extremely serious business of art for art's sake while for him it meant nothing more than the frivolities of mortgage payments and three meals a day, I could not help feeling deeply sympathetic with his plight even at the time.

In the following record of my encounters with later avant garde movements the reader may think he sees the distance between myself and the performers increasing steadily as the years slip by. He may well be right. Just as my harmless second-hand Minor sixths once alarmed a palais musician, so the innovations of later years have often outraged me, although I offer in mitigation of my own attitude the interesting truth that while my revolutionary gestures and those of the Beboppers were still formal enough to answer to names like Minor sixth and Minor seventh, the anarchy of the 1960s, being totally committed, totally uncompromising anarchy, answers to no names at all, remaining free to make what noises it pleases, considerably alarming the natives in the process. But in Stevenson's *The Beach of Falesa*, the banjo strings in the tree being likewise free to make what noise they pleased, likewise alarmed the natives, without ever producing any coherent music. Whether or not present-day critics, chastened by the dreadful mess that was made with the entry of Charlie Parker, have quietly decided that it is safer never to condemn anything out of hand ever again I cannot say, but certainly in the years since I began reviewing, the streets have become positively congested with kings walking about with no clothes on.

For the record, I got to Lords later that day in time to see Compton bowled by Broderick for 85. It was another five days before Hobbs's mark was equalled, again at Lords, in the match against Lancashire. I do not seem to have been present on that day, and cannot imagine what kind of engagement it was that seemed important enough to keep me away at such a historic moment. Certainly not another audition.

Miles Davis (1961)

The myth that jazz is essentially a good-time music was finally laid to rest last week when the American trumpeter Miles Davis opened his long-awaited British tour. At the Gaumont, Hammersmith, Davis somehow managed to recreate, and even intensify, the hypnotic effect of recordings which have obliged us all to stop in our tracks and ask once again, 'What *is* jazz anyway?'

The power of Davis's originality is most effectively proved by the astonishing way in which his playing places that of the rest of his quintet on a subordinate plane. His saxophonist, Sonny Stitt, prolific and irresistible, is an instrumentalist of immense culture and personality. It is hard to imagine even a partial eclipse of so dynamic an artist. But Davis, with a few notes selected with diabolonian cunning, forces us to examine the classical methods of players like Stitt from a new perspective.

The one very real dilemma of jazz music is the problem of the limitations of improvising on chord sequences. Within the framework of a harmonic progression the musician is free to trace whatever melodic patterns he can. But one senses, in the work of the most gifted soloists and in the fidgeting of younger rebels, a certain resigned acceptance of the theory that the utmost limits have almost been reached.

The attempt by Davis to solve this problem was admirably posed at Hammersmith by the sharp contrast between the material Davis first introduced on his albums, and the more orthodox themes which form perhaps half of the quintet's repertoire. Significantly, Miles opened and closed his first British concert with two themes from his *Kind of Blue* recording, one which questioned the tenets of jazzmaking more searchingly than anything since Charlie Parker. With those two themes, 'Freddie Freeloader' and 'All Blues', Davis cast a spell already familiar to those who know the recordings.

What is it about this spell which makes it so very different from any other jazz? To put it briefly, Davis has succeeded in introducing into the jazz context a new aesthetic. Every note he plays is tinged with the disturbing melancholia of a highly sophisticated and super-sensitive artist. Nowhere is there any trace of the unselfconscious joy at being alive of Louis Armstrong, or the irrepressible good spirits of Davis's great contemporary, Dizzy Gillespie. Suddenly, through the prism of Davis's conception, all other jazz appears a Panglossian affair concerned with the release of tension rather than the exploration of it. With Miles Davis, introspection enters the jazz world, and just as Lester Young, when he introduced the qualities of wit into the idiom, used new weapons, so Davis has been obliged gradually to evolve an approach of his own.

Tonally he has dramatically distilled the sound of the trumpet, so that it now possesses a deathly purity evoking all kinds of poetic images. Vibrato has almost disappeared completely, and forgotten is the old avowed intention of the instrumentalist to suggest the overtones of the human voice, still very apparent in contemporaries like Ellington's Clark Terry. When Miles, using a mute, improvises on 'Green Dolphin Street' and 'Round Midnight', he achieves a spectral evocation which makes even Lester Young's pre-war legerdemain sound like jolly extroversion. Were I limited to one adjective in reference to Miles Davis, I would probably settle for 'crepuscular'.

The *Kind of Blue* material reflects Davis's attempt to escape from the cage of normal progression from discord to resolution without shattering the jazz form entirely. The themes are based less on chord progressions than on a series of modal scales, whose possibilities Davis probes with consummate delicacy, employing a more rigorous selection and economy of note than anybody before him. To find any parallel at all with this introversion I can think only of the piano fragments of Bix Beiderbecke thirty years before, although these were necessarily quite different in harmonic conception.

Davis's originality is underlined by Stitt when the group plays a conventional blues theme like 'Walkin''. Here Stitt is positively brilliant, playing with masterly execution and producing a cascade of ideas completely overwhelming to the listener bred on a diet of derivative homegrown jazz. The contrast between Stitt and his leader serves also to remind us that Davis is limited by the very nature of his development to a single mood, but that within its confines he is one of the great jazzmen.

The presentation of this new approach has given rise to some touching confusion on the part of audiences. Davis says not a single word throughout his concerts. He makes no announcements and even leaves the stage when not actually playing. Some people have used this austerity as an excuse to talk of Miles Davis's 'failure to project' or even his bad professional manners. The truth is that Miles projects with his trumpet, and that his so-called snubbing of the audience is merely a flattering assumption that any audience which pays to see him knows enough about what is going on to be spared announcements of the 'For my next number' variety.

As for the benumbing jocosities of most jazz group leaders, Davis is quite justifiably contemptuous of such attempts to milk his followers. He is trying to invest a jazz performance with the same dignity and self-assurance which he himself possesses to such a remarkable degree. Those knockabout comics, the Modern Jazz Quartet, would do well to study him a little more closely. Rarely have I witnessed a more impressive concert of jazz.

JOHN COLTRANE: *AFRO-BLUE IMPRESSIONS* (1977)

The nature of John Coltrane's performance on this album demands that it be taken in its historical context. In order to understand what he is doing and why he is doing it, the listener must acquaint himself with great thoroughness to the prevailing winds of style at the time the performance was made. To some extent, of course, this is true of every jazz musician at every juncture of his career, but it is particularly so of Coltrane, who, in a comparatively brief and extremely brilliant career, advanced with a kind of desperate courage to the very frontiers of lucidity and even, it should be said, occasionally beyond them at the very end of his life. One has only to hear half a chorus of Coltrane to perceive that he was a man chafing under the restraints of traditional jazzmaking, a man struggling to establish some new kind of method which would somehow reconcile a thirst for adventure with a respect for the canons of logic. In other spheres creative artists like James Joyce, Pablo Picasso and Béla Bartók made the acquaintance of the same enigma, creating new techniques to solve new problems. Did Coltrane succeed? The answer is that sometimes he did and sometimes he didn't. What is important to the understanding of him is the fact that he was one of the most intrepid explorers in jazz history, which raises the question of how much, by the time he arrived on the scene, there was left to explore.

Not so very much. The historians will certainly see Coltrane as a musician who, having inherited the vast new harmonic territories bequeathed by Charlie Parker, sought to consolidate those gains and to build upon them. The problem was to know *how* to build upon them, for Parker, in opening the way for the incorporation into jazz of an all-embracing harmonic system, had, like a westering pioneer too successful for his own eventual good, reached the sea; after Parker, where else could an experimenter wander without violating the bounds of formal logic altogether? In this album that is the question which Coltrane is constantly asking himself; what makes it fascinating is that there are some moments when he appears to have found a few answers. The difficulty inhibiting players like Coltrane and Sonny Rollins, who was caught on the horns of the same dilemma, is that you can only build so many chord changes into the structure of a solo. The old-timers used to make one harmony stretch over four bars; the virtuosi of the pre-war Swing Age preferred the idea of harmonies which shifted from bar to bar; with Parker came the idea of chromatic bridges linking the main harmonies, much as a series of subjunctive clauses can lend colour to a simple sentence. Coltrane himself often sounds like a player cramming a chord change into every *beat;* but where lay the ultimate?

Much of the relevance of what Coltrane played is to do with certain experiments conducted by Miles Davis a few years earlier, in which the question was asked: Are conventional chord sequences necessary at all? In one or two Davis albums, harmonies as such were laid aside in favour of modal patterns, that is to say, instead of finding himself confronted by a series of resolving chords, the soloist was offered a scalic line, a melodic rather than a harmonic pendant on which to hang his improvisation. Or perhaps he might use harmony only in the limited sense of a theme consisting only of two chords, with the dynamism of the performance based on the pendulum-like swing of the solo from one of those harmonies to the other. The aim was to liberate the jazz musician from his self-made prison of discord-to-concord resolution and in so doing increase the likelihood of his finding fresh patterns of thought. It was intended to be an uncluttering process, but the irony was that in uncluttering the harmonic freeway, the experimenters inadvertently encouraged an even more cluttered melodic line. When a man has no laws of perspective to observe, his inclination will be to doodle. That is why so many people mistake avant garde frippery for a phenomenal technique, forgetting in their excitement that virtuosity in music consists not of playing a lot of notes fast, but of playing a lot of notes fast within the constraints of form.

But Coltrane is an exception to that rule which makes us doubt the claims of so many experimental pretenders. For whatever one thinks of Coltrane's playing, the one charge which can never be laid against him is of posturing or insincerity. For this reason he is one of the most important figures in any attempt to appraise the validity of the avant garde. The truth is that no matter how far he sometimes strayed from the harmonic fold, Coltrane always retained a mastery over conventional jazzmaking methods which was total. Some of his performances were so fine that they literally took the breath away; both in cleanliness of execution and beauty of tone Coltrane possessed classic virtues, so that when he turned away from this control and deliberately courted disaster, and by so doing implied that the constraints of form were now intolerable to him, we cannot do what we are inclined to do when we hear the same story from younger men, which is to wonder, if their mastery is all that complete, where they have hidden the evidence. Coltrane left the evidence all over the place; had he never conducted a single experiment in the improvising art, he would still have been one of the great soloists of jazz.

There is something else about Coltrane which needs to be said, and that is that not even the limits of his instrument were sufficient for his purpose. Within a few moments of starting to play in 'Lonnie's Lament' he is straining after notes far higher than those originally considered to be a practical possibility by the instrument's inventor Adolphe Sax. The listener should also take note of the fact that once into his stride, Coltrane becomes implicated in a duet with drummer Elvin Jones. There occur several parallel passages during the album, where McCoy Tyner and Jimmy Garrison drop out, and it is safe to assume that each time they do so, it is a hint that Coltrane is to an extent chancing his arm, following in the wake of his own inspiration, or 'freaking out' as it subsequently became known. The consummation of this approach comes in the coda of 'I Want To Talk About You', a passage so extended that it may be nominated as a remarkable example of the tail wagging the dog, in so far as the coda virtually obliterates the performance it is meant to be tying up. At this point in the concert, Coltrane is like a man transported by self-absorption into a room on his own, where he can blow his instrument and finger runs and arpeggios for the sheer naked pleasure of playing them. There is a sense in which this sort of thing is a confidence trick, because the content of the ruminations is attached to no known system of thought or notation. However, I can think of no saxophone player who will not attend closely to this remarkable opening of the saxophonist's Pandora's box and admire the wonderful variety of its contents.

As the concert proceeds, Coltrane brings up his reserves, as it were, only instead of cavalry he deploys the soprano saxophone, an obsolescent instrument which he did more than any other saxophonist of the period to revivify. If the tricks he was attempting on the tenor were impractical, then they should have been downright impossible on the soprano, where the player can do so much less with his embouchure and fingers to render the execution more pliable. In the album's one theme drawn from the conventional popular repertoire, 'My Favourite Things', Coltrane the soprano player achieves his best strokes. This was the theme which always appeared to him to be the one perfectly suited for his soprano experiments; he never tired of playing it on the instrument, and it can be discerned quite unmistakably that he was able somehow to add the theme to the horn and arrive at some marvellous solutions. His soprano playing as typified by 'My Favourite Things' consists of passages of furious endeavour punctuated by other, exquisitely beautiful, interludes whose most precious virtue of all is that they are starkly original; in the passages where the soprano takes wings in 'My Favourite Things', Coltrane is genuinely extending the frontiers of improvisation, that is to say, he is annexing new territory without resorting to methods of musical barbarism.

The frightful problems which Coltrane set himself in his career were never really resolved; Coltrane himself would have been the first to admit that. Shortly after this concert he was dead, still a young man and still with his evolutionary cycle uncompleted. This album, which catches him at a point of balance between the comparative orthodoxies of the mid-1950s and the maelstrom of his last performances, is as graphic an illustration of jazz in the instant before dissolution as any I can remember hearing.

Joe Turner and the Blues (1975)

As it is around fifty years now since Joe Turner first began shouting the Blues, and around forty since he first came to New York and established a national reputation, people have had ample opportunity to sit down and drive themselves half-crazy puzzling over the enigma of the music Joe makes. Its form appears to be infantile, its content extremely limited. And yet its effect is devastating. In spite of its apparent simplicity, it is so hard to perform with any real conviction that today Joe Turner is especially prized by the jazz lover as almost the only man left alive who can take hold of a traditional Blues piece and do it full justice with all the authority of a founding father. The explanation is, of course, that it is its very simplicity which makes the Blues so challenging a business, because the performer, unable to hide behind the palisades of harmonic obscurantism or literary subtlety, has nothing to rely on except the quality of his voice and the natural swing of his style.

The academic theorist, faced with the fundamentals of an artist like Joe Turner, would soon find himself impeded by a lapful of limitations and negative assessments. Beginning at the very beginning, there is the voice, which no more conforms to the conventional bel canto demands of the outside world than Fats Waller's did, or Billie Holiday's, or Louis Armstrong's. I have never undertaken a strict analysis of Big Joe's practicable vocal range, but I would be greatly surprised if a single octave did not encompass all his requirements with room to spare. Moreover, many of the musicians who have played for Joe testify to a predilection on his part amounting very nearly to a prejudice, for the key of C Major. As to the matter of repertoire, Big Joe either writes his own Blues or borrows other people's, which means that more or less the entire residue of art-songs famous for the literacy of writers like Hart and Porter, is a closed book to him. It is true that on *Nobody in Mind* he does sing one or two songs which fall outside the Blues category, but of them, 'I Want A Little Girl' is one of those thirty-two bar standard songs which leans so heavily on the Blues structure that without that support it would fall flat on its face. As for 'Red Sails In The Sunset' and Joe's version of it, thereby hangs a cautionary tale, of which more in a moment.

So our picture of Joe Turner does not look a very promising one. He has a strictly limited range, a strictly limited choice of keys, strictly limited vocal effects and a highly specialized repertoire. In which case, so much for mere facts. For the moment we stop peering through the wrong end of the academic telescope and start to see things plain, Joe's appearance undergoes a dramatic transformation. To begin once again at the very beginning, his voice has a body to it, a certain aural succulence, which makes its impact very nearly a physical sensation. Like Jimmy Rushing, he has an arsenal of vowel sounds and glottal shocks which you can very nearly reach out and touch. Moreover, his range is perfectly suited to the nature of his material, and that material is perfectly adequate to express the essence of his personality. In other words, Joe Turner has done, no doubt by pure instinct, what every creative artist ought to do but what few ever manage: he has contrived an ideal marriage of form and content.

Joe Turner started out on the Blues trail performing double duty – tending bar and singing. In the freewheeling atmosphere of after hours jam sessions in Kansas City, Turner would frequently take off his apron and sing a few easy rocking songs with the house band whenever business was quiet. Many times the last show ended at 5 a.m. and Turner would have plenty of opportunities to sing. He remembers those impromptu performances serving as invaluable apprenticeship.

'I got acquainted with a lot of musicians,' he has recalled in *Living Blues*. 'They used to help me a lot, you know, teach me all the gimmicks and things. I got so I was pretty good at it. So from then on I just took it up for a profession.'

Half a century later, Joe Turner is the grand doyen of big city blues singers. Still performing in 1978 with a jaunty vigour of a younger man, he has a durability unmatched by most of his peers. Nonetheless, his health isn't what it used to be. He suffers from diabetes and carries more than 300 pounds on his 6ft 1½in frame. He walks with a cane and finds it more comfortable singing while sitting in a chair.

The singer considers his weight a sensitive issue and won't discuss the exact figures. 'That's personal,' he declares, turning his palms face-up. 'I used to be skinny. People called me "TB Joe".'

Nevertheless, his rich baritone is still strong enough to shake a room. It jumps and booms with a power that carries it into every nook and cranny without benefit of a microphone, much like the old days when he stood flat-footed roaring out waves of lyrics.

Within the restriction of the Blues form, Turner is a great melodist. And unlike many Blues vocalists, he is a genuine improviser, ever altering the melodic content, inflections and rhythmic accents of his material. It's no accident that he has a gift for the impromptu. As a native of Kansas City, he grew up around the shining musicians who lived and passed through the urban area that was the last great germinating spot for jazz outside New York. Turner performed and socialized with Count Basie, Buster Smith, Lester Young, Hot Lips Page, Ben Webster, Jo Jones, Andy Kirk, Mary Lou Williams, George and Julia Lee – and, of course, Pete Johnson.

What an experience it must have been to hear that magisterial voice ringing out nightly from behind a bar or the edge of the bandstand – accompanied by some of the loftiest instrumentalists.

In the best tradition of a gladiator, Turner has always welcomed the company of the most challenging hornmen. On *Everyday I Have The Blues* he meets Sonny Stitt – surprisingly – for the first time on record. No stranger to the Kansas City tradition, Stitt is persistently associated with Charlie Parker, one of the most eminent exponents of the city's cultural heritage. Their musical styles, however, were both alike and dissimilar. The story goes that as a young man, when he was in Tiny Bradshaw's band, Stitt went to Kansas City looking for Parker. After finding him and jamming for an hour, Stitt said Parker exclaimed: 'You sure sound like me.' Some water has gone under the bridge more than once since and Stitt has carved out his own musical personality, much of which is evident on this disc. He has an imposing sense of melodic decoration and plays the blues with an elegant lyricism and earthy whimsicality. The saxophonist knows when to stretch out phrases in easy-rider fashion or cut loose with a torrent of double-time statements.

Their collaboration on 'Lucille' is a stately discourse on the familiar – the loss of a romance. Stitt plays tenor saxophone and Turner phrases like one. The tempo is a slow walk and the men pace themselves at an ambling gait. Stitt's deep-throated, moaning solo, incidentally, is marvellously constructed, building dramatically in speech-like fashion with a variety of long-held quarter-notes, and ending with jetstreamed eighth- and sixteenth-notes.

In the last twenty years the Blues tradition has been pillaged and burglarized by half a dozen different marauding armies from the commercial world. To the lover of authentic Blues, the 1970s fad for Rock music seems as sensible as a child's passion for chewing gum would to M. Escoffier. For Rock is a corruption of Rhythm & Blues which was a dilution of the Blues, so that today's mass-marketed noise is a vulgarization of a vulgarization. In Joe Turner and company resides the real thing. He is the original article, and on *Nobody in Mind* he has a few original articles pumping out the instrumental support. Roy Eldridge must have entered into this session with absolute glee and delight, for the ambience of the music is meat and drink to him. Historians of the jazz art will take due note of the fact that each time Roy arrives at the end of the bridge of 'I Want A Little Girl', he defines a neat little sequence which is the very soul of the harmonic life of the 1940s, and that each time the heat he is generating reaches his own imagination Roy soars ever onward and upward. In 'The Chicken And The Hawk', the first thing to catch the ear is the way that Milt Jackson, ostensibly playing a subsidiary role behind Joe's vocal, in fact executes one of the best solos on the album, playing a marvellous sequence of phrases which can span the gap between his own period and Joe's without his even thinking about it. A further footnote ought to be added regarding that flat, bland guitar tone of Pee Wee Crayton. I had almost forgotten about players like Eddie Durham, the extent to which that bold, no-messing tone could add to the gaiety of the proceedings. There remains 'Red Sails In The Sunset', that great pre-war hit with the faintly bathetic lyric and the simple but attractive chord sequence. It is something of a postscript to the album, being much shorter than the other tracks, and being played by a much smaller group in the absence of Milt and Roy. Nevertheless, it tells us something of vital importance about blues shouters of the Joe Turner school, and that is the way they transmute all raw material into the style of the Blues. Within the compass of the first eight bars of the vocal, it has been made perfectly clear that Joe has no intention of following the melodic line; Instead he is flattening and contracting the shape of the melody until almost the entire vocal chorus is packed in within the range of a fifth, between Tonic and Dominant. It is, of course, a very simple thing to do – until you try to do it, and that is why albums like these are so welcome. The art they represent is a dying art, and therefore doubly demands our scrutiny.

There remains Joe Turner and the Blues as poetry. Once again a case of apparent simplicity. Three lines of iambic pentameter, with the first two lines repeated, and the rhyme at the end of third line is not always a pure rhyme at all. To make the most of this structure, the singer's voice should be both sinuous and succulent, sinuous because unlike all other singers the blues shouter has no written melody from which to divert his vocal line, succulent because the Blues treats with the juicier realities of life. Not much of an itinerary, and yet throughout jazz history, hardly any men have been able to meet its demands. Joe Turner is one of the very few who sing the Blues as though born to it, which in a way he was, for he was born in Kansas City, and people who are born in Kansas City often have the damnedest way of making good jazz.

The point comes home with particular force at the start of 'Too Late, Too Late' on *In The Evening*, where the lyric actually has the effrontery to begin as follows:

Too late, too late
Too late, too late,
Too late.
Too late, too late,
Too late, too late . . .

The structure is hardly Byronic in the ingenuity of its rhyme schemes, hardly Tennysonian in its development of imagery, and the casual listener might therefore make the beginner's mistake of assuming that Joe Turner is just droning on in an idly hypnotic sort of way. But, as the philosopher has pointed out, to a blind man a picture gallery is a dull place, and closer textual examination soon reveals that Turner sings those nine 'too late' phrases in nine different ways, varying his inflections, his pitch and his stresses to produce nine effects which are almost identical but not quite. And it is in the not-quietness that the essence of the great Blues artist may be found. In a way it is all a kind of game, just as playing jazz is a game, except that the Blues comprises its own sub-division, where the rules are slightly amended. The ideal blues vocal performance, for instance, takes no note of wide range, or spectacularly inventive phrasing. Instead it concentrates on vocal texture and buoyancy of performance to produce its effect of direct emotional impact. A blues singer ought to have a succulence in his voice, he has to have a fat sound and yet imply agility. Like the great instrumentalist, a blues singer ought to be able to rivet one's attention by sounding a single note and holding it, no matter what the intelligence of the lyric happens to be.

Misunderstandings often arise with albums of this type; singing the Blues is all very well, says the devil's advocate, but not all the songs are blues. It makes no matter. The blues specialist has an instinctive urge, you might call it a compulsion, to reshape all material in his own image, that is to say, the image of the Blues. In this album there are at least four songs which are popular standards rather than blues (and perhaps five; 'Corrina Corrina' is a borderline case), but in each instance Turner takes hold of them and contrives to give the song a blues personality by flattening the vocal line. A newcomer to, say, 'Summertime', would get no faint idea of what Gershwin's melody originally sounded like, because the singer has moulded it to suit his own stylistic ends. There is even one juncture, in 'World On A String', where the vocal bridge has been so radically amended as to sound very nearly like recitative.

I am not sure how Harold Arlen would feel about it, but to me it seemed not only permissible but essential to the integrity of the performance. The blues singer's prime function is to tell stories, and I know of no contemporary figure who tells them better than Joe Turner does. At first sight these stories are not always told with quite the narrative logic one might expect. In 'Too Late', the singer informs us that it is 'three o'clock in the morning' and then wonders where his lady can be 'tonight'. In 'JT Blues', the lyric says that 'some people make love in the winter, some people make love in lover's lane', which suggests that lover's lane is closed down for the summer. Once again, it makes no matter. The imagery of the Blues contains its own logic. The stories tell of a world of frightful betrayals, where, as in 'Too Late', you 'ask a small favour, and they even stop coming round', a world where, when you are up, everything goes so well that 'women beg "please take me"', and, when things go wrong, you light out for Denver, for reasons unstated.

Turner is marvellous playing this sort of game. For some obscure reason his intuition tells him to repeat the word 'Lorraine' at the end of his first vocal chorus of 'Sweet Lorraine', to repeat it with a slight inquisitorial edge which creates an effect out of all proportion to the smallness of the gesture.

'Summertime' goes along at a livelier lick than is usual, although there is an excellent precedent; the first jazz recording ever made of the song, while *Porgy and Bess* was still running, was by Billie Holiday at roughly the tempo that Joe Turner uses. The instrumental accompaniment is, as one would expect, a perfect facsimile of pre-Modern small-group jamming. Bob Smith in particular evokes nostalgia for the old days by repeatedly raising the ghost of Johnny Hodges, especially in the coda of 'Two Loves', and in bars seven to eight of his 'Sweet Lorraine' solo.

But albums of this kind always turn out to be examples of the whole being greater than the parts. The individual voices merge to create a different entity. And presiding over the delicate chemistry is Joe Turner, literally the voice of Jazz.

'Every now and then I get the urge to get up on the stage and "do my thing", as the people say,' he told *Living Blues*. 'And I enjoy it.'

∾

OSCAR PETERSON AND JOE PASS: *LIVE À SALLE PLEYEL* (1975)

So far as jazz is concerned, there are only two conventional instruments capable of providing their own rhythmic and harmonic accompaniment. These two are the piano and the guitar, and on this album it is the piano and the guitar which set the scene. There is no doubt that the two players involved give a remarkable demonstration of the orchestral possibilities of the jazz duet, and I use a word like 'orchestral' deliberately, aware as I am of its incongruity in a context involving no more than two musicians. The subtle gradations achieved by the two voices, between solo, solo with accompaniment, duet, and collective improvisation, can only be described as orchestral in their ingenuity, their richness of texture, their constant shifting of focus.

Both Oscar Peterson and Joe Pass are well known as players who can, when the occasion demands it, perform without any accompaniment at all. Peterson in particular in the last few years has demonstrated a growing preference for the splendid isolation of concert recitals where nobody else is on stage, and it is not very long since Pass recorded a solo album which immediately took its place among the outstanding exhibitions of guitar virtuosity in the modern era. Nor are Pass and Peterson strangers to each other, having appeared several times on the same album, and many times on the same stage. The point is important, because a duet of the kind to be found on this album is not the sort of thing to be entered upon lightly, nor carried off without trial runs in the past.

There is, of course, a third musician involved in these performances. He is affiliated to no union, and his name has never appeared in any personnel lists or critical puffs. The English poet A. E. Housman was a professional pessimist who wrote once, 'Far I hear the steady drummer/Drumming like a noise in dreams'. There is a steady drummer present on this album and he does indeed play like the drummer of our dreams. He never obtrudes at a delicate moment, his feeling for the tempo is infallible, and most important of all, he is never too loud. He is the drummer who resides inside the heads of Pass and Peterson, and it is his phantom performance which renders the music vertebrate. This does not mean merely that the players are able to maintain an unflagging tempo without benefit of percussive prompting, but also that they are able to agree on the pulse of their joint performance. And that pulse is to do, not with tempo, but with Time, which in jazz anyway, is a different thing. Two musicians may observe meticulously together this or that tempo, and yet be at such hopeless odds when it comes to Time that their marriage is doomed before it starts, as it was in the days when Lester Young worked for King Oliver, and on that extraordinary occasion when Artie Shaw recorded in the same group as Jelly Roll Morton. (A player of the Red Nichols–Miff Mole school, say, had a firm enough grasp of tempo; his concept of Time has killed him stone dead so far as posterity is concerned.) Tempo can be expressed by a metronome, Time only by the musician. For want of a more precise definition, a player's time is the mark of rhythmic style he imposes on the tempo, which is an idea complicated in words but obvious enough in performance; the late Charlie Christian is an ideal example of the Modernist manqué whose prescient glimpses of the future of jazz harmony were contradicted by a sense of Time rooted irrevocably in the old Swing Era.

In the solo tracks the factor of Time is not a difficult one, for Pass when he is playing unaccompanied, or Peterson when working alone, are each their own man, and are obliged to arrive at no compromises, which is of course the great beauty as well as the great challenge of playing with nobody else. But when the two men come together, to create what must surely rank among some of the most brilliant and witty duets ever recorded by jazz musicians, then Time rears its head. Its presence can be clearly discerned at key junctures, especially where one soloist is taking over from the other, at which points we realize that Peterson's sense of Time is not quite identical to Pass's. That is not only because they are different instrumentalists but also because they are playing different instruments. The nature of instrumental mechanics is a vital factor here; a tuba player's sense of Time is likely to be rather differently expressed to a flautist's, and when the piano keyboard hands over the baton to the guitar keyboard, then infinitessimal adjustments are made to the concept of Time.

In the normal jazz performance this adjustment is hardly ever noticeable when great players perform, because the presence of the drums is a buttress against rhythmic disintegration. But here there is only the drummer of Housman's dreams, which means that Pass and Peterson are dicing with death the moment they join forces. Of the solo tracks there is little new to be said, except in reference to specific songs. I find the manual dexterity and the colossal brio of the opening of Peterson's 'Indiana' almost terrifying in its omniscience, although I cease to be affrighted when the solo shifts into the more genial pace of the middle section of the performance. There then follows an ending of even more furious virtuosity, at which point the listener finds himself almost laughing out loud with the exhilaration of it. The Ellington medley has the obvious advantage of being the fruit of two great minds rather than one, especially 'In A Sentimental Mood', a composition whose exquisite pathos demands a musician as great as Peterson to do it justice, and which shifts into a beautifully leisurely tempo in the first bridge which says in a few bars what jazz is about. 'Sweet Georgia Brown' is another awesome exhibition, not just of technique, which is obvious enough, but also of speed and clarity of thought, without which the technique would be of no avail; playing of this kind is an intellectual as well as a musical exercise.

Peterson injects into 'I Got A Right To Sing The Blues' all kinds of funky allusions to the Blues, an interpretation which can stand as an oblique comment on the extent to which Harold Arlen has depended on the Blues structure for the emotional impact of his songs 'Stormy Weather', 'The Man That Got Away', 'One For My Baby', 'Blues In The Night'. As for 'It Never Entered My Mind', the sweet gravity of Peterson's interpretation is quite perfect for this most original of ballads. Originally written by Rodgers and Hart for a 1940 musical called *Higher and Higher* (which was overshadowed at the time because the same team's *Pal Joey* opened in the same year), the song has always demanded the very best artists to do justice to it, and has always brought out the very best in them. In an anthology of the best American popular music, 'It Never Entered My Mind' would have to be included.

In his solo tracks, Pass includes almost the only song which provides a legitimate excuse to introduce the name of William Shakespeare. The dream referred to in the title 'Darn That Dream' is none other than the midsummer night's dream of Shakespeare's play, for Jimmy Van Heusen and Eddie DeLange wrote the song for a Broadway experiment called *Swingin' the Dream*, whose cast included Benny Goodman, Maxine Sullivan, and, most incredible, Louis Armstrong as Bottom. But the most surprising fact of all about 'Darn That Dream' is that it was composed as long ago as 1931, when the questing chromatic nature of its melodic line must have appeared incomprehensible to a great many people. In fact it is arguable that Van Heusen's song sounds at least as fiercely contemporary as Michel Legrand's theme from *Summer of '42*.

But the real fun begins when the two soloists join forces. Clearly, both Pass and Peterson have to arrive at certain tactical conclusions in carrying out their roles, especially with regard to what to do when the other is taking the solo, and the listener will find that while Pass behind Peterson tends to drift into collective improvisation fairly quickly, Peterson often uses the left hand in the lower reaches of the piano to define the kind of harmonic spine which a bassist might otherwise have provided. The moments when both men are frankly taking solos simultaneously are especially brilliant, and there are many moments like the one in the third chorus of 'Stella By Starlight', where the song goes into tempo and the two instrumental lines somehow convey the contours of Victor Young's original melody without actually stating it for even as long as a single bar.

The most difficult challenge of all is accepted in 'Honeysuckle Rose' when Pass and Peterson between them break up the choruses. It is now that the ghostly drummer comes into his own, providing an imaginary beat inside the heads of the two musicians which is so compulsive that it informs every note being played and thus arrives in the listener's consciousness also. But at least 'Honeysuckle Rose' begins and ends with a tempo described by both men. In the very up-tempo 'Blues For Bise', we finally arrive at the ultimate in jazz duet performance, where one man plays a chorus of the blues, not only at the required tempo, but also using the Time concept peculiar to himself, and then waits while the other soloist repeats the operation, obviously accepting the laid-down tempo but obliged to express a different sense of Time of his own. That split-second pause at the end of the first chorus, where Peterson had done but Pass had not yet started, is the most dramatic moment in the entire recital, because it is the moment where we can almost see one soloist coupling his mind to the concept of the other without any assistance from a rhythm section. What we hear is silence; but what is going on in Pass's brain at that moment can only be defined by whatever the word is which is silence's opposite. That Pass and Peterson carry off their complicated gambit with unqualified success will be obvious to anyone who sits through the contents of this album. It is a marvellous effort and I don't remember its equal.

∾

Last Rites (1973)

In the late 1950s, when I became jazz critic for the *Observer*, very few of us inside the jazz world had yet learned to live with the possibility that there might conceivably come a day when there would be no jazz and no jazz musicians to play it. Certainly the deaths during the 1950s of men like Art Tatum, Charlie Parker, Django Reinhardt, brought home the fact that one definition of the unique musician is that nothing remotely like him will ever appear again. But at least there was still Oscar Peterson, Sonny Stitt, Wes Montgomery. If great players were dying, other great players were maintaining the tradition. The idea had still to sink in that jazz, like the century which saw its rise, was approaching old age, and that the art of basing melodic variations on a given harmonic base might turn out in the end to be finite.

The appearance in 1960 of Miles Davis's *Kind of Blue* was a straw in the wind so far as conventional jazzmaking techniques were concerned, and by the time the 1960s were under way, so was Ornette Coleman, with his creaky dialectic and meandering music. And while this assault against the castle was being mounted, those within its walls began dying off at an ever-increasing rate. The obituary columns were still short enough at the start of the period covered by this book to be novelties, long enough by the end of it to cause genuine fears as to the prospects for a jazz future.

It was obvious, for instance, that the death of Coleman Hawkins was rather more than the passing of a great saxophonist. Hawkins in his career encompassed more or less the complete history of jazz on his instrument. At the start of his playing life he had worked for Mamie Smith, and at the end of it his conception of how the instrument should sound was evidently still giving a figure like Sonny Rollins food for thought. With the death of Hawkins passed our last chance to witness in the flesh the technique and the temperament of the jazz saxophone's founding father. If Pee Wee Russell was less significant, he was no less spectacular in his way. He epitomized an era and an attitude long since vanished, of unrefined, intuitive musicians with a limited vocabulary, who nevertheless managed to produce the music they wanted to produce. Russell was a representative of the Chicagoans, that boisterous and fairly unsubtle bunch of romantics who had in the end the choice of going for the fleshpots, like Benny Goodman, or staying with their own beginnings, like Russell. (It is very possible that the Russell stay-putters were that way inclined, not because of rampant aesthetic integrity, but because their peculiar techniques precluded them from ever subsiding into the conformity of a saxophone section.) In any case, Russell, at the very end of his life, had the laugh after all, in a most surprising way. In his dotage he became a successful abstract painter who sold his canvases for far larger sums than ever he had received for playing the clarinet.

If Sinatra's notice involved a man who although by no means dead, had expressed a desire to lie down, the case of Glenn Miller was much more unusual, of a man who, although very dead, was refusing to lie down under any circumstances. Although from the jazz purist point of view Miller is no more than a peripheral figure, like so many peripheral figures he is useful in the way he defines the boundaries of the art along which he so adeptly flitted for most of his life. His orchestra marks the point at which the diluting of the pure jazz spirit to suit the ends of ballroom entrepreneurs caused the music itself to change form. Ellington and Basie ran jazz bands. Goodman and Dorsey ran dance bands whose source of inspiration was the jazz talent of many of the musicians comprising the groups. Miller ran a dance band whose jazz content was virtually nil, and the cynic is free to draw his own conclusions from the fact that Miller, with the least jazz content, won the most public support. But before dismissing him, it may be as well to remember that whenever he wanted a marketable idea, he was inclined to borrow one from jazz.

As to his posthumous career, with its psychic junketings and massed ranks of impersonators, one can only say that he remains the only figure in the history of popular music whose life after death has been maintained not by a ghost but a regiment of ghosts. Shrewd marketing and a hard core of fanatical support has had something to do with the phenomenon, but no amount of this kind of thing can ever create the kind of demand for a dead man's art that Miller has enjoyed. There does indeed seem to be a genuine hunger for his music, and one assumes that this hunger will continue to assert itself at the box office until the day when the last man who proposed to the strains of 'At Last' finally passes over into that condition of nebulosity which Glenn Miller, all rumours to the contrary notwithstanding, has most certainly been enjoying ever since his plane disappeared over the English Channel so long ago.

Pee Wee Russell (1968)

The death of Charles Ellsworth 'Pee Wee' Russell at the age of sixty-two removes from the jazz scene one of the most puzzling oddballs in its history. Russell was a much-loved clarinettist of the Chicago school whose legendary reputation perhaps in the end outstripped his actual achievements. The trouble was that there was no way of knowing where technical ineptitude left off and gnarled originality began. Many of his solos were faltering affairs which often redeemed themselves from total collapse apparently by accident and always at the last moment.

The result of this bewildering tightrope act was that inside the jazz world, which has always been too ready to equate technical crudities with sincerity, Russell was elevated in his own lifetime to something between a genius and a talisman of the good old days. One possible explanation for his very remarkable and utterly original style, with its crabbed tone and vagaries of direction, may lie in his diffidence as a man. If this were so, it would go far to explain the often drastic improvement in Russell's performance the moment he subsided into the ensemble, where his experience and cunning left him very few superiors in the Dixieland jazz field.

A coterie figure content to be overshadowed by the shrewdly marketed virtuosity of contemporaries like Benny Goodman and Artie Shaw, Russell was one of the last active links with the mythical days when jazz was a dirty word and Capone was the musician's best friend. It was Russell who shared with Bix Beiderbecke the ownership of a broken-down Buick, whose front mirror never reflected anything more mobile than Russell's own craggy face as he shaved each morning; Russell who was found living in a shack whose front porch was sagging under the weight of forty unopened quart bottles of milk; Russell almost alone of the Chicagoans who never trafficked with the commercial orchestras, where his eccentric tone would no doubt have been something of an embarrassment.

He also enjoyed what must surely be the most incongruous dying fall of any jazzman. In the last few years of his life he took to abstract painting and began receiving hundreds of dollars for his canvases. But it is an archetype from bootleg days that he will be remembered, and the recordings with Bud Freeman and Jack Teagarden that will preserve his reputation. He was probably at least half as good as the idolators said he was, which is really very good indeed.

The Club Eleven Reunion (1986)

It was a very good night. In fact, it was one of the best nights you could possibly have imagined. There were people there you had not seen for years, for decades even. In some cases, time had erased their features from your recollection; in others, the face was still there, but the name had gone. In the past you had sometimes wondered whatever happened to them all, and now it turned out that they had sometimes thought exactly the same about you. There they all suddenly were, in Ronnie Scott's Club, to celebrate an ancient occasion.

They stood in the semi-dark, beaming with pleasure at having come this far, the Lennies and Tommys of my adolescence, the Harrys and Tonys of a long-lost apprenticeship, the Joes and Johnnies, Roys and Geoffs, Petes and Lauries of a bygone period in the history of British music. And yet not bygone. When you circulated and chatted with these old friends, it was surprising how high a percentage of them still played.

Some had fared better than others. Some had distanced themselves from their musical indiscretions of nearly forty years ago. Some remained shy, while others whooped and screamed at the sight of a familiar face. Many of them had grown-up children, who themselves had children. Others seemed hardly changed by the years at all. But whatever their corporate fates, one link bound us all together. We were all jazz musicians on the day thirty-seven years ago when an institution called the Club Eleven was first formed. It was created out of the altruism of ten young players, with their manager, Harry Morris – hence the title – who were determined to be self-employed at least part of the time, and not to be dependent on bandleaders for the opportunity to produce music.

In the late 1940s, British popular music was still dominated by those tuxedoed dodos of the music business, the bandleaders, many of whom had formed their own orchestras because they couldn't get a job in anyone else's. The eleven instigators of the Club Eleven represented the usual process. They were the ever-present younger generation knocking on the door. Only this time, there were two differences. The first was their resourcefulness. When the door would not open, they decided to build their own, which is how the Club Eleven came into being.

The other difference was much more profound, and was bound up with the technical evolution of the jazz art. In the 1940s in America, a group of younger musicians made some revolutionary harmonic departures from the old ways of improvising. This group, and especially the saxophonist Charlie Parker and the trumpeter Dizzy Gillespie, pioneered a new improvising method, one so strange-sounding to conventional ears that figures as far apart musically as Benny Goodman and Louis Armstrong reacted in the same way, by dismissing the new music as wrong notes. They lived to eat their words, and so did a lot of other people.

In the meantime, with the end of the war, the gradual seeping into Britain of obscure new recordings – and the occasional trips to New York by our young players masquerading as ship's musicians – meant that the latest developments in America were being monitored. News of that kind travelled fast, and by the late 1940s a small nucleus existed in London of teenage musicians, capable of playing the new music with some degree of fluency.

The Club Eleven comprised two groups, the Ronnie Scott Quintet and the John (in those days Johnny) Dankworth Sextet. The rules of the game were elastic; for instance, any other musicians who wished to play at the club were welcome to do so. All that was required was a standard of efficiency. That standard seemed to me at the time frighteningly demanding. Although this was my own generation blazing its trail, I would not have dreamed of attempting to play at the club. Scott, Dankworth and company were light years in advance of most of the rest of us. People like myself attended the club in the spirit of students hoping to pick up a few rudiments. Hearing the recordings made at that time you begin to wonder exactly how advanced the Eleven were. But then you might realize you are listening with hindsight, and that however naive some of it sounds today, it is not half as naive as you yourself sounded at the time.

Considering the rigours of the road, and that nearly forty years has passed by since the Club Eleven opened, it was truly extraordinary that no fewer than ten of the original eleven musicians turned up for the reunion at Scott's. The eleventh, the pianist Tommy Pollard, died some years ago. As Scott put it: 'He is no longer with us. In fact, he's no longer with anybody.' The rest of them then played; first the sextet, then the quintet, but the real show was in the audience. All those ecstatic faces; all those friendships, so long in disrepair, suddenly working again; all the old stories and anecdotes; so many nights in someone's club, on somebody's bandstand, at someone's party.

One man I spoke to there – for the first time since 1959 – said to me truculently, 'They used to say none of us would make forty. Well, here we all are.' A few moments later we were interrupted by a man I swear I have never seen before, who clapped me on the back, told me how wonderful I was not to have changed a hair in forty years and then took his farewell with, 'Great to see you, Harry.' Who he thought I was is immaterial. What mattered was that he was there, and so was I.

Although it was upstaged by the social importance of the occasion, the music turned out to be as exciting as ever. It was striking how, after all these years, nothing much has changed. Scott and Dankworth are the best players now, as they were then, natural leaders today, as they were in 1948. My own part in the evolution of the Club Eleven was non-existent, except as an occasional customer, sitting open-mouthed and watching the young professors at work.

And, sitting there in the dark of Scott's club, it struck me that of all the creative artists I have mingled with, among the writers, actors, singers, dancers and poets, it was this tiny group of jazz musicians who had shown the most ferocious commitment to their art. We all dissemble at some time or another, all do the commercial thing from time to time. But this crew of so-called dissolute, anarchic jazz musicians were uncompromising in their dedication to a music which in those days was hopelessly uncommercial.

But that is not why the night at Scott's was so memorable. It was something more personal. Looking round, at Ace, Flash, Eddie, Mike, Jack and Tommy, I was joining hands once more with my own youth. For an hour or two the past was tangible in that room. You could reach out and touch it, put an arm round its shoulder, drink to it. What it will look like on the screen I have no idea. But I know what it will not look like. It will not look like a solemn wake. Cheerfulness will keep breaking in.

In another thirty-seven years it will be AD 2022. I do hope that the BBC cameras will be there for that reunion too.

COLEMAN HAWKINS (1969)

The recurring nightmare of the middle-aged jazz lover involves a world where all the elder statesmen of the music have at last disappeared, leaving only the young men in possession. That inevitable situation has now drawn one step closer, with the death in New York of Coleman Hawkins in his sixty-fifth year.

The jazz world may be excused for being utterly shattered by the event, even though Hawkins's physical appearance had telegraphed its coming for some years. Like Louis Armstrong and Duke Ellington, Hawkins has been a central figure for as long as there has been awareness of jazz as a method of making music, and, more than either of those two contemporaries, he could be said literally to have invented the instrument he played so sublimely, the tenor saxophone.

When Hawkins began as a teenager, the saxophone was little more than a vaudeville joke. He became the first man to lend it beauty of tone, coherence of thought, brilliance of execution. Recorded evidence suggests that it was around the late 1920s that the authentic Hawkins style finally matured. Before then his work, although scattered with hints of the grandeur to come, was still flawed by the angularity and the asthmatics of the early saxophonists. And then in 1929 with his famous recording of 'One Hour' it was suddenly clear to all that a classic jazz style had flowered.

Its features were easy enough to recognize: a rich ultraromantic tone symbolizing the phrase of the period 'hot jazz', cascades of arpeggios reflecting extreme harmonic sophistication, and above all that rarest of jazz virtues, a sense of form. When Hawkins played an extended solo, some intuitive gift made it possible for him to transmute bars and phrases into a single unified statement. The legendary version of 'Body And Soul', made in 1939, is as good an example as any, with its climaxes placed so exquisitely and its raw materials developed with such dazzling wit. When the listener grasps that this was a purely impromptu performance and that Hawkins claimed it was nothing special in his career, the architecture of the music becomes positively miraculous.

As a style setter, Hawkins was challenged in the late 1930s by Lester Young, and perhaps superseded ten years later by Charlie Parker. But his influence has been so profound that there is literally no prominent saxophonist anywhere who does not owe him a vast debt. In his last years Hawkins became a far coarser player, yet, although the decline from the great years was dramatic, he still retained enough art to startle the listener from time to time. London had proof of this less than two years ago with his unaccompanied performances of 'September Song'. Beyond any question he will be remembered as one of the half-dozen instrumentalists who made possible the development of jazz.

Is There Jazz After Death? (1969)

Although we are only halfway round the course, there is already no doubt at all that the outstanding musical figure of 1969 is destined to be that Mrs Brown of Balham whose astral creativity is currently confounding the entire world of music. Mrs Brown's perfectly innocent remark that Liszt, Beethoven, Schubert and others drop in frequently to give her musical dictation has been received by the worldlings either with sneers of scepticism or what her spectral accomplices might have called hosannas of joy. The only thing that surprises me about all this is that anyone should find it in any way unusual.

After all, psychic manifestations are common enough in the world of music. Some years ago, when employed briefly with Lew Stone's Orchestra, I found myself working with a saxophonist who conversed regularly with the dear musical departed. There was also an orchestrator who swore that an extremely bitter heavenly feud was going on between Glenn Miller and Jelly Roll Morton, each of whom apparently felt that the other had been consigned to the wrong place.

So far as Mrs Brown's supernatural odyssey is concerned, I have no doubt that she is telling the truth as she knows it, that she does see and hear Liszt, and that she has indeed achieved every musician's ultimate ambition in becoming an instrument rather than an instrumentalist.

For the rest of us, we can only wonder why the giants have waited so long to put in an appearance, and why they should have chosen this particular moment in what Santayana would have called sidereal time to do so.

It seems inescapable that if there were any logical moment for Liszt to have returned home, it would have been during the making of the film of his life, when he might have struck a shrewd blow for the Republic of Art by setting fire to Dirk Bogarde's cloak and planting mousetraps in the studio piano. Still, if Mrs Brown is to believed, only now have the great composers seen fit to re-enter the game. I hardly dare think of the commotion going on in Valhalla at this moment, of petulant creators jostling each other in the queue for Balham, of Bix Beiderbecke's concern whether he will be able to get a drink there, of George Gershwin's refusal to make the trip in case heaven won't be able to get along without him, of Paderewski's doubts about the strength of Mrs Brown's eminently suburban piano frame, of the certitude in Buddy Holly's mind that nothing he might do in Balham could possibly improve the already flourishing state of his posthumous career.

I now await the sequel to Mrs Brown's apotheosis, the return to terrestrial parts of the great writers. The reappearance of Charles Dickens in particular would be most welcome, if only to resolve the question of whether Edmund Wilson or Felix Aylmer is right about the projected ending to *The Mystery of Edwin Drood*. But until Dickens does arrive, my thoughts about whether there is any cultural life on other planes yield pride of place to serious misgivings as to whether there is any on this one.

Father Figures (1973)

From 1943 to 1948, a period which in retrospect I can see constituted my apprenticeship, all my contemporaries conducted fierce tribal wars in support of their chosen heroes. There was, for instance, a Benny Goodman camp and an Artie Shaw camp, a Tommy Dorsey set and a Harry James set, a Gene Krupa clique and a Charlie Christian lobby, while for comparative electics like myself there were such issues as Bix Beiderbecke or Muggsy Spanier, Fats Waller or Teddy Wilson, Bud Freeman or Coleman Hawkins. Generally the movement tended to be a progressive one, towards the giants of the Swing Age, the pathos of the debate being heightened by the fact that, unknown to us, the issues over which we squabbled were dead ones, for the Swing Age and all its heroes were already disappearing over the horizon. Of course there existed concurrently with our world several antiquarian sects whose members, mistaking the recorded ineptitude of some New Orleans pioneers for a musical style, tried inexplicably to reproduce it, with horrific results. However, as I encountered none of these sects, with their reverence for Baby Dodds's chairleg drumsticks and their confusion as to whether the Charleston Chasers ever caught anybody, until long after their excesses could appear anything but comic, I take no account of them in this reminiscence.

Although none of us yet suspected it, by acquiring Swing Age nuances which were already beginning to lose their relevance, we were creating awkward stylistic problems for ourselves in the future. I recall one trombonist who appeared for a while in one of the many amateur groups with which I became involved during those years. Always in these groups we would rehearse with manic fervour against the arrival of a yearned-for first engagement which was destined never to come, and this trombonist shocked us all by conducting an endless debate with himself over the relative merits of Miff Mole and Jack Teagarden. Our surprise was due to the fact that we credited him with a modernity which his style did nothing to confirm, although now I come to think of it he did possess a pair of rimless spectacles which endowed him with a certain superficial resemblance to Benny Goodman, Glenn Miller and Tommy Dorsey. I remember very clearly doing an audition for an extremely trendy semi-professional sextet whose method of testing my abilities was to confront me with the printed transcript of the Artie Shaw Gramercy Five recording of 'Special Delivery Stomp', complete with all the trite riffs and pointless chromatic excesses, my disapproval of such fripperies being quite unconnected with my total inability to play them. This was in

1945, when Shaw had already made several final appearances, and Charlie Parker was embarked on his quintet recordings with Dizzy Gillespie.

Presiding over this gently anachronistic world were two dominant figures, twin deities who did not feature in our disputations at all, Louis Armstrong and Duke Ellington. It would be comforting to pretend that the reason for their absence was that they were considered by us all to be beyond criticism. Unfortunately this would be quite untrue. As far as I remember, of all the dozens of clarinettists, electric guitarists, one-key boogie-woogie pianists and Dixieland drummers who marched across the drawing rooms and youth club halls of the period, not one was familiar with any Armstrong or Ellington recordings. As my own researches had begun, not along the usual route of the local palais and the big bands, but with the more esoteric deliberations of Bix Beiderbecke, it might be expected that I at least was acquainted with this vast body of utterly indispensable music. In fact, my ignorance was as unblemished as anyone else's. It is true that I had been familiar with the work of the Ellington small-groups, with particular reference to Johnny Hodges, almost since I had first begun learning, but my interest abruptly ceased the moment such groups grew beyond eight pieces. So far as the full Ellington band was concerned, I agreed with all my contemporaries that it was no more than a glorified dance band whose integrity must be suspect because of the high proportion of orchestrated, notated music it played. As for Armstrong, it was too obvious for words that he was a New Orleans relic whose significance had faded with the years, and who had himself acknowledged the fact by turning to a career in Hollywood and Variety. The interesting thing about all this is that up to a point we were quite right. Ellington's *was* a glorified dance band. Armstrong *was* a professional comic. What the fierce bigotry of inexperience prevented us from conceding was the possibility that they might also be something more. It was not until long after I had come to take my own professional daily round for granted that I came to see this.

Armstrong's primacy was, of course, unavoidable. It impinged at too many points of jazz experience to be ignored. There was Bunny Berigan's 'I Can't Get Started', a brilliant and passionate composition – of Armstrong's phrases. There was the Goodman big band, sparked by the orchestrations of Fletcher Henderson – who had doubled the power of his own band by persuading Armstrong to join it. There was the beloved Chicagoan Jack Teagarden, who was rumoured to be working with Armstrong in an authentic jazz environment once more. There were those curious moments in movies where something Armstrong did made you tap your foot or catch your breath. There were the hundreds of testimonies from virtually every jazz musician of any stature, that Armstrong was supreme, that Armstrong had started it all, that Armstrong remained as powerful as ever, that jazz would never see a more completely equipped soloist, and so on. It finally became necessary to examine the evidence, if only to refute it. And then the truth began to emerge. Gradually I learned never to be surprised by anything Armstrong did. The last time he ever shocked me was in 1957, when I heard his album of Fats Waller themes, at a time when I had assumed him to be an ageing lion, too old to strike many more sparks. But his Waller album was one of the masterpieces of his life.

My introduction to the body of Ellington's music was altogether more bizarre. No doubt in time I would have discovered it for myself one way or another, which is to say that in time some more enlightened friend would have been sure to thrust it under my nose. But the actual circumstances are comic, and perhaps very faintly pathetic. One day in 1952 a fellow saxophonist called Klein, one of the wisest of musicians and most loyal of friends, announced that he had finally broken off diplomatic relations with a girlfriend of long standing. Returning from her suburban front room one night for the last time, he had come laden with the bric-à-brac of such affairs, arrived at Charing Cross Station depressed by their weight and their romantic connotations and, rather than continue his journey with them, had dumped them at the Left Luggage office, where, for all he cared, they could moulder till the end of the world.

Always prepared to make efforts to improve my musical outlook, Klein on this summer afternoon thrust the Left Luggage ticket in my hand, advising me that if I cared to take the trouble, I would find among the debris of his late love affair four Ellington sides which would do my musical soul the world of good. In the end, determined that I should not duck out of an improving experience, as was my tendency then and since, he accompanied me to Charing Cross himself, where, at the Left Luggage counter, under the glazed eye of a cunning uniformed effigy of a railway porter, we rummaged among the relics, and from the gallimaufry of souvenirs of Cuba, toilet bags, dog-eared paperbacks, post-cards from scattered watering places, a table lamp and an ocarina, we found four sides by the Ellington band which Klein ceremoniously handed over with the advice that I should spend enough time with them to convince myself of their merits, taking care to remind me that it was me that was on trial and not the music. As one of the four sides happened to be 'I Got It Bad And That Ain't Good', my conversion was effected almost before it began.

There were three features of that masterpiece which bowled me over. One was the soprano playing of Johnny Hodges which, although I had been acquainted with it for many years already, never failed to overawe me. The second point was the beautiful economy with which Ellington, or perhaps Billy Strayhorn, had compressed the unusually wide leap of the interval of a Major ninth which occurs in the first bar of the melody, simply by dropping the higher note by an octave, and making the resultant phrase part of a sequence spreading over the first two bars of the last eight of the last chorus. This paraphrase was played in unison, fanning out into harmony after a dramatic though muted sforzando at the beginning of the third bar, the whole section being so finely conceived and so meticulously executed as to leave no doubt of the originality of the mind which had conceived it. There was a third point which interested me for rather different reasons. The vocal was sung by Ivie Anderson, whose elfin voice and personality had made an impression on me which had lain forgotten somewhere at the back of my mind ever since my first attendance, some time in the mid-1940s, at a performance of *A Day at the Races*. In the famous stable sequence of that film she had sung 'All God's Chillun Got Rhythm' with the kind of style and sense of irrepressible joy which Hollywood usually managed to suppress with such ruthless efficiency. Away from the vo-de-o-do of that scene and the distracting genius of Groucho Marx, she was suddenly revealed to me as a unique jazz singer.

From this moment of discovery, the vast corpus of Ellington's recorded music became a continent to be charted, a task whose enormity has been complicated by the fact that Ellington has never stopped adding to it ever since. He was born in the reign of Queen Victoria, during the McKinley administration, a few months before Armstrong, and as the years of my jazz life have raced by, the fear that either or both of these men might soon die has haunted the consciousness of almost every musician of my acquaintance articulate enough to discuss jazz at all. There was a feeling among my generation that if and when those catastrophes occurred, then jazz itself would be permanently diminished.

The only words Armstrong ever addressed to me were 'I'm sure glad to meet you English cats,' but Ellington I did come to know a little better. I was once hired by a television company to write a script for him, which was of course impossible for me and insulting to Ellington, as anyone but a television company would have known, and when I explained my difficulty to him, he advised me to collect my cheque while he spoke his own words, which he did, talking sweetly throughout a programme whose producer had had the interesting idea that everything would sound much better if Johnny Hodges blew his solo in 'Mood Indigo' perched on a podium of unspeakable vulgarity twenty-five feet above the rest of the orchestra. There was also a night once, after a London concert, when Ellington sat in his hotel drawing room and did one of his party pieces, recalling his early days as a bandleader in and around his home town of Washington during the First World War. The talk was so intriguing that even as I was enjoying it I made a resolution to memorize it and write it all down. And I did memorize it; unfortunately I delayed the writing down until in time the recollection of everything that had been said began to blur, until now, ten years later, there remains only the recollection of Ellington's smiling face, and the well-bred effrontery of the British freeloaders phoning down for more whisky; also a curious impression of one of those luxuriant pink clouds which figure so prominently in Ellington's programme notes, and which one day will itself evaporate just as surely as the conversation has.

∾

The Duke (1969)

This year Edward Kennedy Ellington celebrated his seventieth birthday, and predictably everybody celebrated with him: radio and television tributes, testimonials from other composers and musicians, even a reception at the White House, where his uncle and father were once employed as butlers.

While Ellington accepts the honours with his characteristic smile of ducal modesty, the jazz world scratches its head and ponders yet again the enigma of its indisputably greatest figure, the man who typifies more than any other the evolving art of jazz and yet outrages all the sacred cows of jazz convention, even to the extent of not accepting the jazz pigeonhole.

Jazz is supposed to be above all an improvised music, yet Ellington has committed it to manuscript and outdistanced all rivals. Jazzmen are supposed to live by a code of integrity so narrow that the outside world is hardly acknowledged at all, yet Ellington will bring to a performance of 'Mood Indigo' or 'Who's Afraid Of The Big Bad Wolf?' the same smile of self-absorption.

Leading a large jazz orchestra is so arduous a task and so desperate a gamble that nobody succeeds at it without deploying the tactic of the iron fist in the iron glove, yet in the Ellington band discipline in the conventional sense is so lax as to be virtually non-existent.

> *At one time, when we were at the Cotton Club, around 1927, we did have this system of fines and things. But then, you see, Arthur Whetsol was with us. One look from Whetsol . . . everybody started getting into line. We don't have that kind of thing in the present band. It takes too much energy.*

Whetsol, a trumpeter whose work can be heard on many recordings from the early 'jungle' period of Ellington's bewildering development, was one of the very few musicians who joined the band and was not content to spend the rest of his days there. Whetsol left in 1936 to study medicine, but on the other hand a recent discography showed that thirty-one important musicians who have been Ellingtonians averaged sixteen years each in the band. Harry Carney, the band's present baritone saxophonist, has been sitting in the same orchestra chair for the last forty-three years. When asked to explain this very unusual kind of mutual loyalty, Ellington sidestepped the issues with his customary agility and answered, 'I guess Carney will stay for as long as he can afford me.'

Ellington's musical career began in his home town of Washington DC during the First World War, in one of those rare interludes when for a moment the demand for dance band musicians exceeded the supply.

> *I put an advertisement in the telephone book bigger than anyone else's. Whenever anybody wanted anything in Washington, they looked in the telephone directory. If somebody wanted to hire some music and didn't know what musicians they wanted, I figured they were just as likely to pick on the biggest advertisement in the book. My hunch worked out pretty well, and before long I had about three bands working.*

Ellington is full of detailed reminiscences of this kind. He was once quoted as saying that the memory of things past is important to a jazz musician, and certainly his own past has made a deep impression on him. Probably for Ellington the best-loved period of all is New York in the early 1920s: work was scarce, but there were heroes to worship and experience waiting to be picked up on every street corner.

It is in the New York of the 1920s, that great time and place of the solo piano masters, that Ellington's own instrumental origins can be found, in the striding right hands and thumping cross-rhythms of James P. Johnson, Willie 'The Lion' Smith and Thomas 'Fats' Waller. Ellington describes these men as his university, and although it is a long time since he amended their Stride piano style to his own ends, to this day the influence of Johnson and Waller can be discerned in his playing, although he is always quick to insist that he was never in their class.

In the past the jazz world has tended to take him too literally on this point and to have underrated him as a piano soloist, for he is an outstanding technician of unmatched harmonic subtlety. It is his lack of pretension about himself rather than any technical weakness which has caused him to be regarded more as a composer-bandleader who happens to play the piano.

His first band had five musicians, including himself, and for some time its members were too preoccupied with finding work to bother very much about changing the course of jazz history. He remembers how he recruited his drummer Sonny Greer in 1919.

> *We decided to give him the works and see just what sort of guy he was. We stood on the street corner and waited for him. Everybody used to stand on street corners then and try to look big-time. Here comes Sonny. 'Whatcha say' we all ask him. I take the lead in the conversation because I'm sure that I'm a killer with my new shepherd plaid suit, bought on time. Sonny comes back with a line of jive that lays us low. We decide he's O.K.*

Greer stayed with Ellington for the next twenty-eight years.

Not until the episode of the Cotton Club in 1927 does Ellington's dossier begin to link with jazz history. By now the band had more than doubled in size and was recording prolifically, mostly Ellington themes composed in the small hours.

His appetite for work was enormous, then as always, and his touching naiveté about the mechanics of the musical life was beginning to give way to the extreme sophistication of later years. No longer was it possible for him to try selling a song to a publisher without first equipping himself with a written copy of the work, or to get trapped by circumstances as he did soon after arriving in the big city.

> *I was in New York a week and the man came to see me and says, 'You're not working tonight, we got to write a show.' So I'm stupid, I don't know any different. I says, 'Really? Yeah, good', you know. So that night we wrote the show.* Chocolate Kiddies *with Adelaide Hall. It went to Berlin, played two years and the guy who took it there came back a millionaire.*

After the Cotton Club, Ellington's music evolved steadily, until by around 1934 his orchestral textures had moved far beyond the jungle period to a rich impressionism. The original 1937 recording of 'Caravan' is so cunningly wrought that it is impossible to define the moments when the melody disappears and re-emerges on the tide of the harmony. Many connoisseurs feel this was Ellington's golden period, with the 1938–42 band, billed as Duke Ellington and his Famous Orchestra, running it a close second. But Ellington refuses to be drawn, and understandably finds the weight of past achievements distinctly oppressive. 'You see, I'm competing against myself. First the 1920s, then the 1930s, the 1940s, the 1950s. Each time it gets a little tougher.'

In a jazz world filled with experts trying to trace the rising curve of his career, Ellington himself looks back only to reminisce, not to analyse. The newest project is the most important one, whether it is a major suite or a four-minute trifle for the dancers.

Most disheartening of all for the musicologists is the virtual impossibility of engaging Ellington in any extended discussion of his methods. But even he must know that there have been great peaks of achievement in his life: *Black, Brown and Beige* in 1943, his first extended concert work, and the one that finally gave the lie to Constant Lambert's famous appraisal of him as a *petit maître*; the *Liberian Suite*, the incidental music to *Timon of Athens*; the series of Shakespearian vignettes, *Such Sweet Thunder*; the sacred music of the 1960s. Also many band performances of standard jazz themes never since surpassed, either by Ellington or anybody else.

But with Ellington it is very difficult to know. No major artist of this century has a more profound distaste for analysis of and theorizing about his work, even though it is more strongly qualified than most to stand such a scrutiny. And to forestall such discussions, he has cultivated that other side of his personality for which he has become world-famous, the bon-vivant who accepts the lionizing with graceful good humour. The role is easy for him because he happens to have a most extraordinary gift for courtly behaviour: this would appear quite ridiculous in anyone else, but in Ellington it can charm the birds from the trees.

Most remarkable of all is his effect on women. So far as they are concerned, Ellington once seen is never forgotten. Like Disraeli he believes in laying on the flattery with a trowel. A man escorting a lady off the premises will be gently admonished, 'Never take beauty from a room.' A perfect stranger will be asked, 'Tell me, do you always look as beautiful as this?' A lady who once complimented him on the cut of his jacket was flattened by the response, 'Yes, I was up all afternoon sitting at the loom, weaving it to impress you.' It is all an elaborate joke which offends none of the men, rejuvenates all the women and observes one of his golden rules, to make people feel good.

And yet the deeper one digs under the public persona the more serious a man one discovers. Behind the accomplished social diplomat is a dedicated musician who runs an orchestra for the most hardheaded of reasons. 'I don't want to have to wait around for somebody else to play my music. When I write something I want to hear it now, tomorrow.'

And behind the musician is a deeply religious man whose sacred music bulks largest of all in his mind.

> *The sacred concerts are to me the most important thing of all, because they do not constitute part of my career. We don't do it for profit. We play for some churches who have a lot of money, we play for some who don't have any money at all. And whether we win or lose it doesn't make any difference.*

Yet on stage nobody cuts a more worldly appearance.

He is, in fact, the sum of many contradictions, a jazz artist who knows that the definition is misleading, if only because music is music and only the unmusical insist on pigeonholes. He is an intensely romantic artist with a superlative shrewdness in dealing with the harsh practicalities of his profession, a generous praiser of other people's work who has never been influenced in the slightest by the shifting tides of fashion in the jazz world, a conjurer who has always insisted there is nothing up his sleeve, and has exasperated the cleverest musicians by the elusive quality of his work. André Previn voiced the bafflement of thousands when he said, 'Stan Kenton can stand in front of a thousand fiddles and a thousand brass and make a dramatic gesture and every studio arranger can nod his head and say, "Oh, yes, that's done like this." But Duke lifts his finger, three horns make a sound, and I don't know what it is.'

Part of the secret lies in Ellington's discovery that the way to write for a group of individuals is to acknowledge their individuality. While every other composer alive writes for instruments, he writes for specific men, so that an unadorned C Major chord can be made to wear a dozen different personalities, depending on the human permutations involved in producing it. For this reason Ellington's music is inimitable.

It is also the reason why he never gets rid of anybody. A new musician is a new texture to be assimilated into the master sound. Yet even here there is a contradiction. Much of his own music can stand without him. Some of his songs (he ranks with Porter, Rodgers and the rest of them as a songwriter) are completely performer-proof.

The biggest irony of all, is that his most famous composition, 'Take The "A" Train', was not written by him at all, but by his beloved partner Billy Strayhorn, who died in 1967.

Broadway's failure to use Ellington's talent ranks as one of the gross musical blunders of our era. An even grosser one is the attitude of the musical world at large, which has usually regarded him as a clever jazz trickster, not much more. Posterity will no doubt reach its own conclusions, and may well decide that he is one of the few authentic melodic stylists of the twentieth century.

But then, as Duke would say, such talk stinks up the place. And, whatever posterity might think of him, he never thinks about posterity at all. He is far too preoccupied with the cut of his clothes, the pattern of his diet, the contentment of his musicians and audiences, his next project, the itinerary for the next tour. Jazz, he once said, is a parade of individuals. Ellington continues to lead the parade.

Louis Armstrong (1970)

For sheer power to excite, no popular artist of this century has remotely approached Louis Daniel Armstrong, trumpet virtuoso and singer extraordinary, who celebrates his seventieth birthday today. His name has only to be mentioned for people to smile in recollection of something they once saw or heard him do.

And yet, as the tributes and the telegrams pour in, the affection of the jazz world at large will surely be tinged with certain pangs of uneasiness, almost as though it were the music itself and not just its most renowned practitioner who was moving into the dangerous age. For ever since he came out of New Orleans nearly fifty years ago, a chubby young man bursting out of a single-breasted dinner suit, to take his music to the cities of the north. Armstrong has been accepted the world over as the physical embodiment of jazz.

He has always managed to look the part without even trying. The staring banjo eyes, the rivers of honest sweat dabbed away by a whiter-than-white handkerchief, the slack lower jaw which has given him the nickname of 'Satch' (satchel-mouth), the illusion of row upon row of sparkling white teeth, the fixed smile and the alarming gravel voice which can somehow make even the most excruciating jive-talk seem witty – all these trademarks, already a little larger than life, have become magnified on cinema screens to be accepted by the average citizen as an accurate representation of what jazz looks like.

Armstrong contrived to preserve this essentially youthful image of himself far longer than anyone could reasonably have expected. Long after most of his New Orleans contemporaries were either dead, or forgotten, or both, and at a stage in life when most people are looking for the nearest armchair, he continued to stick to the kind of working itinerary that would kill a horse. It did seem at times as though his managers were pushing him too hard, or, as somebody recently put it, 'They'd have booked the old man eight days a week if they could.' But the victim appears to have enjoyed every minute of it. Although his life resolved itself many years ago into a crazy dash in and out of aeroplanes, from night club to sound stage to concert hall to recording studio, almost never did his music show signs of fatigue.

Not until very recently did the image begin to fall apart. In the early 1960s came the two heart attacks which have halved Armstrong's effectiveness as a trumpeter, and which have given rise ever since to rumours that he is dead or about to die. Even more drastic have been the effects of his morbid curiosity about the behaviour of his own bowels. This obsession with laxative processes, which began as a joke, has now developed into a mania, reducing the chuckling cherub of the vintage years into a nine-stone wraith whose features can appear shockingly unfamiliar.

Customers at his last British season, at Batley in 1968, were dismayed to find that the handout photographs showed a keyhole through which the great man could be seen smiling from his vantage point on a lavatory seat.

It is very doubtful if Armstrong can ever work at full throttle again. His lips, or 'chops', as he has always affectionately called them, can no longer stand the strain of those high notes scattered around with such liberality over the past fifty years. Not that he has lost his grasp of the idiom. An understanding of the nature of music which runs as deep as Armstrong's can never really be damaged. It is simply that physical decline has forced him to accept the fact that if he does play again, it can only be in short, calculated bursts. Not even the bookers who would be pleased to see him perform purely as a singer are able to tempt him out of semi-retirement. Only days ago he was offered $10,000 a night for as many nights as he cared to stipulate, just to sing. But the offer was declined.

Armstrong turns his back on this kind of proposition, not just because he is too tired to accept it, but also because he can afford to indulge the luxury of saying no. There has always been a great deal of uncertainty inside the jazz world as to exactly how rich he is. Probably not as rich as he should be. But although he and those connected with him have always kept the cards very close to their chests in this respect, it is safe to say that he has not had to worry about how much he earns for at least the last twenty years. Perhaps he never did worry too much. To play jazz has always been his way of enjoying himself, a fact which explains much about the effect his performances have. There is even a sense in which he might be said literally to have invented jazz single-handed.

Armstrong the musician is impossible to explain away in purely technical terms. Raised in New Orleans in wretched poverty, at a time when that city was throbbing with the rhythm of the new music, he not only possessed every talent required to master it, but was denied the chance to acquire any talents which might have got in his way. It is important to remember that Armstrong, like so many of his race and generation, is a self-taught musician, not from choice but from necessity.

Ironically, the social prejudices which barred his way to formal training only had the effect of increasing the depth and power of his originality, so that he was obliged to make up the rules of improvisation as he went along, and to break those rules whenever his instincts told him it was right to do so. To this day he is not much of a sight-reader of music, and he recalls his home town less in terms of studies completed than of life lived riotously, and perilously close to the bone.

His love affair with New Orleans, and particularly with its notorious red-light district of Storyville, is probably the most overworked piece of background information in jazz history, not least because Satch himself retains an unquenchable affection for the good old days which keep spilling out in conversation: 'Ever since I was a little boy selling newspapers, my mother and father – when they were living together – would tell me lots about Storyville, to kind of frighten me from spending my newspaper nickels down there.' It was just as well for jazz that the advice was ignored, because the Storyville joints were the nearest thing to a university campus he was ever to enjoy.

In any case, New Orleans at that time was so crammed with casual vice, with jazz as its incidental music, that it would have been impossible for any small boy to have avoided it:

> *I would delight in delivering an order of coal to the prostitute who used to hustle her crib right next to Pete Lala's cabaret, just so I could hear King Oliver play. I'd just stand there in that lady's crib listening to Oliver. All of a sudden it would dawn on her that I was still in her crib very silent while she hustled those tricks, and she'd say, 'What's the matter with you, boy?'*

And yet Armstrong, who still remembers the layout of the streets and the nickname of every madam, parts company with many of his idolators in his refusal to sentimentalize the music. One of the most surprising and unSatchlike remarks he ever made was, 'You get cliques in a band. Want to play this way and that way, full of that New Orleans fogeyism.'

That remark alone is telling enough to suggest that there is something more to Armstrong than the childlike buffoon with the trumpet. But he once told a few of us something even more revealing, something which actually hints at deviousness and diplomatic shrewdness. He was explaining the astounding fact that for many years he has not been responsible for the choice of musicians who work for him. It has always been assumed that this is merely one more example of his Uncle Tom passivity in the face of overbearing managers. Not a bit of it. 'I never pick my own bands,' he said. 'There are too many good musicians around, and it makes bad friends.'

The Uncle Tom issue has, inevitably, bulked much larger in the past few years, and one has only to examine the sentiments of an Armstrong hit like 'Wonderful World' to see why. He has been accused of selling out to the white commercializers, of having become a kind of one-man Black and White Minstrel show, of embracing the old White-Man-Boss relationship with a willingness which says nothing for pride of race or awareness of his own special responsibilities as a figurehead. If the other popular musical figure born on Independence Day, George M. Cohan, is seen as the musical embodiment of Uncle Sam, then Armstrong is just as surely the musical embodiment of Uncle Tom. Or so his detractors say.

They regard him as an old buffer with no relevance to the contemporary scene, and whose popularity is built on the acceptability to the white exploiters of the red-beans-and-rice ethos he has marketed so consistently. They cannot understand why so rich and so gifted a musician should fool about singing 'Hello Dolly' with Barbra Streisand, how he can mouth the lyrics of 'Wonderful World' without baulking at the incongruities.

The interesting thing is that the complaints have all come either from purist critics or political rebels. There is not one single musician of any consequence who takes exception to the personality Armstrong projects on stage, and for a very good reason. It takes a performer to know a performer, and musicians have grasped an obvious truth that the commentators have overlooked, which is that Armstrong's stage life is as much a performance, the projection of an artistic image, as any actor's.

He may sing in public of an idyllic Deep South where the banjos are forever strumming, but the words are no more than musical cyphers to fill up the bars. If Armstrong were really marketing the myth implicit in a song like 'When It's Sleepy Time Down South', he would hardly have sent a bitter telegram to President Eisenhower, as he did when the latter was dealing in his own sweet way with the schools' desegregation issue at the time of Little Rock.

Armstrong has not been walking around for fifty years with his eyes closed. He knows all too well what the colour bar has cost him, in the 1930s for instance, when the ballroom bonanza was the exclusive preserve of the white orchestras, or in Hollywood, where he has played a long succession of grooms and valets to a string of leading men who were not fit to wipe his boots, musically speaking. In 1927 he led the first desegregated jazz group to make a record, but he must have noticed that reciprocal gestures from white musicians have not been as frequent as they might have been.

The musicians can't fault him, either on grounds of Uncle Tomism or of anything else, simply because of his infallible professionalism. The respect he commands from fellow professionals is without equal in the world today and this is because he has been able to do naturally what others have strained to do without ever matching him. It is always forgotten that, in spite of his magnificent legacy of recorded jazz, Armstrong has not for many years been able to make a record in the accepted sense. Nobody is able to book him for a specified number of hours to cut a specified number of sides. His touring commitments have meant that recordings are something achieved on the march, in the middle of the night, piecemeal, between planes and hotels. Had it not been for his freakish stamina and his sense of obligation, Armstrong would hardly have made any long-playing albums at all.

Satch's sessions are like no others. Although not nearly so sophisticated an operator as the moderns, he can pick up an orchestral routine in quicker time than it takes to rehearse it. In fact there are virtually no rehearsals at all. 'It would be a waste of time,' says one man who has recorded him many times. 'You give him the song copy or the lead-sheet, he asks you what you want him to do and then he does it, straight off.' Hardly ever is a second 'take' necessary. He is, in other words, the recording executive's dream, a man who can defy fatigue to produce high quality work in the fastest possible time.

There is even a sense in which Armstrong has been too professional. So completely does he regard himself as an entertainer, and so comprehensive are his gifts, that he will put on record whatever is asked of him, even if it happens not to be worthy of his talents. There is a story about him which is so mawkish that the only excuse for repeating it is that it is quite true. He had come to the end of a particularly gruelling day, ending up in the small hours in a recording studio. The session was over and the musicians packing their instruments. It was then discovered the projected album was one side short.

Armstrong, already heading for the exit, was asked when he could come back to cut one more track. His reply was 'Now.' He sat in a chair and studied the song copy of an old Irving Berlin standard that he had never played before. Would everyone mind waiting just two minutes while he learned the song? Before the two minutes were up he had fallen asleep and tumbled out of his chair, the music still in his hand.

But it would be wrong to see him as a hero martyring himself for the cause. His good humour is irrepressible, and when things go wrong he laughs his way out of trouble, refusing to be pompous about either his own music or anyone else's. When he came to London to appear with a symphony orchestra at a charity concert for the victims of the Hungarian rising, neither rehearsals nor performance went quite according to plan.

At one stage the conductor played the piano while Armstrong ran through one of his routines. At the point where he was to play a four-bar cadenza, Armstrong played eight bars instead. The conductor stopped playing and acidly inquired if Armstrong intended on the night to play a four-bar break or an eight-bar break. Armstrong thought about it for a moment and replied, 'I may do both.' On the night of the concert, orchestral chaos wrecked the performance of one of his favourite spirituals, 'Nobody Knows The Trouble I've Seen, Nobody Knows But Jesus'. Ploughing on through the chaos about him, Armstrong sang, 'Nobody knows the trouble I'm in, nobody knows – but JESUS!'

Basically he is a primitive, an artist with a boldness of approach which has reached heroic proportions. He had no schooling, musical or otherwise, and anyone who can imagine what life was like for a poor black child in the Deep South of sixty years ago must see that it is Armstrong's great triumph to have survived at all. Incapable of intellectualizing his part in the evolution of jazz, his rare attempts at critical percipience have usually been disastrous ('These damn Beboppers are killing the business'), while the suggestion that without him, jazz might never have happened at all, would appear to him to be preposterous.

Probably the tributes he prizes most are the ones paid to him by the pioneers of that vanished time and place of his early years. All his rivals loved him in those days, and one of them, a trumpeter called Mutt Carey, said more than all the verdicts of the musicologists put together. When asked what he thought of Armstrong, Carey replied, 'You know it's a pleasure just to hear Louis tune up. Why, just warming up, he blows such a variety of things that it is a wonder to the ears, and a real pleasure.' Carey was right. For more than fifty years, Louis Armstrong has been a wonder to the ears and a real pleasure. His style has that quality of apparent simplicity which only the complexity of real genius can achieve. Anybody can learn what Armstrong knows about music in a few weeks. Nobody could learn to play like him in a thousand years. Unfortunately, the language of jazz criticism is a currency hopelessly debased by thirty years of hyperbolic lunacy, but Armstrong, with his masculine beauty of tone, his endless inventive resource, his vast instrumental range, demands all the superlatives. The towering, heroic extroversion of his style, shot through with a brio which enabled him to bring jazz to a world which frankly cares very little for it, will prove in time to have been one of the artistic triumphs of the twentieth century.

II

London: Jazz Decade

Ten Years at Ronnie Scott's 1959–1969

39 Gerrard Street

In 1959, there was nothing to distinguish Number 39 from the other houses on the south side of Gerrard Street. Following the schizophrenic pattern of life in the area, it had for some time led two quite independent existences, its upper floors housing a gown manufactory by day, its cellar coming to frenetic life after dark as an obscure near-beer joint employing a succession of hamfisted house pianists and relying on the whim of passing musicians to augment its orchestra. Through the 1950s it gradually became the kind of place a professional jazz musician might visit in the small hours to get some practice, or become acquainted with a new mouthpiece, or simply gratify a sudden urge to play. One night in 1954 I had gone there to explore the possibilities of a newly repaired soprano saxophone away from prying ears, and found Joe Harriott there, playing 'Deep Purple' over and over again in an attempt to become familiar with the chords. On a later visit I had seen a legendary eccentric called Reggie Dare* play two choruses of 'Crazy Rhythm' on the tenor saxophone and fall off the microscopic bandstand three times in the process. What the proprietors and their customers made of us we never discovered, but because we were jazz musicians who sometimes gave our services free, they admitted us without hesitation to the odd freemasonry of their tiny world.

And then, in the spring of 1959, the pattern in the cellar at 39 changed. The old club vanished, to be superseded by a new and rather more respectable one whose constitution was non-existent but which was vaguely understood to refer in some way to taxi drivers. Once again, jazz musicians succeeded in infiltrating the premises, this time to scoff fried bread and play endless rounds of rummy with their allies the cabmen. But the new

---

* 'In the jazz world, a man who doesn't eat meat is a Reggiedarian.' Anon. *circa* 1952.

establishment was doomed from the beginning. Intended to be the successor to a highly successful club of a similar kind which had recently expired, it possessed neither the tradition nor the facilities necessary for survival, and within weeks of its birth was limping irrevocably towards its own funeral. By the nature of things, the cellar should have reverted back immediately to the status of near-beer joint in a street devoted to that peculiar social institution. Instead, it turned into something very different, a place where the music, instead of being a drone in the background, became the most important facility the management could offer. It was also about to become the first, and as time proved, the only permanent jazz club in Britain to be owned and administered by a jazz musician rather than by an entrepreneur. Probably for this reason it was regarded by what are sometimes laughingly called the businessmen of the jazz world as a typically lunatic gesture certain to degenerate into low farce before the paint on the walls was dry. In the event everybody was wrong, except for the small nucleus of practising jazz musicians who knew something of the personality of the man involved.

The musician in question was Ronnie Scott, and in view of the startling success of his venture, it might be revealing to take a closer look at his unique temperament. The apparent contradiction in his nature between an intense romanticism about jazz music and an utterly realistic approach to making it, has always resolved itself into a series of idealistic actions accompanied by a running barrage of his own sardonic comments on those actions. A natural straightfaced comic, Scott has always presented himself to audiences as though the whole thing was a joke, and then proceeded to play as though his life depended on it, which in a way it does. An established soloist while still in his teens, he has always indulged this tendency to carry buffoonery right up to the moment when the music has actually to be delivered, but the true assessment of his achievements may be gauged not from the things he says, but the things he does. Even before the idea of opening his own club had entered his head, he had for a long time shown a talent for organization inside the chaotic world of Modern jazz. As early as 1947 he had been a dominant influence in the formation of the country's first Modern jazz club, the Club Eleven, and had later led a series of groups ranging in size from a quartet to full orchestra, and in degree of success from moderate acceptance to hysterical acclaim. This gift for marshalling the resources of others into some kind of ordered unity was less a question of administrative capacity than of force of personality. In fact the knack of making life more interesting for other musicians is at once the most nebulous and the most valuable asset Scott possesses, and it has undoubtedly had a great deal to do with the success of many of his experiments.

The first time I ever heard him mention the idea of a jazz club was in the bandroom of the Orchid Ballroom, Purley. The year was 1953, when Scott, myself and seven others were waging a bitter, and in the end, triumphant campaign to keep alive a co-operative orchestra whose strategy was to get itself booked into the dance halls, and then play uncompromising jazz once it got there. Already most of the country's bandleaders had conceived a deep loathing for us, which we did our best to aggravate on all possible occasions. The trouble was that an orchestra which splits the profits is a violent blasphemy against the dance band convention that the musician is a hired hand pledged to making the fortune of the bandleader, with whom he is expected to reach a relationship somewhere between medieval serf and lickspittle accomplice. To the non-playing maestros of the period, our co-operative enterprise must have smacked very strongly of syncopated Marxism. If our little cell proved to be the first of many, then the nation's bandleaders, doomed to the tumbrils of redundancy, would have no choice but to go and get an honest job. And yet, had our enemies been able to see us that night at Purley, they might well have tempered their distaste with a little sympathy. The evening had been a disaster.

Scott and I were sitting in the bandroom, slowly changing into what, for the lack of a better phrase, might be called our street clothes, and pondering the implications of the box office returns. For the last five minutes we had been trying to work out how many times nine went into £14 6s 5d. Such mathematics are not good for the soul, so I was astonished when Scott remarked that he intended investing his share of the profits from our orchestra in a jazz club. 'What profits?' I asked. 'I won't always be like this,' he said, 'Not every date will turn out to be like this one.' As it happened he was quite right. On the following Thursday we played at Acton Town Hall, where this time the mathematics resolved themselves into nines into £12 10s 6d. So it is not really surprising that it took Scott another six years to realize his ambition.

Being a born night creature, Scott had naturally been one of the musicians who frequented 39 Gerrard Street in both its near-beer and cabman's refuge phases. On his visits there he must have made a mental note that this was one of several possible sites for the jazz club he still intended one day to open, although it was by no means the first choice. It was too small for the type of club Scott had in mind, and there would obviously be acoustic difficulties, for audiences if not musicians. It was in a lamentable state of repair and clearly would have to be renovated and redesigned throughout before the public could be invited there. There might also be trouble complying with London County Council's Fire Regulations because the premises had only one entrance, on to the street. On the credit side, the rent was comparatively cheap, and it was located in the right place, Gerrard Street being at the very heart of the area which followers of the music had learned over the years to associate with Modern jazz. Whether the close proximity of the Flamingo Club, less than a hundred yards away in Wardour Street, would be a help or a hindrance neither Scott nor anyone else knew, but at least the premises were available at not too prohibitive a cost.

In order to gauge the magnitude of the task Scott was setting himself, it is necessary to examine the state of the Modern jazz club world during the late 1950s. Saturday night business was usually good, Sundays moderate, the rest of the week more or less non-existent. In the early 1950s, Studio 51 had provided Modern jazz on week nights, but by the time Scott was contemplating moving into Gerrard Street, had long since reverted to a policy of the crudest Revivalism. All the known facts suggested that Modern jazz in London was essentially a weekend affair, patronized by a tiny nucleus of loyal followers who were not prepared to turn out during the working week.

Apart from the consideration of sheer numbers, there was a more serious problem to be faced, and that was the pitiful shoestring economy on which all jazz clubs were based. Both in range of admission prices and fees for musicians, the London clubs limited themselves to the scales of the dance halls without possessing the dance halls' vast potential public. The result was that even with consistently full houses no jazz club could remotely consider the possibility of booking regular international attractions, or even of acquiring its own permanent premises. By the time the small profits had been divided, there was never anything left for improving amenities. And when from time to time musicians tried to break out of the cage by running their own clubs, the profits left to them at the end of the evening were usually even smaller than the fees they could expect from clubs like The Flamingo and Studio 51. It is true that both these establishments were housed in premises either owned or leased by the proprietors of the jazz club, but it was true also that both these proprietors, being business speculators rather than musicians, were eventually tempted into fields more lucrative than Modern jazz, The Flamingo to Rhythm & Blues, Studio 51 to New Orleans pastiche.

These were the daunting facts, and there was no getting round them. They had applied for at least ten years, and nobody who believed they could be reversed had a scrap of tangible evidence to support his argument. Scott, however, had always been convinced that something better might be done. Throughout the penny-pinching era, he had himself been the biggest local attraction in any of the London jazz clubs, and these years of experience had left him with the conviction that a new potential audience, much larger than any existing clubowner dreamed of, was available to jazz musicians if only there was a radical change in the way the music was presented.

Very briefly, Scott's theory may be summarized as follows. If the existing clubs were imitating the pattern of dance hall prices, then proprietors would never draw enough money to make expansion a practical possibility. If, on the other hand, something approaching a nightclub policy were attempted, both the size of the audience and the prices it was prepared to pay would increase vastly. Of course, running costs would increase proportionately, but provided the musical attractions really were attractive, and not just further permutations of the same few faces, enough money would come into the box office to meet the increased overheads. And this brought Scott face to face with the most frustrating problem of all.

Jazz is basically an American art form, which means that any club claiming to present the best jazz had to send to America for it. Now apart from the expenses involved, there was in operation at the time Scott was considering opening his own club, a

Musicians' Union edict barring all American jazz musicians from appearing in British clubs or dance halls. Although this sounds, and indeed is, a shortsighted rule with only the crudest of sophistical arguments to justify its application, it actually represented a distinct advance on the rules governing entry of American musicians which had operated from prewar days through to 1956. For those twenty years Americans were not allowed to work in Britain at all, but then the ban had been lifted on concerts. Why concerts and not clubs, and why classical virtuosi and not jazzmen, has never been satisfactorily explained, but Scott knew that if he did open his club, he would not be permitted to import American attractions unless the rules governing their entry were changed. There is no question but that he gambled on this change coming about.

When Scott finally went ahead and opened the club in Gerrard Street, with a provisional policy of British jazz four nights a week, the general reaction was typical of the dismally parochial attitude of the British jazz world in general. Nobody took the project seriously enough to assume it would last more than a few weeks. Rival proprietors smiled and went on with their business. Musicians applauded and wondered how long it would be before the restless Scott moved on to some other dream-scheme. The public read the Jazz Club columns in the trade press and made a mental note that another tiny mushroom had sprouted in the barren field of Modern jazz. I suppose my own reactions were typical enough. Like most musicians who had worked with Scott over the years, I had a healthy regard for his initiative, but it was not enough to convince me that he could ever come remotely near his end of a high-budget club importing Americans. I thought he had a good chance of surviving as just another local clubowner, but even this, I knew, would be a very difficult thing to do. I had myself run a jazz club in the previous year, and had seen my backers' status slump from plutocracy to penury within the space of seven weeks. Scott was to open his club in the autumn, and I felt that if he was still operating on New Year's Eve, he would be doing better than he could have hoped.

The builders finally moved out of 39 Gerrard Street in October, and on Friday the 30th the musicians moved in. There were five sessions that first weekend, Friday evening, Friday all night, Saturday evening, Saturday all night, and Sunday evening.

Attendances were excellent and the gate receipts poor, much of the clientele being composed of professional comrades of the proprietor who assumed, quite correctly, that their names must go automatically on to any free list with which Scott was concerned. The two groups which opened the club were both quartets, one led by Scott himself, the other by a relatively obscure teenaged saxophonist called Peter King.

Mention of one Peter King demands mention of the other Peter King, a retired tenor saxophonist who had worked in many bands with Scott during the 1950s, and who had graduated, by the time the Ronnie Scott Club finally opened, into the position of Scott's general business manager. On King would devolve a great deal of the paperwork, administration of staff, booking of musicians, regulation of finance, and all the other essential jobs which do not normally fall within the experience of the working jazz musician. Basically King's job would be to translate into practical terms Scott's somewhat visionary intentions. As the two men had been close friends for so long, there was little chance of business strains destroying their partnership, and there was no question that King himself was just as excited as Scott about the prospects before them. Both men were determined to achieve independence of the existing jazz club proprietors, both were convinced that, being musicians, they knew more about running a jazz club than the speculative amateurs who had dominated that field till now, and both were utterly convinced that the audiences could be doubled again if only there was a radical change in methods of presentation. The next few years were to try their beliefs very severely indeed. For the moment the club was open, and apart from Scott and King, there was a general feeling that before much longer it would be closed again.

THE OLD PLACE

Already in this history reference has been made to that quirk in Scott's temperament which impels him to lampoon everything about the music he plays except its actual execution, and unless this point is taken, the early history of Ronnie Scott's Club will become totally incomprehensible. An outsider coming to the study of the subject with nothing to help him but the customary printed sources, would very speedily come to the conclusion that the club, so far from being a gesture of defiant idealism, was no more than an elaborate private joke which no one connected with it believed would survive more than a few weeks. In fact, so unorthodox was the early publicity that the average customer reading about the club might be pardoned for assuming that the club literally did not exist at all. The whole approach to the running of the club was that blend of derision and dedication typical of the man behind it, derision in selling the music, dedication in playing it. A symbolic example is the method employed to advertise each night's attractions at 39 Gerrard Street.

Every weekend unofficial conferences were held between Scott and his professional friends, in which private jokes were sifted through and edited to the point where they might be printable. Anybody could contribute to these councils, and it soon became an issue of some pride to have an item officially accepted. For many years, of course, the trade press had carried jazz club advertisements as stereotyped as they were misleading. Adjectives like 'fabulous' and 'immortal' were appended to the names of soloists of quite modest ability, including at one time myself, and the innovation had become a convention which nobody thought of ignoring. It is quite possible that the reason why this tactic was pursued for so long has something to do with the fact that jazz club proprietors knew so little about the music they were selling, that they really believed the idiotic hectorings they composed and paid for each week. But when Scott was first faced with the responsibility of inserting these advertisements announcing the week's attractions, it was characteristic of him that he should transform a menial task into an exercise in slapstick. Solemn students of the music studying the Jazz Club columns of the musical comics, as Scott himself used to describe them, were bewildered to find that the relevant information was cloaked by moonshine so impenetrable that it was sometimes difficult to know how far the joke was meant to be taken. Was there a Scott's Club at all? And if there was, what went on there? It was certainly hard to know what to think when you picked up your weekly and read:

TUESDAY:	*The Ronnie Scott Quartet will play music from the film of the same name.*
WEDNESDAY:	*'The best cuisine in town.' Fifty million flies can't be wrong.*
THURSDAY:	*Lecture on Jazz by the eminent Indian critic, Pandit Badly.*
FRIDAY:	*Yehudi Menuhin with Strings.*
SATURDAY:	*Try our buffet. Food untouched by human hand. Our chef is a gorilla.*
SUNDAY:	*Mystery guest who's just finished variety in the north, now here to finish it in the south.*

Nor were these advertisements the only outward sign of levity. In the very early days of Scott's Club those concerned with its life were constantly thinking up ways of varying the diet placed before members. One of several gambits which was soon abandoned involved myself in a series of record recitals. The audiences paid reasonable attention, but any chance of real success was destroyed by the claque of hecklers standing at the back of the room by the snack bar, shouting ribald comments on my opinions and the way I delivered them. The fact that this claque consisted in its entirety of my brother-musicians, and that more than once their number included the proprietor, shows why there was no alternative but to agree with their criticisms and retire gracefully.

A more successful experiment was the resuscitation, after five years, of the co-operative band which had once been so successful touring the country. Its first appearance at the club drew a packed house, but as most of the band library had been left in provincial bandrooms, eaten by mice or disfigured by spittle from mouthpieces, the band's entire repertoire consisted of four titles, which we played three or four times each before giving up a morbid experiment in nostalgia.

Once his club became established, Scott became intrigued by the possibilities of a room which he alone administered. One obvious way of extending activities was the use of the premises as a rehearsal room, an innovation which was to bring about a farcical exercise in jurisprudence, as we shall see. Another of Scott's departures was his contribution towards the development of dramatic art in Britain. For a time in 1960, when the premises were cleared on Tuesday nights, they were reopened after midnight for the running of a small Actors' Group presided over by Lindsay Anderson and attended by talents as disparate as Maggie Smith and Georgia Brown.

Predictably, Scott cast himself as a parody of the waiter in *You Never Can Tell*, dispensing Cokes and coffee to the actors and actresses, most of whom had not a suspicion who Scott was, and carrying everything through in a mock-Shakespearean voice strongly reminiscent of Sir Donald Wolfit, except of course that Scott is a rather better actor than Wolfit. The guise of tragedian even spilled over into Scott's daytime routine, and was only discarded when the proprietor of the local betting shop threatened to suspend credit when Scott kept asking him, 'Prithee knave, what fanciest thee in the half past meridian at Sandown Park this afternoon?'

But confused with all this buffoonery and never affected by it, was the intense jazz atmosphere which Scott succeeded in creating in the club. In a very short time he was operating seven nights a week, thus becoming the first owner of a fulltime professional jazz club in London. Rival club owners folded their tents and stole away to more lucrative pastures, and it very soon became accepted that Scott's Club was the one place where the audience could be sure of finding jazz of the highest quality local musicians could provide. For the moment, neither club finances nor Union politics made it possible to carry through the plan to make the club's attractions international, but in the meantime, much ingenuity was brought to bear on the problem of creating balanced and interesting bills.

In these early days, the outstanding music was provided by the same tiny nucleus of soloists who had already dominated the British jazz scene for the past few years. Tubby Hayes, Jimmy Deuchar and Scott himself were three examples of local musicians whose standard of play was much closer to American criteria than many club members suspected. Indeed, in later days, when imported players became the norm, more than one thoughtful reassessment of British players was made by those who came to hear the American soloists and were surprised to find that, for the last ten years, local men had been suffering because of geographical rather than musical shortcomings.

Deuchar in particular is an example of a British jazz musician with a dash of originality about his playing. A natural improvisor with a distinct melodic gift, Deuchar had worked alongside Scott over the years in a succession of groups of all sizes, and it was natural that he should be appearing at the club so frequently. Deuchar was double value because of his ability to compose and arrange themes for whichever group he happened to be working with.

By the time Scott opened his club, his friendly rival Edward Brian 'Tubby' Hayes had already acquired a prolific technique and an intimate familiarity with every twist and turn of Modern harmonic convention. A soloist of furious energy and an insatiable appetite for playing, Hayes had been Scott's partner in the last of the groups with which Scott was involved before the experiment of the club, The Jazz Couriers. By the 1960s he had also turned himself into an accomplished vibraphonist and a flautist of infinite possibilities. Some idea of his prowess on instruments other than the tenor saxophone may be gathered from the fact that when Victor Feldman returned to England for a working holiday and appeared at the club, Hayes happily shared vibraphone duets with him without any suggestion of being the junior partner.

At 39 Gerrard Street the bandroom was too tiny for comfort, especially as it served as an office during the day; but visitors to the club, which was now becoming something of a landmark, usually managed to find a seat on the upturned instrument cases which filled the room. Sonny Rollins used to practise his lip-twitching exercises there, and the poet Robert Graves once delivered the definitive harangue on the efficiencies of romantic love there. Even in the club's earliest days there was an undercurrent in this room of greater things to come. The air was pregnant with all kinds of possibilities, and dominating all was of course the hope that some time, very soon, Scott would be able to bring in the Americans. Rumours came and went with no tangible results. Finally a rumour came which was only half-dispelled, and which then evolved into half-fact and finally into a definite statement. Union agreement had been reached, Ministry of Labour blessing granted, fees agreed upon and contracts exchanged. Those of us who had taken an interest in the club since its beginnings, and for whom the club had indeed become virtually a way of life, were half-delighted, half-incredulous, when we were told that an American saxophonist, one of the outstanding figures in the jazz history of the last decade, was to come to London to play a season at Scott's. With this announcement and its eventual confirmation, ended the embryonic stage of the club's growth. It had lasted four years, had begun with buffoonery and grown into seriousness that had never been allowed to sag into solemnity. Parochial attitudes, typical of British jazz ever since there had been such a thing, were to go forever. Scott had fulfilled his original ambition at last.

Zoot Sims

John Haley 'Zoot' Sims was an especially happy choice with which to open a new period of expansion. At a time when jazz was already beginning to reflect its own dire uncertainties in the tortuous convolutions of the avant garde, he had remained a soloist in the classic tradition, observing scrupulously the laws of discord and resolution without ever sounding restricted by them. Ever since his rapid rise in the late 1940s, he had always been designated a Modernist, meaning a post-Charlie Parker musician, but by the time he arrived at Scott's, it had been obvious for a long time that he was a player whose roots went far back beyond the line which Parker had drawn so dramatically across the face of jazz history. When compared with contemporaries like Sonny Rollins and John Coltrane, his effect was positively venerable, and there was at times an almost Dixieland geniality about his structures which reduced the pigeonholers to total confusion.

But there is in jazz a modernism of inflection as well as a modernism of harmony, and it was in this sense that Sims could be described as an authentic Modernist. Possibly the least fussy of all the important tenor saxophonists in jazz, he created an unmistakably Modern effect by the technical mannerisms of his playing, through his conception of where the pulse of each performance lay, and in the way he executed his phrases. As the years went by, the administration at Scott's was to become much less preoccupied with this esoteric issue of who was and who was not a Modernist, but at the time it first acquired the services of Sims, such considerations were still of vital importance to a club which was catering for the Modernist diehard if it was catering for anybody at all.

In any case, the stylistic bona fides of Zoot Sims were authentic enough. Both tonally and in the aural shapes he deployed, Sims belonged to a school of tenor saxophone playing which had just begun to flourish when he was in his formative years, a school pioneered by that remarkable innovator Lester Young. Adherence to Young's precepts demanded a honking, metallic tone and a high degree of subtlety in shaping arpeggios to produce an astringent effect. It also implied a mastery of the series of false fingerings which Young had perfected, and whose value lay in their property of creating different densities of sound on the same note. In all these aspects Sims was the model Young disciple, the most outstanding, in fact, with the possible exception of his great rival Stan Getz. There was, of course, and still remains, a vast contrast in musical temperaments between Sims and Getz, but the two men comprise a fascinating proof of the proposition that jazz musicians may stem from the same source and yet be utterly dissimilar in the effects they produce. In time the audiences at Scott's were to be given the chance to discern this difference for themselves, but for the moment it was Zoot Sims they were being asked to listen to.

In assessing the impact of Sims's debut at Scott's, there was one other serious consideration, and that was the quality of the accompaniment. At the time Scott opened his club, it was a truism in the British jazz world that playing standards among rhythm sections were much lower than those to be found among the front-line instrumentalists. In being granted permission at last to import American attractions, Scott had overcome his most daunting diplomatic problem, only to be faced now by a musical one of just as serious proportions. So far as British drummers and bass players were concerned, it was less a question of technique than of subtlety and sophistication, and there was a very real danger that even the most accomplished visitors might feel themselves hamstrung by the solecisms going on behind them. Scott did the best he could, and in the event, whether from politeness or genuine satisfaction, very few of his imported guests ever conveyed displeasure about the quality of the support provided for them, although a crisis was very soon to occur, as we shall see.

Sims proved to be a brilliant success at the club. He had worked in London only once before, in 1958, when he was part of an unfortunate gallimaufry of American stars browbeaten into a subordinate role by the despotic bass player Oscar Pettiford. On that occasion, Sims, like several of his colleagues, had stepped quietly into the background while their self-appointed leader edified concert audiences with an endless stream of deafening bass solos. But judging from his recordings, Sims was ideally the kind of musician who would flower in the intimacy of a small group in a small club, and this proved to be the case. Away from the inhibiting atmosphere of the recording studio, which was the only environment in which most of us had heard him before, he was even more impressive than we had hoped, producing a succession of fluent solos whose main features were melodic wit and a vigorous rhythmic power. It is difficult to exaggerate the significance of his visit for most local jazz connoisseurs. The vagaries of Musicians' Union policy had caused a twenty-five year hiatus in the education of the British to authentic jazz played in natural surroundings, and Sims was the first musician to break this sequence with official blessing. He played nightly at Scott's through the month of November 1961, and was so evidently comfortable playing there that it seemed almost certain that he would be back again.

But if audiences expected a stream of Americans to follow Sims into the club, they were to be sorely disappointed. The financial burden of hiring men of his calibre was increased by the fact that no matter what the attraction, a full house was a full house. The club's capacity was a mere 150, which meant that it would prove virtually impossible to show any profit from a season like Sims's even if every seat were occupied every night. Also, the Union had by no means relented its previous obstructionist policy, and was rationing the club's quota of Americans with a parsimony which would have been comical had it not also been irritating. Zoot Sims departed at the end of November. It was to be another seven months before another guest of his class succeeded him.

In the meantime there occurred a curious interlude which

began to the strains of 'Whatever Lola Wants' and ended in the unlikely precincts of the Law Courts. Although it was a thought which surely struck nobody who frequented the club, 39 Gerrard Street had remained for most of its ratepayers a conventional house of business. The gown manufacturers on the ground floor locked up and retreated to the pink mirrors and cocktail cabinets of suburbia each night long before the club came to life, and because of this fortuitous Box-and-Cox situation the inevitable clash of interests took a long time coming. But as the club became established as a fixture of London nightlife, the first rumblings of discontent began. They came from the tenant on the ground floor, whose musical tastes evidently did not quite run to the neologisms of the post-Parker jazz era. Gradually the polite requests for silence modulated into irritated demands for peace and quiet and then into hysterical outbursts of extreme bitterness. Rehearsals grew longer and tempers shorter, and as the gown trade has never been particularly distinguished for the patronage of any art other than making money, the legal profession was at last called in to perform a gig of its own.

Ronnie Scott – Witness for the Defence

One Wednesday morning in the summer of 1962, Scott went to the Law Courts to defend his right to make musical effects on his premises during normal business hours. The plaintiff was a nervous little man who would probably have been flattered by moribund violins, but who felt there was something subtly corrupting about the phenomenon of jazz music seeping up through his floorboards. Obviously the outcome would hinge on the musical rationale of the judge himself. If the defendants were unlucky enough to be saddled with one of those disingenuous wigged effigies who think an affected ignorance of all subjects apart from jurisprudence is a substitute for wit, then the cause was lost. If, on the other hand, the judge was the kind of person who did not feel that the inducement to tap one's feet while stitching hems was necessarily the first step on the road to Sodom, then the rehearsals, by now an integral part of the club's routine, might be allowed to continue.

In the event the plaintiffs produced only one witness, a middle-aged woman of about twenty-five who worked as a secretary in a room almost directly over the club bandstand. She claimed that there were times when the noise downstairs was so bad that it was impossible for her to take important telephone messages. An odd statement. What about unimportant telephone messages? And the very preference of the word 'noise' over 'music' or even 'sound', significantly suggested an inability to distinguish between the two. It was at this early stage that the judge showed to which of the two juridical categories he belonged. Leaning forward and speaking in tones of gentle remonstrance, he observed, 'Some people like jazz. They might consider you lucky to have it while you work, without paying for it.'

The witness was plainly baffled by this remark, which is perhaps not quite the kind solicitors anticipate when coaching a witness. After a pause she mumbled 'Yes,' looking rather as Bill the Lizard must have done when Alice snatched his pencil away. Much shaken, she continued with the rest of her evidence, which appeared to consist in its entirety of two visits downstairs to request less noise. On the first occasion, she said, the place was occupied by a group of buglers rehearsing on the bandstand: 'I told the conductor he was too noisy, but he told me he didn't want to know.' The idea of a group of buglers being led by a conductor in a jazz club was rich indeed, but before anyone present could savour its richness, the evidence progressed from absurdity to sheer impossibility. When she descended into the club a second time, the witness said, there was nobody there at all. Somebody pointed out, very gently, that if there was nobody there, then there could not have been any noise. The witness seemed utterly confused by this sophistry, and did not so much leave the box as evaporate out of the case. It occurred to me, sitting there watching this extraordinary charade, that possibly the entire staff of the plaintiff's establishment was suffering from delusions. Two days before, Scott and I had stood in the passage outside the gown manufacturer's office. With us had been a young man with a sound-measuring machine; downstairs in the club, directly beneath us, Ella Fitzgerald rehearsed 'Whatever Lola Wants' with rhythm accompaniment. The singing was quite inaudible, and the machine had registered only a few decibels, the result of our heavy breathing.

I now glanced across the courtroom and studied the man who had brought this action. He was bald and small, and kept working his mouth in the oddest way, as though he had recently been nibbling nut chocolate. His expression, which remained unchanged throughout the morning, was one of nervous insensitivity. It dawned on me that he felt righteous about the whole thing, that he had picked up from somewhere the curious notion that selling something for more than it cost you was, in some obscure way, more respectable and necessary to the welfare of the community at large than playing a few choruses of the blues.

During the luncheon interval Scott conferred over steak and kidney pie with his solicitors, who smiled uncertainly when the defendant suggested he enter a plea of Guilty but Insane when the case was resumed. To lend forensic authority to the idea, Scott kept addressing the waitresses as 'M'Lud' and quoting as a precedent the case of The Crown versus Schpeilke, 1904. It should be explained that at this time Scott was deep in the Schpeilke fantasy which slowly faded out of his life in the next few months. For part of 1962, the name had been inscribed on the card over the bellpush of his flat behind Marylebone Road, and none of his visitors ever had any doubts about which bell they ought to ring. Scott later defined this harmless aberration as a splinter movement, and it is a pity that an intimate knowledge of dog Yiddish is required to appreciate the pun.*

Just when it was promising to move into the realm of slapstick, the court case faded away into the tamest of endings. A few whispered conferences and the dispute was settled out of court, after which the dynamics of the groups working and rehearsing at the club seemed to be no less and no greater than they had been before. The only practical outcome of the case may have been that the club acquired a new member. While the case was in progress, Scott's solicitor had demanded as part of

* Shpilke is Yiddish for a sewing pin.

his fee life membership of the club. Scott had replied, apparently quite in earnest, 'Whose life, yours or mine?'

The point was not pursued.

Lucky Thompson

It was in this same summer of 1962 that the club's second American visitor arrived. He was the tenor saxophonist Lucky Thompson, who opened in Gerrard Street on 1 June, exactly seven months after Zoot Sims had left. Thompson's had been one of the oddest careers in post-war jazz. A superlative technician with a brilliant gift for improvisation, Thompson had somehow missed the status he once seemed certain of achieving, and, let it be admitted, he had never quite fulfilled the promise of his startling debut. He had burst on the then parochial ears of the British jazz fan with a mid-1940s recording of 'Just One More Chance' which placed him clearly in the long and honourable tradition of rhapsodic tenor playing founded by Coleman Hawkins and sustained later by men like Chu Berry and Don Byas. His tone was sumptuous, his technique blinding, and his talent for inventing melodic phrases quite ravishing. An outstanding career seemed to be under way.

But then a combination of unfortunate circumstances proceeded to rob Thompson of his success. At just about the time he appeared, jazz was about to fly off the chromatic tangent which disturbed so many apparently well-founded careers. The art of improvisation was never to be quite the same again after the advent of Charlie Parker, and suddenly it was men like James Moody who were regarded as the pacemakers on Thompson's instrument. Nevertheless, Thompson was still a very young man, even as jazz soloists go, and there seemed every chance that he would move with the times and absorb the ideas of the new school without damaging his basic talent. In fact, a player of his extreme sophistication seemed the ideal type of musician to prove capable of grasping the subtleties of the new Modernism. That Thompson never did this, or even seemed to care very much about doing it, is one of those puzzling facts about jazz over the last twenty years for which there is no satisfactory explanation. He had divorced himself from the jazz centre by living in Europe, and had built up over the years a reputation for being 'difficult', whatever that blanket criticism may mean. His inability, or refusal, to fit in with the arrangements at Scott's seemed to manifest itself in two different ways, an impatience with the shortcomings of his rhythm section which may well have been justified, and a deep contempt for critics, which certainly was justified in his case.

Most of us made the mistake of expecting him still to be producing the romanticism of 'Just One More Chance', and when he turned out to have moved on since those days, the sentimentalist in each of us was sorely disappointed. In what seems to me now to have been a wrong-headed review, I doubted the wisdom of a player of Thompson's gifts expending himself on the tortuous complexities of Modernism, when the obvious reaction should have been to congratulate him on not resting on twenty-year-old laurels. For there was no question that, however one might have preferred the congenial Thompson of 'Just One More Chance', the Thompson who presented himself at Scott's was a saxophonist of remarkable command and distinction. The fact that his musical personality was probably best suited to the passion of his early work is beside the point, which is that only the most gifted musicians are able to make even a half-successful transition to a newer style.

Most jazz musicians, when faced with critical obtuseness, are inclined to shrug their shoulders and get on with the job, but not Thompson. One of his more engaging habits was to contact those reviewers who he felt had misread him, and challenge them to explain themselves. No doubt life is too short for this kind of thing to become accepted practice, but in this particular case it was a highly salutary device for bringing the adjectives out into the open. It is also interesting that not many of Thompson's critics took up his offer, and that their failure to do so seemed to justify Thompson's opinion of them. One critic who promised to appear and then ducked the issue received a letter from Thompson, which arrived after the latter had returned to Paris. It contained a sheet of blank notepaper. As for my own tea with Thompson, it proved to be a very civilized conversation about tenor saxophone playing in which Thompson stated his case with some lucidity.

He had excited some unfavourable comment among local musicians while he was in London, because on one or two occasions he asked the accompanying rhythm section to stop playing because they were cramping his style. People said it was unpardonable of him to have done such a thing, but hardly anyone asked himself whether perhaps the accompanying section really had been cramping his style. His actions do suggest that perhaps he took his own work a little too seriously. Jazz history is crammed with examples of gifted players prepared to indulge the shortcomings of their colleagues. If Bix Beiderbecke could bear to live with the solecisms of Howdy Quicksell and company, Louis Armstrong take no deep offences at the gaucheries of the Carrol Dickerson Orchestra, and Charlie Parker endure the yelpings of a background choir of indeterminate age and sex, then Thompson might have been charitable enough to wink at the limitations of his London accompanists. On the other hand, it is understandable that a musician should sometimes feel obliged to express dissatisfaction in this way, and certainly one or two who received the *coup de grâce* at Thompson's hands at Scott's had themselves been known once or twice to regard their own music with rather more solemnity than perhaps it merited. It is a very vexed question, this issue of knowing how far to go in criticizing the playing of people with whom one is involved professionally, but whether or not Thompson really was guilty of indiscretion, his uncompromising refusal to pay lip service to conventional standards of politeness certainly did his social standing no good.

Thompson is an outspoken man whose intense pride might be mistaken at times for arrogance, and who has deduced from long experience as a freelance artist that suffering fools gladly usually pays poor musical dividends. By the time he arrived at Scott's he had long since passed the point of charity. Totally honest men are, of course, an acute embarrassment, and it takes very few in a tiny principality like the London jazz world to make relations virtually unworkable.

It was not hard to see how Thompson had acquired this reputation for being unco-operative, but he had after all been brought into Scott's to provide jazz of a quality the locals could not match, and this he certainly did. Thompson, on the three occasions I heard him play, was literate and prolific. It was sad that he never fell in love with everyone he met in London, sadder that he never bothered to conceal the fact, saddest of all that his bluntness off the stand excited more comment than his fluency on it.

Dexter Gordon

Thompson stayed for five weeks, to be followed on the last day of August by a very different type of player and personality, the giant Dexter Gordon. This was an extremely imaginative piece of booking on Scott's part, because for most followers of the music Gordon was that very rare bird in these copiously documented days, an unknown quantity. He had been one of the pioneers of the Bebop era, blending the honking tone and stark arpeggios of Lester Young with some of the more obvious harmonic innovations of the Parker school. Most people felt that through the 1950s he had not quite retained his place in the forefront of tenor saxophonists, but this might have been an illusion brought about by his absence from British recording catalogues. Whatever the reasons, by the time he came to Scott's, he was regarded more as a past hero than a present leader. It was not till he started to play that it became clear that most of these vague impressions were false ones. Reputations in jazz, as in all the arts, depend on several extraneous factors to be fashionable among the kingmakers.

He was soon to show, however, that he remained a very formidable player indeed. Not the kind of musician to be bothered very much by working conditions, he immediately established a rapport with his rhythm section and swept through his sessions with an ease and enthusiasm that was almost contemptuous. The possessor of a booming tone and irrepressible rhythmic vitality, Gordon outblew many saxophonists with more exalted reputations, and watching him work, it was apparent that he was one of those soloists who would just as soon be playing as doing anything else. Like Zoot Sims, he fitted perfectly the description of an earlier age, the playing fool.

Singlemindedness, however, was not one of his virtues. If punctuality is the politeness of kings, Gordon was a devoted republican whose appearances on the bandstand did not always coincide with the advertised times of his sessions. And yet his geniality and transparent good intentions contrived to make his season at the club successful if slightly chaotic. Before he had been in London very long, he and his employer recognized mutual humorous tendencies, and more than once during his five weeks at the club, Gordon would play his part in a slapstick bandstand charade in which Scott, looking up at the enormous bulk of Gordon, would inform him that there was not enough money in the till to pay any wages. There is more point to recording this mild buffoonery than might seem apparent, because it illustrates the generous spirit which prevailed. However, all the mutual goodwill in the world would have been pointless without Gordon's basic musical talent.

When he left at the end of August 1962, the customers at Scott's still regarded appearances by men like him as an occasional treat rather than part of a continuous policy, and indeed, for the next three months, members had to make do with a succession of British groups whose one drawback as box office attractions was their availability over long months or even years. It becomes impossible to instil a sense of occasion in those who are paying to hear them, and even though the actual standard of performance might be very high, the lack of novelty is likely to become a serious problem at the box office. Having tried three Americans and found that the increased financial burden could be borne, Scott was naturally keen to maintain the policy. But the Ministry of Labour, working in close if incongruous harness with the Musicians' Union, was still rationing the number of imported musicians allowed.

Al Cohn/Zoot Sims

But a small landmark was finally passed on 11 December 1962, when the club presented not one American musician but two.

Admittedly one of them was the now familiar figure of Zoot Sims, but in pairing him off with Al Cohn, Scott was doing much more than just doubling the number of strange names on the programme. For Sims and Cohn formed a single entity as surely as any two men in jazz, and their union dates back to the day in 1947 when the Woody Herman Orchestra recorded 'Four Brothers' and in so doing revolutionized the whole conception of the saxophone section. Until 'Four Brothers', most large orchestras had deployed two altos, two tenors and a baritone. This unwritten law applied to everyone from Duke Ellington to Glenn Miller. But with 'Four Brothers', Herman introduced an entirely fresh conception based on three tenors and a baritone, with Herman himself available for the occasional sub-Johnny Hodges alto voice when required. But what lent vital interest to the 'Four Brothers' sound was not just its composition but its stylistic origin. The choice by Herman of Zoot Sims, Stan Getz and Herbie Stewart (soon to be replaced by Al Cohn) was the final belated vindication of Lester Young's one-man revolution of ten years before. In pioneering a dry metallic tone Young, in the 1930s, had very bravely been contradicting the hot breath of Hawkins and the Romantic school. All three of Herman's young recruits were unmistakably Young disciples, and the orchestral result was something quite new in saxophone textures. Because of its concentration on an academic, purer tone, and its drastic curbing of the extravagant vibrato effect, the Lester Young method of blowing a tenor saxophone is ideally suited to the demands of a tightly voiced section. In fact, it is so idiomatic a way of playing as almost to demand a certain type of harmony and a certain way of moving inside the frame of that harmony. It is a method that was evolved before the jazz world ever heard of Charlie Parker, which is why its most accomplished exponents, Sims, Cohn, Getz, have closer affinities with the pre-war era than, say, exact contemporaries like Rollins and Coltrane, who were stimulated much more by Parker than by anyone else.

In the days since 'Four Brothers', Sims and Cohn had gone their own professional ways without ever losing musical contact. In the days since 'Four Brothers' Sims had steadily developed into one of the great natural soloists, a musician whose playing was unusually pure in the sense that it dispensed with all fripperies and went straight to the heart of the problem, which must always be to generate swing and conjure up melody. In this sense, Sims is one of the most direct of all jazz musicians, highly sophisticated without ever being affected. Cohn, on the other hand, had gradually come to neglect his tenor playing for orchestration and composition, two skills in which he was highly gifted. Over the years the demand for his writing had tempted him to become a semi-retired instrumentalist whose periodic jaunts with Sims were in the nature of working holidays from the manuscript paper and the stopwatch. But he had never lost his talent as a saxophonist, and it says much for his ability that even in company with so gifted a player as Sims he was never eclipsed.

Although the two men stemmed from the same stylistic source and had worked alongside each other in many ensembles and small groups, each retained his individuality and no practised ear would ever have much trouble in distinguishing one from the other. Sims was the more fluent, no doubt because of his unwavering devotion over the years to the art of constructing instrumental solos, while there were now small signs from time to time in Cohn's playing which hinted at technical difficulties. The very different disciplines of a writer's life had obtruded to the point when the execution of ideas was proving more troublesome than it once had. Cohn also had the heavier, rather gross tone, and his phrases occasionally sounded slightly more pedantic than his partner's.

The collaboration was ideal because it stimulated both men. By exposing himself to the uninhibited music of Sims, Cohn was refreshing himself with that whiff of the real thing without which his orchestral writing would in time no doubt stultify. He in turn brought to his partner the kind of organizing mind which is never content to play the same standard themes, and which expresses its discontent by concocting neat original themes in which unison and close harmony alternate, to form a charming echo of the 'Four Brothers' sound both men helped to popularize. As each man is, at least musically speaking, the other's alter ego, the little songs Cohn wrote for his season at Scott's with Zoot Sims fitted the Sims style as perfectly as they did his own, so that listeners who came to the club expecting to hear the same kind of programme Zoot had given them just over a year before, found themselves confronted with something just as delightful but subtly different.

Cohn had come to London armed with at least two original themes which pointed back clearly to the inspiration of both men. 'P Town', a racy Minor piece, instantly evoked memories of Lester Young's 'Tickle Toe'; and 'I'm Telling You', a basically simple and very relaxed tune, might have fitted into the Count Basie Band's pre-war repertoire without a single raised eyebrow. In ensemble passages, if two men playing saxophones can be called an ensemble, the tonal blend and balance was so perfect that it was not always easy to know which of the two men was playing the lead part.

This was Cohn's first-ever visit to London, and the fact that the city was sprinkled liberally with relatives he had never met soon showed itself as a distinct social disadvantage. I found him one night between sets, leaning against the counter of the snack bar debating whether or not to go out and get some fresh air. It seemed odd that anybody should worry about so unimportant a decision, until I realized what was keeping Cohn pinned to the club premises. It had not taken long for his British blood brothers to find out where he was working, and ever since the discovery had been made, a stream of rubbernecking aunts, uncles and cousins had laid siege to the club premises, not daring to enter but daring Cohn to leave. Some nights he would stick resolutely to his lemon tea at the bar, on others shuffle up the wooden steps into the street shrugging philosophically as he went to meet whatever fate that the unpredictable quirks of consanguinity had prepared for him. Under such trying circumstances, it was reassuring to know that at least so far as his musical experiences were concerned, Cohn's first trip to Britain was a happy one.

Johnny Griffin

The succession of tenor players was maintained when at the beginning of February 1963 Johnny Griffin began a three week season. Griffin, who had made his home on the continent, was already recognized by this time as a prolific technician capable of trading phrases with the very finest musicians. An album of duets with Eddie 'Lockjaw' Davis called *Tough Tenors* had revealed Griffin as a man who could make the notes fly out like bullets from a machine gun, but the real significance of his art was not so much its technical precision, which is after all only to be expected in a player of Griffin's reputation and experience, but its high musical content. Griffin can be classed as an advanced harmonic expert, familiar with the most sophisticated harmonic devices of the 1960s. A textual analysis of any of his solos would reveal the most intricate system of amendment to and substitution within the chord structure. At first hearing, his playing is so furious in its sheer pace as to give an impression of overwhelming confusion, but as one becomes more familiar with it, there is revealed the fact that at the centre of the maelstrom lies an ice-cool brain capable of subdividing the beat into the smallest and subtlest fractions, and at the same time keeping a tight hold on the general direction the harmony is taking.

In a way this superb control is the one great threat to the symmetry of Griffin's style. For the up-tempo themes there is no greater master, but when the ballads arrive so does the intrinsic problem for a player with Griffin's ability. Should the ballad retain at least enough of its own personality to be identifiable as a ballad, or should the player unleash his own armoury of demisemiquavers and prove his own virtuosity at the expense of the theme? Each musician must find his own answer to this problem, and Griffin's has always been to work up as ferocious a pace as possible, leaving the contours of the original melody to survive as best they can. The effect this strategy created is in the end one of unremitting attack, with moods and tempos blending into each other. In this sense can the listener complain that there is little discernible change of pace in a Griffin recital, but once one learns to accept this, there is very little that his playing leaves to be desired among Modernists.

Roland Kirk

Johnny Griffin saw out the year with a return booking which began on 17 December, but three months before he arrived, one other very fascinating instrumentalist had been and gone, leaving in his wake a trail of speculation which has continued to this day. It might not be stretching a point to describe Roland Kirk as the most astonishing single phenomenon to hit the jazz world in the last twenty years. Not that he is in the class of a Charlie Parker or Dizzy Gillespie as a soloist. Kirk is phenomenal for other reasons, which have in fact tended to obscure his more conventional talents as a soloist, which are considerable. To put it very briefly, Kirk has devoted his attentions to achieving the impossible and has to a very large extent actually succeeded. In order to gauge the extent of his ingenuity as well as its intrinsic musical value, it is necessary to pause for a moment and examine the peculiarities of the saxophone.

The instrument, invented by the Belgian Adolphe Sax, requires for the production of many of its notes the use of two hands, although some can be produced with the left hand alone, and one, middle concert B, with no hands at all. It immediately becomes clear that to play two saxophone keyboards at once demands the creation of an intricate system of fingering, in which the notes procurable by one hand alone can somehow be blended to produce the relevant harmony. In order to play *three* saxophones at once, the task remains the same in theory but becomes infinitely more complex in practice. And in addition to the nightmare task of making three instruments respond to the fingers at the same time, there is the incidental consideration of being able to blow a stream of air through three mouthpieces simultaneously. Kirk is the first man in the history of jazz to consider these points with any seriousness, and the technique he has evolved can only be described as utterly remarkable.

If we add to these observations the fact that Kirk is one of the very few Modern musicians to sense acutely the difficulties inherent in making modern jazz commercially acceptable, it is not surprising that we end up faced with an enigmatic artist who has deliberately confused several issues in the cause of commercial appeal. For all practical purposes, the three instruments Kirk plays are soprano, alto and tenor saxophones, but by building them himself and imparting to them a quaint Heath Robinson appearance, Kirk has been able to claim mastery over at least two instrumental mysteries called the manzello and the stritch. The result has been that faced with the onslaught of a talented musician playing three instruments at once, two of which have never been heard of before, the public and the professional critics alike have come to accept Kirk as the freak he sometimes appears to be.

Now Kirk is a man with an impish sense of humour, and a very healthy contempt for reviewers who presume to evaluate the work of professional musicians without themselves having taken much trouble to acquire the rudiments of musical grammar. Much of his humour consists in experiments to see how far gullibility can be stretched, hence his surrealistic statements regarding his ability to blow a note indefinitely without seeming to take a breath. He has said at different times that he is able to do this because there is a hole at the top of his head through which he can draw air, and that he can inhale and exhale through his ears, neither of which slapstick theories has ever been rejected as forcefully as one might have expected. The truth of Kirk's everlasting semibreves is much simpler than holes in the head or respiratory ears. Any student who has observed Harry Carney protracting the bottom B with which he ends his concert versions of 'Sophisticated Lady' will know that it is possible to draw in breath without disturbing the outward flow of air which produces a note. It is this time-honoured method which Kirk deploys, and one assumes that his outlandish explanations of how he achieves this effect is yet another manifestation of his humorous tendencies.

What is much more to the point is, that by diligent research over the years, Kirk has found a working method of operating three saxophone keyboards at once. By using the open note on one of the instruments, that is to say by incorporating into his three-part harmonies the B natural which can be produced without the use of his fingers, and by operating a system involving elastic bands and added keys, Kirk can actually play a theme like 'Mood Indigo' as three saxophonists would harmonize it. Quite clearly this is a feat so bizarre that even were he to cheat a little by simplifying the written chords, Kirk would be doing something too astonishing not to demand the closest attention. In fact, Kirk's three-part exercises are not only fabulous in the old-fashioned meaning of the word, but technically correct. Possibly he points the way to a future in which every soloist will become his own orchestra. The recent invention of the Varitone, for instance, a gadget which can be attached to a saxophone to produce a duplicated note an octave below the note being fingered, already means that with his three saxophones and three varitones, Kirk could easily simulate six men playing at once.

Obviously it is impossible to compare the multi-instrumentalist Kirk with anybody else, because nobody else even attempts what he is doing. But on his debut at Scott's he did at times put aside his manzello, his stritch, the swanee whistles, the hunting horns and the assorted special effects, and play an orthodox tenor solo, and it was at these moments that his status became much easier to judge. Kirk at such times is revealed as a highly intelligent, post-Charlie Parker modernist with a fine technique and a lively imagination; a clown who not only dreams of playing Hamlet, but can when the mood takes him, actually play him.

Kirk is intensely proud of his ability to think along two or more musical lines simultaneously, and will even go to the lengths of producing a musical box with two themes built into it in order to confuse a new acquaintance. He will listen intently to tape recorded jazz solos in taxi cabs, and will look constantly for ways to enlarge his public appeal. His nose flute, a gadget which produces music when an adequate supply of air is snorted down the nostril, might serve as a symbol of his approach to audiences. It looks comical, is very nearly absurd, but redeems itself finally by sounding like an authentic if somewhat eccentric way of producing cleverly constructed jazz.

Kirk has an ambivalent attitude towards his own ingenuity. He must know that musicians will have no difficulty distinguishing the horseplay from the real jazz, the buffoonery from the intensely felt moments of musical climax. And yet he can persist in his own comic theories with disconcerting vehemence when he chooses to. My own tendencies, for instance, which include a desire to reassure people that in reality Kirk breathes the same way as everybody else, through his mouth and nose, have inspired a comically misguided belief on his part that I am bent on revealing him to the world as a charlatan. In fact, I am bent on revealing him to the world, but as anything but a charlatan. Kirk is a thrilling soloist with a powerful, instinctive talent for jazz, and it seems to me important that the gadgetry and the clowning, amusing as they sometimes are, should not obscure the fact of his genius gift for improvisation. To the superficial eye and ear Kirk may appear to be a freak, but no theory could be more wrong-headed, or potentially injurious to his eventual placing in the context of Modern jazz history.

At Scott's he was a riot, and soon became established as one of the club's favourite sons, a player who came to enjoy a wide allegiance from London jazz fanciers. His rambling introductions to his own themes, his furious absorption in his own playing, his desire to enlighten as well as to please, made him the ideal attraction, one of those rare musicians who tried hard to sell his music because of his conviction that it was worth selling. Ever since his debut at the club, his name on the billboards has ensured flourishing business and good music. Kirk was the sixth successive tenor saxophonist to be imported by Scott, and the thought was beginning to occur to some people that he intended never to book any other kind of instrumentalist. The fact that all six tenor players had been virtuosi was sometimes forgotten in the heat of the moment. And then, at the beginning of March 1964, the succession of tenor players was extended still further by the importing of the greatest master of all.

Stan Getz

Ever since Zoot Sims had started the convention of Americans at the club, the hope had been in the air that somehow Scott would succeed in producing for audiences Sims's contemporary and rival, Stan Getz. There were serious difficulties. For one thing, Getz is one of the very few jazzmen to break through into the fleshpots of commercialism without compromising his art. Almost alone of the Modernists, he had come to know the delights of best-sellers and large royalty statements, which meant that his price tended to be higher than most other people's. Also he was in great demand in all areas of musical entertainment, and quite clearly could pick which engagements he preferred to accept. Most important of all, Getz had earned the reputation for being a most demanding artist, who would expect as his right, perfect working conditions, an efficient rhythm section and a proper degree of respect from those around him. Finally, on 6 March, he made his debut at Scott's.

The extent to which Getz posed extra-musical problems for his employers has become almost as legendary as the standard of music he produced while working for them. In some players the nature of their style is a reflection of their temperament, in others a contradiction of it, and certainly Getz, the most exquisitely tender of saxophonists, did not impress many people with his tendencies to exquisitely tender behaviour. Shortly after his season ended Scott was taken to hospital with a slipped disc, and he may or may not have had Getz specifically in mind when he told a BBC interviewer that his ailment had been brought about by leaning over backwards to please the musicians who worked for him. So far as the standard of performance Getz achieved, nobody could possibly have faulted him. In spite of the peculiar snobbery which refuses to admit that any contemporary player can become a classic until he is either dead or retired, it has been clear to many people in the last ten years that Getz will always be recognized as one of the outstanding saxophonists of jazz history, and his case is unique in that almost alone of the great personal stylists of jazz, he began as a purely derivative player. Clearly he has been tremendously influenced by the school of thought embodied in the vintage work of Lester Young, and more than once on the stand at Scott's he would quote verbatim even if unconsciously, from famous Young recordings like 'Lester Leaps In', 'Twelfth Street Rag' and 'Dickie's Dream'. But if, when he began as one of Herman's Four Brothers, Getz was still seeking an identity of his own, by the time he arrived for his first London club date he had long since found it. Like Zoot Sims, Getz had taken as his starting point the inventions of another man, but steadily, by natural assertion of personality, had arrived at a kind of method highly subjective and original in its own right.

But whereas Sims had pared the style down to the bone, dispensing with extraneous grace notes and superfluous flourishes,

Getz had adopted a tactic diametrically opposed, making a virtue out of ornamentation, constantly in pursuit of the romantic, until by the 1960s he had perfected a glorious rococo style demanding a virtually perfect technique, extreme presence of mind and overwhelming self-confidence. There was an insolent ease about the way he made the keyboard respond to his demands. No tempo could scare him and no chord sequence confuse him, although seen in the context of men like Griffin and Gordon, he was very much more of a Swing player than a Bebopper, if one may be pardoned for slipping into the crudities of pigeonholes for a moment. Like Sims, Gerry Mulligan and a few others of his generation, Getz was never afraid to go for the simple interpretation of the harmonies, and he would often trace out the chord sequence by going for the third of the chord in the authentic pre-modern way.

Tonally also Getz had arrived at a personal effect. While evoking memories of the honking sound of Lester Young, he had distilled it still further, so that it was now a sweet, feminine (but not effeminate) instrumental tone sought after by many copyists but never really captured by any of them. He used the entire range of the instrument, and ranged over all periods of jazz in his search for sympathetic material. It is not surprising that so consummate a master of melody should prove to be a faultless judge of the melodies of other people, and his nightly repertoire, though it varied from item to item, never deviated from the very highest thematic standards. The bonuses which accrued to the listener were considerable, and on the first night I heard him it was with delight that Getz should have remembered so grossly neglected a song as Jerome Kern's 'Why Was I Born?' Apart from a classic version by Billie Holiday in the mid-1930s, this theme, like so many of Kern's, had hardly been used at all by a generation of jazz musicians so preoccupied with writing their own themes; but Getz's 'Why Was I Born?', one of the peak moments of his season, could have stood comparison with the Holiday version itself.

Getz's appearance in Gerrard Street pointed out one more truth about the economics of jazz in Britain, which is that, provided the music is of a sufficient quality, people will pay even what might appear to be inflationary prices. For the Getz season, the club raised its admission fee, a tactic justified by the wages Getz demanded and also by the 'House Full' notices which were put up virtually every night for a month. People sensed that in watching Getz they were watching one of the great players of jazz history, and that to miss the chance for the sake of a few shillings would be something they might one day bitterly regret. Indeed, since that month at Scott's, Getz has hardly set foot in this country.

What was it about Getz's playing which made him stand out so clearly from all other tenor saxophonists who had preceded him? There was nothing remarkable about the adoration of all the local musicians, for as Scott himself had written in 1962 in a brief but glorious interlude as a record reviewer, 'Musicians believe that the sun shines out of Stan Getz's tone-holes.' But audiences too sensed the supreme command of Getz even if they did not understand all the technical reasons for it. Probably what marked Getz off from his rivals (and 'rivals' is an apt word to use in reference to a player who feels the competition of other musicians so intensely) was the fact that his style was more highly polished than anybody else's. No doubt a player like Griffin could match him for technique. Dexter Gordon conveyed a far greater sense of physical strength, and Sims could claim to swing as well as ever Getz did. And yet there was an unmistakable sense in which Getz asserted his superiority over all these players the moment he put the instrument to his lips.

The solution lies in the nature of Getz's style, which unlike those of the other tenor players, is an essentially artificial thing, shaped meticulously, painstakingly, over a period of many years. Getz is a self-conscious player in the sense that every nuance is calculated and fitted into the context with infinite care. There is a certain cuteness about a Getz solo which marks him off from the playing fools, and which indeed in the early 1950s marred his general effect. But as he moved into the 1960s Getz came to full maturity, at least as a musician, so that his work possessed a stimulating nervous tension created by the perfect balance between his precocity and a fearless attack. The unique thing about Getz's playing, the one that marks it off from everybody else's, is the fine contrast between the tenderness of his tone and the delicacy of his fingering on the one hand, and the sinuous strength of his patterns on the other. Or to put it another way, his work is attractive because it combines the pleasantness of a commercial artist with the uncompromising vitality of real jazz.

Sonny Stitt

Wherever Getz appears, there is a serious danger of anti-climax crippling those who follow him. In all the jazz world, there is only a tiny élite of musicians who can stand comparison with him, and Scott was fortunate, or shrewd, in procuring one of these to play at the club during May 1964. In a sense the club even outdid itself, because the musician it employed was not only in Getz's class as a tenor player, but was also one of the best alto saxophonists in the world. In his four weeks at the club, this musician switched from one instrument to the other with no apparent trouble, and in so doing, posed a very interesting problem for the student of style.

The musician's name was Sonny Stitt, who began his career as a carbon copy of Charlie Parker, later switched to tenor, and ever since had been dividing his time between the two. At one time there was a strong feeling among the carpet knights of jazz criticism that Stitt was some kind of a counterfeiter because of his ingenious facsimiles of Parker's solos. The charge was always an unjust one, if only because Stitt is instantly recognizable as himself, not because he tries to copy Parker and fails, but because he copies him and yet succeeds in producing something intrinsically his own. But the riddle of Stitt's musical personality becomes even more inscrutable when he starts to play the tenor. We have here apparently a man who follows the precepts of one man when he blows one instrument, and another one entirely when he blows the other. Stitt as a tenor player has at least one thing in common with Getz in that he will occasionally quote Lester Young verbatim.

It is true, of course, that Young's aphorisms have passed into the jazz vocabulary so thoroughly that the modern player can hardly help echoing them from time to time, but Stitt's relationship to Young was, and is, much more than a question of mere quotation. Not only is his tone a heavier version of Young's beautifully balanced honk, but his aural shapes also look back to the period when Young was blazing his private trail. One of the quaint psychological results of Stitt switching to the lower instrument is that he switches also, at least in part, to a less complex harmonic convention. It should also be said that whichever instrument he plays, Stitt at his best is a musician of passionate splendour. The tone on alto has the same rich texture as Parker's, and on tenor the kind of booming muscularity that Dexter Gordon had displayed. Like Parker, Stitt likes to construct phrases in double time producing cascades of perfectly placed semiquavers, and then underlining them with a much simpler phrase of bold, direct power bringing the solo back to its original pulse.

I was in the fortunate position of having seen Stitt work in a jazz club environment before this, and by a coincidence the man who sat next to me on that occasion was Scott himself. In 1957 he had taken a small group on an American tour, and I, unable to believe that any jazz lover could dislike New York as much as I had on my one previous visit, went with him on a holiday. One night he had burst into the hotel room and said, 'Come to see the greatest saxophone player in the world.' And so we went out to Newark and found Stitt playing in a small club which had been presenting Getz the week before. Whether or not there was real rivalry between the two men I could not say, but regular customers certainly sat there trying to decide which had the greater command of his instrument. It was, of course, a pointless exercise, because Getz and Stitt are utterly dissimilar players who have each achieved total mastery over the style that has attracted them. And now the sequence in Newark was being repeated in Gerrard Street. No sooner had Getz packed his instrument away than Stitt was occupying the bandstand, bowing with exhilarating power and freedom.

Ben Webster

One other musician of special interest worked at Scott's during 1964, the saxophonist Ben Webster, who finished out the year and stayed till early January 1965. Webster is one of those musicians who carry about with them the heady aroma of a glorious past. For such men the burden of private history can be an embarrassing item of luggage, especially if customers and critics alike turn up expecting them to recite old party pieces instead of attempting new ones. In the thirty years that he had been in the jazz eye, Webster had changed considerably as a stylist, and changed in the most natural way possible. What Webster had managed to do was what very few of his contemporaries had even attempted, and that is to grow old gracefully. In his younger days with the Ellington band he was rightly recognized as one of the most talented tenor players to spring up about Coleman Hawkins. Webster has told how at first he desired nothing better than to be mistaken for Hawkins, and how one day he suddenly decided that this was absurd, and that the real wisdom lay in sounding only like himself.

This he had achieved. His work with Ellington in the 1930s bore the hallmark of class. It is hardly remembered today that when Webster joined the Ellington band in 1934, he contrived by his very presence to push Ellington's evolution one step further, for he took nobody's place but merely increased the size of the saxophone section. On recordings like 'Cottontail' he had demonstrated his ability to move fast when required, and in 'Just A Sittin' And A-Rockin'' he had shown how superbly Ellington and an outstanding soloist could create an exquisite dialogue between single voice and ensemble. Webster's work in this period was exalted enough for analysts to dismantle it and theorists to wonder about it. Echoes of his playing were still in the air twenty years later, as when Paul Gonsalves, playing the tenor solo in a remake of 'Cottontail', acknowledged the greatness of his predecessor by quoting the opening few bars of the original Webster solo.

But the Webster who arrived at Scott's in December 1964 was a very different proposition indeed. Middle age had slowed down his reflexes, so that he was no longer able to indulge in virtuoso performances at fast tempos. His jazz was as genial as his physical appearance, avuncular, reassuring, gently entertaining. A textual analysis would have revealed the simplest harmonic patterns, and virtually nothing to indicate that since his own prime a revolution had taken place in jazz thought. He played nothing he had not already played a thousand times before, and could have been reviewed quite accurately without actually being heard at all.

But jazz has still not quite reached the regrettable stage when everything can be assessed by harmonic content. Webster's playing in his later years had acquired one extra dimension, rendering it exquisite and admirable. Almost as though seeking a compensatory quality for his loss of mobility, Webster had developed quite the most sumptuous tone in jazz. He had always possessed a fine resonance, but in recent years this had grown progressively richer until in the late 1960s its beauty had become almost a fetish to which everything else was subordinated.

That excellent judge of saxophonists and completely unselfish observer of other people's work, Roland Kirk, declared during Webster's visit that such a tone ought to be impossible to produce, but evidently for Webster it was simply the normal way to play.

Very few musicians have ever managed to justify their existence by sheer beauty of tone alone, but Webster's Indian Summer had produced a sound so romantic as to be almost over-ripe. In fact, so impressive was it that it tended to obscure the fact that when the right vehicle was travelling at the right tempo, Webster could still build a solo whose virtues were not entirely confined to the cello-like depths of the tone through which they were executed. One of his pet themes was Gershwin's 'Our Love Is Here To Stay', which he played at medium rather than ballad tempo, constructing his solo of short, two- or four-bar phrases which saved him the trouble of taking too deep a breath, and caused him to produce a perfect succession of epigrams arising out of the key chord changes of the melody.

It very soon became apparent to Scott that in producing a guest out of the past, as it were, he had stumbled on a musician who could always be relied upon to draw crowds and please them once they had bought their tickets. In future Webster was to be one of the club's standbys, and it is no coincidence that more than once he has found his way on to the bandstand during Christmas.

Webster's is the perfect holiday jazz, thoroughbred in quality and not overbearing in the demands it makes on the listener's thought processes. Webster is a comfortable man to listen to because he is a comfortable man himself. As he stares out across the room, focusing his eyes on different customers, completely detached from what his fingers and embouchure are doing, he is virtually demonstrating that the playing of jazz can be a simple thing if you get your priorities right. The booking of Webster also pointed to another very significant fact for Scott. Until now, the club had dealt exclusively in Modern musicians, that is to say, men whose reputations were still unmade when the conspiracy of Parker, Gillespie and company upended all the conventions. Webster belonged to a generation whose improvisations had congealed into mannerism long before the Modernists were under way, and yet, in a club rightly rewarded as the very heart of Modern jazz in Europe, he had won everybody over. This was entirely unexpected. One of the healthier features of the 1960s had been the gradual crumbling of the barriers which once separated the old from the new. Good jazz is so evidently good jazz, and Webster had so evidently produced it, that nobody could possibly have complained about him without being revealed as a cloth-eared bigot. And in any case, if there were a few unspoken disappointments about the break in the modern convention at Scott's, the man booked to follow Webster certainly rendered them superfluous. Not since the notices went up for Stan Getz had any musician's arrival caused more speculation than that of Sonny Rollins.

SONNY ROLLINS

Even his most fanatical supporters would admit that Rollins is faced with a terrible dilemma in his playing, and that this dilemma is one which threatens jazz itself. Quite simply, the issue is whether or not the art of jazz is finite, whether or not we have all been quite logical over the years in assuming that the music would go on evolving and evolving indefinitely. It is the old argument between Cassandra and Pangloss all over again, but what is amusing is the point at which different commentators choose to swap the later role for the former. The pioneer British critic Rex Harris marked the death of jazz at 1932, and the French dialectician Hughes Panassie at somewhere soon after 1940. Many people of my own generation, including sometimes on bad nights myself, wonder whether the 1960s will not see the last rites.

Rollins's career poses the problem in a nutshell. He began as a brilliantly gifted disciple of Charlie Parker, moved on to maturity with classic performances like those in *Saxophone Colossus* and *Way Out West*, and then, quite suddenly, suffered a loss of faith and retired from the battle for two years to rethink his approach. On his return as an active musician, Rollins bewildered most people by the sheer inconsistency of his playing. This was not the normal inconsistency of the man who feels better one night than he does the next, but the inconsistency of a man who can slide from sublime heights to abject depths within the space of a single chorus, a man who can sound like a lampoon of himself in the eighth bar and then justify everything with a stroke of genius in the twelfth, a man evidently concerned with the problem of finding fresh avenues of escape from the rutted highway of discord and resolution, a man who above all is maddened by the paradox that no matter how original a solo might sound to other people, it is bound by the very mechanics of making music, to sound overfamiliar to the man who actually conceives it.

The problems of listening to Rollins were, and still are, compounded by the eccentricity with which Rollins himself presents his music. His eccentric haircuts and dabbling with mysticism are irrelevant to the issue of his music, but the average customer might be pardoned for losing control for a moment when he realizes that Rollins has begun his first number while treading his way from bandroom to bandstand. And when that first song of the recital proves also to be the last one, Rollins not being the man to bother about starting a new theme when he is still interested in the old one, then all the accepted canons of judgement seem to be crashing down.

The fact that all these mannerisms are intriguing does not alter the fact that they are also irrelevant to the main theme of Rollins's innate ability as a jazz musician. When Rollins plays nonstop for forty minutes, he is not necessarily restricting himself to one theme, but playing others without going through the formality of stopping and starting. When he gets bored with a song, Rollins will baldly start playing another one without indicating his intentions to anybody, so that what starts out as an interpretation of 'Yesterdays' somehow changes into 'I Want To Be Happy', which then turns out to be the Blues after all, except that by the time the final chords have been rolled up, it is the Jerome Kern estate which is about to collect some more royalties because Rollins was playing 'Yesterdays' after all. More to the point is the fact that when he plays, Rollins shows the influence of all kinds of saxophone players before him. Certainly he can evoke Charlie Parker with a furious burst of semiquavers shaped in an ingenious pattern, but he can also produce eight bars of perfect Lester Young, a few phrases couched in the rich tone of Hawkins, and then subside into the gaucherie of an Italian beginner in white shoes blowing for the edification of tourists in an Adriatic summer resort. Ronnie Scott, who took weeks to recover from Rollins's visit, described the experience as watching the history of jazz go flashing by every night. This is only partly true, because one or two of the weapons in Rollins's armoury had no precedent in any history at all. By manipulating his embouchure and experimenting with false fingerings, Rollins had discovered how, at certain convenient junctures in a solo, to play two notes at the same time. As he had also mastered the same trick as Roland Kirk of being able to extend a note indefinitely by breathing in at the same time as maintaining a flow of air through the mouthpiece, any recital of his tended to overwhelm even if it did not always entertain.

It is always difficult for the commentator to know what attitude to adopt towards an artist like Rollins. It would be absurdly unfair to demand of him the conventional felicities of tone or neatness of execution. As he is attempting to achieve something known only to himself, it is equally unfair to accuse him of failure. The only course left to accept Rollins for what he is, and to enjoy whatever beauty in his playing can be found there. If poetic genius consists among other things in keeping open the pipeline to childhood, then there is a touch of genius about Rollins in his childlike ability to ignore the conventions of presentation and performance. But it must also be said that there is often a touch of charlatanism about his antics. Undoubtedly he produces passages of greatness. Undoubtedly also he produces other, longer passages of excrutiating clumsiness. At the risk of being thought self-idolatrous, I reproduce the closing lines of my original review of Rollins for the very good reason that even after all this time I can think of little else to say:

> *Plainly this kind of music is a different proposition to all the jazz that has gone before. Rollins is no mere Modernist chord sharper, neither is he the moulder of neat 32 bar packages. It may well be that what he represents is jazz at the moment of dissolution, an art stretched to breaking point by sheer ingenuity.*
>
> *Whatever the truth, the usual measuring rods are useless. The only man who might know what standards to judge by is Rollins himself, and even he has confessed his uncertainty. In the meantime his playing at Scott's is an extraordinary thing, a great rubbish dump sprinkled with pearls of wisdom.*

It ought not to be necessary to say this, but so far as personal experience may be trusted, I found no reason to believe, as some appeared to do, that Rollins was some kind of semi-lunatic. Perhaps his behaviour, or even his haircut, encourages this canard, but as he sat in the tiny bandroom flexing his lip muscles in preparation for the coming session, like a prizefighter limbering up before ducking under the ropes, he seemed to me to be a very serious man troubled by the problems which the creation of any art presents. Above all, he is a man of unquestioned artistic courage. It might have been easy for him to go on indefinitely as he had been in the 1950s. The mere thought of his brilliant paraphrase of the written melody in an old recording of 'The Way You Look Tonight' is always enough to curb me when I feel that perhaps Rollins is an impostor after all. Like John Coltrane, he has too many genuine achievements to his credit ever to be suspected of imposture.

BILL EVANS

Three weeks after his season ended another small milestone was passed when, for the first time, the club was able to present not just an American musician, but an American group. This was more than just a commercial tactic. Indeed, as the leader involved was the pianist Bill Evans, it may be described as an aesthetic necessity. More than most Modern jazzmen, Evans requires fellow musicians of long experience so far as his own playing is concerned. The essence of Evans's art is the ingenuity with which he reshapes the harmonies of any given standard theme, and clearly, unless the drummer and bassist are familiar with his patterns, his own playing will suffer in proportion.

Evans's debut also presented another problem of a very different kind. He is the antithesis of the jazzman who is able to sit down in any room at any piano and start playing. He is the most exquisite of the Modern jazzmen and his style perhaps the most fragile that exists today. It exists on a knife-edge of sensibility, and unless all the factors are perfect, the chances are that the final subtlety which gives Evans his appeal will be lost. It was therefore imperative that whatever else might go wrong, Evans had to be provided with a piano which would satisfy him. His touch is so delicate and his whole conception so highly refined that an uncongenial keyboard could wreck his effects. The first priority was therefore to find, somewhere in London, an instrument worthy of him.

Now those who frequented the original Scott Club will remember that the only access to the premises was down a tortuous flight of narrow wooden steps whose construction had not been carried through with any mind to the transportation of grand pianos. The day of Evans's debut was a day with less affinities to the administration of a jazz club than the staging of an early Laurel and Hardy comedy. Pianos went up and down the wooden staircase with the steady rhythm of a pendulum. Firms who hired the best pianos were unwilling to release their best instruments to so low an establishment as a jazz club. One firm even refused to SELL their piano to the club for fear of it being outraged by the clumsy technique of some barrelhouse thumper. It was only at the last minute that an instrument was acquired which met all the considerations, good enough for Evans to play on, common enough for a firm to release it, narrow enough to be carried down the staircase. The audience which watched Evans on that first night could have had very little idea of the exertions made on its behalf all day.

The only really valid criticism to be made against Evans is that his playing appears to lack a rhythmic spine. The criticism is just, but as it touches on the very effect that Evans strives to create, it hardly seems fair to chastise him for it. In any case, the true merit of the Evans style is the sumptuous richness of the harmonies he produces. Indeed, he could without stretching the point too far, be described as the most outstanding harmonic improviser in jazz, as distinct from the melodic improvisers whose value lies in the new tunes they are able to conjure out of the old ones. Evans is virtually an orchestral improviser in the sense that he orchestrates the chords as he goes along. In view of all this, it is not surprising that Evans made up his programme of old standards with interesting chord sequences, rather than original themes with which most Modern musicians equip themselves. And it is here that Evans finally proves his ability. In playing perhaps overfamiliar themes like 'Summertime' and 'Come Rain Or Come Shine', he is somehow able to invest them with a quality they have never possessed before, so that whatever he happens to be playing, the illusion he produces is that we are hearing it for the first time. He is a studious, devoted musician whose popularity inside the jazz world is a rare tribute to the perception of audiences who might perhaps have been forgiven for dismissing him in favour of the more robust delights of men like Oscar Peterson and Errol Garner.

Wes Montgomery

On 5 April 1965, a week after Evans and his two accompanists, Larry Bunker and Chuck Israels, had moved on, the Scott Club introduced an even greater jazz musician, the undisputed leader on his instrument, a dazzling self-taught virtuoso and, most important of all, one of the few Modernists capable of resolving the complexities of Modern harmony into melodic coherence. One might take exception to the invertebrate felicities of Bill Evans, or the protean violence of Sonny Rollins, the derivative origins of Sonny Stitt, or even the stylized deliberations of Stan Getz, but from a purist jazz point of view there seemed to be no arguing about the supreme jazz talent of Wes Montgomery.

Montgomery played the guitar, an instrument with a curiously chequered history in the jazz world. At one time, in the sensitive hands of Charlie Christian, it had promised to play a prominent part in the evolution of Modernism. But Christian died in 1942, at precisely the point when the Bebop revolutionaries were struggling for recognition. Since Christian, the guitar had been mastered by Christian disciples like Barney Kessel and Herb Ellis, without ever really producing anybody with a wholly original approach. Montgomery therefore had a doubly dramatic impact when he first arrived, and his appearance at Scott's was not only a piece of inspired programming, but a triumph of faith over logistics. Wes and his two musician Brothers, Buddy and Monk, were renowned throughout jazz as resolute haters of the aeroplane. Dozens of stories have passed into the apocrypha of jazz about one, or two, or sometimes all three Montgomeries rushing off a 'plane at the moment of takeoff, unable to conquer their fear of the air. But Wes had somehow been persuaded to fly over for this season, and although once he touched down he vowed never to fly again, except possibly for the purpose of getting home again, once he began playing, the ordeal he had undergone seemed well worthwhile, at least so far as audiences were concerned.

Like most of the great self-taught instrumentalists, Montgomery possessed a technique which was in certain aspects highly unorthodox. He was able, for instance, to play the most intricate passages twice at the same time, or to put it in musical terms, he could state a melodic line and produce octave effects with every note. It was quite clear watching him that no matter how difficult the passage might be, it presented absolutely no difficulties at all. Montgomery on the stand presented the most relaxed appearance of any jazz musician. A smile usually played about his features, and he seemed at times to be casually observing the movements in his room around him rather than wrestling with the problems of his own art. A truly astounding musician whose brilliant technique was subordinated at all times to the rich melodic inventiveness of his style, Montgomery must surely rank alongside Stan Getz as one of the most richly endowed musicians ever heard in Britain. His youthful appearance belied the fact of his status of grandfather, and it came as a totally unexpected tragedy when he died suddenly of a heart attack in the summer of 1968.

Wes Montgomery's visit ended on 7 May 1965, and by this time it was becoming apparent to Scott and his manager Pete King that very little further could be achieved under the prevailing circumstances. The capacity at Gerrard Street was not large enough to produce enough profit to improve facilities, musical or social, and the need for larger premises was becoming urgent. It was to take another six months before the Ronnie Scott Club found a new home, but in the meantime the attractions continued to draw in jazz purists and fringe followers alike.

Don Byas/Benny Golson

On 13 August arrived Don Byas, the one-time Basie saxophonist who had emigrated to France after the last war and remained based there ever since. Like Charlie Christian, Coleman Hawkins, and a few others, Byas had attempted to carry the banner of the older generation into the new Modernist era. Gifted with an extraordinary technique, a ripe, very nearly overripe tone, and a good grasp of harmony, Byas had been involved in some of the best early Modernist recordings with Dizzy Gillespie, and it was interesting to discover to what extent his self-imposed exile had cut him off from the main stream of development since.

In the event Byas proved to have changed very little, which so far as connoisseurs of classic style are concerned, was a good thing. Stemming both tonally and harmonically from the school of Coleman Hawkins, Byas remained as prolific a technician as ever, the kind of artist to send other saxophonists away stunned with the intricacy of it all. A fetish for the augmented chord is a characteristic rather than a blemish in Byas's playing, and on the evidence of his work in London, twenty years away from the centre of the action had damaged his art not in the slightest.

His visit was important in another sense. It helped to impress on those who saw him the sense of continuity in the evolving jazz tradition. Byas is a fascinating figure in that he represents one of the very few links between pre- and post-Parker jazz, and it is always important for the student of the music to observe as closely as he can the methods of such a musician. Byas stands in the line of classic tenor players, beginning with Hawkins, and moving through Chu Berry and Ben Webster down to the Paul Gonsalves of the current Ellington band. His material reflects his period, and at Scott's he produced ravishing embellishments of 'Stella By Starlight', 'What's New' and 'Tenderly', although he also included in his programme a deferential nod to the younger generation with Parker's 'Billie's Bounce'. When listening to him, one could not help wondering how he might have sounded had he been born into Modernism, instead of being required to make a conscious effort to work his way into it.

By one of those flukes of circumstance which occur so often at Scott's that they may not after all be flukes, the answer to that hypothetical question was there for all to decipher in the next saxophonist to arrive at the club, and the last American musician ever to play in the Gerrard Street premises. Benny Golson is a richly gifted musician in rather a different sense to anyone else mentioned in this history. As an instrumentalist he is a cultured and technically impressive soloist with the same warm tone of the Byas–Webster–Hawkins school, but with a much more sophisticated corpus of harmony to assist him. But in addition Golson is perhaps the most talented composer of melody that jazz has produced since Duke Ellington, although perhaps not quite the most prolific. Almost alone of jazzmen, Golson has the ability to write instrumental themes with the shape and texture of the best Broadway stage material. The most famous of his themes, 'Whisper Not', is certainly worthy of somebody like Cole Porter, except of course that it has the added muscularity of the jazz idiom in every bar. In the 1960s Golson has succumbed, if that is the right word, to the same processes that have changed a musician like Al Cohn from a saxophonist to a writer, and it may well be that with his visit to the club, Golson was not only presenting the last American jazz to be heard in Gerrard Street, but the last Golson instrumental jazz to be heard in Britain.

Golson closed on 27 November 1965, by which time the builder's men were already in operation two hundred yards away preparing a bigger, more comfortable Mk. II version of Ronnie Scott's Club. If the history of the six year Gerrard Street experiment is preponderant with American names, that is because it was the Americans who put the club on a workable financial basis, and who steadily raised Scott's status to that of one of the leading jazz proprietors in the world. It should not be forgotten, however, that all the time the visitors were coming in from New York or San Francisco, British musicians were present at all times, either in the supporting groups or actually accompanying the Americans. Reference has already been made to the consistent brilliance over the years of Tubby Hayes, the beautifully poised trumpet playing of Jimmie Deuchar before he left for Cologne, the scholastic contributions of John Dankworth, and the succession of drummers, pianists and bassists who slowly but surely raised their game to the required international level. All of these men contributed enormously to the practical success of the importing of American soloists, but one player stands out from all of them. In a club such as Scott's, a house pianist is an absolute necessity. He must be not only a capable soloist in his own right, but must also possess the very rare gift of being able to adapt his own conception to the demands of whoever is the current guest. At Scott's this function was performed by Stan Tracey, one of the most controversial of all British musicians, a player whose work is characterized by jagged rhythmic effects and the calculated dissonance of the devoted harmonic adventurer. Often Tracey's playing hovers on the rim of ugliness, and it must be admitted that there are times when to some ears he appears to fall in. But over the years he has sustained a remarkable consistency in grappling with the appalling problems of constant accompaniment.

Players like Getz and Rollins represent opposing poles in the jazz tradition, the felicities of one being mocked by the stridencies of the other. And yet Tracey had to work not only with both of them but with all the other players who represented various compromises between the two extremes. All the musicians who have worked at Scott's Club have had their well-earned publicity, but Tracey was often in the position where the bouquets he should have won found their way elsewhere. A gifted composer and arranger in his own right, Tracey during the Gerrard Street period was content on many occasions to perform the donkey work for others. He played an integral part in the consistent high standards which Scott was able to achieve in the six years.

When Benny Golson left at the end of November, one era was ending and another about to begin. What had begun as a personal whim, grown into a demanding occupation and developed imperceptibly into a virtual crusade, had now outgrown its beginnings and was changing in scope. The thought occurred to many people that perhaps now there would also be a change in manner. A larger club requires a larger income, and a larger income requires a more commercial policy. If this was what was about to happen to Scott's Club, it would not be the first child born of jazz forced to turn its back on the purists to survive. The new club might be an improvement. Then again, it might not. In any event, it was hard to see how the music itself could be much better than what had been on display in Gerrard Street. But all these considerations were academic. New layouts were being designed in new surroundings. New policies were being formulated, new tariffs agreed on, new amenities being dreamed up. In December 1965, for the first time in six years, there was no Ronnie Scott's Club in operation. Golson blew his last cadenza, the cleaners swished their brooms around the floors of the basement, and the cash boxes slammed shut for the last time. Phase One was over.

THE NEW PLACE

The new Ronnie Scott Club opened in Frith Street on 17 December 1965, and was such an event in itself that the actual quality of the music, provided by Yusef Lateef and Ernestine Anderson, tended to be overshadowed. It was obvious the moment one stepped inside the door that the atmosphere had changed. What people in general and musicians in particular wondered was whether the musical policy would change with it. Whether or not this suspicion sounds cynical, it was justified by the surface evidence. It is one of the inscrutable economic laws that the greater the overheads, the more diluted the music, with the intense jazz performances being given in cellars like the one Scott started in, and the complete fake being found at the other end of the scale, in plush-walled nightclubs. A very accurate assessment of a club's music may be made without actually hearing it, simply by calculating the weekly running expenses, and it was obvious that Scott had increased his overheads enormously. There was now a small army of waitresses, barmaids, doormen and ushers. The lighting was more sophisticated, the tables, chairs and upholstery more ambitious, the footage much greater, the facilities vastly improved. In order to make ends meet Scott would now have to attract at least twice as many customers as he had in Gerrard Street, and very often the only way to double attendances is to halve the effectiveness of the music. This fear that in attempting to improve itself, London's one authentic jazz centre might in the process destroy itself, proved in the end to be unfounded, and after a season of the organist Lou Bennett and Mark Murphy, yet another stroke of imaginative programming brought the historians as well as the floating fans running to the club.

Lee Konitz

In booking the alto saxophonist Lee Konitz, Scott could hardly have resorted to a more intriguing device for launching the new premises. Konitz had been one of the great heroes of the late 1940s, a unique figure in the confused landscape of emergent Modernism. The genius of that age had obviously been Charlie Parker, who happened to play the same instrument as Konitz. Parker's personality as a musician proved to be so strong that it is true to say that almost nobody who ever encountered it was able to resist its attractions. It was, in fact, irresistible, and the fact that Konitz alone had managed to defy logic and resist it makes him one of the most remarkable characters of his era. There lies in BBC archives at least one tape recording which makes this point with great force. It is simply an account by Sonny Stitt of how he spent his day on the day of Parker's death. Stitt is an infinitely resourceful musician, in his heyday one of the greatest of all the jazz saxophonists. And yet in this highly subjective account of a tragic day, he makes not the slightest attempt to conceal the fact that he sees himself as nothing more exalted than trainbearer to the processional of Parker's turbulent career. Stitt is a born jazzman, gifted prolifically in all departments of the art, and yet he reduces himself to a cipher in his attempt to convey the degree of veneration which he, and many of his fellow musicians, felt towards Parker. This veneration Konitz appeared to have avoided, at least if imitation is its only valid evidence.

Konitz as a teenaged musician had made a series of recordings whose contours were as unusual as their atmosphere was precious. Adherence to the four-in-a-bar pulse was not so much sidestepped as deliberately avoided. Abstruse variations on existing harmonies, the deployment by all the musicians in the group of cool, detached tones, the reduction of width of vibrato, and the adaptation, especially by Konitz himself, of much more formal melodic patterns than had hitherto been heard in jazz, patterns which sounded at times as though their sequential felicities had been lifted straight out of nineteenth-century music primers, all these facts contributed towards a very curious overall effect of nonvertebrate resilience, of limpid animation, of an ingenious decadence which produced a form of valid jazz which nevertheless dispensed with one of jazz's vital ingredients, animation.

The Konitz style was never commercial, even by jazz standards. Slow but steady erosion by circumstances reduced Konitz's room for manoeuvre, until by 1953 he was in Britain, not with the kind of group one might have expected from his recordings, but with the Stan Kenton Orchestra. There had been one other visit, a totally unsuccessful one, with an All-Star group in 1959, whose inner politics, manipulated by the autocratic Oscar Pettiford, had reduced Konitz to a cipher, a musician so paralysed by indecision that listeners did not so much reject him as refuse to count the occasion as a test at all. Since then little had been heard of him, either through the professional grapevine or on record, so that his return to London as Scott's solo attraction was one of the most intriguing situations which the club had so far managed to set up. The results were very curious indeed.

Yet again the discographers were caught with their trousers down. Konitz at Scott's bore only the most superficial resemblances to the Konitz of the Tristano partnership and the arcane revival of collective improvisation with Wayne Marsh. It was evident that Konitz had abandoned his old stand many years before, either because it had proved a dead end or because maturity had made its originality seem like mere precociousness. Whatever the reason, the strength of musical will which had enabled him to resist the siren song of Parker's style had wilted in the face of newer fashions, so that now his solos peeped through for a while, only to be swamped by groping and uncertainty.

Here was one more example of youthful self-confidence melting away through years of public indifference. The one factor which the early Konitz recordings had needed to exist at all was faith in the music, and that faith was now lost. Instead, Konitz played like a puzzled man, not sure in which direction to head, technique hampered by vagueness of purpose, clarity of mind smudged over by the bewildering changes of fortune that have characterized jazz history over the last twenty years. And there was a dramatic irony behind all this, which may or may not have occurred to Konitz as he struggled with the problems of his own disarrayed sensibilities. Any doubt that he had been on a wild goose chase in his youth had for some time been dispelled by the eventual emergence of an alto player who had followed Konitz's precepts very closely, and not only won jazz acceptance but also captured the large public following that Konitz in his days with Tristano and company, must sometimes have dreamed of. Konitz had sowed the seed and Paul Desmond had reaped the harvest, and what we were seeing at Scott's sounded very much like a disgruntled ex-farmer.

Possibly Konitz's standards would have sounded higher had we not still in our minds the echo of those early recordings. Judged purely on current form, Konitz was no worse than several of Scott's guest stars and better than some. But he had once had pretensions to leadership, or at least critics had thrust leadership upon him. All we were hearing now was one of the followers of the newer modernism. Musicians who read this kind of criticism of themselves usually react in the same way. They say that only the weakminded can really expect an artist to stand in the same place forever. This is perfectly true. Nobody can blame Konitz, or indeed anyone else, for attempting to develop. But the unfortunate truth remains, that the earlier work sounded more impressive than what came later. If, like F. Scott Fitzgerald's Tom Buchanan, Konitz's life reached a certain limited excellence at an early stage, it is pointless for any witness to pretend otherwise. During March 1966 music at the club was provided by Sonny Rollins and Ernestine Anderson, both of whom in their wildly differing ways remained true to form, Rollins with his chaotic mixture of beauty and ugliness, Ernestine with a recital of well-known standard songs intelligently and timefully delivered. But for once, even the eye-catching behaviour of Rollins was not enough to distract patrons of the club from thoughts of what was soon about to happen. It must be a rare event for a player like Rollins to be upstaged by a more violent revolutionary, but the truth is that compared to what might be expected in April, the music Rollins was dispensing in March was made to sound quite conventional.

Ornette Coleman

April, in fact, was the time when we were all about to catch up at last with what we had become tired of regarding as the ultimate musical experience. After several years of rumour, promise, adulation and insult, after a thousand crazy dialectical battles on the back of record covers, in the columns of periodicals with large egos and small circulations, after much diplomatic hedging by established players who refused to commit themselves, and some blatant puffs and some equally blatant deflations by others, the issue was finally to be resolved, at least for Scott's audiences, by the arrival of a new American group in the second week of

April 1966. What followed was something utterly intriguing, an apocalypse for some, a nightmare for others. The episode of Ornette Coleman may be described either as high comedy or low farce, depending on the degree to which one finds it possible to take Coleman's pretensions. By the time he arrived at Scott's with his quartet he had already achieved the remarkable distinction of having been a newcomer on the jazz scene for at least seven years, and appeared to be one of those endearing characters who surface from time to time on artistic waters, promising everything but too intrigued by the melodrama of their own adolescence ever to leave it behind. For years his spokesman had been attempting to forestall criticism by insisting that Coleman must be granted more time to formulate his findings and produce his masterpieces, but as he was by now older than many great soloists had been at the time they produced some of their most significant work, the legend was beginning to curl up around the edges.

A far deeper irony was the fact that by the time he arrived in London, Ornette Coleman, the most outrageous of all the experimentalists, was a general in serious danger of being outflanked by his own troops. There had been a time, not so long before, when it was quite impossible to imagine jazz more anarchic than Coleman's, but sadly that had turned out to be an attitude of pathetic naiveté. Musicians like Archie Shepp and Albert Ayler were already further advanced into this wasteland than Coleman, which should in a way have been a comfort to him, because it meant that his chances of being appreciated by London club audiences were greatly improved. We had, in effect, been conditioned by his rivals to expect any conceivable musical sound – or so we thought. In the event there proved to be one or two new quantities in the Coleman equation we had overlooked, and it was due in no small measure to these unknown factors that Coleman was able to preserve the sublime incoherence of his art.

In the meantime, local critics began sharpening their sensibilities and burrowing through their bags of adjectives in readiness for the stern test ahead. For as they well knew, it was not really Ornette Coleman who was on trial at all, but themselves. It was an absurd situation, and in order to explain how it came about, it is necessary to glance back for a moment to an earlier chapter in local jazz history. Until the advent of Charlie Parker in the late 1940s, jazz criticism in Britain had been largely an affair of backing all the wrong horses and flogging all the dead ones. Jazz, it appeared, had very conveniently achieved a kind of status, with the ubiquitous Jelly Roll Morton forever promising to disappear over the horizon in pursuit of Freddie Keppard but never actually doing so, and whippersnappers like Coleman Hawkins and Roy Eldridge representing an illimitable future. A glow of Panglossian optimism suffused the entire landscape. It was accepted as a truism that the music would continue to evolve onwards and upwards in an everlasting ascent to godhead, although nobody ever explained why this should be so. But although it was agreed that styles would naturally evolve and the face of the music be changed accordingly, it was agreed also that these changes must occur so imperceptibly that nobody would be able to notice them.

And so, while some of the critical brotherhood used a slide rule to measure the distance from New Orleans of a player's origins, others wrestled mightily with the problem of whether after all Jimmy Dorsey was the best alto saxophonist of all time. Obscure monographs were composed which surprised themselves in the last line by stumbling on the truth that Red Nichols was not after all quite so gifted as Louis Armstrong. Some critics worked their own little allotments and became local specialists on arcane issues like the interrelationships of Bunk and Dink, or which kind of chairleg Baby Dodds preferred as a drumstick. Others tried to locate the day and hour when the music had lost its pristine innocence. 1927 said the diehards. 1931, insisted the more adventurous. 1933, suggested the real revolutionaries. Recordings were cherished less for their musical merit than for their unavailability to the general public, and players were deified, not for their art but for their mannerisms of dress and temperament. British jazz criticism was in fact a dedicated little principality which operated all the better for being totally unaware of what was happening beyond its own constricting borders.

For Charlie Parker suddenly to have erupted into this syncopated Ruritania was a gross breach of aesthetic morality, and most of the brotherhood took its revenge by refusing to recognize him as a jazz musician at all. Why, they had not even got around to Lester Young and Charlie Christian yet, so how could they possibly be expected to allow an upstart like Parker into their pantheon? And that was how when he arrived, despite all their obstructive tactics, they were caught hopelessly on the wrong foot, and very understandably fell flat on their faces.

They attacked the new Modernism as one man, assuming that they were not able to sing Parker's solo in 'Anthropology' as they had been singing Armstrong's in 'West End Blues' for the last twenty years, then Parker's solo in 'Anthropology' must by definition be composed wholly of wrong notes. They felt that the whole Modern movement was either a confidence trick or a joke in the worst possible taste, and being honourable men, they said as much in print. The fact that in so doing they damned their profession forever more, at least so far as the British musician was concerned, was not something they were ever able to grasp, then or since. Parker had given them their one great chance, and they muffed it.

It was only very gradually that the enormity of their mistake dawned on them, which made the joke more priceless than ever. One by one the Parker albums slipped into the country, slowly the locals began to acquire the nuances of the new style, and even more slowly a tiny but intensely loyal audience began to build and to patronize new hole-in-the-wall clubs where no Traditionalist was ever seen. By the minutest degrees it became apparent that Parker had in fact turned out to be what so many younger musicians had always said he was, an improviser touched with genius. The critics realized with slowly growing horror what had happened. They had speculated all their capital on a single horse, and as usual it had turned out to be the wrong one. What were they to do? As a group they had rendered themselves bankrupt, and the sound of derisive laughter was in the air. There remained only one escape route, to welsh on their debts, and this they proceeded to do with admirable efficiency. There now began the ceremony of the turning of the coat.

Quietly, and certainly imperceptibly because nobody took much notice of them any more, the defaulting judges began reversing their decisions, until by the time Parker died in 1955, most of them had adjusted so well to the new critical climate that they were able to compose pietistic obituaries with a perfectly clear conscience. Not that it really mattered very much. A man may be pardoned for being wrong about the work of an artist with whom he has no affinity. To call a good player a bad one is no terrible thing (except for the good player in question), and it is at least arguable that the recanting critics of Old England took themselves just a little too seriously. In any case, most of them became accustomed after a while to wearing their Charlie Parker hats. They breathed a sigh of relief, congratulated themselves on having survived such a perilous passage, and settled down once more to their occupational duties, which appear to consist mainly in composing critical gaffes outrageous enough to make amusing reading to the next generation.

But jazz criticism had learned a terrible lesson, which it was never likely to forget. When a man has dared on one occasion to commit himself and has been proved disastrously wrong, he will usually vow never to commit himself again, and this explains the comical reversal of roles on the occasion of Ornette Coleman's testing time. The frame of mind in which most critics trooped down to Scott's Club to hear the ageing *enfant terrible* may best be described by reciting the false syllogism which had become the first rule of conduct for all jazz reviewers. 'Parker sounded mad, and he turned out to be a great musician. Ornette Coleman sounds mad. Therefore Ornette Coleman must be a great musician.' Whether or not Coleman was himself aware of the peculiar critical climate he was walking into, of whether indeed it was the same climate that he obtained in New York and San Francisco it is impossible to say, but certainly if he had the slightest misgivings about the nature of his reception when he first stepped on to the bandstand at Scott's, he was just wasting valuable nervous energy. Charlie Parker had won his battle for him at least fifteen years before.

Now it so happened that the onslaught to which Coleman subjected his critics was of an even greater severity than his record albums might have led them to expect. His assaults on the ear proved even more terrible than anything known from past campaigns. The pessimists came expecting a *blitzkrieg*, and what they got was an earthquake. What had happened was, very simply, that in the past two or three years, Coleman had become a multi-instrumentalist. Part of his early fame had rested on the fact that he preferred blowing a plastic alto saxophone, although why this should have contributed to the legend of his genius it is hard to say. So far from being a crazy novelty, plastic saxophones had been tried and found wanting many years before Coleman took up their cause. In any case, it is difficult to understand on what basis a man can see something spectacular about a plastic instrument who has never handled a metal one. Coleman's choice of instrument had no more relevance to his originality than the rumour that he always wore an overcoat in the summer, but it had been seized upon all the same by the type of commentator who finds more interest in a false nose than in the brain lying just above it.

But Coleman had come to London armed not only with his plastic saxophone, but with a trumpet and a violin as well, and if it is true to say that he was at least reasonably familiar with the technical problems of playing jazz on a saxophone, it is also true to say that he apparently had only the most rudimentary notions of how to handle the two new instruments. Coleman as a saxophone player is a fascinating curiosity, an artist whose technique is a bewildering patchwork of dexterity and the most shocking ineptitude. Some phrases tumble out with the authentic fluency of the professional Modernist. Others stumble out behind a smokescreen of squeaks and whistles which are no doubt taken by the cognoscenti as further evidence of his greatness but which are, nonetheless, further evidence of his failure so far to win complete control over the instrument. But to the practised ear it is quite clear that Coleman has tried very hard with the saxophone, just as it is obvious to the trained musician that he has very definite gifts as a composer of themes.

But what of Coleman the trumpeter or Coleman the violinist? What he actually succeeded in doing at Scott's was to defy all rational criticism. Once he began to struggle with the trumpet or to saw savagely at the violin, the process of ratiocination collapsed entirely. There was no criterion by which to judge. It was not so much bad playing as no playing at all, not so much poor music as antimusic. It was certainly original in the sense that nothing remotely like it had ever been heard before, but whether it had any musical validity depended entirely on your own personal attitude. For the reasons I have already defined it was useless looking to the critics for enlightenment. Even though several of the working reviewers were too young to have been involved in the Parker debacle, there is such a thing as a group memory, and I believe this to have been an extremely potent subconscious factor in determining the reaction to Ornette Coleman. The professional commentator, having trusted to his ears once before, and found those ears sorely wanting, had evidently decided never to trust to those ears again. The press generally ranged in its reactions from quiet approval to sheer ecstasy.

My own reactions to Coleman's music certainly have no more validity than those of my colleagues, but the reverse is also true, and it was rather pathetic that my strictures on Coleman should have drawn the comment from his supporters that I must be wrong simply because I was in a minority. In reacting as I did to the Coleman recitals, I was, of course, well aware what to expect. In 1962 I had published a book on jazz in which I had questioned the proposition that given time, Coleman would come up with his masterpieces. In an otherwise extremely generous review of the book, Mr Nat Hentoff intimated that my fall from critical grace in the last few pages involving Coleman was probably due at least in part to the fact that I was British, and therefore congenitally incapable of understanding the social significance of the New Jazz. But if I am British and therefore unable to grasp the essence of Coleman's work, then it must also follow that Hentoff, being American, cannot grasp the essence of mine. In any case, time was on my side. Four years had passed since the publication of my book, and still Coleman had not apparently arrived at a definitive version of himself. In reproducing here my original review of Coleman's season at Scott's, it needs to be said that contrary to the layman's belief, a bad review is not more pleasant to compose than a good one, any more than sitting in a club and being outraged is more pleasant than sitting there and being profoundly moved. This is the review which inspired what one neutral party later defined as 'a small Ornette's nest'.

It ought to be clear to anyone visiting Ronnie Scott's Club in the last few days that it is not possible to criticize the playing of Ornette Coleman. The act of criticism is necessarily connected with what the artist is supposed to be doing, and as I haven't the remotest idea what Ornette Coleman is supposed to be doing, all criticism is stilled. It remains only to report in factual terms what happens when he arrives on the bandstand.

Coleman begins with what might be laughingly called an alto saxophone solo at a fast tempo, brief and to the point, lasting, say, ten or fifteen minutes, in the course of which both harmony and melody are given the brush. Next comes a change of mood, that is to say, the same thing is played slow instead of fast. The violin interlude which follows is even more startling. Coleman staggers through some mysterious pattern of his own devising, sawing away with a ferocity which belies the dolorous expression on his face.

Finally, there arrives what will probably come to be known in jazz history as Coleman's Trumpet Involuntary, in which this unique artist plays a series of strangulated bugle calls and high chromatic runs with a fine disregard for all precedent.

He is not, however, completely without shrewdness. By mastering the useful trick of playing the entire chromatic scale at any given moment, he has absolved himself from the charge of continuously playing wrong notes. Like a stopped clock, Coleman is right at least twice a day.

To me the most remarkable thing of all is the sycophancy of his audiences, who sit in awed silence throughout each number, and then applaud like a barbarian horde hailing the fall of a great city. Unquestionably Coleman is king of the avant garde, but I cannot help wondering how many people have noticed he is wearing no clothes.

This reaction drew other reactions in turn, including a letter from Coleman himself which accused me of personal prejudice. Now of all reactions to a review, this kind is the saddest, because it implies on the artist's part an inability to conceive the possibility than anyone could dislike him for purely artistic reasons. The ironic thing is that I happen to approve of everything about Coleman except for his actual jazz. He is obviously a talented composer and he has shown considerable moral courage in sticking to his aesthetic guns. He has always displayed precisely that kind of adventurous determination without which any art form must curl up and die. His attempt to find an escape from the cage of Dominant-to-Tonic resolution is utterly necessary to the future of the music, and if the cheers of his supporters have been tempered with less good sense than one might wish for, Coleman himself is hardly to blame for that.

In addition, Coleman, lacking the prestige of the big crowdpullers of the British jazz concert circuit, has not found it easy to get himself taken seriously. Whatever one might think of his gifts as an improviser it is, of course, unpardonable that he should be prevented from exhibiting them, which is why, about a year after his season at Scott's was over, I helped organize a petition to the Ministry of Labour at a moment in the career of that remarkable organization when it was pondering whether Coleman was a worthy enough artist to be allowed to give a British concert. In other words, I ought, and indeed would, do anything I could to give work like Coleman's maximum exposure and try to help protect it from bigotry. The one thing I was unable to do when confronted by his actual music was to say that I liked it.

Buddy Rich

Till now Scott had progressed steadily in his administration from British soloists to American soloists, from American soloists to American duets, on to quintets, and now, for two days in April 1967, he arrived finally at the most ambitious point of all. Arrangements with the Harold Davison office made it possible for him to present at the club on 10 and 11 April the entire Buddy Rich band. It was inevitable that delight at the news should have been tempered with a few misgivings. For one thing there was the question of jazz content. Although bigotry against larger orchestras in jazz clubs is not as blind as it once was, there was certainly a departure from policy in presenting a group whose main virtue was an orchestral rather than an individual one. Rich's band had established itself in an unprecedentedly short space of time in Britain, and although the ensemble sound was impressive enough, one could hardly say that the soloists were making history. There was the leader himself, of course, and it was largely because of the widespread admiration for his drumming that audiences supported the experiment.

There was another doubt in many minds. To what extent would the eardrums be damaged by the assault of a full brass section blowing treble forte in the restricting confines of the Scott Club? We had for so many years been deprived of the chance to find out how loud an American big band would be in a club as distinct from a concert hall, that several of us wondered whether we would survive the experience. In the event, the fears were misplaced. Both the Rich band and the Woody Herman Orchestra which was featured in a similar experiment, contrived somehow to blow in their usual uninhibited manner without appearing to become overbearing.

In any case, the jazz student ought to be prepared to go through worse ordeals than a mere split eardrum to savour the technique of Buddy Rich. Whether or not Rich is the ideal drummer for all jazz groups is beside the point. There comes a stage where technical excellence arrives on such an exalted plane that it can be enjoyed for its own sake, and Rich is so comprehensive a drummer that nobody with any interest in any kind of music could fail to be at least intrigued by the mechanics of his art.

Rich is something of a unique figure in jazz. In a sense he belongs more to the vaudeville tradition than to music, and indeed began as a professional in his parents' comedy act when he was still literally a babe in arms. He made his entry into jazz history proper when as a teenager he joined Joe Marsala's band in 1939, but before long he had become associated in the minds of most people with the big bands of the 1940s. His several spells with the Tommy Dorsey band helped to give him the kind of exposure that wins popularity polls, and to this day the *Guinness Book of Records* includes the surprising information that Rich is the highest paid orchestral musician in world history, the generous employer in his case being Harry James.

Any ideas that the vaudeville tradition was left behind him a long time ago are soon displaced at any Rich public performance. He is soon revealed as a genuinely funny stand-up comic, a reasonable singer, a good dancer, and, if the record books are accurate, a competent straight actor. In the late 1950s, when he suffered two heart attacks, Rich actually announced his retirement as a drummer, and began appearing on American television in dramatic roles. But by 1961 he was back again as a bandleader, and his belated but complete victory over British audiences reached its climax with his band's appearance at Scott's Club.

In presenting Rich and the orchestra, Scott was maintaining his reputation for thinking up impracticable ideas and then showing they are practicable. By the time Rich's orchestra was booked into the club, members had been trained to expect anything. If Scott had told them that Buddy Bolden was to give a recital, half of them would have come along in good faith. Scott himself showed the occasional partiality for exploiting this faith of his members. More than once he announced a 'brief appearance by Toulouse-Lautrec,' after which he would lower the microphone to the appropriate height and then leave the stand. There were always two or three customers who craned forward in expectation of the promised miracle.

By the end of 1967 the Scott Club had a registered membership list of 25,000, although a high percentage of this figure consisted of floating customers who had not renewed their connections. Even so, by the end of the year, the club was averaging 40,000 customers a year, which was not so far short of the one-time absurd figure in Scott's mind of 50,000 patrons per annum. Scott felt that with a thousand customers a week coming into the club, he could claim that his point was proved. More important, attendances of this size would supply additional capital needed to improve amenities and expand the scope of the club's activities.

Occasionally, Scott would become a promoter at stage concerts featuring the musicians appearing at the club. Some of these ventures were more successful than others. There was also his attempt to create a small chain of clubs across the country which would book his guests, and therefore lighten the load of expenses involved in bringing men across from the States. This experiment failed, but more indicative of the importance of the club's survival in the general jazz scene was its influence as a propagator of the cause among people influential enough to help the cause themselves. One of the most enthusiastic visitors was, and is, the actor John Neville, who during 1967 booked in some of Scott's guest musicians at a series of highly successful Sunday jazz recitals at the Nottingham Playhouse. Another regular visitor, the comedian Spike Milligan, showed a distinct partiality for one or two of the regular musicians at Scott's when he appeared in a music-and-poetry series on television.

What in fact had happened was that for the first time in London there existed a place where those with a curiosity about or an affection for jazz, but without any knowledge of the inner workings of the local jazz world, could attend and find a reasonable standard of bodily comfort allied to a high standard of musical skill. In the past you could always get the comfort in two or three of the more civilized London night clubs, and you might have found the musical skill in some of the jazz clubs of the 1950s. But as the night clubs always did, and still do, favour forms of public entertainment which veer drunkenly between the pathetic and the imbecilic, and as most predecessors to Scott's in the jazz club line had the aspect of punishment boxes, it is obvious that Scott's was unique in the sense that there was nothing with which you could really compare it. By the time it was established in Frith Street and its old premises were continuing to function under its management as a kind of avant garde outhouse called The Old Place, it had evolved to the point where it was not a Modern jazz club so much as a central jazz point from which the music radiated. If any further proof was needed that the old civil war between Trad and Modern had long ago been revealed as the irrelevance it had always been, that proof was forthcoming on 24 April 1967.

Bud Freeman

Ever since his opening night Scott had shown an understandable partiality towards tenor saxophonists, until by now a list of those he had employed would look very much like a complete jazz history of the instrument. There were, however, one or two gaps still in the record, and one of these was now plugged up with the arrival on the bandstand of Lawrence 'Bud' Freeman. Ten years before, Freeman's appearance in a Modern London jazz club would have been unthinkable, but now his booking caused no more than a few mildly raised eyebrows. People often grumble about the disadvantages of the jazz attitude in the 1960s, with particular reference to the efforts of the avant garde to break up the traditional forms of jazz. What is often overlooked is that running concurrent with this tendency to artistic mayhem, is another set of attitudes which no longer see jazz so rigidly divided into two armed camps. The advance of stylistic tolerance in the 1960s has been a vast one, although only those who remember the vitriol that was flung around in the late 1940s and early 1950s will notice the extent of the improvement.

In booking Bud Freeman, Scott was reaching much further back into the history of the music than he ever had before, because unlike the younger heroes who had preceded him on the stand, Freeman belonged to origins so obscure to the younger generation that he could be defined accurately and without any overtones of mawkishness, as legendary. He had been actively involved in making jazz music for roughly forty years, and had long survived most of his contemporaries. Of the men who surrounded him as a youngster, Jack Teagarden was dead, Benny Goodman retired, Venuti still active but no longer connected with jazz. Eddie Lang had been dead for a quarter of a century by the time Freeman arrived in Frith Street. Eddie Condon had evolved into a lampoon of himself, and Freeman's closest musical partner, Charles Ellsworth 'Pee Wee' Russell, had discovered in his sixties that his unsuspected talent for modern painting was more lucrative than dipping the clarinet in the brine of his own temperament, as he had been doing all his life. Freeman was, in fact, the sole survivor from the days of the Chicagoans to retain both his enthusiasm and something of his original fluency. Like Hawkins, he had won the right to be judged, not so much on what he now was, as on what he had always been.

The saxophone style of Bud Freeman is so highly personal to the man that it deserves a footnote of its own in any history of the music. Freeman is in fact a minor but very fascinating figure in the landscape of jazz history, a man who just scrapes into the pantheon by passing the most difficult test of all, creating a style wholly original and musically valid. At the time Freeman was moving from apprentice violinist to professional tenor player in Chicago in the late 1920s, Coleman Hawkins was literally inventing the jazz tenor saxophone. Before Hawkins there was no such thing as a tenor saxophone tradition, which meant that for a long time after he created one, everybody tried to sound like him. Until the arrival of Lester Young in the mid-1930s, the Hawkins approach swept the field, and of all the countless tenor players who rose to prominence in the years between, say, Hawkins's 'One Hour' with the Mound City Blue Blowers and Lester Young's 'Lady Be Good' with the Count Basie Quintet, Bud Freeman alone owed nothing to anybody else in the formulation of his own method. If this were all that could be said for him, it would still be enough to guarantee him a mention in the history books. In fact, Freeman achieved rather more than this.

Freeman's tenor style is one of those curiosities which occur from time to time in jazz, that have no visible ancestors and no really considerable descendants. It exists, as it were, only within the compass of its inventor's own active life, and has no conceivable influence on those who come later. In tone alone, Freeman was a startling innovator when he first began winning his solo reputation. He made a windy, asthmatical sound which seemed flimsy when you compared it with Hawkins's rich tone, but which was curiously well suited to the idiom Freeman was using, the Chicago style, with its compromise between ensemble and solo. Technically Freeman was very good for his time, and although today the chromatic arpeggios of 'The Eel' might sound naive to ears accustomed to the endless codas of the Modernists, that recording is still not quite as simple to imitate as it sounds.

Freeman was also capable of good melodic construction, and probably reached his peak at this difficult game around the end of the 1930s when he fronted an excellent Chicago-style band featuring Teagarden, Russell, Max Kaminsky and Dave Bowman. Together with the Muggsy Spanier Ragtimers, this band represented an odd retrospective climax to Chicago small-group jazz, and not least impressive about the achievement was Freeman's own technically resourceful playing.

But the most praiseworthy thing about the Freeman style was its one incalculable property, its resilience. For reasons which are probably intimately connected with breathing, fingering and bodily relaxation, and which expressed themselves through Freeman's technique in a wholly intuitive way, his playing at its best had the same springy energy of a bouncing ball, which meant that it had a great rhythmic strength which made it workable jazz even at those moments where the melodic thought was not particularly distinguished. The outstanding Freeman recordings all have this peculiar dynamism of their own, although at a few odd moments they seem, misleadingly or not, to hint at what Lester Young was soon to do.

Young has denied ever having been influenced by Freeman, and as Young has always been generous enough to acknowledge the inspiration of as incongruous a figure as Frank Trumbauer without seeming embarrassed by it, we can take it that he is speaking the truth. On the other hand, there really are a few of Freeman's aphorisms which might almost be pearls of Young's wisdom. In particular a 1939 recording by Freeman of 'I Found A New Baby', where, in the last middle eight of the performance, Freeman constructs one of those academic patterns based on the E Minor arpeggio which might have come straight out of Lester's solos in 'Dickie's Dream' or 'Twelfth Street Rag'. One possible explanation for the similarity has never been offered, and that is that it was Young who influenced Freeman. After all, by the time he made that recording of 'I Found A New Baby' Freeman had had at least two years in which to savour the subtleties of Lester's best early work with the Kansas City Five. A much more likely explanation, however, for this tantalizing distant relationship between antipathetic artists, is simply that men can work independently towards the identical end and never be aware of each other. Whatever the answer, when Freeman came to Scott's Club, he certainly arrived, stylistically at least, as a man from outside the Modern camp.

His fortnight there was a charming interlude between Modernists, and the press he received was predictably respectful. However, Freeman approaching sixty was not quite the master he had been back in the much-recorded great days of Chicago. He could still bounce his fingers with the same resilience, but in the later years he had acquired a vibrato which tended to make most of his slower themes sound too sentimentalized for comfort. Also, a few of his phrases had congealed into formal devices he resorted to again and again, although this is something which happens to all original players sooner or later. On balance Freeman had weathered the forty years of his career remarkably well, and with the exception of Jack Teagarden, who had died two or three years before Freeman reached Frith Street, could be nominated as the Chicagoan with the longest effective career as an active soloist.

Yusef Lateef

The next instrumentalist to appear was the eccentric Yusef Lateef, although he was eccentric in the instruments he played, rather than what he played on them. Lateef, a fluent tenor saxophonist, represents the logical extension of the theory which first came into circulation after the last war, and was based on the idea that a platitude becomes mysteriously original when it is transferred from the expected to the unexpected instrument. A Herbie Mann, therefore, could change in a matter of months from an average alto player to a flautist of apocalyptic significance. Oddly enough the reverse also seems to apply; witness Jimmy Guiffre, who chose to alter himself from a rather good tenor player into a rather boring clarinettist. Lateef has taken this game into more refined areas altogether. During the 1960s, Lateef had made it his business to corner the market in exotica. Not only had he tended towards compositions reeking of the hothouse orientalism of vintage Hollywood, but he had come to play them on a battery of rare and sometimes even non-existent instruments, whose usefulness would probably be better appreciated among snake charmers than among Modern jazz fanciers. Once again we all fell into the trap of prejudging a man by his recordings. On the stand at Scott's, Lateef reverted to type, that is, to a muscular extrovert who verged time and again, not on MGM rococo flourishes but on the world of Rock'n'Roll. It was obvious from his first few bars that he was a very accomplished player indeed, and listening to him the thought was irresistible that much of his dabbling with spurious musical mysticism has been prompted by the entirely understandable desire to dish his rivals. The once small company of competent Modern saxophonists had swelled by the time Lateef arrived in London to a vast army, and in order to stand out from the crowd even the best player might be tempted to the most outrageous devices. Sonny Rollins had cut all his hair off. Charles Lloyd had refused to cut his at all. One assumes that Lateef's occasional imitations of Syrian shepherds calling the flock home were his devices for attracting attention to what he could really do.

At Scott's, Lateef alternated his tenor playing with some fine flute interludes which pointed a stark contrast to his more robust work. At one moment he would be waving his tenor saxophone around like a peashooter, playing a fast blues that put one in mind of all the changes Charlie Parker brought about in the jazz world, and at the next he would switch to the most contemplative flute playing which showed what an advantage a limited technique can be to a prolific player. Obliged to build with less notes, Lateef the flautist produced highly musical and starkly economical passages which underlined still further his intrinsic ability. The contrast between the public entertainer and the private artist was further underlined by the fact that when invited to appear in a jazz TV programme, Lateef instantly whipped out a wooden pipe which played two notes at once, and informed the viewer with the utmost solemnity that such instruments were unknown outside the foothills of Syria.

Coleman Hawkins

But if Ronnie Scott's Club could be said after all this time to have finally reached its peak as a jazz centre, that peak was undoubtedly scaled on 27 November 1967. It was on this day that Scott could claim once and for all to have caught up with jazz history, to have raised the local game to the point where the last vestiges of parochialism were wafted away. What it must have meant to Scott personally to be able to employ Coleman Hawkins, another saxophonist like myself can only imagine, but the dullest of all laymen must have realized at the time that it does not fall to all musicians, or indeed artists generally, to be able to work with a man who literally invented their art.

Hawkins by the time he appeared at Scott's had been active in jazz for at least fifty years, and he looked it. Patrons who associated Hawkins with his photographs over the last twenty years were profoundly shocked to see a man shamble on to the stand who looked less like a jazz musician than the model for Hemingway's Old Man of the Sea. A grizzled beard and a stooping body were the first impressions, instantly superseded by the fear that the old man's trembling legs would not be able to get him to the bandstand safely. Hawkins did negotiate the journey from the bandroom, and although drowsy in a smiling sort of way, played his sets without any crises occurring.

Who could criticize Coleman Hawkins? The myth of the dispassionate, objective critic is always revealed for the fraud it is on such occasions. In any case, objective criticism is a platonic impossibility which would not even be desirable even if it were possible. The only criticism which is readable is the fiercely prejudiced, fiercely subjective criticism by a man who cares enough to show his enthusiasms. I for one would no more have felt like finding fault with Hawkins than I would with apple pie or sunshine.

But there has arisen a critical cliché over the last few years which persisted in the lunacy that Hawkins in 1967 was as good as ever he had been. Sentimentality is always understandable, and perhaps even excusable with a figure as venerable and as venerated as Hawkins, but the point was that in saying he was as good now as he had been in his prime, was only another way of saying that he had been no better in his prime than he was now. And that was a critical affront for which there can be no forgiveness. As all serious students of jazz know, Hawkins in the 1930s and 1940s had achieved perfection on record, not once or twice, but time and time again.

Apart from the famous version of 'Body And Soul', which Hawkins himself has always insisted was nothing special in his career, there are dozens of recordings to remind us that apart from being the greatest rhapsodic ballad player ever to play a saxophone, Hawkins has in his time generated more swing, created more musical climaxes, conjured up more sheer beauty than anybody else with the possible exception of Louis Armstrong. Hawkins's vital importance as a jazz figure is that he offers incontrovertible proof that jazz is after all an art form, although perhaps a minor one. His mastery of form, that is his gift for weaving a succession of phrases and choruses into a single unified statement, is the greatest and the most elusive jazz gift of all, and the fact that in the last few years this gift has been slipping away from him, makes it doubly important to stress the fact that, however well he plays today, there was a time when he played better. Without this acknowledgement, Hawkins's superlative career ceases to make any sense at all.

There were hundreds, perhaps thousands of saxophonists in London alone whose lives had been profoundly influenced by Hawkins's music. It would have been impossible to calculate how many active musicians in this country have first been tempted to become professional musicians because of some ravishing recording by Hawkins, heard perhaps by accident but then never forgotten. I had been asked by the Educational Broadcasts department of the BBC to prepare a programme which dissected a perfectly formed jazz solo, and had inevitably chosen something of Hawkins's, a miraculous paraphrase of 'Out Of Nowhere' made in the late 1930s. I had even worked in my apprentice days for a bandleader who had himself worked for Hawkins during the latter's barnstorming European period before the last war. This bandleader, Bertie King, was only one of a whole army of men who had crossed Hawkins's path and never forgotten the experience. And here were people like myself presuming to sit there and judge Hawkins.

In fact, we were trying to do nothing of the sort. We were simply congratulating ourselves on our good fortune in getting one more opportunity to see the old Master in a congenial environment. As for myself, as I sat there waiting for Hawkins to make his appearance, I could not help wondering about the absurd twists of fortune that had put me in a position where somebody was to pay me for listening to him. I was aware that we would not be getting the Hawkins of 'Body And Soul' and 'Out Of Nowhere', aware also that the differences ought to be stressed, and aware most of all that no critical carping would have any real relevance. Eventually, after much nostalgic daydreaming, I composed the following review, which in sentiment, echoed most other reviews:

If tomorrow Shakespeare were to turn up in a state of advanced decrepitude with a mediocre play under his arm, where would be the critic to attempt a dispassionate assessment? Because jazz history has been telescoped into a brief fifty-year period, that is precisely the dilemma awaiting those who go to Ronnie Scott's this month to hear Coleman Hawkins playing the tenor saxophone.

Hawkins was the first man ever to give the instrument any kind of coherence. Before he arrived, saxophones were a vaudeville joke; after he had done his work, they were recognized as machines which could, in the right hands, create music of sumptuous beauty. All jazz criticism today is based on the standards of a handful of men like him, and even if a few players like Charlie Parker and Lester Young have managed to survive the comparison, Hawkins still stands first because it was he who started the whole business. Without him there would have been no saxophone tradition in jazz at all.

But Hawkins today is long past his prime, and not even the vast fund of goodwill that has accumulated over the years on his behalf can hide the fact. Admittedly, some people are so delighted that at sixty-four he is still playing at all, that they go completely wild and insist that the old man is as good as ever. This is not only to overrate his current playing, but to place his earlier masterpieces in an unflattering light.

In the 1940s, there was no tenor player who could live with him. The greatest improviser at slow tempo of his generation, Hawkins also possessed the most remarkable sense of form ever heard in jazz, so that instinctively he could make a few random choruses grow into a single unified statement. There was no harmonic subtlety he could not grasp and no technical problem he could not cope with.

The contrast between then and now is underlined by the way he tackles 'Sweet Georgia Brown' at Scott's Club. The speed of the piece seems to cause him problems, and he is struggling so hard to keep up that there is no time left for invention. Exactly thirty years ago in Paris, Hawkins recorded the same theme with a brilliance that was an inspiration to thousands of other jazz musicians. In the same way his present version of 'Moonglow' suffers largely because of the great achievements of the past which overshadow it. Here is a leisurely tempo Hawkins can settle into without strain, but although the old harmonic sense still flickers into life, the melodic stream has dried up.

And yet Hawkins today, frail in body as well as spirit, retains the courage of a lion. This has always been one of the most admirable things about him as an artist. When the post-war Modernists first arrived breathing fire, almost alone of the established masters he fraternized with them, studied their methods, and even gave them jobs. In this way he probably prolonged his life as an influential soloist by at least ten years, although it was not the instinct for self-preservation which impelled him, so much as his burning curiosity about music. And he remains curious to the end.

At Scott's he plays 'September Song' out of tempo and unaccompanied; no rhythm section to lean on, no pleasant piano chords to hide behind. It is a stroke of great defiance, because the unaccompanied saxophone solo is the cruellest test of all, invented by Hawkins himself half a lifetime ago. And yet in 'September Song' he produces his best playing of the evening.

Gruff as the tone is, long as the pauses are between phrases, a vast map of Kurt Weill's harmonies is unfolded and transformed into a landscape by the innate romanticism of the soloist's style. It may be jazz played from memory, but at least Hawkins is remembering his own work and not other people's.

While he was in London, disturbing reports filtered through of Hawkins's increasing disenchantment with the delights of senility. A BBC producer seeking a taped interview with him discovered that Hawkins was in the habit of locking himself in his hotel room and staying there all day, much to the bewilderment of the chambermaids who were supposed to make his bed and clean his room. But perhaps the really significant point is that the interview, when finally it was obtained, proved to be perfectly lucid, and indeed sprinkled with a few observations whose wisdom is so often lacking in reported conversations with jazz musicians. Certainly the customers who paid to see him went away acutely aware of the fact that they had watched in action a type of musician whose like will certainly never occur again in jazz history.

∾

KENNY CLARKE

February was taken up by a nostalgia not altogether dissimilar to that evoked by Hawkins's visit, although it was nostalgia of a subtly differing kind. Regret for the good old days of the jam session and widening of narrow frontiers is one thing. Fond memories of the emergent days of Bebop, with its hiccuping clichés and perverse rhythmic figures is quite another. For many years the Modern drum veteran Kenny Clarke had been relegated to the background by the kingmakers of jazz criticism. He was, however, alive and well and living in Paris, and now came over to Scott's with his own trio to show how little he had declined.

Clarke is one of those rare figures who retain an interest quite independent of their actual musical prowess at any given moment. No matter how indifferently these men play, they hold the glamour that comes with the invention of new effects. Once a pioneer always a pioneer, and Clarke had without any question been the first of the post-war drummers to integrate the disconcerting mannerisms of the early Beboppers into a coherent system. Perhaps it was sad that London audiences should finally get to hear Clarke in congenial surroundings so long after his history had been made, but paradoxically it was his very distance from his own past which made Clarke easier to assess as a musician. In his early prime, Clarke shocked by the sheer uncompromising novelty of his bass drum accents. But today, when a whole succession of players from Max Roach down to Tony Williams have removed the element of surprise from what was once such a shocking style, Clarke can be judged on intrinsic musical worth rather than as a novelty.

The first thing to emerge when Clarke began playing was that in spite of his long self-imposed exile, he remained a great musician. The marked change was not in his music but in the reaction of the listener. Whereas twenty years ago his 'bomb-dropping', or destruction of the regular pulse of the rhythm section, could sound like sheer perversity, we were by now educated to the point where we could see what he had been getting at. By extending the range of the drummer's opportunity for improvisation, Clarke had helped to elevate his own role from animated metronome to a vital participant in the long chase of the extended solo.

The most impressive proof of his mastery at Scott's was the degree of his anticipation. Like all great players, he had a telepathic gift for knowing what the next musician was about to play, and adjusting his accents accordingly. The result was that even as the soloist executed a phrase, he found Clarke executing a counterpoint against it, so that the soloist himself was continually being spurred on by an accompanist in full sympathy with what he was trying to do. In fact, Clarke's two supporters, organist Eddie Lewis and guitarist Jimmy Gourlay, benefited so enormously from the subtle tattoo of Clarke's drumming that they were perhaps made to sound rather better players than they really were. Their jazz was assured enough, but to Clarke, who in the great days of the revolution provided the rhythmic stimulus for men like Charlie Parker and Dizzy Gillespie, it might have all sounded just a shade innocuous. Clarke in his own lifetime had achieved so much in his playing, acquired so comprehensive a technique and changed the face of jazz drumming so radically, that only utter genius could surprise him now, and neither Lewis nor Gourlay fell into that category.

Phil Woods

Two more saxophonists appeared at the club during the spring of 1968, Phil Woods and Hank Mobley, neither of whom had been seen in Britain before, that is if we discount a fleeting concert appearance by the Thelonious Monk band in the previous winter, where Woods had played only one thirty-two bar chorus, much to the bewilderment and extreme disappointment of the audience. Both Woods and Mobley articulate their instrument with the clarity which indicates a thoroughly organized mind, and Woods in particular showed at Scott's that in spite of an enormous stylistic debt to Charlie Parker, he is a musician of some originality. He elected to extend his stay in Britain after his season at the club was over, although most of his activities in Britain have been restricted to studying and writing, rather than playing.

It was during the Woods visit that patrons of the club first began to hear rumours of a further extension of the club's premises, and it was not long before rumour evolved into vague certainties. Once again, Scott had found himself trapped by his own success. The rising costs of importing well-known musicians had forced upon the management the confession that a larger capacity was necessary if the whole experiment was not to collapse under its own weight. In 1967 alone, more than £30,000 had been paid out in fees to artists, and it became increasingly clear that unless more people could be accommodated at a single sitting, the club would find itself in deep financial waters. And so the site next door to the existing club was acquired, walls knocked down and the new premises opened in October 1968, almost nine years to the day since the Gerrard Street club first opened its doors.

The enlarged premises included a downstairs lounge-bar and an upstairs discotheque, but the focus of attention remained the ground floor jazz room, where the Buddy Rich band opened to the leader's typical remark that he was not used to working on a building site. The transition was smooth enough, but it would take several months before anyone could know whether improved facilities would lead to the larger attendances which are vital if the new Scott Club is to survive its own expansionist policy. In the meantime London possesses the major European jazz club, and one which outdistances most of its American rivals. There was a time when Americans, and American critics in particular, were comically patronizing in their attitude towards their British counterparts. Time and again we were told that we were too far from the source to have any real valid opinions. We judged too closely from recordings, we were told, and recording only gave us a falsified because over-simplified picture of the jazz truth. The argument was always dubious and today, with the existence of the Scott Club, no longer has any validity at all. We are all New Yorkers now, and have in fact become so blasé that we no longer consider it a tragedy if we do not bother to see one or another of Scott's guests at all. There will always be a next time, we tell ourselves, and if this is a rash tactic to adopt, it does at least bear witness to the astonishing transformation from parochialism which the success of the Scott Club experiment has brought about. Nightly jazz of the very highest quality has at last become a fact of life for the London enthusiast, and this is so because Scott himself, being a totally impractical romancer, has obstinately refused to take the excellent advice that has been offered to him, and has reduced all his own arguments to their logical conclusions. His success is perhaps the most astounding victory of hope over experience that the local jazz scene has ever witnessed.

Postscript: Jazz Decade

A decade is a neat and tidy period of time from which to draw conclusions. In the jazz world it represents roughly a generation, in the sense that at no point in the history of the music have ten years elapsed without bringing with them radical changes in the art of improvisation. At the time Scott's Club opened, 'Modern' meant Sonny Stitt and Oscar Peterson, or perhaps the early modal experiments of Miles Davis. By 1969 all these musicians and their musical approaches had been relegated, if that is the right word, to the comfortable past. They and their contemporaries had all been drawn by time into the main body of jazz culture or, to put it another way, when their work came up for review, it was no longer the music but the reviewer who was on trial.

The 'New Modernism' of the late 1960s was a very different affair indeed, a music which very courageously, and perhaps a shade truculently, rejected the canons of the last fifty years, cut itself adrift from the inscrutable laws of discord and resolution, substituting for them new anti-laws of discord and revolution. Scott, and all others whose livelihood depends on the selling of jazz to a large enough public to make the whole operation workable, have been faced throughout the 1960s with a nice problem in professional morality – to play safe and book the established masters, or reflect the changes and give an airing to the most violent and anarchic of the New Wave. Scott has done both, booking Bud Freeman one minute and Ornette Coleman the next, and in so doing has contrived to give the British jazz audience much more than a glimpse of the latest trends in the music. He has done this, but also shown them that 'new waves', whatever their vintage, always coexist with the established methods they seek to overthrow.

Sometimes this determination to show all facets of the jazz world is achieved accidentally, as in the ironic case of Stan Getz's return to Scott's a few months before the decade ended. Getz had always been regarded, and rightly so, as a custodian of those traditional methods of jazzmaking which had applied to all tenor saxophonists ever since the great days of Coleman Hawkins and Lester Young. He had exemplified the musician whose desire to create melody transcends all schools and all dogmas. And yet Getz on his return, at the dangerous age for a young jazz musician of forty-one, proved to be a new player altogether, one whose fluency was now destroyed by attempts to echo the jagged dissonances of the new generation.

But perhaps more important than incidents of this kind, more important in fact than anything else which was to be seen and heard at Scott's Club throughout the decade, was the steadily increasing tendency to broaden the spectrum of musical activity. In the beginning the club was a bastion of Modernism, that is to say, the only musicians seriously considered as attractions were those who could loosely be designated as post-Charlie Parker players. Very gradually, as audiences became more catholic in their attitudes, this rule was broken, so that by the end of the decade, the only criterion being applied was pure ability.

Not only this, but even jazz itself was dropped as a measuring rod. The booking, within a few weeks of the end of the decade, of the classical guitarist John Williams, was certainly a radical departure in the sense that Williams is not remotely connected with jazz at all, but the important point here is that he maintained the very high musical standards with which the club has become associated in the last ten years. Audiences listened to the delicate nuances of Williams as respectfully and as intensely as ever they had listened to Getz and company. The engagement of musical satirists like The Scaffold is another example of the way in which Scott has tried to broaden the commercial appeal of the club without compromising its artistic intentions.

In the last reckoning, these amendments to original policy all reflect the personality and the opinions of the man who owns the club. Scott has always believed that jazz can be made attractive to listen to if only it is presented in the right environment in the right way. He has also never stopped insisting that good music is indivisible, that the customer who has the patience and the ambition to plumb the depths of a complex player like, say, Bill Evans, will by definition be able to appreciate also the work of a musician like Williams. As for laughter, Scott has always insisted on its place in the jazz environment. If he had his way, which is another way of saying if he had a larger budget, the music would be sandwiched between recitals by stand-up comedians. And as all frequenters of the club well know, he has done what he could to compensate for this lack by becoming something of a comedian himself. His announcements of future attractions and his curious conspiratorial relationship with his audiences are now well-known aspects of the experience of a visit to the club. If he could sing and dance, he would do that too.

In the twenty-five years of Scott's career in jazz, he has always occupied a unique position, especially with his fellow musicians, who learned a long time ago that he has a knack of making life more interesting for those around him. In the old days this manifested itself in the formation of countless groups led by him and countless schemes dreamed up by him to improve the general health of the jazz life. Easily the outstanding feature of the last ten musical years in Britain has been the way that all this energy, all this residue of goodwill inside the profession, all this devotion to what is after all a much underrated and sat-upon musical art, has been focused in the administration of one of the most unusual and interesting of all the artistic emporiums to be found in Britain. What the second decade in the life of Ronnie Scott's Club will bring, nobody knows. Except possibly Scott himself.

III

From Broadway to Hollywood

The Art of the Songwriter

Broadway

In 1967 a *Punch* essayist, extracting what humour he could from the jazz life, in passing lamented the fact that I appeared to be becoming progressively more distracted from my jazz interests by musical comedy, much as to say that it is a sad portent for the future of theology when the monks start frequenting the local brothel. I was not sure of the exact point of the observation, but understood it to mean that the demands of jazz criticism are too rigorous for any man to be able to meet them for very long without risking permanent damage to his mental faculties. Although I thought I recognized a grain of truth in the idea, I considered its generalizations to be too sweeping, but, rather flattered that anyone should have bothered to observe my movements at all, kept my objections to myself. In any case, I had by then already been writing about jazz in continuing good health, for long enough for the mere fact of my survival to be in itself a sufficient contradiction of the theory. I have to admit, however, that a great many people believe that Jazz and Musical Comedy are incompatible, and frankly I find this extraordinary.

For it so happens that the world of jazz and the musical stage, so far from being antipathetic, are aesthetically much more closely allied than the friendly reproach in *Punch* would imply. In fact, the proposition that there are moments when the two have become so intertwined as to have become very nearly the same thing might be an extremely difficult one to discredit. Consider, for instance, my own experiences as an apprentice musician. The first recordings which influenced my conception of how jazz ought to be played were the Billie Holiday–Teddy Wilson pickup bands and the assorted small-groups formed by Benny Goodman, both of which series of recordings I started acquiring through the 1940s with as much speed as a teenage budget and the delays of wartime would allow. By 1945 I had gathered enough items to start making a few deductions, one of which was that without Broadway, it might have been difficult at times for the jazz musician to know what to play. Among my Goodman items were 'Lady Be Good', 'I Know That You Know', 'I Surrender Dear', 'Exactly Like You', 'More Than You Know', 'Body And Soul', 'I Got Rhythm'. Billie Holiday had recorded 'Summertime', 'I've Got My Love To Keep Me Warm', 'More Than You Know', 'Can't Help Loving That Man', 'The Man I Love', 'Night And Day', 'Why Was I Born?' and 'I Can't Get Started'. I also possessed the famous Lester Young recordings of 'Lady Be Good' and 'Lester Leaps In' (a disguised version of 'I Got Rhythm'), also Hawkins's 'Out Of Nowhere' and 'Body And Soul'. For a time I was too preoccupied by the astonishing inventiveness displayed on these recordings to start theorizing about their genesis. But the day had to come when I began drawing conclusions.

I have listed nineteen items, four of which occur twice, leaving fifteen actual compositions. Fourteen of them come from either musical comedy or revue, and the only way in which the fifteenth item, 'I've Got My Love To Keep Me Warm', differs from the others is that it was written for Hollywood instead of Broadway, which, so far as musical comedy is concerned, is no difference at all, as all the outstanding Broadway composers were eventually enticed out to Hollywood. Soon I started to break down the fifteen items in a different way, discovering that the name Gershwin appeared four times, Johnny Green, Vincent Youmans and Jerome Kern twice each, Irving Berlin, Vernon Duke and Cole Porter once each. Of course I possessed other recordings, and of course the names of other composers were often mentioned, but I list these names because of the consistency with which they began to confront me. Nor did their dominance fade when jazz styles altered. Indeed Modernism, when it arrived, paid Broadway the ultimate tribute of burglarizing it so persistently that before long there was nobody apart from the musicians themselves who could be sure what was and what was not being played. 'Rifftide' was really 'Lady Be Good', 'Hot House' was 'What Is This Thing Called Love?', 'Bird Gets The Worm' was 'Lover Come Back To Me', 'Anthropology' was 'I Got Rhythm', 'Ornithology' was 'How High The Moon', 'Koko' was 'Cherokee' and so on. And where the camouflage was dispensed with, the preponderance of Broadway became more noticeable than ever. The greatest soloist of the movement was Charlie Parker, and his recordings of the period which I possessed included 'Why Do I Love You?', 'All The Things You Are', 'Smoke Gets In Your Eyes' and 'The Song Is You', all by Kern, 'Embraceable You' and 'Strike Up The Band', both by Gershwin, Johnny Green's three outstanding songs, 'Body And Soul', 'Out Of Nowhere' and 'I Cover The Waterfront', one item from Rodgers and Hart, 'I Didn't Know What Time It Was' and two by Vernon Duke, 'I Can't Get Started' and 'Autumn In New York'.

Even in the midst of the excitement of the discovery of these performances, by Billie Holiday and Benny Goodman, Charlie Parker and Dizzy Gillespie, even in the grip of my midsummer madness, a kind of notated frenzy which did not in fact subside for twenty years and from which I have never completely recovered, there was a kind of half-realization somewhere at the back of my mind that the source of this music must surely be located at a considerable distance from the jazz world. There were occasional brief overtones in the performances, especially the vocal recordings, which could only be explained with reference to some other system of thought, some other world whose motives and actions were very different from those of Billie Holiday or Coleman Hawkins.

It needs to be said that during all the time I was acquainting myself with this body of recorded jazz, I never once saw a musical comedy, and it was not until 1954 and the London revival of *Pal Joey* that I witnessed for the first time the creaking artifice and unique logic of the musical. However, long before I ever set eyes on *Pal Joey*, that curious mutilation by an author of his own original work, I had already weathered the storms in a thousand teacups of Fred Astaire and Ginger Rogers, Nelson Eddy and Jeanette MacDonald, Judy Garland and Mickey Rooney, Alice Faye and John Payne, Crosby, Oakie, Durbin and all the rest of the two-dimensional warblers whose careers happened, most unfortunately, to coincide with the perfection of a machine which took audiences down gullets magnified ten thousandfold by the miracles of modern technology. My long if quite accidental education in the art of the musical taught me among other things that those enchanting verses, on whose construction composers and lyricists often seemed to lavish more attention than they did on the choruses, and which to this day are usually neglected by professional singers, were not the gratuitous artistic flourishes I once thought they were, but had been originally designed for the strictly functional purpose of making bridges to span that awkward gap in conception between dialogue and song. And as my jazz education proceeded it became clear to me that, by some vast irony, none of the artists for whom these songs had originally been commissioned had ever been able to extract from them anything like the same depths of passion as the jazz champions, which means, among other things, that to this day, having once been infected by the art of Billie Holiday, I can never take the great mistresses of the musical comedy world seriously. I am sometimes told that in comparing a Billie Holiday with, say, an Ethel Merman or a Judy Garland I am confusing two categories. But a song is a song, and I am confusing nothing. I sometimes wonder if George Gershwin ever knew that the one occasion on which 'I Loves You, Porgy' was expressed with the dramatic intensity and earthy power it demands, was when Billie Holiday recorded it.

My faltering musical advance to professional status incorporated hundreds of nights on palais bandstands where the sheer wretchedness of most of the repertoire we were so handsomely paid to play forced me into other diversions, one of which was reading all the small print on my music parts, a diversion which not only acquainted me with the addresses and telephone numbers of every tripe-peddling music publisher in Britain, but also impressed on me yet again that whenever a song did happen to possess some kind of style, very likely it had been composed by one of that small group of composers, perhaps two dozen men who, I was now beginning to realize, represented a kind of professional élite. I noticed also that the number of new songs of this type appeared to be shrinking steadily, and that if the output of the Gershwins and the Kerns was anything to go by, there had been something very like a golden age between the two great wars, a period when apparently some sort of accidental balance had been struck between the sophistication of the best composers and the musical instincts of their audiences, before the moguls, mistaking their own musical imbecility for that of the general public, which really had quite good taste, had destroyed that balance by deliberately debasing the coinage of popular song.

Still later, I became a member of a co-operative group which, having no leader, was composed entirely of leaders, a unique fact of its existence which had a great deal to do with the impeccable government of its affairs and the immense success of its artistic policy. In this group, one of my extra-musical chores was to collect each night from the manager of whichever ballroom to which our agent had banished us, one of those printed sheets on which the performer is required to enter the titles and, where known, the authors of every song in his recital. The completed form is then sent to the Performing Right Society, which is thus able to gauge the frequency with which any song is being performed, and, therefore, the amount of the royalty accruing to each composer and lyricist. Now the co-operative group to which I refer was existing in the real world and not, sadly, in the Euphonia of Berlioz's dreams, which meant that we were obliged to include in our programmes at least a few items beneath our contempt. Under the circumstances the least I could do, on behalf of my partners as well as for myself, was to deprive the wretched composers of these wretched songs of the royalties to which they were rightfully entitled, by omitting their names from the sheet, which was filled instead with the names of my élite. My defence against accusations of unethical conduct is that I was at least meting out some kind of aesthetic justice, and that in any case, if the law will insist on equating three minutes of garbage with three minutes of artistry, then it must first breed a race of ballroom managers whose musical imbecility is mitigated by the ability to read the titles of songs on a slip of paper. Whether anyone ever analysed the sheets we returned each night I have no way of knowing, but on paper at least, we must have been the first jazz band in all history whose repertoire was limited to Gershwin and company.

It was around this period that, for a short interlude, a band came into being whose repertoire really was limited in this way. Serving for one round trip as a ship's musician on the New York run, I found myself in a quintet which had been sentenced, for no misdemeanour that any of its members knew of, to play nightly for the patrons of the first class nightclub. We were not two hours out of Southampton Water before the five of us reached a decision. In order to make the time crawl less slowly, we would see how long we could continue playing the music each night of one selected composer. We worked at our lists, and on the home run actually succeeded in producing a whole night of Gershwin, another of Porter, and another of Kern, even though our performance was seriously impeded by the odd fact that our pianist, who had been press-ganged by a demented purser minutes before we sailed, had until that moment restricted his professional appearances to the saloon bar of a public house just outside Eastleigh. Each night we half-hoped that some discerning member of the audience, by which we meant someone who was still breathing, would approach the bandstand and say something to indicate that he had noticed what we were up to, but none ever did. Perhaps it was symbolic of the anarchic games we were playing on that trip that throughout the voyage home the elements flung our ship like a cork across the waters, causing the bass drum time and again to crash over the edge of the bandstand and go rolling like a juggernaut across the dance floor, where it would come to rest rocking gently to and fro against the tables, rattling as it did so with the noise of the contraband stuffed inside it. Magically the storm endowed smoked salmon sandwiches with the ability to fly at the same time as it deprived those who carried the sandwiches of the ability to walk, and eventually causing almost the entire passenger list to retire behind closed cabin doors, until, by the time we were back within a few hours of Southampton Water the long, lit corridors of the first class quarters looked like a reconstruction of the *Marie Celeste* the morning after. But still we ground out our medleys, too intrigued now by our self-imposed task to bother about a minor detail like going down with all hands. While the plates flew across the galley and the cutlery, dropped soundlessly on to the carpeted fringes of the nightclub floor, while silent waiters laid the tables with cloths dampened to hold the glasses, we presented our resumés of Gershwin and company, watched only by a couple of drunken honeymooners, the kitchen hands leaning against the galley doors, arms folded, legs braced against the storm, and a few social climbers who had sneaked in from the tourist deck.

If that bizarre audience was ignorant of the nature of our repertoire, who can blame it when the jazz and musical comedy worlds themselves often betray the same ignorance? There is the well-known story of the trumpeter Oran 'Hot Lips' Page announcing to his club audience that in honour of the great Cole Porter, sitting over there at that table, it would give him great pleasure to play one of Mr Porter's best-loved songs, at which he then proceeded to play two rousing choruses of George Gershwin's 'Embraceable You'. A view from the other side was once given in a *New Yorker* profile on Porter, which included the hair-raising claim, 'Some of the Swing boys are inclined to pout at Porter's musical tricks as compared to their own.' Even if we agree to overlook the fact that a writer whose experience embraces the extraordinary apparition of pouting Swing boys is not one to inspire a reader's confidence, it still has to be said that the statement is not so much false as senseless, and it is senseless because the true relationship between songwriters like Porter and the jazzmen who sometimes use his songs as a point of departure has not been perceived. Only when the nature of that relationship is appreciated does it become clear why there should have existed so strong a link between what might appear at first glance to be two unconnected musical forms.

The jazz musician is someone who, by definition, is not concerned with the published melody. On the contrary, he is only in business at all because he presumes the ability to create superior melodies of his own. His concern is not with the melody which a Cole Porter might produce, but with the harmonies underlying that melody. The sole currency in which the jazz soloist deals is harmony. Harmony is his job, his profession, his vocation, his one abiding interest. The jazz art is the art of creating melodic variations based on an existing harmonic structure, and so it follows with the inevitability of truism that, so far as the jazz soloist is concerned, the most interesting composers must be those whose harmonic sequences are the most favourably constructed with a view to improvisation. It was therefore inevitable that the moment the jazz soloist perceived the complexity of Kern's harmonic legerdemain, the apparently endless harmonic resource of Gershwin's mind, the stark originality of some of Irving Berlin's inspired guesses, then all these writers should be drawn into a world of which they had no knowledge. Ira Gershwin once remarked in a letter to me that 'at one time I thought jazz meant absolute improvisation on the melody of a song'. The truth is that the melody doesn't come into it. By substituting the word 'harmony' for 'melody' in Mr Gershwin's statement, we can arrive at an extremely useful working definition of jazz.

For this reason, that the jazz musician has usually relied on the musical comedy composers to supply him with a high proportion of his raw material, it is understandable, perhaps even inevitable, that the apprentice musician, who began by learning Lester Young's solo recording of 'Lady Be Good' parrot-fashion, should have found himself twenty years later watching the London revival of the show for which that most durable of jazz themes had originally been composed.

Porgy and Bess: Ray Charles and Cleo Laine (1976)

In 1935 when the first public performance of *Porgy and Bess* took place, the immediate result was a cultural confusion which would have been comical had it not also been unfortunate for its performers and costly for those who had invested in its finances. It was also acutely disappointing for its composer, who never lived long enough to enjoy the eventual vindication of the work, although perhaps we need not feel too badly on that account, for George Gershwin, buttressed by an impregnable and wholly justified self-esteem when it came to his own work, appears to have known perfectly well that the ultimate survival of the opera was a foregone conclusion. Unlike a great many composers whose premature death has sadly anticipated the belated acceptance of their work, Gershwin is utterly lacking in that pathos which comes from unjustifiable rejection. On the contrary, the ghost of that confident Gershwin smile, wreathed in cirrus clouds of cigar smoke, seems to preside over every performance of *Porgy and Bess*, just as the Cheshire Cat's did over Wonderland. Gershwin could afford to smile, because he knew what he was bequeathing to us.

The critics, however, did not know. Their disarray on the morning after the New York premiere of *Porgy and Bess* may reasonably be described as prodigious. Virgil Thomson described what he had half-heard as 'crooked opera and halfway folklore,' while Olin Downes in the *New York Times* grumbled that 'the style is at one moment of opera and another of operetta or sheer Broadway entertainment,' no doubt leaving the opera lovers dismayed at his implication that opera can never be entertaining. Of course every creative artist worth his salt has to endure this sort of twaddle, and Gershwin, having paid his tormentors a tribute that none of them deserved, by answering their complaints in an article in the *New York Times*, got on with his next score. Later the critics, shamelessly continuing to conduct their own education in public, recanted. Thomson decided that the crooked opera was in fact 'a beautiful piece of music whose melodic invention is abundant and pretty distinguished,' while Mr Downes, by now mysteriously reconciled to hybrid strains in the work, revealed that 'Gershwin has taken a substantial step, and advanced the cause of native opera.'

But the critical structure which really gave the game away was one by a Mr Gilman of the *Herald Tribune*, who wrote, apparently with a perfectly straight face, that the tunes in Gershwin's opera were too *good*. Bringing the mighty engines of his musical intellect to bear on the problem of *Porgy and Bess*, Mr Gilman decided that though Gershwin had incorporated into his score some song hits 'which will doubtless enhance his fame and popularity,' it had been mistaken of the composer to do so, for, so far as these song hits were concerned, 'they mar the work. They are its cardinal weakness. They are the blemish on its musical integrity.' Happy world, in which the thematic balance of an operatic score might so easily be adjusted by a mere telephone call to the offices of the *Herald Tribune*. Fortunately for posterity, Gershwin omitted to ask Gilman's advice before finalizing his score, and no more was ever heard on the subject from that perceptive gentleman – which is a great pity, for it was Gilman, who, for all his carping foolishness, had touched on the heart of the matter. In retrospect we can sympathize with a critic whose sensibilities have become so benumbed by constant exposure to legitimate opera devoid of melody that the sudden confrontation with a hybrid opera bubbling over with it should prove too rich a dish for his enfeebled musical digestion to cope with. Gilman's predicament, which may be taken as representative of classical criticism in general, is enough to make a cat laugh. Having learned to live with musicians who possessed every attribute of the great composer except the ability to write a good tune, the Gilmans of this world had actually conditioned themselves to the point where the presence in a musical-dramatic work of a good tune actually disqualified it from inclusion in the operatic category altogether. The false syllogism of the Gilman school of criticism ran as follows: X is a much venerated opera of the modern school; X has no discernible melodies; therefore no venerated opera of the modern school must possess any discernible melodies. It was as though the British Admiralty, having noticed how well Lord Nelson was doing with one eye, were to cashier every officer with two.

Gershwin, however, had been raised in the toughest of all schools, where you either came up with a good tune or you went out and found a job. That is the vital fact about his background which separates him from every other operatic composer who ever lived. When you were selling a song like 'Swanee', there was no tenor's rich vibrato and throbbing jugular to help the demonstration, no lush orchestral effects to prop up the structure, no pretentious wedding of plot and characterization to excuse a hackneyed harmonic pattern. Most significant of all, your singer was performing *in English*, so there was not even the mysticism of an incomprehensible foreign language to cow the listener into humble respect. All you had was your melody, and it had better be a good one. These ethics of the songplugger's booth are as remote from the European world of opera as the isles of the Hesperides, but that is not to say that Tin Pan Alley writers remained in total ignorance of the world of so-called classical achievement. Gershwin as a child had been sandbagged by Rubinstein's *Melody in F*, just as Harry Warren as a juvenile had been stunned into reverence by the arias of Puccini. It was Gershwin, however, who became the first, and also the last, gifted popular songwriter to aspire to the classical form without paying the price of his own melodic vitality.

Now, at the time of the composition of *Porgy and Bess* the American public at large had little interest in or understanding of conventional classical opera. Sensing the fundamental absurdity of a heroine complaining that she is dying of consumption when it is plain to see that she is thirty-five pounds overweight, and bravely refusing to be browbeaten into an enthusiasm it did not feel by the orotundities of operatic Italian, America stayed away in its millions. There was, of course, the occasional exception to opera's lack of verisimilitude; when Enrico Caruso appeared at the Met in *Tosca* in 1906, the *New York World* reported next morning that 'so great was the realism in the torture scene that a man in one of the orchestra stalls fainted. The auditorium was in darkness and the affair caused some commotion. When the usher started to drag the man out someone attempted to help him, but in his excitement he grabbed the usher's leg and threw him. Finally the victim of his emotions became conscious and peace was restored.' As for the German variety of operatic inscrutability, in this regard the American public was as one with the Englishman in the Wodehouse story who, stumbling into a dark room where a stolen prize pig has been hidden, runs out screaming, 'There's a man in there. And he's speaking German.' In fact, so resolutely was the popular face turned away from opera that its more outrageous absurdities became a target for the philistines. In 1936, the very year in which *Porgy and Bess* was fighting for its artistic life, the continent rocked with laughter when Otis B. Driftwood, alias Groucho Marx, discovering that a great operatic tenor might get paid as much as a thousand dollars a night, replies incredulously, 'A thousand dollars a night? Just to sing? Why, for seventy-five cents you can get a record of Minnie the Moocher. For a buck and a quarter you can get Minnie.' The essence of that joke is that Gershwin belonged in the same huckstering world as Driftwood, and yet was now attempting to cross over.

The attempt cost him considerable professional heartburn, for apart from the difficulty of selling the opera itself, Gershwin soon found that he had compromised his own commercial standing with the Driftwoods of showbiz with whom he was obliged to parley. In that same year of 1935, the RKO producer Pandro S. Berman had attempted to make Lily Pons a popular movie star. The attempt failed because, as Berman later observed, 'I don't think the bulk of the American public ever listens to opera. Opera has never made any money on the stage, it's always been supported by the community. The songs aren't popular and the people who do them are not attractive enough for the most part.' Berman's quixotic campaign to launch Miss Pons on screen ran concurrent with his production of the Astaire–Rogers movies which ushered in a new era of screen musicals and rescued his studio from insolvency. And Berman was a fanatical fancier of the great school of American songwriters. He had recruited Porter, Berlin and Kern, and when the time came for him to desist from Miss Pons and make the picture which eventually became *Shall We Dance*, he wanted the Gershwin brothers very badly. He wanted them simply because he revered them and knew what they were capable of. But now, in 1936, the existence of *Porgy and Bess* stood like a giant impediment across the path of the plan. There were people in California who believed that once you write an opera you become artistically damned. Producers and moneymen actually sat down and asked each other whether Gershwin had now become too esoteric a writer for Hollywood to trade with any longer. That was the extent to which opera was considered to be an utterly un-American, minority interest.

In retrospect we contemplate the score of *Porgy and Bess* and wonder what the moguls were worried about. Above all we wonder what Gershwin felt. On the one hand the Gilmans of this world admonished him for putting hits in an opera; and on the other, movie people admonished him with equal solemnity for not having put enough hits in. Who was right? Gershwin was right, as always. Whatever the virtues and demerits of *Porgy and Bess* as an operatic work – and its acceptance across the world was confirmed a generation ago – we can see that when he came to write his score Gershwin brought to the task all the wonderful thematic inventiveness which had for the past fifteen years been elevating the popular song form to a kind of art. No wonder the mixture was too heady for the sobersides of musical criticism. Till now operatic writing had come from the conservatory side of the great divide but now, for the first time, an opera appeared which came from a world where the melody was the beginning and end of musical life. America was, of course, extremely fortunate to get a George Gershwin, someone capable of synthesizing the classical European tradition with indigenous American styles. *Porgy and Bess* and *Rhapsody in Blue* are to American music what *Huckleberry Finn* and *Life on the Mississippi* are to American literature, a sign of the emergent native school. And just as Twain's novels have come to enjoy a dual life, as works of art and as repositories of the best jokes and the deepest compassion, so Gershwin's opera has also come to enjoy two independent careers, as a work of art and as a repository of some of the loveliest ballads and wittiest up-tempo swingers that he ever achieved.

All of which means that the material of *Porgy and Bess* has two faces; it is familiar to people in the dramatic context of DuBose Heyward's folk tale, and it is familiar also to quite a different set of people as part of the repertoire of performers who have no intention of reading DuBose Heyward's novel, and probably wouldn't approve if they did. What has happened to the opera is that its main themes exist today not only as arias but also as songs, and before somebody complains that 'aria' means 'song', let us acknowledge yet again the cultural gulf between the two words; one stands for an imported culture executed in an alien style; the other for an American form expressed in a colloquial style. No greater difference could ever exist between two synonyms, and the most eloquent proof of that is to place the score of *Porgy and Bess* alongside that of, say, Puccini's *Girl of the Golden West*, a bizarre attempt by an Italian to put Bret Harte to music. Both are valid works of art; both are tuneful operas; both look like passing into the traditional repertoire. But the contrast between them is so profound that the writer despairs of ever finding a metaphor to express it – until he remembers the simplest metaphor of all. *Porgy and Bess* is the stuff of which memorable recordings by Louis Armstrong, Ella Fitzgerald and Billie Holiday are made; *Girl of the Golden West* is not. I have no desire to slaughter Puccini to make a Gershwin holiday; for one thing, Harry Warren would never forgive me. In any case, the two works are not rivals for my affection, or indeed for anyone's. But what is significant if we are to grasp the enormity of what Gershwin was attempting when he wrote his opera, is that they are utterly different, and that it did not take the popular singers and instrumentalists of America very long to grasp the nature of that difference, and its vital importance to them. The process which culminates in the music on this album began as early as 10 July 1936, only nine months after *Porgy and Bess*'s New York opening. On that day a small group of jazz musicians, known in the vernacular as a pickup group, gathered to accompany Billie Holiday to cut four sides. One of the four was a blues, and two of the others were the work of that highly gifted and undeservedly forgotten songwriting contemporary of Gershwin's, Walter Donaldson; the fourth item was 'Summertime'. The session is famous enough today, but what has been overlooked about it is that not only was it the first session ever in which an accepted jazz artist plucked one of the themes from *Porgy and Bess* out of its context and recast it in a jazz mould, but also that this was the first Gershwin song Billie Holiday had ever recorded. Clearly to her, and to the musicians who accompanied her, who included Bunny Berigan, Artie Shaw and Joe Bushkin, something in the mood and structure of 'Summertime' had commended itself to their essentially jazz view of things. At the time Billie Holiday made that recording, Gershwin was in Hollywood, blithely dismissing the doubts of the moguls as to his commercial talent by writing two of the prettiest arias of his life, 'Foggy Day' and 'They Can't Take That Away From Me' (for two different productions), and it would be instructive to know if Gershwin ever heard that recording, and if he did, what he made of it. We know that he was not only sympathetic towards improvisations based on his songs, but also flattered by them, and that he considered that when Art Tatum played 'Liza' it was a great compliment to the song. But what, one wonders, would he have made of the drastic amendment to his work which the jazz performers had undertaken?

For the Holiday recording of 'Summertime' is, in its way, one of the most eloquent testimonies to the universality of Gershwin's music that was ever offered. From the first bar it is obvious that this is not Catfish Row or anything remotely like it. Any lullaby connotations have vanished. The tempo is up, and the interpretation, to use an old phrase of Don Redman's, hot and anxious. The instrumentalists, particularly Berigan, revel in the climacteric of the song's melodic line which comes on the 'hush little baby' phrase, as the song is suddenly uplifted from the Minor to the Major tonality. What Holiday, Berigan and company had done was to put Gershwin's work to the only honest test there can ever be for any work of art, that is, to look it straight in the eye and ignore all the extraneous social factors; they had dismissed from their minds any thought of the portentous issues of native American opera, of the red plush and chandeliers of the archetypal opera house, of composers with alien names and beards like horses' tails; they had chased all that mumbo-jumbo from their minds and discovered what the music itself actually sounded like. Today we tend to forget that a beautiful theme like 'Summertime' ever required to be prised out of its operatic setting in order to be rediscovered by jazz performers. But in 1936 that simple act of aesthetic justice must have looked like the most wilful heresy. 'Summertime' blazed the trail, and as the years went by and more and more successful revivals of the opera took place, other items followed into the popular repertoire. 'I Got Plenty O' Nuttin'' was next, and then 'It Ain't Necessarily So'. For the sumptuous rhetoric of the love ballads to seep into the mass consciousness, rather more time was required. 'Bess, You Is My Woman', 'My Man's Gone Now', 'I Loves You, Porgy', ballads as tender and as compassionate as any the Gershwin brothers ever created, became widely known much more gradually. How such specialized items passed into the standard heritage is uncertain, except that in such cases, where the material is good enough, a kind of musical osmosis always seems to come joyously into operation. Perhaps it was a matter of the occasional enlightened night club singer or ambitious jazz vocalist slipping one of the *Porgy* items into an act somewhere; perhaps fragments were heard on radio or glimpsed on television sets. But whatever the process, today it is complete; forty years after the New York opening, the bulk of the score of *Porgy and Bess* is intimately familiar to millions of people who would not step inside an opera house if you paid them Musicians' Union scale for sitting there.

Since the introduction of the long-playing record made it practicable to release at one time a substantial proportion of the work, there have been several jazz or pseudo-jazz versions, only two of which seem to have had much importance. Both were collaborations, and both were interesting for the way they jettisoned the DuBose Heyward aspect of *Porgy*, the plot and dialogue aspect, in favour of an examination of the quality of the songs. The first of these was the orchestral exhibition which Gil Evans once staged for the benefit of Miles Davis; the other, very much more germane to the present discussion, was the album in which Norman Granz brought together the two greatest jazz singers of the age, Louis Armstrong and Ella Fitzgerald. What was enlightening about both the Davis–Evans and the Louis–Ella versions was the way they demonstrated that there are as many ways of interpreting 'Summertime' and 'It Ain't Necessarily So' as there are artists prepared to attempt them. The connoisseur may revel in the Louis–Ella album without feeling in the slightest that by doing so he is thereby compromising his own reaction to the opera in its conventional form. In the same way, there is no reason why the Louis–Ella version should be considered the last word on the subject, and for some time the idea of a Ray Charles–Cleo Laine partnership had been in the wind.

Nobody will be surprised by the choice of Ray Charles, who of all male singers today is the one whose idiosyncrasies of style and diction are perhaps best suited to the treatment of the songs from the opera. The grainy quality in Charles's voice, a kind of vocal chiaroscuro which makes it so easy to identify, is especially well suited to themes originally written for characters who lived life so desperately close to the bone and who were no strangers to wretchedness as well as to exultation. In fact, Charles's performance recalls the point which was first raised all those years ago by Billie Holiday's 'Summertime'. Gershwin had written his material so that it might eventually be filtered through the conservatory correctitude of singers like Todd Duncan, the original Porgy, a man so steeped in the operatic attitude that when the invitation to sing for Gershwin first arrived, he refused: 'I just wasn't very interested. I was teaching in a university in Washington, and I thought of George Gershwin as being Tin Pan Alley and something beneath me.' But once the jazz performers got hold of the material, and began to sing and play it without the constraints of dramatic situations, which faction was then interpreting Gershwin's music the more appropriately? I remember that years ago, when I was a working musician, there was a general feeling among my fellow players that there was a certain incongruity about the meticulous pronunciations and the unbending textual readings of the score as rendered by conventional opera singers; we used to wonder how far the process of exactitude might not go, and whether one day we would wake to hear some musical purist 'improving' 'It Ain't Necessarily So' to the point where it had become 'It Is Not Necessarily Thus'. We suspected that it was Billie and Ella and Louis who were being truer to Gershwin's operatic muse than he ever knew, and that it was performers like them – and Ray Charles – and not the academy-grilled voices from the operatic schools who really brought the characters of Catfish Row to vibrant life. Were we right to think that? Or were we just displaying the cultural bigotry of which young jazz musicians, over-eager to compensate for the scandalous neglect of their art, are often guilty? A fascinating question, but the duality of *Porgy*'s reputation renders it unanswerable. Both approaches are valid, and both work, but I do feel that the versions by Louis and Ray Charles have enriched my understanding of the music Gershwin wrote for the opera. Now that Charles has actually done the job, it seems inevitable that he should eventually have had a shot at it.

The case of Cleo Laine, however, is very different indeed. You might call it unique. If one wanted to find a locale as far as possible spiritually as well as geographically from Catfish Row, Southall in the county of Middlesex in the south of England would not be a bad choice. That was where Cleo was born, and where the vowel sounds of her small-talk acquired that slight but delightfully whimsical flattened effect which is the hallmark of the true Cockney. For more than twenty years before she made this album Cleo had been working steadily, at first in London jazz clubs, then in British dance halls, later on television and across Europe. Her marriage to her boss, composer-bandleader John Dankworth, had much to do with the fact that through the 1960s she began extending her repertoire in the most unorthodox way, adding to the usual items like 'Riding High', 'I Got Rhythm' and 'Happiness Is Just A Thing Called Joe', certain works by gentlemen not previously acknowledged as effective songwriters. These included T. S. Eliot, W. H. Auden, Thomas Hardy and William Shakespeare. There arrived a juncture at one highly prestigious music festival when everything was ready for a performance of Kurt Weill's *Seven Deadly Sins* except the proximity of the lady supposed to sing it, Miss Lotte Lenya. Cleo deputized, and has retained that difficult work in her repertoire ever since, where it jostles with Ellington and Schoenberg, Marie Lloyd and Gershwin, in the most variegated corpus of material ever assembled by a vocal artist.

There is an extent to which she has remained a prophet unsung in her own country, at least comparatively speaking, because although she has been acknowledged in Britain for many years as by far the most gifted specialist in her field, and also as an actress whose ability was for a long time neglected by purblind, tone deaf impresarios, it is in the United States over the last few years that something like a popular understanding of her singing has come about. To the challenge of the songs from *Porgy and Bess* she brings several qualities which are rare and one or two which are surely unique. Perhaps the most astonishing aspect of her vocal equipment is its range, over several octaves, and the apparent ease with which she is able to navigate its upper limits. Because this is an album devoted not to the opera but to transcriptions from the opera, the sacred texts of the songs have no more been strictly observed than the text of 'Body And Soul' was strictly observed when Coleman Hawkins played it. At a juncture like the last cadenza when Cleo sings 'My man is dead', the voice soars above the written text in a way which is highly dramatic as well as musical, for up to this point the listener has not suspected the extent to which Cleo is liberated in her singing from any of the conventional worries about range. The same effect is created in her second verse of 'Summertime', and again and again after that right across the entire album. Perhaps the most moving use of range is to be found in 'Bess, You Is My Woman', where Charles and Cleo, possessors of two highly individual and subjective styles, arrive at a fusion which gives that most lovely song one of its loveliest readings ever.

As the cardinal truth about improvisation is that in order to justify its intrusive presence it must always improve on the original, the question arises about the degree to which the two singers have succeeded in bringing to *Porgy and Bess* anything which singers of the Todd Duncan–Anne Brown school were unable to give it. The shortest answer is the Ray Charles version of 'There's A Boat Dat's Leavin' Soon For New York'. From the moment that he foreshortens the word 'leaving' and makes 'soon' a syncopated accent, Gershwin's design undergoes a rigorous amendment without its texture being damaged by so much as a single blemish. If a word like 'swing' has not by now been muddied by misuse to the point where it ceases to have any meaning at all, then it could be applied to this track. In fact, the 'Boat Dat's Leavin'' is part of a group of three songs, with 'It Ain't Necessarily So' and 'I Got Plenty O' Nuttin'', which brought to the original score, whether Gershwin meant them to or not, the unadulterated spirit of jazz music, which is why in the past those musicians I spoke of always felt slightly unsure of their own reactions to strictly correct operatic renderings of the opera. On the other hand, the popularizing of fragments from *Porgy and Bess* has occasionally been done at the expense of some of the best lyrics. Through an accident of circumstance 'I Got Plenty O' Nuttin'' has generally come to be regarded as a man's song, so that when once again we are reminded of the woman's part in the original setting, as we are in this album, then we realize that some of the lyrics which Cleo sings are not only excellent but hardly ever heard outside an opera house.

Operas are not like sheaves of songs or even like musical comedies. They are musical works whose calculated artificiality is based on the convention that there is a world in which nobody ever says anything without singing it. This means that in addition to the songs or arias, there are always fragments which have been composed for the expression of small or passing thoughts, or fragmentary observations by the characters. When you are a Gershwin, possessed of such profligate melodic invention, you are always likely to fling away the most priceless thoughts on some of the most transient moments in your libretto. It is virtually impossible for a popular singer to record a performance of 'Honey Man' or 'Strawberries' or 'Crab Man'; they are altogether too brief and too nebulous to sustain such a treatment. But in the context of any treatment of *Porgy and Bess* they emerge as they do here, as brilliant miniatures of the composer's art, which contribute to the conjuring of the Catfish Row mood out of all proportion to their fleeting brevity. Even more valuable, because much less well known, is the theme which Cleo sings, 'They Pass By Singin''. When this album was being prepared, Ira Gershwin suggested to Norman Granz that this small musical moment, utterly overlooked whenever discussion of the opera has been mounted, might bear a close examination. It does indeed; in a world where the recording companies waited forty years after that New York opening before releasing any complete operatic version of *Porgy and Bess* – imagine Puccini and company being kept waiting half as long – the presence on this album of 'They Pass By Singin'' is at once a bonus for the listener and a salutary reminder that when dealing with a great creative artist it is never wise to assume that there remains nothing of his work with which we are not familiar. Even the most blasé Gershwin buff is likely to be reduced to tremulous adolescent excitement by the brief episode of 'They Pass By Singin''.

There remains the question of improvised music, of the kind which so intrigued and delighted Gershwin whenever he heard it. Unlike several of his fellow composers, Gershwin took no offense when jazz musicians borrowed his themes to use them as a pretext for improvisation; instead, he took the juxtaposition of jazz and his own songs as a high compliment, which indeed it was. And just as in the original Louis–Ella version of *Porgy and Bess* Louis played the dual role of singer-instrumentalist, so in this new version Ray Charles the singer gives way at regular intervals to Charles the instrumentalist, with two important differences from the Louis–Ella session.

One of those differences constitutes an innovation of great importance in the method of presentation. Performances where a singer-musician plays both roles within the compass of a single performance are common enough; ever since Louis popularized that combination and men like Teagarden followed his example, we have become accustomed to the jazz man who lays aside his instrument to sing a chorus or two. In this version of *Porgy and Bess*, instrumental jazz has been used in a revolutionary new way. Instead of singing and playing on the same track Charles reserves his keyboard interludes for separate independent tracks which, intervening between the vocal tracks, have the effect either of telegraphing the nature of Gershwin's raw material so that when the vocal version arrives we are already conversant with its contours; or alternatively following the vocal version to show us what remains of Gershwin's operatic achievement when the words are subtracted from the equation.

The outcome is both enjoyable for the quality of Charles's playing and extremely revealing so far as Gershwin's melodic innovation is concerned. When themes like 'I Got Plenty O' Nuttin'' and 'It Ain't Necessarily So' are divested of their lyrics, we can see more clearly than before how very close Gershwin managed to get, in the purely musical sense, to the ambience of Catfish Row. For the themes from *Porgy and Bess*, when placed in the hands of a practiced jazz performer, are seen to be not just suitable themes for improvisation, but surprisingly, themes suffused with the spirit of the Blues. I say surprisingly because Catfish Row notwithstanding, Gershwin was the product of Tin Pan Alley and Broadway; that he should have understood the nature of the challenge before him, and to have assimilated the essence of the characters in his opera can be seen in retrospect as one of the most astounding feats of even his astounding career.

The other important difference between Louis's instrumental playing in *Porgy and Bess* and the playing of Ray Charles is that while Louis was restricted by the nature of his art to one instrument, Charles has been able to vary the keyboard effect of the piano by switching instruments from time to time. The appearance of the electric piano on this album is one of those fairly rare instances where its presence is not an intrusion while the choice of celeste for the 'Strawberry' track has the most wonderful effect; it's rhythmic balm in the midst of performances bursting with animation. It's worth mentioning in passing that in the conventional piano tracks, particularly 'I Got Plenty O' Nuttin'', there are several manneristic reminders that a long time ago, when he was beginning his career, Charles was a slavish admirer of Nat Cole. But such is the nature of public response to *Porgy and Bess* that whenever news of the opera is received the instinctive reaction is to go for 'Summertime', Gershwin's marvellous simulation of a folk lullaby. Charles plays organ, and achieves a reshaping of the whole conception of the song, which somehow remains respectful to what Gershwin had in mind. Which brings me to my one reservation about this whole album. The only thing seriously wrong with it is that nobody has yet discovered a way of letting George Gershwin hear it. If only he could have heard it, I think I know what his reaction would have been.

Pal Joey (1970)

I find it gratifying to discover thirty years after the event what *Pal Joey* is really about. Its true theme was apparently missed when John O'Hara first published it – even the astute Edmund Wilson mistook it for a satire which 'represented a contraction of O'Hara's interests' – and any chance there might have been of a reappraisal vanished when the original became hopelessly overlaid, first on Broadway, later in Hollywood.

For years I had assumed that *Pal Joey* was more or less as Lorenz Hart and Frank Sinatra painted him. I should have known better. Because of its musical transmogrifications, *Pal Joey* has always been regarded as a lightweight item even for a mere welter-weight like O'Hara, a loose bundle of picaresque episodes with no central vision, a book about nothing of any more consequence than a few desultory seductions. All of which is unjust, because if it is about anything, *Pal Joey* is about a revolution, a social revolution which overturned the leisure habits of a continent, seen through the puzzled eyes of one of its victims.

At the start of the story, Joey is a nightclub singer, what Wilson describes as 'an amoeba of the nightlife of the Jitterbug era', an opportunist reasonably content with his lot. His work seems congenial enough, and it gives him ample openings to indulge a septic ego by pursuing, and usually catching, a long succession of attractive girls. But soon this picture begins to alter. Joey is not so pleased with his existence after all. He changes jobs with ominous frequency, seems to be haunted by the fear of a vast professional abyss opening up at his feet, and is aware that both his working conditions and those who impose them upon him are often contemptible. We begin to realize that Joey is a man whose options are closing in on him, but it is only through his correspondence with his old friend Ted that he is made to see this for himself.

At first Ted and Joey seem to be equals, a couple of also-rans who have shared a common musical past and who are still struggling, each in his own way, to escape second-class status. There is a strong camaraderie between them. When the story opens Ted has loaned Joey fifty dollars and Joey is returning thirty. But as the letters cross the professional gulf separating the two men widens, slowly at first, then more quickly, until in the end they are too far adrift ever to make contact again. Ted is a national, an international figure, while Joey is – what? Only a name which might crop up from time to time when Ted reminisces, an embarrassment whose failure can be rendered palatable to old friends only when thrust deep into a romanticized past.

Why has Joey failed where Ted succeeded? We know that Ted is a violinist, that he forms a band, that he breaks attendance records, becomes a brand image. Joey makes passing reference to Ted's triumphs at two places, the Palomar and the Paramount, and sends out cries for help which his own pride renders so oblique that Ted can have found no trouble ignoring them. At the very end Joey erupts violently. He is alone in a rooming-house writing to Ted when he suddenly reveals that he is not a singer after all, but a failed musician:

> *I often think to myself that what if I turned out to be a Channcey Morehouse and a Dave Tough? That would mean I was a really good drummer, but not the lug that does not know a flammadiddle from a high hat. I put on such a good act here in Chi that I kid myself and think I do not remember how to play.*

Finally he is too maddened to care what he says:

> *Ted old friend, how the hell are you and how does it feel to be rich? Will bet you put your dough into an insurance annuity and send the rest home to your mother. I never saw you even pick up a tab for four mocha Java coffees, you cheap larceny jerk if ever there was one.*

We leave him sitting there awaiting the arrival of a prostitute, embittered by the suspicion that Ted has had all the luck, that if only the cards had been dealt differently it might have been him, Joey, in the money. And he is absolutely right.

In 1935, not long after the repeal of the Volstead Act, a Chicago clarinettist called Benny Goodman conceived the plan of forming a jazz-orientated dance band. It was the best idea Goodman ever had. Now that Prohibition was ended, the jazzmen of Capone's speakeasies needed a new public. Inadvertently Goodman stumbled upon it. On 21 August 1935, in the Palomar Ballroom, Los Angeles, he saw that the dancers were congregating round the bandstand. The Swing Age had begun. Less than two years later, at the Paramount Theatre, New York, 21,000 paid to hear him in one day. He and his rivals, Artie Shaw, Tommy Dorsey, Harry James, became film stars, millionaires, world figures, and, long before the Swing Age petered out in the 1940s, dance hall jazz had become a mechanistic thing administered by baton-waving businessmen. It was the New Style, and relics like Joey were done for at thirty.

It is Joey's dawning realization of all this that makes him send Ted harebrained moneymaking ideas, but not so harebrained that they could not work. At one stage he advises Ted to anticipate the coming war and get his band into the forces, 'the first Swing band in uniform'. It sounds mad, but O'Hara wrote his book in 1939, and five years later the missing body of Major Glenn Miller had already become one of the cultural curiosities of the twentieth century. Joey and Ted are complementary figures in the American Dream, and for every Ted there have to be ten thousand Joeys, stranded by the shifting tides of showbiz fashion, cut off by a revolution whose terms they cannot or will not accept. A generation later Ted's own group was jettisoned from a base in a Liverpool cellar. One day in the 1980s the Liverpudlians will themselves meet the same fate. And when that day comes, we could do worse than quote Joey, 'Merry Christmas, as the saying goes.'

Songwriters (1989)

I met my first famous songwriter in a New York apartment in the autumn of 1957. His name was Sam Coslow, and I had retained enough of my elementary education in the local picture palaces to know that he had been responsible for putting a great many words in Bing Crosby's mouth. This did not interest me much. There had always been something about the gradient of Crosby's ears that put me off him. But there was one point about Coslow which did interest me. In 1934 he and his partner, Arthur Johnston, had been the first team to grab at the commercial opportunities presented by the belated repeal of Prohibition. Their song, 'Cocktails For Two', a celebratory hymn to the joys of getting tipsy, had been one of the great moneymakers of its year. It had then been quietly forgotten.

Years later, during the war, a maverick drummer named Lindley Armstrong 'Spike' Jones seized upon 'Cocktails For Two' and subjected it to such vicious derision that in three minutes it had been reduced to a pile of rubble which nobody would ever take seriously again.

Jones's slapstick version of 'Cocktails For Two' was for a while one of the world's most popular recordings. Now that I was face to face with its composer, it seemed too good an opportunity to miss. With the bald callousness of youth, I asked Coslow to describe his feelings when the Jones outrage first reached him.

Without hesitating, he replied: 'My first instinct was to reach for my attorney, but when they told me the Jones version had sold a million, I reached for my accoutant instead.' And then, having done his anecdotal duty for the benefit of a brash stranger with a funny accent, he turned away and chatted of other things.

That exchange between us, brief as it may have been, was profoundly educational, because it taught me, at the very outset of my pursuit of distinguished songwriters, never to believe a word they told you. It was perfectly clear that Coslow, who must have been confronted with the same unfeeling question a thousand times, had formulated a stock reply, mildly amusing and pleasantly flavoured with just a tincture of modesty and self-reproach.

In later years, during other close encounters of the absurd kind, I was invariably offered the same kind of glib anecdotal response by writers who had learned to their cost that most interviewers are more interested in a good story than a good song. The truth is that neither Coslow nor most of his contemporaries had much of interest to say about their big successes. They had written them, that was all, and most of the recollections were bogus.

The temptation to believe all the alluring white lies is a danger in tracing the history of any of the arts. Did John Stuart Mill's maid really burn the only existing copy of the first volume of Carlyle's *The French Revolution*? Did John Steinbeck's dog really eat the first draft of *Of Mice and Men*? Did Webster Booth really keep goal for Aston Villa?

The seductive nature of this sort of thing is always likely to distract from or even eclipse the real issues. The problem looms especially large in the songwriting world, which has always been hopelessly unacademic, insanely cavalier about its own annals, and forgetful of itself to the brink of amnesia. The delver into the musical past realizes the magnitude of his task only when he does come across the rare exception. Ira Gershwin's *Lyrics on Several Occasions* saves many brands from the burning, and P. G. Wodehouse's *Bring on the Girls* is the most revealing as well as the most readable theatrical memoir of its epoch. But if Gershwin and Wodehouse can fill in so many thousands of missing details, what further millions must have been lost beyond recovery by men too busy or too disingenuous or too lazy to save anything, say anything, write anything?

There have been a few notable exceptions, men who took the time and trouble to work up a genuine relationship with their inquisitors, and who told the truth as far as they could remember it. Among them was E. Y. Harburg, a lyric writer of great wit and whimsicality whose biggest popular success, 'Over The Rainbow', has distracted attention from much finer work.

It was Harburg whose ready-made, all-purpose reply to the inevitable inquiry was so diverting that it constituted a cunning evasion of the question rather than a reply to it. In 1932 Harburg, whose flourishing electrical supply business was wiped out by the Wall Street Crash, turned to songwriting. With his very first effort, he became celebrated. Collaborating with a man called Jay Gorney, Harburg produced the definitive song of the Great Depression, 'Brother, Can You Spare A Dime?'.

Forty years after the event, I asked Harburg if 'Brother, Can You Spare A Dime?' had been the first popular song to take the Depression as its theme. Harburg's reply: 'Listen, until I wrote that song there *was* no Depression.'

Just as memorable, and extremely wise, is a remark credited to Jerome Kern by the English composer Vivian Ellis. As a young man, Ellis was constantly being advised to make his music simpler if he wished to make any money. One day at a reception he spotted Kern, the Grand Master of the notoriously complex, and decided to ask his advice. Kern's reply: 'Go on being uncommercial, young man; there's a lot of money in it.'

Kern's life is more fully known than some, largely because his apprentice years in Edwardian London have proved surprisingly accessible to the intelligent researcher. He was also fortunate enough to be partnered for several years by P. G. Wodehouse, who has left all sorts of quaint glimpses of Kern going about his day-to-day business.

We know from Wodehouse that Kern was an insomniac, that he could be irascible, and that his pride in his craft turned him into a bully capable of browbeating even the Hollywood moguls. Once, when David Selznick asked him to play a few new tunes,

Kern stormed out saying, 'I don't give samples.' We know from the heroic researches of Andrew Lamb that in his bachelor days Kern shared a flat in Jermyn Street, that he married at Walton-on-Thames the daughter of the manager of The Swan public house and lived happily ever after, that he retained all his life a fond affection for the music of the Lancashire music hall composer Leslie Stuart.

One of the more sensational stories about the genesis of a popular song was circulated about himself by Noel Coward. It described the circumstances surrounding a sumptuous ballad of 1934, written for Yvonne Printemps to sing in *Conversation Piece.*

Inspiration for the ballad proved so elusive that Coward at last decided to ask C. B. Cochran to put back the opening by six months:

> *I poured myself a large whisky and soda, dined in grey solitude, poured myself another, even larger, whisky and soda, and sat gloomily envisaging everybody's disappointment and facing the fact that I should never write any more music until the day I died. The whisky did little to banish my gloom, but there was no more work to be done and I didn't care if I became as fried as a coot, so I gave myself another drink and decided to go to bed.*
>
> *I switched off the lights at the door and noticed that there was one lamp left on by the piano. I walked automatically to turn it off, sat down and played 'I'll Follow My Secret Heart' straight through in G Flat, a key I had never played in before.*

Coward evidently believed that the unfamiliar key only compounded the mystery. In fact, it may go some way towards explaining it. The unfamiliar alignments of a strange key can sometimes have the most inspiriting effect on the executant. But the anecdote, which is almost certainly true, underlines the baffling nebulosity of the songwriting craft.

The American composer Arthur Schwartz used to consider 'How did you write that?' to be a rude question, yet was always ready with an amusing story to explain himself. His most successful song, 'Dancing In The Dark', is unusual in that it attempts a wider range than the usual theme of romantic love.

Schwartz once described to me how he and his lyric writing partner Howard Dietz, resolved to write a song with some sort of philosophic content, took the title from a book on the shelves, and produced a song in which dancing is an allegory for life.

True or false? In his autobiography, Dietz says of the song: 'I thought it was dull. Time and applause have taken the dullness out of it.' Schwartz so admired Dietz's facetiousness that when he heard I was to compile a radio obituary of his old partner, he took me to lunch just to make sure I knew all the jokes.

There was the apology to an outraged hostess for having been sick in mid-dinner. 'Don't worry. I brought up the white wine with the fish'; the defence against his employers at MGM who accused him of arriving late at the office each morning: 'Yes, but I always go home early'; and the one occasion on which he acknowledged defeat, when his invitation to Greta Garbo to come to dinner with him next Monday received the riposte 'How do I know if I'll be hungry on Monday?'

But the best subject for interviewing was certainly Ira Gershwin, who accepted you as an intellectual peer even though it was comically obvious that you were not. Ira's conversational style was curious. He never answered a question directly, but would go into some ancient anecdote whose point was that it did answer the question after all. I think that everything he said to me was truthful. But he was over eighty years old at the time and was no longer sure. When I complimented him on the charm of an ancient lyric to a song called 'Do What You Do', he looked surprised and denied ever having written the song.

> *'But all the reference books say you did.'*
>
> *'No. I think Gus Kahn wrote the words. He and I shared lyric duties in a show called* Show Girl, *and that was one of Gus's.'*
>
> *'Oh, I see.'*
>
> *'Just a minute. I think maybe I did write it.'*
>
> *He then hums a few bars.*
>
> *'I don't know if I did write it or not. I can't remember.'*
>
> *Then a pause, followed by, 'I wonder if Keats and Shelley ever had that sort of problem.'*

For all the loftiness of the allusion, Ira was the most modest songwriter I ever met. The writer Arthur Kober used to tell a story of an evening at Ira's house when, after a long card game, the company decided to go out to eat. Ira went and telephoned a fashionable restaurant and returned with the sad news that no tables were available. Kober then offered to try. He returned in triumph, saying that their table was awaiting them. When Ira asked him in amazement how he had managed it, Kober said, 'I told them I was Ira Gershwin.'

One truth of the human condition which appears to have evaded most social historians is that people tend to measure their lives, not in coffee spoons, but in popular tunes. A song begins as the adjunct to some emotional moment, until at last, being the only surviving element able to evoke the original emotion, it actually *becomes* the experience.

The Golden Age of popular song, which flourished, very roughly, for the first half of this century, has left us with a residue of words and music without a codified history. And, contrary to popular legend, that residue was not bequeathed by a body of men exclusively untrained, exclusively poor, exclusively the children of immigrants. The great popular composers came from every social stratum and their melodies mysteriously bear proof of the fact. Cole Porter's songs exude gilded elegance; Irving Berlin's social squibs like 'Puttin' On The Ritz', and 'A Couple Of Swells' are cries from the underprivileged. When we come to examine the lives of the two men, we find that Porter was born to millions, Berlin to beggary. The difference between them was that while Porter knew how to talk to waiters, Berlin had actually been one.

The trouble is that the survivors of the Golden Age are very old men. And because with dotage comes anecdotage, the history of the standard song has become the depository of the tall story. And yet, if a story is tall, does it follow that it must be untrue? Jerome Kern always insisted that he filched the melody of 'I've Told Every Little Star' from the song of a Cape Cod Sparrow which once perched on his bedroom window sill.

∾

FATS WALLER AND *AIN'T MISBEHAVIN'* (1979)

It is always unwise to take the public image of a musician at its face value. As the face of Thomas 'Fats' Waller was always seen to be smiling, on marquees and theatre bills (The Cheerful Little Earful), in photographs, on stage, on screen, the researcher is not surprised to discover the discrepancies between the public performer and the private man to have been even starker than usual.

Waller's problem was that he was able to do very well several different things which most people assume are aspects of the same thing but which are actually antipathetic, and that his earning power with these different, disparate things went in inverse proportion to their artistic value. Waller was a slapstick comedian, for which the world paid him handsomely; he was an unusually richly endowed composer, for which the world paid other people handsomely; and he was one of the greatest of all jazz pianists, for which very few people ever paid him anything at all.

The syndrome is familiar enough. Every jazz musician knows perfectly well, even if he sometimes pretends not to, that the only way for him to get rich is to dilute his art to the point where it is insipid enough not to upset the feeble musical digestion of the wider public. This need not necessarily be a tragic or wasteful process. There were friends of Thomas Fats, like Louis Armstrong and Duke Ellington, who were able to fool around for money and remain musicians of genius. Waller too had this ability, but it was his ironic fate to preserve his beautiful gift while the bankroll which he should have collected for putting it at risk was abstracted by a succession of those peculiarly odious felons which only showbiz ever seems to produce.

The truth is that Tin Pan Alley, one of the most burglarious conspiracies of the twentieth century, was made with victims like Waller in mind. To this day publishers lie awake all night praying for someone like him, a prolific commercial songwriter with the commercial acumen of a babe-in-arms. In July 1929, having written some songs for a successful Broadway revue called *Hot Chocolates*, he sold all rights for $500; the package included

'Ain't Misbehavin'', which has probably been earning that amount in royalties per week ever since.

In the 1920s, Waller would think nothing of selling a piece outright for twenty dollars or thirty dollars, committing that classical mistake on which the entrepreneurs of this world always count, which is to assume that because something comes easy to you, it cannot therefore be of much value to anyone else.

What is puzzling is that Waller appears to have appreciated, if not the pricelessness of his own work, then at least the immorality of the publishers who were stealing it from him. His method of reprisal was not to demand a good rate, but to sell the same song to several different crooks on the same day, going from office to office improvising different variations of the same song and collecting a few dollars for each new 'composition'.

Had he been just a song writer, his story would be much too sad to be told. As it was, he could always earn money performing (in 1937 at the London Palladium he topped the bill over Max Miller and Florence Desmond) and recording, which raises another awkward point about his art. Waller was renowned in his own lifetime as an inspired lampooner of run-of-the-mill Tin Pan Alley sentimentality. To this day his recordings of long-forgotten pop songs of the mid-1930s are considered by many to be the last word in the art of musical pasquinade.

In fact most of these buffooneries are tiresome and sometimes even embarrassing attempts to jolly along some musical fragment beyond redemption. What is curious is that often these songs were not so far in spirit from some of his own; it is as though Waller the great jazz musician is poking wry fun at Waller the darling of the variety halls.

For in jazz terms, Waller had seen Shelley plain. Born in New York in 1904, he found himself in just the right place at just the right time to form part of something almost unknown in jazz history, a School. The teachers were the pianists James P. Johnson and Willie 'The Lion' Smith, the star pupils Thomas 'Fats' Waller and Duke Ellington.

It was a school where you taught by precept and learned by playing the sedulous ape, which meant that Fats and Duke picked up the secret of Stride piano by watching and listening. Stride piano, so-called because of the movement of the left hand as it marches across the lower reaches of the keyboard playing a series of tenths, is a style demanding a ten-fingered dexterity from the player; it is essentially a solo style, with the left hand providing its own rhythmic accompaniment and the right hand implying all kinds of harmonic variations as well as melodic shapes.

Waller is the only instance in jazz history of the imitator becoming a greater creative artist than his master; long before his death in 1943 on a Chicago train headed for New York, he had become acknowledged as the greatest Stride pianist jazz had ever known.

And so he remains to this day, because not so long after his death the style became obsolete with the final overwhelming triumph of the opposing school, in which the right hand plays single note patterns. But where is the evidence? If Waller made so many hundreds of recordings featuring his own high-pitched vocal mischief, sometimes as many as twelve sides in a day, where are the great jazz classics? The answer is, on the same records.

There is no body of work in jazz which contains elements as antipathetic as Waller's recordings. The most outrageous fooling is followed by sixteen or thirty-two bars of piano unsurpassed either for rhythmic vitality or for harmonic imagination. Even more absurd, very often the Stride master and the singing fool are performing together, with Waller laying down the most exquisite accompaniments to his own perverse vocal frivolities.

The ultimate irony is of course that, a generation after his death – a generation, by the way, in which legal battles over his estate have been proceeding with the usual acrimony – his music should be packaged in a style acceptable to audiences who, in the normal run of things, not only are indifferent to jazz but actually disapprove of it. It is possible that by flinging together some of Waller's best songs, plus a few others with which he was associated, producers have been able to create something wonderful. But in the last reckoning, the only judgments which have any relevance to the musical issues at hand are those of the jazz musicians with enough practical experience to be able to take Waller's measure. And one of them at least, who has just studied the Broadway cast recording of 'Ain't Misbehavin'', cannot help thinking that it is crammed with precisely the kind of interpretations which Thomas 'Fats' took such pleasure in murdering. And if you were to ask me to define what is wrong with that album, I would refer you to the most notorious of all Thomas 'Fats' Waller's aphorisms: 'Lady, if you have to ask, forget it.'

COLLABORATIONS

Most men, if they are honest with you, will admit that at odd moments in their lives they have seen themselves as songwriters. 'Anyone can write a song', they feel – and when one hears some of the masterpieces unblushingly performed by pop groups, it sometimes seems as if anyone has done so. Perhaps anyone *can* write a song, but few can write a good one. What the man in the street, or the discotheque or the record booth, overlooks is that songwriting is a doublesided art, in which each side, the words and the music, is a rare skill in itself. Only a tiny élite, including Cole Porter, Noel Coward, Irving Berlin and a handful of others, has ever mastered both halves of the act. So a third factor enters the songwriting equation – collaboration. And that's where the trouble starts, and also the comedy.

Many composers can hardly put two words together, let alone write a lyric, and almost all lyricists are so totally ignorant about music that they'd confuse a quaver with a physical tremor. In such cases each partner easily believes that the other's contribution is unimportant, and as all royalties have to be split down the middle the tensions this can produce can be imagined. Sometimes private contempt even spills out into the open, as in the most famous of all songwriting partnerships, that of Gilbert and Sullivan. These two men were so antipathetic in temperament, background and attitude that they had only to work together for a while to end up loathing each other, refusing to talk or meet, slanging each other in public, and threatening the law courts at the slightest provocation, or indeed without any provocation at all.

A second-rate dramatist with a genius for rhyme, William Schwenk Gilbert established with Arthur Sullivan, a hack composer of oratorio with a sublime gift for light music, the most successful words-and-music partnership of the last one hundred years. But all the time he was rhyming the Savoy operas, Gilbert thought that the world was being deprived of his dramatic masterpieces. Sullivan was meanwhile equally convinced that posterity was being denied all those pious oratorios. Worse still, Gilbert felt (not without reason) that Sullivan was a social-climbing toady, while Sullivan (also not without reason) felt that Gilbert was a rude overbearing bully who never knew what he wanted. Sullivan would rather have assaulted Queen Victoria herself than sit through one of his partner's excruciating blank-verse dramas, and Gilbert thought that all music was a waste of time unless it happened to be graced by his own lyrics.

Here was a comic situation no writer of fiction would dare invent. Indeed, the more we think about it, the more surprising it becomes that Gilbert never thought of writing a comic opera about it. Here were two men, indispensable to each other, and yet consumed by a withering mutual contempt. In any civil war Gilbert would have waited to see on which side Sullivan aligned himself, and then promptly volunteered for the other. Each one tried different partners without success. Each kept vowing never to work with the other again, and then changed his mind. The truth was that both Gilbert and Sullivan loved money even more than they hated each other, so that even though they might refuse to speak, or even to meet socially, they continued to collaborate.

Today, because the gifts for wit and ridicule were all on Gilbert's side, it is Sullivan we tend to laugh at. In dismissing the art to which poor Sullivan had devoted his whole life, Gilbert once confessed: 'I know only two tunes. One of them is "God Save The King" and the other one isn't.' About to embark on a new opera, he gave Sullivan a searching look and inquired: 'Now you're quite sure you're not sickening for another oratorio?' As he put it later in a pretended fit of gloom: 'If that man had his way, he'd put the whole Bible to music.'

The pattern of incompatibility, if not open hostilities, set by the Savoy team has been repeated by most of the partnerships responsible for today's standards. In the 1920s the influx of mid-European composers into Broadway brought new opportunities for discord. Many of these melodic masters hardly bothered to learn their new language, so that there occurred the anomaly of a composer drawing royalties on songs whose words he not only had no interest in, but scarcely understood. One night the Hungarian-born Broadway master Sigmund Romberg, who had made a fortune out of his collaboration with Oscar Hammerstein in *The Desert Song*, found himself on the losing end of a rubber of bridge. His partner and lyricist, trying to think of some way of letting Romberg know he was holding only one trump, had a sudden brainwave and started humming one of Romberg's big hits from *The Desert Song*, the ballad called 'One Alone'. Obtusely, Romberg ignored the hint, led the wrong card and lost the rubber. Later his partner asked him:

> *'Ziggy, what happened? I gave you a clue. I hummed your song.'*
> *Romberg looked blank. 'What song?'*
> *'You know. "One Alone".'*
> *'Ach', Romberg replied, 'who knows from lyrics?'*

A rare case of harmony on both the musical and personal fronts was the family team of the Gershwins. It was a happy accident that, after trying several lyricists, George suddenly realized in 1923 that his own brother Ira was better than any of them. No two brothers have ever presented a greater contrast in temperament, yet the Gershwins formed one of the most amicable as well as successful songwriting partnerships of this century. George was the egotist, modestly admitting that he happened to be a genius, while Ira, the bookish one, stepped into the background and provided his brother with some of the wittiest rhymes in the popular repertoire.

The Gershwins also illustrate one of the few advantages of having to take a partner, which is that no matter how brilliant you might be, another man's judgement can sometimes be sounder than yours. While engaged on the score of a Broadway show, George had concocted an excellent melody intended for a fast tap-dance chorus routine. One night after a gruelling day at rehearsals, George sat pensively at the piano playing some of his favourite music, which was of course exclusively Gershwin music. He began playing his tap-dance song, only at half the normal speed. Ira looked up, listened for a few bars and then said: 'I think that's the tempo it should be.' George agreed, and an hour or so later Ira had completed the lyrics of the song which came to be known as 'Someone To Watch Over Me'.

The personal success of the Gershwin partnership was the more surprising in that George was not the easiest of colleagues. Intensely proud of his position as the leader of the songwriting profession, he knew he was its most gifted member and saw no reason to pretend he wasn't. Oscar Levant has told how he went on an overnight rail trip with George. When the time came to retire for the night, George took the lower bunk without even offering to discuss the point. Levant said nothing but meekly climbed into the upper bunk. After a few minutes silence George poked his head round the curtain and remarked: 'Upper berth, lower berth. That's the difference between talent and genius.'

Gershwin often exhibited this naive vanity, once almost causing a permanent breach in an old friendship. One of his favourite sports was handball and one of his closest associates the successful songwriter Harry Ruby. One afternoon while the two of them were playing handball, George suddenly withdrew, explaining that his hands were too valuable to be exposed to possible injury. Ruby's answer was obvious: 'So what about my hands?' Without intending any hurt, Gershwin replied: 'Well, it's not the same thing.'

Ruby avoided Gershwin for the next two years. One day they met by chance at Atlantic City, and Gershwin, innocent as always, asked Ruby what was wrong. Ruby reminded him of the handball incident, ending with the words: 'And then you said it wasn't the same thing.' Gershwin stood there saturnine in the Atlantic sunlight and considered Ruby's grievance. Then he pronounced: 'Well, it isn't.'

Still, Gershwin had a cross of his own to bear, though a lovable one, in the form of his own father Morris, who combined an intense pride in his son's work with the first-generation immigrant's utter inability to comprehend what that work was. To Gershwin *père*, the complexities of 'Fascinating Rhythm' were resolved into 'Fashion On The River', and he always regarded his own special song as 'Embraceable You', with its line 'Come to papa, come to papa, do'. 'Go on, George', he used to say, 'play them that song about me.' It was Gershwin's father who clinched the arguments about the merits of *Rhapsody in Blue* with the comment: 'Of course it's important. It lasts fifteen minutes, don't it?'

Such was the strength of his musical personality that the quality and originality of Gershwin's music would probably have remained unaffected no matter who his collaborator might have been. But a change of partners can sometimes effect a most dramatic change of musical personality, as evidenced vividly by the two independent careers of Richard Rodgers. For his first twenty years of composing, Rodgers worked with Lorenz Hart, for the second twenty with Oscar Hammerstein, and even the most casual study of his output reveals an astonishing variation in the style of his music during the two periods. It seems likely that despite the gargantuan success of Rodgers–Hammerstein shows like *Oklahoma!*, *The King and I*, *South Pacific* and *The Sound of Music*, Rodgers will eventually be remembered for, and measured by, the brilliant sophistication of the earlier songs he wrote with Hart (a partnership romanticized in the musical *Words and Music*).

Hart was perhaps the most gifted versifier since Gilbert, a polyglot who could move at will between sentiment ('My Funny Valentine') and satire ('The Lady Is A Tramp') – both songs, incidentally, written for the same show. Compare items like 'My Heart Stood Still', 'If They Asked Me I Could Write A Book', 'Manhattan' and 'Mountain Greenery' with more recent Rodgers successes like 'If I Loved You' and 'Climb Every Mountain', and the truth begins to emerge that Hart touched a chord in Rodgers' make-up that Hammerstein never even knew existed. With Hart, Rodgers was capable of astringency, with Hammerstein only sentimentality. The question immediately arises whether this contrast was due to the power of Hart's personality or merely to altered methods of technique, for when Rodgers changed partners he also changed his working approach. With Hart the music was always done first, with Hammerstein always the lyrics.

Does the priority matter? Yes, according to Johnny Mercer, four-time Academy Award lyricist, and the man responsible for, among others, 'That Old Black Magic', 'Charade', 'Moon River' and 'Days Of Wine And Roses'. He believes the music should come first because otherwise the words will be nothing more than rumpty-tumpty. 'Write the words first,' Mercer told me, 'and it's odds on you end up with doggerel. No lyricist in the world can produce enough variations of rhythm to create a satisfactory lyric.'

Mercer's analysis makes sense when we remember that Gilbert, who wrote the words first, was primarily the greatest master of doggerel the popular song has ever known. In limiting himself to the rhythms of Hammerstein's words, Rodgers evidently sacrificed a great deal of his invention, even though he himself has always seemed to be happier with his later work than with the youthful fireworks of the Hart period.

There is a polite fiction in the songwriting business that Rodgers only formed his alliance with Hammerstein after Hart died. This is untrue. It was not Hart's death that made Rodgers look for a new partner. It was his alcoholism and his gradual loss of professional self-discipline. In fact, the ailing Hart was in the audience for the first of the Rodgers–Hammerstein first nights. This was *Oklahoma!*, the show inexplicably regarded by critics as the point at which the musical arrived at maturity. All his life Rodgers had been pursuing something which he called the 'integrated score', by which he meant a musical in which every song arose naturally out of the action and characterization. In *Oklahoma!* he felt he had realized it at last. Rodgers was surely mistaken. There can be no such thing as the integrated score, for the good reason that in real life nobody ever breaks into song unless he happens to be drunk. For my money, Hart's impudent rhyme schemes and vast vocabulary remain to mock the pretensions of those who have followed him.

But at least Hart has been deified by the theatre which is more than can be said of another of the great lyricists, P. G. Wodehouse. In the years since he dropped out of the Broadway theatre and became the creator of Jeeves, Wodehouse has been forgotten as a songwriter. Yet on his eightieth birthday, Rodgers sent him a congratulatory wire saying that in the early days Hart, Ira Gershwin and the rest of them had all worshipped Wodehouse's work in the theatre and cribbed from him unmercifully. Wodehouse's triumphs as a novelist have of course overshadowed his musical work, but his great contribution to songwriting was to give it the same comic levity one finds in the dialogue of his English country house fiction. During his partnership with Jerome Kern, Wodehouse made the popular song lyric conversational and casual, and did much to rescue it from the stagey pomposities of the old mock-Viennese style.

To Wodehouse everything has always been a big joke, and in a book of reminiscences he has given highly coloured accounts of how he and Kern would try to sell songs to the impresarios.

The best of all the Kern–Wodehouse numbers, 'Just My Bill', had been hanging around for twenty years when the two partners decided to build a trap for Ziegfeld to fall into. Invited to the great man's yacht for a weekend, Kern, a master-tactician at this sort of thing, wangled an invitation for a certain lady singer, who was then carefully coached to sing 'Just My Bill'. At the psychological moment aboard, the musical broadside was fired at Ziegfeld and hit him between wind and water. He offered to buy the song immediately. Eventually, twenty-one years after Kern had written the melody and fifteen after Wodehouse had put words to it, 'Just My Bill' was slipped into the score of *Show Boat* to become one of the great standard songs of the decade.

Even among those rare spirits who can manage the whole thing themselves, words and music with no outside assistance, severe conflicts occur between the composer and lyricist sides of the same man. During the First World War, Irving Berlin the composer wrote a tune for Berlin the lyricist, who proceeded to botch a potential winner. The result was a ditty called 'Smile And Show Your Dimple', which appeared in a revue for a few weeks and then died a speedy and well-deserved death. In Hollywood fifteen years later, Berlin, stuck for a good melody, remembered 'Smile And Show Your Dimple', threw out the lyric and wrote a new one. Every year since then the amended song has earned Berlin vast royalties during the month of April. The new lyric which Berlin wrote was called 'Easter Parade'.

These one-man teams often show more talent in one department than the other. Berlin is primarily a great composer, Coward a great lyricist, and even Cole Porter, richly endowed in both departments, seemed to decline as a lyricist towards the end of his life, though his music went from strength to strength. Lionel Bart, the most successful British one-man band of recent years (*Oliver!*), complains of the loneliness of doing it all yourself, but the general feeling is that the advantages of self-help far outweigh those pleasures of collaboration which can so easily turn into civil war.

What kind of man is the songwriter? He is a man who works in furious bursts of inspiration. (Johnny Mercer took fifteen minutes to write the words of 'I Remember You', only five to complete 'Days Of Wine And Roses'.) It also helps if he is a stoic with the ability to laugh at himself, because much of his life will be spent watching other people butcher his brainchildren. The Gershwin brothers had the mortification of seeing one of the greatest popular songs ever written, 'The Man I Love', thrown out of three successive musicals, because either the star or the producer didn't like it. 'The Man I Love' never did reach the Broadway stage, and only won its status in the end through the underground movement of cabaret.

Ira Gershwin once described what happened to a musical called *Funny Face*, later filmed with Fred Astaire and Audrey Hepburn. During the six-week out-of-town tryout, the *entire score* was rejected, so that by the time the show arrived in New York for its Broadway run, the two brothers had composed an entirely new score. Ira explained: 'George always felt that writing a new song was less trouble than arguing about an old one with the money men.'

Finally, of course, come the perils of the *third* member of the collaboration, the indispensable, but unpredictable, performer. Consider the feelings of Johnny Mercer, who wrote the words to the romantic 'Laura' and then attended a concert at which the vocalist changed the last phrase from 'but she's only a dream' to 'but she's only a fool'. Between houses the culprit was quickly informed of his error, and promised to get it right for the second house. He then went on and gave a word-perfect rendition till he arrived at the last phrase. This time he sang 'but she's only a drool'.

Irving Berlin: the First One Hundred Years (1988)

In 1888 there was a great noise in Germany, where they were crowning a new Kaiser. The French pointedly ignored the event, being preoccupied with a constitutional crisis, as usual. Meanwhile, at Hatfield House, the Prime Minister, unconcerned at agitation for a public performance of that dangerously seditious tract *A Doll's House*, expressed his political philosophy by tricycling through the grounds. An obscure colonial called Kipling was creating a furore with a volume of Indian short stories called *Plain Tales from the Hills*, and in America Mark Twain was being praised for his new novel, *Huckleberry Finn*. As for the fattest head in Europe, Tsar Alexander III, he was so excited by his new discovery (which was that autocracy was good for you) that he paid no attention to the condition of Russian music, which happened to be good in at least four respects. Tchaikovsky was doing well in London, Borodin was plodding away on *Prince Igor*, Rimsky-Korsakov had nearly completed *Scheherazade*, and in the Siberian village of Temun on 11 May, a Mrs Baline, wife of the local kosher slaughterer, gave birth to a son, Israel. Four years later a bunch of Cossacks rode into the village and began slaughtering the residents. As this was the only military engagement they had ever won, the soldiers were understandably exuberant, expressing their high spirits by setting fire to what was left of the place before galloping off to their next appointment with glory, unaware that they had just laid the foundations of the modern American song.

The terrified Balines fled to New York, to find the theatrical profession dividing its energies between the burglarization of Gilbert and Sullivan and rapt contemplation of the amplitude of Lillian Russell's thighs. The drunks in the Bowery were singing 'Where The Sweet Magnolias Grow'. Irving Berlin – the new name was the upshot of a printer's error – would remember that song. He remembers more or less everything, even those flames lighting up the Siberian landscape. Not surprisingly, the affair at Temun tended somewhat to colour his views on the Russian psyche, and he has been adamant about the anti-Russian aspect of a waltz he wrote in 1927 called 'Russian Lullaby', insisting on its validity as a political tract, with its reference to 'a land that's free for you and me'.

It is this dogged recollection of his origins that has made a jingo American of him. His 'God Bless America', unofficial anthem of his adopted land, is a perfectly serious expression of his feelings. Always profligate with his talents in support of the army, navy, Red Cross, boy scouts, girl guides among others, his fervid love of country is the patriotism of a waif who was allowed to go unmolested, to make a huge fortune from the practice of the innocent craft of writing words and music, and to collect among his souvenirs a Medal of Merit, the Congressional Gold Medal and the Légion d'Honneur.

Bewilderment persists over the issue of his musicality. How can it be that a man responsible for many of the most pervasive airs of his time should be a musical illiterate? His piano playing, comically awful, is limited to the key of F Sharp, and the contraption which was built into his upright, a handle to crank the keyboard into new keys while he continued playing in the old one, was so freakish that today it resides at the Smithsonian in Washington, bizarre proof of what you can achieve if you don't try.

Berlin has never bothered to conceal his limitations. On the contrary, his laughing insistence on sharing the joke with the world at large has given rise to some of the best Broadway stories. P. G. Wodehouse has told of being terrified of the two ferocious toucans perched on either side of the entrance to Berlin's New York apartment in the 1920s. When Wodehouse asked him if he wasn't worried that they might do him an injury, Berlin replied, 'One of these days, those goddam birds are going to bite me in the finger – the one I play piano with.'

Being completely unschooled has had its advantages, enabling him to carry off heresies which a trained writer would not only never think of perpetrating but would never think of at all. 'Top Hat, White Tie And Tails' (1935), written to order for Fred Astaire, has a middle section of two five-bar phrases, a resort to asymmetry unparalleled in the popular field. 'Cheek To Cheek', from the same score, has not one middle section but two. The opening arpeggio of 'The Best Thing For You' (1950), is so ingenious that not even the master strategist Jerome Kern could have thought of it. One of the most striking examples of this brilliant empiricism is 'Let's Face The Music And Dance' (1936), a song with so many exquisite ambiguities that a full treatise deserves one day to be written on it. In tonality it drifts so sinuously from Minor to Major and back again that the performer sometimes wonders which tonality he is actually working in. Structurally, too, it is unpredictable, for though it sounds like the conventional thirty-two bar A-A-B-A structure, it is in fact an exotic A-B-C-D contrivance with the bars running to 14-16-8-18 respectively. Berlin, one of the most underrated lyricists of his time, imposed on this song one of his subtlest plots, using the cliché of romance/chance/dance for the obligatory rhyme, reserving his wit for the opening line of each set, all of which rhyme:

> *There may be trouble ahead.*
> *Before the fiddlers have fled.*
> *There may be teardrops to shed.*

Another aspect of his genius has been the tendency to recycle anything which he feels might be further improved. The wonderfully spry modulations in the middle passage of 'I'm Putting All My Eggs In One Basket' (1936) received their trial run in 'Not For All The Rice In China' (1933). The famous trio of ascending phrases beginning with 'When the things you planned' in 'Always' (1924) turn up again nine years later in 'Maybe It's Because'.

A much deeper insight into his working methods is disclosed by an extraordinary tale whose pieces I was able to put together by sheer fluke. After Berlin had completed his work on *Follow the Fleet*, he agreed to write the songs for a Twentieth-Century-Fox film called *On the Avenue*, starring Dick Powell. His eventual score was a masterpiece, but the revealing thing is how he went about the writing of the big love song. He remembered that five years earlier he had published a piece called 'I'm Playing With Fire', which Crosby had made into a minor success. The song was now quite forgotten, except by Berlin. He saw that the metaphor of its title, of love as a generator of heat, might be used again. There was something else he remembered about the song, its little-known, never-sung verse. Berlin found that by halving its tempo and amending its rhythm, he had an excellent basis for a new main theme, which he decided to call 'I've Got My Love To Keep Me Warm'.

Forty years after the event I was in Beverly Hills interviewing Berlin's old producer at RKO, Pandro Berman, who was effusive in his praise of Gershwin, Kern and Porter. When I asked him about Berlin, he instructed me to switch off the tape recorder. This is what he told me.

It happened that while Berlin was working on *On the Avenue* his RKO picture, *Follow the Fleet*, was going the rounds and making huge profits. Berman decided to hold a celebratory party, which Berlin attended. (Each of them, including Astaire, was cut in for 10 per cent of the profits.) That night something unexpected happened. It rained. When the party broke up, Berlin, a tiny man, asked Berman, who is just as tiny, for the loan of an overcoat. The coat was forthcoming. At this point in his narrative Berman became animated, indignant, irate. He told me that the overcoat was a new one, that it was handmade, that he had never worn it. Berlin took it and left. Time passed and it began to rain again. Berman went to find his overcoat. It wasn't there.

He telephoned Berlin to demand its return. Berlin denied possession, and an argument developed, ending with Berlin's 'Who needs an overcoat? I don't need an overcoat.' Those remarks appear, more or less verbatim, in the middle section of 'I've Got My Love To Keep Me Warm'. The real joke lies in the fact that until I pointed it out to him, Berman had never connected the coat with the lyric.

Berlin would probably abhor that anecdote. For many years now, he has refused to countenance the most innocent speculations on his private life and the links between that life and his songs. Yet the links are there for all to see. 'Russian Lullaby' is one example. An even more obvious case is the great tragedy of Berlin's young manhood and the song which came out of it. In 1913 he fell in love with Dorothy Goetz, the sister of the songwriter Ray Goetz. The lovers married and honeymooned in Cuba; on their return the bride fell ill and died. Berlin then wrote the simplest of waltzes, 'When I Lost You', incorporating a lyric whose imagery is so hackneyed that it can be excused only by the grief-stricken sincerity with which it was written. The words consist of a catalogue of loss, embracing sunshine and roses, a heaven of blue, beautiful rainbows and the morning dew. One has only to imagine Noel Coward, say, or Lorenz Hart writing such a lyric to see how hastily they would have shied away from it. But Berlin, unabashed by his own banality as always, put the words on paper, thereby winning the allegiance of millions of ordinary folk whose only difference from him is their lack of creativity.

Johnny Mercer, generally acknowledged as the most gifted of the lyricists of the generation which followed Berlin's, has said that Berlin was able to write 'for the girl in the Five-and-Ten'. Someone like Porter not only couldn't do it but would never have wished to. He and Berlin represent opposing social poles of the American songwriter, the one born to millions and massively overeducated at Yale *and* Harvard, the other risen from the gutter and never educated at all.

Yet it was Berlin who became the head of his profession, bestowing fatherly advice and encouragement on his rivals. When Porter, harassed by the philistinism of Louis B. Mayer, was obliged to write a song he hated, and was then mortified to see it become a great moneymaker, it was Berlin who wrote him a word of comfort. The song was 'Rosalie', and Berlin's message: 'Listen, kid, take my advice, never hate a song that sells half a million copies.' Quite apart from the fact that only Berlin could have got away with calling Porter 'kid', the advice reflects his ruthless pragmatism when it comes to making money. One of the most striking features of Berlin's vast output is its dizzying range, from the crudest ethnic jokes to the sumptuous sophisticated rhetoric of pieces like 'Let's Face The Music And Dance' and 'Change Partners'. Anyone who asks Berlin which type of song he enjoyed writing best gets the same answer: Hits. No doubt Berlin is proudest of all about 'White Christmas', because its record sales passed the hundred million mark years ago. Yet no experienced musician would place it among Berlin's fifty best songs. To this day the division of the spoils in songwriting remains absurd, with the composer and lyricist splitting one half and the publisher taking the other. Some writers have campaigned for reform, but not Berlin. Ever the pragmatist, he decided before he was thirty to become his own publisher, after which he proceeded to buy back all his early work. It is hopeless to speculate on what Berlin is worth today, but a hint is provided by the fate of 'Always', which he presented as a love-gift to his second wife. She is said to have collected royalties amounting to $60,000 in one year alone.

These days Berlin discourages such talk, and refuses to allow anyone to speculate about his life or music. No great man this century has been more resolutely opposed to his own fame than Berlin, who has been incommunicado for years, and who guards his life's work so closely that not even the most disinterested academic is allowed to quote chapter and verse. Even his British publishers are not allowed to circulate books of his songs, even though this is standard practice for every prominent Broadway composer. The best that Berlin would allow was a cardboard folder containing twelve of his most famous songs, the act of a man raised in an age when a songwriter computed his wealth and fame by the number of people who bought the sheet music and played it on the parlour piano. Sometimes his cussedness seems inexplicable, although the most recent example was mitigated, as usual, by his sense of humour.

Last year one of Hollywood's young lions applied for permission to use 'Always' in a new movie. The response was a blanket refusal, and when the intrigued producer asked why, Berlin said: 'I'm saving it for a future project.'

And it is true that his longevity has itself become a sort of joke, making nonsense even of Congress's copyright arrangements. The original law granted songwriters sole rights in their own work for fifty-five years after publication. But Berlin made his first fortune, from 'Alexander's Ragtime Band', in 1911. When the fifty-five years were up, he was still a mere sprig of seventy-eight. So Congress changed the law in deference to him. That was nearly a quarter of a century ago and Berlin is still collecting. He has also been known to make the occasional joke about his physical prowess. On his eightieth birthday, he lunched with the composer Arthur Schwartz, who, indulging in pleasantry, asked him about his love-life, to which Berlin replied, 'Listen, Arthur, a man of eighty is not like a man of seventy.' Schwartz's favourite Berlin story concerns the old boy's wispy voice, of which someone once said, 'To hear him you have to hug him.' Schwartz swore that he was in a recording studio one day when he overheard two engineers editing a vocal version by Berlin of 'Oh, How I Hate To Get Up In The Morning'. One engineer listened and then said to the other, 'If the guy who wrote that song could hear what this son-of-a-bitch has done to it, he'd turn over in his grave.'

In his extreme old age, having argued with everyone, Berlin has beguiled the time by becoming a keen amateur painter, applying to his canvases the same simple rule-of-thumb which once energized his music. When one of his favourite sons, Fred Astaire, reached the age of seventy, his birthday gift from Berlin was a painting. Astaire was moved by the gesture but puzzled by the picture, which showed a man with no hands. Was there some dark symbolism in the omission? Was this Berlin's way of confessing that when it came to piano playing, he never did have any hand to speak of? Finally, Astaire had to phone Berlin to ask him. 'The painting was fine, Irving, but why no hands?' The reply was: 'Because I can't paint hands.'

It would seem that we have much to thank the Romanovs for, after all.

ALAN JAY LERNER: *THE STREET WHERE I LIVE* (1978)

Books become indispensable for all sorts of reasons, some because they are masterworks, others because they give the reader a good time, still others because they celebrate language, still others because the author's voice is so starkly original. The musical theatre is a special case, a word sustaining certain links with literature and yet itself irrevocably illiterate. Self-justifying showbiz confessionals are a joke, critical assessments of musical works a disgrace, entrepreneurial musings a pack of lies. Recent memorable additions to the collection in the Stuffed Owl room include the wonderfully awful autobiography of Joshua Logan, which had the remarkable effect of endearing the reader to almost anyone else, and Richard Rodgers's own story, whose effect was roughly equivalent to being hit on the back of the neck with a large shovel. There are only two classics of the genre, Ira Gershwin's *Lyrics on Several Occasions*, which combines literacy, humility and deep wisdom, and a comic masterpiece called *Bring on the Girls*, without doubt the most unjustly neglected book ever written by P. G. Wodehouse.

Now although this is a bad business for the reasonably literate seeker after musical comedy wisdom, it places each new aspirant in a happy position indeed. Faced by almost no competition, he can proceed serenely in the confidence that his feet are treading ground which, if not quite virgin, has been the scene of more exhibitions of factual, literary or musical coitus interruptus than ever Freud could have envisaged. With Lerner our hopes rise in defiance of experience. After all, he more than any other major lyricist for the theatre has dealt exclusively in literary counters; the cover of his book reminds us of that: Shaw, Colette, T. H. White. Surely a man who grapples with three so formidable figures without inflicting grievous bodily or aesthetic harm must have sufficient literary sensibility to compose a readable book? It is with some relief that the impartial witness is able to answer, 'Yes, he has.'

Lerner's book is exceptional in its professional context for three reasons. First, he is actually able to write in a readable way. Second, he is evidently trying to be as honest as the libel laws permit. Third, and really very remarkable, he has not allowed life among the trendies and the phonies to divest him of that eminently humanizing virtue, compassion. One example among many is his barter with Jack L. Warner, the Hollywood mogul who bought the screen rights of *My Fair Lady* for $5.5 million and assumed, like all moguls, that the transaction magically endowed him with more insight into the nature of the work than the men who wrote it. Warner evidently didn't think too much of Rex Harrison and Julie Andrews, demanding in their place among others Rock Hudson and Audrey Hepburn. The battle ended in a draw, one-all, yet all the saintly Lerner says is, 'Jack bowed to the inevitable.'

There is one priceless passage concerning the felonious basis of all movie accountancy, priceless because writers on the subject tend to back away from the simple truth of the matter, which is that Hollywood is a den of thieves. Lerner explains why, because outsiders are invited to take a percentage of this or that production, it is in the interest of the major studios to 'reduce to the shadiest possible minimum the money owed to those who have a percentage of the film'. After remarking that the film companies have 'a well-trained corps of bandits in the book-keeping department', Lerner ends on a declamatory note: 'Ah, Bernie Cornfield! Had you only known that there is a place in this world where your genius would be appreciated, where your unique gifts could thrive with complete immunity – in the bright sunlight of respectability – without fear of penalty, punishment or prison.' Of the villains of the piece, there is one critic: 'George Jean Nathan, who lived in a room without ventilation and so thick with smoke that the elevator man told me that when he brought Mr Nathan his coffee in the morning he could never find him.'

There are several heroes and heroines, the most unexpected of whom is Richard Burton, who emerges from the *Camelot* episode with Arthurian garlands dangling from his brow; Lerner's version of Burton makes an interesting contrast with the journalistic generality on the subject.

The book is indispensable in the end for the knowledge it imparts about the problems of musical comedy authorship. The section describing the genesis of *My Fair Lady* is outstanding, and includes one of the most profound of all anecdotes on the nebulosity of the whole genre. One day Moss Hart asks Irving Berlin, an execrable pianist, to play his finale music for a new revue. Berlin obliges, and there may be those who do not understand what Lerner is saying. For anyone who does grasp the essence, Lerner's book is strongly to be recommended. Here is the anecdote:

> *Berlin sat down and played 'Easter Parade' for Moss. It sounded terrible. Moss was in a dilemma. Finally he said: 'Irving, play "Blue Skies" for me.' Irving played 'Blue Skies' and that sounded terrible. Moss then said, 'Irving, the finale is terrific.'*

∾

IRA GERSHWIN: *LYRICS ON SEVERAL OCCASIONS* (1985)

In 1958, Ira Gershwin was sixty-two years old, his career effectively over. Most people who knew what was what placed him alongside Cole Porter and Lorenz Hart as America's major lyricist of a period that can be seen in retrospect as the golden age of performing art in America. He had composed some of the loveliest and wittiest song lyrics of the century. With verses like 'They Can't Take That Away From Me', 'Embraceable You', 'Someone To Watch Over Me', he had created the counters of love's small talk for the man and woman in the street. In *Of Thee I Sing* he had helped write the only considerable musical pasquinade in the American repertory by playing Gilbert to his brother George's Sullivan. With *Porgy and Bess* he had contributed towards the extraordinary feat of elevating Tin Pan Alley to the opera house without murdering Tin Pan Alley in the process. Any last, lingering doubt as to the quality of his versifying was dispelled by the fact that Hollywood had never awarded him an Oscar. His life's work was complete – at which point the publishing house of Alfred Knopf invited him to write a book, any book, about anything he liked.

It was a reckless step for any publisher to take. Even in those days, the earth was cluttered with the autobiographical maunderings of showbiz luminaries whose approach to the writing of a book too often suggested that they had never read one.

Fortunately for posterity, Ira was nothing at all like the others. A modest, gentle soul whose whimsical brain was crammed with the erudition of the autodidact, he knew enough about the pleasures of the printed word to understand that just any book would not be good enough. He had wanted for some time to publish a collection of his work but knew that to offer the music lover words without music was like giving a thirsty man the H_2 and telling him to find the O for himself. And yet the work was worth preserving. How to transform a set of essentially functional rhymes into something resembling literature?

Now, Ira was what we have in mind when we talk of the bookish man. Almost our first glimpse of him is as a teenaged attendant at his father's abortive Turkish baths on Lennox Avenue, rejoicing in the thought that so long as the customers continue not to roll up, he can go on reading. At the other end of his life, bedridden in Beverly Hills, he slept next to a bay, three of whose four walls were lined from floor to ceiling with books. The nature of the books in the bay give a clue to the kind of book Ira was himself to write, for those volumes indicate that many of his interests were not so much contemporary American as period English.

Stylistically, Ira always saw himself as by W. S. Gilbert out of P. G. Wodehouse. He was steeped in English literature, had found the title 'Nice Work If You Can Get It' in a caption by the Edwardian *Punch* cartoonist George Belcher, had amended Chesterton's 'I think I will not hang myself today' into the lyric 'I Don't Think I'll Fall In Love Today', had paid tribute to the slang of Wodehouse's silly asses in the words of 'Stiff Upper Lip', and had justified his use of 'with a down-a-derry' in 1937 by quoting the work of Thomas D'Urfey, who had perpetrated 'with a hey ding, hoe ding, derry, derry, ding' as long ago as 1719. He had come within an ace of writing lyrics for a musical version of Max Beerbohm's *Zuleika Dobson*, had composed 'The Cozy Nook Trio' in respectful imitation of the linguistic cartwheels of the Reverend Spooner, and was the only man I ever met who had actually read *Amenities of Literature*, by Benjamin Disraeli's bibliophile father, Isaac. To think in terms of literary allusion came so naturally to him that one time, when a conversation between us was interrupted by a nurse, he mumbled to me in the moment before he washed the pills down, 'I'm like Demosthenes with the pebbles in his mouth,' downed the pills, and added, 'Or like Eliza Doolittle with the marbles.'

The volume that Knopf was privileged to publish in 1959 turned out to be unique, an utterly charming amalgam of technical disquisition, personal reminiscence, literary scholarship, and green room gossip. It was also one of the very few books that nailed its colours to the mast *before* the reader reached the first page, for the dust jacket announced it as 'A selection of stage & screen lyrics written for sundry situations; and now arranged in arbitrary categories. To which have been added many informative annotations & disquisitions on their why & wherefore, their whom-for, their how; and matters associative. By Ira Gershwin: Gent.'

Having begun by wheeling on the engines of literary scholarship, Ira proceeds as he started, by offering as an epigraph the remark from John Aubrey's *Brief Lives* 'How these curiosities would be quite forgott, did not such idle fellowes as I am putt them downe!' What curiosities does Ira have in mind? The very first of the 104 lyrics that make up the book is 'The Man I Love'. We learn that notwithstanding the fact that it was this song that persuaded the financier Otto H. Kahn to invest in the show *Lady, Be Good!* it was dropped during the out-of-town tryout; that it was subsequently put into and ejected from two other musicals; that it never did see the light of day as a show tune and only emerged as an American classic through the enthusiastic intervention of Lady Mountbatten.

Any suspicion that this is to be another autobiography in disguised form is swiftly dispelled in the next entry, 'Looking For A Boy,' whose inclusion Ira uses as a pretext for a discussion of the hellish difficulties of finding suitable bachelor rhymes for 'heaven', apart from the weary 'seven' and 'eleven'. As Ira says, '"Devon" was geographically out of bounds; Labourite E. Bevin was probably already married; and what could one do with "replevin"?'

The 'Looking For A Boy' annotations are also revealing for the cunning way in which Ira blends reminiscence, technical niceties, and literary allusion. It so happens that the verse of this song ends with the couplet 'I'll be blue until he comes my way;/ Hope he takes the cue when I am saying . . .' The rhyming device whereby a one-syllable word is made to match the first half of a two-syllable word is commonplace enough in the Broadway marketplace, and Ira had adopted it very early in his career without thinking twice; but it was not until his retirement that he discovered, from a newly published book on poetic technique, that the device was known as 'apocopated rhyme, so called because the end of one rhyming word is cut off'. The news that he had, throughout his life, been an unwitting master of apocopated rhyme absolutely delighted Ira's bookish soul, and he expresses this delight before capping the annotation with the perfect literary allusion for the occasion: 'I am suddenly made aware that long, long ago in the last two verse lines of "Looking For A Boy" the music made me rhyme, apocopatedly, "way" with "saying"; and I now feel one with Molière's M. Jourdain the day he learned he'd been speaking prose for over forty years.'

From the reader's point of view, the effect of this strange melange of erudition and gossip, of discussion and digression, of whimsical verse and informed prose, is curious and utterly beguiling. At one moment we read that Eric Partridge has proscribed over two thousand hopelessly exhausted clichés, only to learn that Ira had used hundreds of them in this or that lyric (he lists twenty-seven examples), to which he then adds one of the profound truths of the songwriting art:

> *The phrase that is trite and worn-out when appearing in print usually becomes, when heard fitted to an appropriate musical turn, revitalized, and seems somehow to revert to its original provocativeness.*

We find him gently chiding the editors of *Time* for deploying false rhymes in advising readers how to pronounce proper nouns; we learn that Paris is a place where

> *girls wear bodices*
> *like goddesses;*
> *that the married state means*
> *. . . signing a lease together;*
> *And hanging a Matisse together!*
> *and that there was once a lady who*
> *had a most immoral eye:*
> *they called her Lorelei.*

We also learn that the title 'Don't Be A Woman If You Can' was inspired by an oldtime Tin Pan Alley poetaster who lost his reason and went around saying things like 'I never liked him and I always will.' We see George and Ira one evening in their apartment awaiting the arrival for dinner of Ira's fiancée; by the time she arrives they have discussed, sketched out, completed, and revised the song 'Do, Do, Do'. We read of the drudgeries and aesthetic injustices of the out-of-town tryout, the vagaries of performers and producers who think they know better, the inexplicable flops, the equally inexplicable triumphs. Best of all, we learn the true nature of Ira's profession. In the foreword to *Lyrics on Several Occasions* (Ira confesses that the idea for the title comes from Mrs Aphra Behn – another one-up for the British), we find a priceless distillation of the contents to come, a touch of rueful irony that tells us much about the job and everything about the man who performed it so brilliantly: 'Since most of the lyrics in this lodgment were arrived at by fitting words mosaically to music already composed, any resemblance to actual poetry, living or dead, is highly improbable.'

Hoagy Carmichael (1981)

Everett Hoagland 'Hoagy' Carmichael, songwriter and publicist extraordinary, died as much an enigma as he had always been. More than any of the other great standard popular composers, Carmichael created contradictions between the artist who produced so many sumptuous melodies and the image projected on the general public.

In whichever stage of an unusually quixotic career, whether as law student, apprentice jazz pianist, professional sophomore, songwriter or actor, Carmichael, perversely or not, tended to confuse the issues. Pink clouds of whimsy followed always in his wake, often obscuring the trail, and the result was a public life crammed with the kind of stories which journalists hunger for in their attempts to get to grips with the ungrippable, that is, with musical composition.

As an example, there is the business of Carmichael's military career. As a skinny youth from Bloomington, Indiana, he was too underweight to be accepted as cannon fodder, so he began gorging himself on bananas to achieve the required poundage. He was eventually accepted for the United States Army on 10 November 1918, ate two military meals and then, to the accompaniment of armistice hysteria, walked out of camp without a pass, it being his little vanity for the next sixty years to describe himself as AWOL.

Even more to the point was the remarkable publicity campaign mounted on behalf of one of the best songs of unrequited love of the 1930s, 'I Get Along Without You Very Well'. Dramatic as the lyric undoubtedly is, it pales before the grand guignol convolutions involved in its launching. There was an anonymous poem comprising the lyric of the song, Carmichael's determination to set it to music, the nationwide search for the poet culminating in a bugle call for help from Walter Winchell, and finally the death of the poetess, an obscure widow, only twenty-four hours before Dick Powell unveiled the song on the radio. By the time 'I Get Along Without You Very Well' was finally in circulation, it had already created more interest, and achieved more publicity than most songs do in a lifetime.

Later, when Carmichael won a new audience by playing himself in a series of Hollywood movies, his show business reputation began to dwarf his real gift, for he was neither a very good singer nor much of a pianist. And even in the area where he truly excelled, in light substantial composition, he never conformed to type.

Most songwriters have risen fairly swiftly to the apex of their art, remained there for a decade or two, and then gently declined. Carmichael's performance was nothing like this. He began with a few masterpieces, then went on to produce some highly talented songs and finally faded away, with his greatest song, 'Stardust', having turned up at the very start, to become the *Citizen Kane* of his life.

Carmichael naturally never acknowledged this. On the only occasion I ever met him, in the 1950s, he brushed 'Stardust' aside as an item of juvenilia.

And indeed, there must have been times when 'Stardust' was difficult to live with. Had Carmichael written nothing else, that one song would be a surety of his flair. Utterly conventional in structure, utterly original in its contours, 'Stardust' stands alongside 'The Man I Love', 'Body And Soul' and one or two others as the classic example of American popular song.

There was, however, another side to Carmichael's art, the side beloved of jazz musicians. With songs like 'Rocking Chair', 'Lazy River' and 'Georgia On My Mind', he succeeded in integrating an element of the jazz spirit into popular music.

Inevitably, there are contradictions between the whimsical music-master of the movies and the hard-headed writer of hit songs. One of Carmichael's most idolatrous disciples, who went on to become one of his most effective lyric writing partners, was Johnny Mercer, who later said that in the early days of their association, Carmichael could be an awkward customer. According to Mercer, it was Hollywood which softened Carmichael and which incidentally gave him only one Oscar, which he shared with Mercer for 'In The Cool, Cool Cool Of The Evening' in 1951.

Of course he published a romantic autobiography. Of course he called it *The Stardust Road*. And of course it included, apart from an idealized portrait of himself, some wonderfully funny-innocent observations on his professional rivals. One day as an obscure youth he heard Irving Berlin playing the piano at a private party: 'Hoagland,' I said to myself, 'by God, if anyone who plays that feebly can write that nobly – you can write a song.'

Guys and Dolls (1985)

The trail which culminated in the National Theatre's revival of *Guys and Dolls* begins on 8 October 1880, in a one-horse town in Kansas, where an itinerant drunkard, gambler, printer and Indian fighter called Runyon was proud to announce that his wife had delivered a son, to be called Damon. American journalism was never to be the same. At seventeen Damon sold a piece to the *Pueblo Evening Post*, drifted through the towns of the Midwest, working on local newspapers, and by 1910 was working for Hearst on the *New York American*. His speciality was sport, and particularly baseball. Runyon liked the screwballs, the eccentrics, the rule-breakers, the troubleshooters. His columns became famous for their celebration of the crazy side of professional sport. He was also a dab hand when it came to horse racing and boxing, and within a year of his arrival in the Big City he was earning enough to marry a wouldbe socialite called Ellen Egan. Sadly, he had chosen a partner who preferred gentility to the typewriter. Runyon plumped for the typewriter every time, wrecking the marriage, estranging his own children, and winning an awesome reputation as a loner, a dedicated, dispassionate observer who kept his emotions corked up and went looking for stories.

He was never much of an idealist. He wrote for money, the more money the better. 'Get the money,' he used to say. And again, 'My measure of success is money.' And yet again, 'Money is not everything; it is only 99 per cent of everything.' He made a great deal of it. Not from his sports reporting, but from those extraordinary short stories, for whose telling he invented a new style, consisting entirely of the historic present. The stories were meticulously crafted. Runyon agonized over every word. And yet when he was hired by Hollywood and the moguls mangled his scripts, he went quietly, and praised them for it, saying that if the movies made money, which they did, then the moguls must have been right to make their changes. In fact, Runyon was near to having no morality as it is possible for a man without actually being dead. He befriended killers, found gangsters amusing, and in his stories very often softened their sins to make everything seem like a whimsical joke.

Most of his plots and characters come from real life. Sky Masterton was drawn from the character of one Bat Masterson, sheriff of Dodge City. Nathan Detroit owes his flair to that colourful gambler and one-time partner of Jimmy Durante, Lou Clayton. Lieutenant Brannigan is based on a man called Broderick, the most feared plainclothes cop in the New York of Runyon's time. Angie the Ox is really one Ciro Terranova, who once cornered the New Jersey artichoke market. And so it goes on, a vast gallery of roughnecks and nuts whose only common denominator was that they would do anything or anybody in order to avoid going to work. For Runyon such friends were a literary gift of incalculable value. Not that he merely transcribed what they told him. Nobody was more ingenious over the structure of his tales than Runyon, nobody took more care in the writing, or expended so much imagination in the atmosphere they exuded. It is very odd, but this Broadway slicker, this consort of chorus girls and chum of hoodlums, was one of the most dedicated creative artists of his epoch. What was even more amazing was that he managed to combine this dedication with being commercial. By the time he died in December 1946, Runyon had had more Hollywood productions made out of his works than any other writer. The seventy-two stories he had written had made him rich, world-famous and probably immortal.

But writing stories is one thing. Transmuting them into words and music is quite another. To take a work of literature and turn it into a musical comedy without either killing the original stone dead or coming up with a very bad musical is almost impossible. To have done justice to Runyon, what was required was nothing short of genius. Runyon's posthumous luck held. Up came a man called Frank Loesser, a Runyon character himself, the smartest cat in Tin Pan Alley, a Hollywood lyric writer whose induction into the United States Army coincided with his realization that he ought to be doing the whole job instead of half of it. Who needed composers? Loesser, who had worked with the likes of Hoagy Carmichael ('Two Sleepy People'), Arthur Schwartz ('They're Either Too Young Or Too Old'), Jule Styne ('I Don't Want To Walk Without You, Baby') and Burton Lane ('The Lady's In Love With You'), now started providing music to his own words. By 1948, the target was Broadway. He wrote a musical based on *Charlie's Aunt*, called it *Where's Charlie?*, and found himself more successful than he had ever been before. The producers were two men called Cy Feuer and Ernie Martin. They gambled on Loesser and ended up with a run of 792 performances. Afterwards Feuer said, 'Frank never came fully to life till that show.' Cole Porter came to see it and was seen shaking his head at its brilliance. Arthur Schwartz came, and wrote an essay in the *New York Times* defining Loesser as 'the greatest undiscovered composer in America'.

He did not stay undiscovered for long. The project to turn Runyon into a musical began. There were problems. The first libretto was no good. The second libretto was still unfinished when Loesser had completed the score. The second librettist, a man called Abe Burrows, realized that all he had to do was write a book which followed the gist of Loesser's songs. The upshot was a more or less perfect musical, one of the very few destined to have an indefinite active life. *Guys and Dolls* is immortal, which, in Broadway terms, means that it will probably last for a hundred years. Its greatest virtue of all is that it remains faithful to the Runyon originals. When the show first opened the role of the bigtime gambler Sky was played by Robert Alda. When Goldwyn made the movie Marlon Brando played it, with Sinatra as Nathan Detroit. Nicely-Nicely was played by Stubby Kaye. One has to quote no further from the cast list to make the point that the show demanded, and still demands, the very highest quality performance from its principals, because not only are they portraying people from an American literary classic, but they are also singing the words and music of another, later American musical classic. In tackling the role of Adelaide, for instance, Lulu is following in the footsteps of, to name but a few, Vivian Blaine and Julia Mackenzie. Norman Rossington's Nathan follows Sam Levene, Sinatra and Bob Hoskins. As for Sky Masterson, he began as Alda, became Brando and then, in a famous recorded version, was portrayed by Sinatra himself which means that Clarke Peters is sure to be on his toes.

The fact that the British are capable of producing *Guys and Dolls* at all is an amazing thing. I suppose the nearest comparison would be a Texan production of *Hamlet* that succeeded in not being funny. And yet the National Theatre production of the show became one of the biggest successes in the theatre's history. What Frank Loesser would have made of it all remains anyone's guess. Surprisingly, he preferred the love songs among his own works. I say surprisingly because he wrote some of the best joke-songs ever written. Watch how *Guys and Dolls* starts, with the three veteran horseplayers discussing in song their opinions about various chunks of horseflesh. The whole thing is positively dazzling. And yet Loesser preferred the tender items. He used to say, 'I'm in the romance business,' and when friends had been to see his work he would ask eagerly, 'Which song made you cry?' One lady who certainly cried was Isabel Quigley. While rehearsing 'I'll Know' for the Broadway opening, she was having problems with the wide range of the melody. Loesser, unable to contain himself, leapt on stage and gave Miss Quigley what Runyon would have called a slug on the beezer. He was, as they say, difficult. His first wife was even more difficult, and was known as the evil of two Loessers. Loesser was a bumptious, freakishly gifted man who used to wake up some mornings and say, 'I feel as good as Irving Berlin today.' And there were days when he was right. When he finally smoked himself to death, on 26 July 1959, he was sitting cross-legged in bed, plugged into a breathing machine – smoking a cigarette. As for Runyon, the greatest irony of his extraordinary career is that one-horse Kansas town where he was born. Talk about prophetic signs. The name of that tiny burg was – Manhattan.

George Gershwin – Then and Now (1988)

On 26 September 1898, Rose and Morris Gershwin, immigrants from St Petersburg living in Brooklyn, celebrated the arrival of a second son, George. Their first-born, Ira, was a mild-mannered child who gave no trouble, so why not another? This was what marriage was supposed to be, wasn't it? If anyone had told the parents that within twenty-five years their new child would be one of the most famous men in the world, their responses would have defined the differences between them. Rose would have said, 'Keep your rubbish to yourself.' Morris would have beamed and said, 'Naturally.'

Morris was right. It turned out to be George's century, and we, living in its dead embers, find ourselves willing parties to the arrangement. George died with the century no more than a third done, yet now, as we drift on into a new millennium, George is as much our constant companion as he was our parents', our grandparents'. His songs permeate our atmosphere, they echo on our romantic silences, their patterns are now in some strange way our patterns. His music continues to fill evenings in the concert hall; revivals of the musicals George wrote with his beloved brother in another world, another life, surface regularly on Broadway like those of no other writer of his day. Not so long ago West End audiences were emerging from *Crazy for You* with smiles on their faces. Yet *Crazy for You*, a melange of an old Gershwin show with other hits thrown in, is based on *Girl Crazy*, written in 1930.

Why should this be? The answer lies in the rapturous melodies. You went to see *Crazy for You*, knowing it was you and not the Gershwins who were on trial. And out they came, the great songs, of love consummated, 'Embraceable You'; of love unrequited, 'But Not For Me'; of love still undiscovered, 'Someone To Watch Over Me'; of lost love defiantly celebrated, 'They Can't Take That Away From Me'; of the sly elusiveness of love's rewards, 'Nice Work If You Can Get It'; and the swinging agelessness of 'I Got Rhythm', whose harmonic structure quickly became second only to the Blues in the equipment of the jazzman.

And there are the other Gershwin songs which were never attached to successful shows. What of the apparently simple but so subtle 'Isn't It A Pity?', the fizzing buoyancy of 'That Certain Feeling', the sleepy eroticism of 'Do It Again', the breathless discovery of love in 'How Long Has This Been Going On?', the mock-military march 'Strike Up The Band', the Viennese spoof 'By Strauss'. Perhaps the most eloquent proof that you can't put a date or a period to George's music is the movie, *The Shocking Miss Pilgrim*, in which Betty Grable, as Boston's first lady typist, goes to work for a besotted boss played by Dick Haymes. The score is remembered mainly for one of the loveliest ballads anyone ever wrote, 'For You, For Me, Forever More'. The point is that *The Shocking Miss Pilgrim* was filmed in 1946, nine years after George's death, and remains the only new posthumous Hollywood musical ever made, and was comprised of songs which George left behind unused at his death. How old is 'For You, For Me, Forever More'? We can't be sure. All we know is that it was nine years old when first we heard it. For how many years before that had it been languishing on Gershwin's shelves? But it is all academic, because Gershwin's work is literally timeless.

There is a postscript attached to this. In 1976, I visited Haymes in California and happened to mention his good fortune in being the one to introduce the world to 'For You, For Me, Forever More'. At which he waved away an entire era of popular song with 'You can't do that sort of stuff any more. It's too innocent. The world isn't like that today.' I could have reminded him that the world never was, that poets show us that pretence can be real too. But I didn't want to argue with the man in his own home. Besides, I didn't believe a word of it, and I didn't believe he did either. A few months later a new Haymes album appeared, and there they all were, the old songs of love found and lost, the songs 'too innocent' for a disillusioned age.

So where lies the secret of Gershwin's achievement? Frankly there is no answer, unless you agree that George was a genius, someone who never had to agonize over what he was writing, someone for whom it came easily. People are constantly writing books about him in attempts to discover the heart of the matter. I, who am by no means a dedicated collector, have a biography of Jerome Kern, one of Harold Arlen, one of Cole Porter, one of Irving Berlin. I have seven on George Gershwin, plus a coffee-table pictorial history, plus several pseudo-technical accounts of his methods. Probably the two men who came closest were his best friend, Oscar Levant, and his favourite brother, Ira. Here is Oscar Levant on the subject:

> *There was nothing frustrated about George. There was no gap between his dream and his doing. No uncertainty. The music was there and it came out, naturally, easily. He was a natural. That's a wonderful thing to be. Pretty marvellous when you come to think about it.*

Ira comes closer but in some curious way distances us even more from the creative processes which sparked the songs:

> *One night I was in the living-room reading. About 1 a.m. George returned from a party, took of his dinner jacket, sat the piano, said, 'There's a spot we might do something about a fog . . . How about a foggy day in London?' We finished the refrain, words and music, in less than an hour.*

Meanwhile we must be thankful that Gershwin was ever around, and that the staying power of his work has been so phenomenal. Today in the concert halls you can hear, in *Rhapsody in Blue*, the most widely known main theme of the twentieth century. Go to the opera and there you will find *Porgy and Bess*, the only authentic *and* popular American opera of our time. Turn on your TV some lazy afternoon and suddenly be confronted by Fred Astaire sitting on a country stile singing that song about a foggy day in London town. And catch up with 'The Man I Love', which was dumped by foolish producers from three successive musicals but made it anyway, to become what some say is the greatest popular song of them all. And then, when you have been through all this, remind yourself of the most amazing fact of all about this amazing man. He hardly ever got started.

IV

The Reluctant Art

Studies in Jazz

Why Reluctant?

Music does not come out of the ether, it has to be conceived and performed by musicians. This is a very unfashionable view in the jazz world, where thousands of people spend their entire lives shoring up the walls of the romantic legend of jazz, pasting over the cracks in those walls which must inevitably be made by the long-range guns of reality. The legend, of course, is very attractive and takes more than one form. For instance, it can be Jazz as the Bawdy Musical Expression of Nonconformity, or Jazz as the Great Artistic and Intellectual Significance of Our Time. On the face of it this may appear strange, because the first version contradicts the second. But this, after all, is the very essence of legend, whose irresistible attraction lies in its independence of the commonplace rules of logic. Galatea may change into a woman and Dionysus into a ram without upsetting in the slightest the reader who approaches these metamorphoses in the appropriate spirit, and by the same token John Lewis may change into an Oracle and Mezz Mezzrow into Pure Fiction without causing much bewilderment in the spectators. Unfortunately the working musician rarely has much time for such diverting sport and has to face the realities of his profession as best he can.

Those realities are hard and uncompromising, and revolve around a single familiar pivot, which is that most people have neither the time nor the temperament to interest themselves in what he is doing. They may embrace the trappings of his world as part of a social cult. They may cherish his music as a private, entirely subjective world of their own, unconsciously using the jazz they hear as the incidental music to a Proustian reconstruction of their own lives. They may support his efforts as part of their sociological homework. But only rarely are they inclined to trouble themselves to discover very much about the music itself and why it sounds the way it does. To most people the evolving styles of jazz occur with the same inevitability as the hands moving slowly around a clockface, and if some explanation must be provided, it usually has something to do with a magical, aesthetic Life Force thrusting the musician onwards and upwards to artistic achievements over which he has little or no control.

The attitude of the musician towards this outside world with which he has somehow to come to terms, usually takes one of three forms. Either he is amused, or he is disgusted, or he believes what people tell him about himself. The first reaction gives us the high comedy of the hipster abroad in a world of dullards, the second the belligerence and pathos of the seeker after cheap euphoria, while the third establishes nebulous messiahs who come to regard the music they play as a kind of free pass into the pantheon of great art.

Now there is one way in which jazz really is the most astonishing of all the arts, invaluable to the student of the artistic process, and that is the highly pressurized rate of its evolution. Jazz music has moved from primitivism to neoclassicism within the space of half a century, and so, just as geneticists may breed a thousand generations of insects to study the effect of environment on hereditary tendencies, so the documentor of art may make a detailed study of jazz and note the effect of economic pressures on the nuances of instrumental thought.

This hypothetical observer will discover a certain disarming naiveté about jazz. He will find that it came into the world conceived in such complete cultural innocence that it never even knew it was a form of artistic expression at all. He will find that even today few people in the jazz world have really got over the joke. For the jazz musician, groping and stumbling forward in his quest for articulate expression, has been rather like a shipwrecked man who, knowing nothing of life on the mainland, slowly and painfully evolves his own primitive kind of alphabet, and is so elated after years of struggle to discover words of two syllables that he sincerely believes he has made a significant step forward on behalf of civilization. And, indeed, how can we laugh at him? He has performed a prodigious feat, and to belittle him because he has not yet evolved the sonnet form or mastered the subtleties of irony would be most uncharitable.

That is why the terms employed in jazz criticism apply only in their own context, in the same way as the literacy of our islander only remains literacy by the standards of the island. The modernism of jazz is not modernism at all to anybody with a reasonable knowledge of nineteenth-century music. It is merely called Modern to mark the point in the evolution of jazz when one of its few real geniuses made the giant step from diatonic to chromatic harmony. In that sense only is the jazz of Charlie Parker modern.

There have been a few men who played similar roles to Parker. For various reasons these men found the conventions of their day inadequate, and attempted to break new ground. Sometimes their reasons were not purely musical. Sometimes they were not the outstanding musicians of their time. Nobody would pretend, for instance, that my inclusion of Benny Goodman in this collection and my omission of Louis Armstrong implies a belief that Goodman was a greater jazz musician than Armstrong. Some artists, and Armstrong is one of them, produce art so indigenous to their own spirit that it never occurs to them to change or evolve in any way. They create masterpieces so daunting that those who follow them are impelled to break away from the pattern and find something of their own. Which brings us to the second of the two huge jokes of jazz history, its relentless advance towards respectability.

As jazz advances technically, as it assimilates harmonies more and more complex, as it absorbs rhythmic variations that would have whitened the hair of the primitives of New Orleans, as it takes chromaticism in its stride without strangling itself, it also advances socially, from the brothel to the ginmill to the dance hall to the concert stage and the cultural festivals of the world. Of course the music itself lost its innocence a long time ago, perhaps in the ballrooms of the Roosevelt era. But its practitioners still wrestle manfully with the terrifying problem of keeping alive the earthy spark of its beginnings. And every time somebody introduces a new harmony into the jazz context, then the task becomes more difficult.

For the production of valid jazz depends on a delicate compromise between acute awareness and complete unselfconscious ease, between extreme artistic agility and consummate relaxation. A jazz musician is a juggler who uses harmonies instead of oranges. So long as he limits himself to the ensemble techniques of early New Orleans he is being very spectacular about throwing and catching the lone orange of dominant-to-tonic discord and resolution. Each time he throws up an additional orange, it becomes increasingly difficult for him to achieve that relaxed poise of the spirit without which no jazz is worth the playing. No matter how dexterous he may be, he will become a bore if his preoccupation with the oranges destroys the charm of his movements and the grace of his attitude. Today our modernists are striving so hard that the air is thick with flying oranges, many of which fall to earth and trip up the juggler.

Jazz criticism often tends to place importance on the wrong aspects of this juggling act. Mr Balliet tells us how the oranges often appear to him as light brown or deep purple in colour. M. Hodeir calculates the velocity and rate of acceleration of the oranges, and then selflessly credits the musicians with a mathematical subtlety which they do not possess. M. Pannassie insists that once the number of oranges passes a limit set by himself, all the oranges cease to exist altogether. For the juggler it remains a tortuous affair. But a few valiant spirits still manage to perform fantastic feats of skill. And they have the questionable compensation of knowing that the background against which they perform their art gradually becomes better upholstered, better ventilated and better patronized as time goes on.

Whether this is really what the jazz musician wants I do not know, because he can be just as insufferable about the glories of the ginmill as he sometimes is about the kudos of the concert hall. But whatever his feelings about the daunting responsibility of the Creative Artist where once there was only the kick of having a blow, the handful of musicians who changed his situation either musically or socially or both at the same time, either deliberately or accidentally, either for better or for worse, are in some ways the most fascinating and significant figures on the entire jazz landscape.

BIX BEIDERBECKE

. . . which is the right man,
Walt Whitman or Paul Whiteman?
COLE PORTER

The curse of jazz music is its hagiography, perhaps only to be expected in an art form possessing so much surface flamboyancy. The apparent glory of the spectacle of a lone soloist pitting his inventive powers against the world every time he stands up to play, combined with the element of the picaresque in so many gifted musicians, has been the supreme misfortune of the music. Popular journalism has found it easy to tack on to the body of jazz a spurious romanticism tending to obscure the art that lies beyond. There has been a surfeit of what Walter Sickert once called 'the recourse to melodrama to which the disinclination for real critical work drives some critics'.

Not all the journalism was meant to have this effect. Some of the very worst critics had the very best intentions. The effect has been deadly nonetheless. Artistic prowess has been neglected in favour of what the twentieth century refers to as 'human interest', a phrase which implies that poking one's nose into other people's business is more edifying than poking one's soul into other people's art.

Now the effect of magnifying the artist's personal foibles at the expense of his creative output is to create a sourceless mythology, an order of saints without divine inspiration of any kind, which is precisely what has happened to jazz all through its history, and precisely why the world at large is consistently baffled by the spectacle of a bohemia seemingly peopled only by eccentrics and degenerates producing music which doesn't sound like music at all. It is as though for every genuine lover of painting there were fifty who knew only that Toulouse-Lautrec frequented bawdy houses.

That Buddy Bolden should be immortalized as a barber and scandalmonger whose trumpet could be heard at a range of one, five or ten miles, depending on the degree of fanaticism to which one adheres to his particular legend, is understandable, for no recordings of Buddy Bolden exist. That Freddie Keppard should be remembered for covering his trumpet valves with a handkerchief to hide his fingerings from covetous rivals is a little less sane, though it may well be aesthetic justice. That Frank Teschmaker should be mourned as an incipient genius cut down by a premature death is hardly acceptable in the light of his recorded work. That Lester Young should be deified as The Man in the Pork-Pie Hat and Charlie Parker fondly recollected as an attempted suicide is quite unforgivable, for by now the legend is devouring the art from which it sprang.

With Bix Beiderbecke the position is already impossible. Sanity long ago fled in wild disorder from the task of interpreting his career. The damage was done many years ago by two agencies, the mawkish contemporaries who grabbed prestige from accidental associations with him, and the disgracefully inept journalism over the years which encouraged the process because it made what was called 'very good copy', which always means very bad copy. Bix is jazz's Number One Saint, and any attempt at a rational analysis of his talent usually invokes the bitterness of a theological dispute.

Today Bix is a kind of patron saint of Improvisation, a beatific figure before whom the idolators kneel in reverence, and at whom the debunkers heave giant brickbats. Of course the circumstances were ideal for this process of deification. The exquisite talent, the weakness for bathtub gin, the seraphic smile, the artistic frustration, the premature death, all played out against the backdrop of the Roaring Twenties. The façade has been building up, brick upon critical brick over the years, until today the man is equated with all kinds of people, objects and causes with which he has only the most tenuous connections. Today, when anybody mentions Bix Beiderbecke, a confused vision is conjured up of all the variegated symbols with which he has been juxtaposed, from Capone to Gatsby, from the crude fact to the artistic synthesis of the fact. The dismal truth awaiting the earnest student of Bix is that his vision will become impaired the moment he breathes Bix's name, and that instead of one figure he will see half a dozen, all interesting enough, but only one of which has much to do with music. The five spurious Beiderbeckes feed on the single reality, the hard core at the heart of the myth, the creative artist. There is the cardboard martyr of the Bixophiles who concoct biographies with acknowledgements to the Princeton dance programmes of the Jazz Age; there is the marvellous boy one critic talked of 'with wisps of genius swirling around in his brain'; there is the whimsy-whamsy superman of the Condon–Carmichael anecdotes; there is the baby-faced apotheosis of the Jazz Age, with glib parallels drawn between the Bix Crash and the Wall Street Crash: '. . . like the stock markets, he was riding high but shaken by 1929'; there is the actual jazz musician, the one-sixth of the legend which has supported the parasitic growth of the other five-sixths; and, finally, and in some ways the most fascinating of all facets of the legend, there is the fictive Bix projected by Miss Dorothy Baker in her novel *Young Man with a Horn*, a book so perfectly symptomatic of the failure of the writer of fiction to perceive the quintessence of the Jazz Life that the discrepancies between it and the reality of Bix's experience should serve as an invaluable guide to the aspiring writer of jazz fiction.

Fragments of the Bix myth are quite true of course. Bix Beiderbecke really is a key figure in the development of jazz. His dilemma really was a new one for the improvising musician, and he really was the first, perhaps the only, white musician to contribute something completely original to the jazz art which was not artistically suspect. Digesting the bare facts of his life one is soon convinced of the peculiar lovability of this amiable goofer Bix Beiderbecke, with his frightful naiveté in a worldly environment and his helplessness or irresponsibility which made a man like Frank Trumbauer desire to father him even at the expense of his own career. But Bix offered up as a martyr on the altar of fine art is more difficult to swallow. Bix's death, by no means the outcome of a self-destructive lust, seems rather to have been, like everything else in his life except his music, a confused accident, the aimless drift of an unsophisticated young man who was hardly aware at any time, of what was happening to him.

There were huge blanks in his musical education, and he evidently became increasingly aware of them. He must also have realized the comic ineptitude of many of the musicians with whom he worked. No great jazz musician ever kept worse musical company than Bix Beiderbecke. He seems to have spent most of his career working with lame dogs and most of his energies in helping them over a style. This apparent indifference to the poor quality of his companions is one of the surest indications of his amazing lack of awareness as a creative artist. To him, the dedicated ruthlessness of the creator would have seemed mere churlishness. Pee Wee Russell once said, 'His disposition wasn't one to complain. He wasn't able to say, "I don't like this guy, let's give him the gate and get so-and-so." He was never a guy to complain about the company he was in.' It is in that last sentence of Russell's, and not in the idiotic talk of selling his soul to Paul Whiteman, that the only real indictment of Bix lies. 'He was never a guy to complain of the company he was in.' No more deadly accusation could be levelled at any artist.

Sensational as Bix's arrival must have seemed to those who witnessed it, it is clear on reflection that nothing could have been more inevitable. Of all the things that had to happen to jazz, Bix had to happen to it more certainly than all the others, and when jazz has finally run its course and its development seen for what it is, a single continuous process, even the time at which he appeared will seem to have been predictable almost to the year. The jazz Bix heard as a boy was born of a sociological phenomenon whose total effect on the history of man has yet to be charted. Jazz was the musical expression of an oppressed minority dumped on an alien society, and in its beginnings was therefore not respectable, certainly not to the kind of middle-class immigrants the Beiderbeckes typified.

By the time Bix was old enough to understand what he was hearing, jazz had already begun its advance north. He was only one of thousands of white youths intrigued by it. And just as surely as jazz was the result of the transference of African native culture into the melting pot of the Deep South, so was the Bixian dilemma of the last years born of the contrast between the hybrid music Bix played and the sensibilities of the essentially European mind which conceived that music, for although Bix is always nominated as the All-American Boy of his period (the notes to the *Memorial* album on American Columbia begin 'The Bix Beiderbecke Story is the great romantic legend of American jazz'), Bix was the son of German immigrants aware of European music who tried to school the boy in what they thought they knew.

There is indeed a sense in which Bix was a martyr, but it has nothing to do with all the puerilities about marijuana nights and bathtub gin. Bix was the first jazz musician who felt obliged to attempt a widening of the harmonic scope of jazz by grafting on to it some of the elementary movements of modern harmony, the first improviser to try to take the patterns beyond the primitive shapes of New Orleans and give them a tint of the subtleties of the Impressionist composers of Europe.

By the end of his short life he had become less interested in the cornet, and obsessed instead by the piano and the half-formulated pieces he composed for it, a change of attitude with the most profound implications. The added harmonic dimensions of the piano, on which he was able to strike several notes simultaneously, were obviously better suited to his purpose. By that time the early days with the Wolverines only seven years before, days when he was a mere boy carrying the entire band on his shoulders, must have seemed far distant indeed, uncomplicated days before his own developing sensibilities forced him far beyond the point for which his training and experience had equipped him.

The body of legend dimly appreciates that a tension of this kind existed somewhere in Beiderbecke's life, but interprets it with unfailing lack of perception. The Bix legend goes very briefly as follows: 'Innocent young white boy with jazz gift. Becomes recognized and records masterpieces in the Big City. Starts to drink. Reaches peak around 1927. Sells his soul to commercialism. Falls ill. Half-recovers. Dies. End of life, beginning of legend.' It will be perceived that this framework leaves convenient gaps for the insertion of gangsters, the Right Woman, the Wrong Woman and the rest of the clumsy farrago which takes the music for granted and delivers a kind of affectionate rap on Bix's posthumous knuckles for being naughty enough to join a band as corrupted as Paul Whiteman's, a band whose only contribution to jazz was the money it poured into the pockets of those who sat in its elephantine ranks.

This artistic defection of Bix's is the one big blot on his copybook, the sole act for which posterity finds it difficult to forgive him. Indeed some criticism cannot find the heart to forgive him at all, being possessed of no heart in the first place, nor a brain nor an ear. Rudi Blesh once wrote with tight-lipped resolution, 'Bix's playing is weak. He just pretended to be a jazz musician because his weakness permitted him to play in the commercial orchestras of Whiteman and Jean Goldkette. Bix was neither a tragic nor an heroic character, he was a figure of pathos.' Leaving aside the curious defective logic of Blesh's second sentence, I am obliged to admit that there is a whole school of this criticism which discounts Bix, and throughout this school great stress is laid on the fact that Bix finally went for the fleshpots when he should have been preserving his innocence.

Now this kind of plot stands up very well when it is transferred to an idiom as crass as itself, for instance Hollywood and the fourpenny library romantics. But as an evaluation of Beiderbecke the artist it is so wildly inept that no deliberate parody of authentic criticism could ever get further from the mark. The truth about what happened to Bix and the motives behind his apparently irresponsible behaviour are obvious to any thinking jazz musician who has himself experienced, even if to a far less vital degree, the process which took hold of Beiderbecke. Educated by his own worldly experience as an artist, the jazz musician looks at the great mound of rubbish which has accumulated about Bix's figure and chuckles in wonder to himself, thinking perhaps that after all it is hardly reasonable to expect much better from such a parcel of fools.

The Artist-Who-Sold-His-Soul-For-A-Hip-Flask theory is useful in one way, because it is so completely, utterly hopelessly wrong that all one has to do to get to the truth of the matter is to reverse all its main propositions. After all, the man who is consistently wrong is just as sure a guide to conduct as the man who is consistently right.

The one significant thing about Bix is not that he sold his soul to Paul Whiteman for three hundred dollars a week, but that he refused to sell his soul, no matter what the consequences, and that he would have been prepared to sacrifice everything, even the one priceless gift he possessed, his jazz gift, rather than compromise musically so much as a semiquaver. The conventionally accepted story of Bix's growing artistic lassitude which finally destroyed him, may be neatly reversed to arrive at the truth. Bix embodies the case of artistic irresponsibility and unawareness which imperceptibly evolves into a growing wonder at the glory of music and a desperate attempt to create something worthy of that glory. It is a process half-aesthetic, half-intuitive, and all the more peculiar for the fact that throughout his adult years Bix remained intellectually unaware of the process that had taken hold of him, unable to rationalize its effects, unable to help the process along, unable even to opt out for the simple reason he was hardly aware he had ever been opted in. Iain Lang struck miles nearer the target than Blesh when he remarked that there was no hard core of intelligence or character in Bix to enable him to cope with his unwieldy fame, although he too goes on to describe the Whiteman episode as a compromise.

What did, in fact, happen to Bix had to happen to somebody as soon as jazz started to travel north into the nation at large where middle-class whites like Bix could hear it and be stirred by it. About Bix's reaction to the tremendous strains imposed upon him by his unique experience at the hands of music, there is something which borders, not on the heroic, but on the comic, and the fact that neither intellectually nor morally was he equipped to cope with that experience does make some belated sense out of Blesh's word 'pathetic'. The most comical thing of all about this battered reputation of Bix Beiderbecke is that there is little opposition to the Sale-of-Soul theory. Instead of opinion being divided between the Bleshes on one hand, who believe that as Bix knew he couldn't play jazz anyway, he joined the highest-paid band in the country and made the best financially out of his own shortcomings, and those like myself who can see quite clearly that joining Whiteman in 1927 was artistically the only honest thing Bix could possibly have done, the field is divided between those who know Bix joined Whiteman and despise him for it, and those who know he joined Whiteman and forgive him for it. Both the Bixophobes and the Bixophiles miss the point.

BENNY GOODMAN

Money is indeed the most important thing in the world; and all sound and successful personal and national morality should have this fact for its basis . . .

BERNARD SHAW

One day while talking about jazz to some students at the London School of Economics, I met a very earnest young woman who told me of her determination to compose a thesis involving jazz. Her chief difficulty was that she had no theme, and so after a brief conversation I suggested she compose a psychological history of the music. She was scandalized. 'You speak,' she reproached me, 'as though jazz were a person as well as an art. How can you possibly analyse an abstraction as though it were flesh and blood?'

And when I explained to her about the guilt complex which runs like a scarlet thread through the weave of jazz history, she seemed genuinely surprised. It had never occurred to her that a creative activity can have its complexes and its repressed desires as certainly as those who practise it, and the sudden revelation that jazz was the victim of its own psychological disorders was a deep shock to her. I believe she took my suggestion as a flippant joke, and never appeared on any of the future occasions on which I was invited to talk to the School's jazz club.

The subconscious awareness of jazz musicians that the art they practise had its beginnings in the most disreputable surroundings is more widespread than even the musicians themselves sometimes realize. A glance beneath the surface of Bix Beiderbecke's career reveals what dilemmas and dividends may spring from the yearning for musical legitimacy, but the process becomes glorious high comedy when the musical desire is wedded to social aspiration. That jazz music of all the arts should have developed bourgeois sensibilities is one of the most comical developments in the history of twentieth-century music, although when the musical results fall on our ears we are suddenly constrained not to laugh quite as loud as we might, possibly because we are yawning so heavily.

Had that young lady only known it, the theme I suggested was rich with possibilities. She was well aware that jazz began as a do-it-yourself music which graduated to the brothels of Storyville. At the time she asked me her question she held two tickets to the Royal Festival Hall for the latest of Mr Granz's importations. Yet she saw nothing incongruous enough to impel intellectual curiosity in the juxtaposition of brothel and concert hall. Perhaps she did grasp it but was daunted by the enormity of the task. She need not have worried, because fortunately for us all, the process may be traced quite simply in an individual as well as in the art form generally, and the individual case has the added charm of being dramatic on the personal level.

In examining the career of Benny Goodman, the most obvious fact to emerge is that the jazz musician, no less than any other creative artist, is captain of his fate only to a limited degree, and that there sometimes arrive junctures in his career when apparent irrelevancies like governmental economic policy, unemployment figures and patterns of popular education will coalesce to mould his musical style despite himself. Benny Goodman, who so beautifully symbolizes the half-witted old Hollywood myth about the poor slum boy who blows hot licks and becomes a national idol ('But, poppa, I don't want to be a pants presser'), is an archetype because in addition to prodigious musical talent, he was subjected to a combination of economic and social circumstances in not quite the same way as anyone else. The imbalance between his talent and the forces which brought pressure to bear upon that talent is so exquisite as to appear too good to be true. The suspicion that one is reading into Goodman's career things which are not there, is only dispelled by the unshakeable evidence of Goodman's recorded work, the only evidence which really matters.

Goodman's life as an influential jazz musician extended, very roughly, from the end of the Jazz Age to the beginning of Modernism, say from 1928 to about 1943, and it is doubtful whether in a comparable fifteen-year period, any sphere of artistic activity has seen such bewildering, hysterical changes. It is literally true to say that a jazz lover who heard Bix's 'Singing The Blues', then went into a monastery, stayed there till the death of Roosevelt, and then came out to hear Charlie Parker's 'Anthropology' would have real difficulty recognizing any relationship between the two recordings. The period between the two saw jazz move from simplicity of conception to complexity, from unselfconscious ease to high sophistication, and it is a diverting spectacle to watch Goodman moving forward hardly at all, beginning the period as an advanced spirit and ending it as a petulant last-ditch reactionary, playing the same music all the time.

Not that Goodman can really be blamed for standing still for fifteen years. Some of his outbursts against the modernists were a little too apoplectic to merit serious consideration, but if Goodman moved forward so little, he moved as far forward as most of his contemporaries. It is true that jazz evolves from one style to another, each more complex harmonically than the last, but its individual musicians cannot possibly keep up with the process, wherein lies their tragedy. This is a truth which all but the musicians themselves seem to overlook. Once a musician matures he is straddled for the rest of his life with the nuances of his formative period. That is why at the advent of modernism Benny Carter was braver than Johnny Hodges, and Hodges wiser than Carter. The fact that though an art form evolves, its practitioners may not, is one which applies particularly to Goodman because by the time Charlie Parker suddenly began extending the harmonic range of the jazz solo, Goodman had long since become a walking anthology of all the mannerisms of the previous fifteen years. Looking back at it, we can see that when we hoped years ago that perhaps Goodman's scholastic quartets, evolving slowly into the stylized sextets, were the beginning of something, we were misreading the evidence, that really Goodman was the exact opposite, the end of something, a fulfilment, a culmination, the sum total of his own past.

Now there are certain truisms about Goodman's talent which are often overlooked, hardly surprising in view of the fact that to the purist Goodman's apparent lack of professional dignity and his obsessive trick of making money, must seem like the work of the devil. But this does not alter the case of Goodman's musical endowment. First, he always had a firm grasp of the principles of hot clarinet playing. He was an intuitive jazz musician, and the red herring of his effortless technique should never be permitted to obscure the fact. He may never have lost his mind, like Rapollo, or suffered a melodramatic death, like Teschmaker, or appealed to the amateur musicologist with the crude excesses of his own style, like Johnny Dodds, but strictly musically, Goodman's was a beautiful talent. Second, he had the kind of nimble mind which can assimilate and correlate the climate of its own environment so well that in time its owner becomes symbolic of that period without necessarily having contributed anything very original towards it. Third, Goodman, once he grew to manhood, never believed that the world of music could be contained within a jazz ensemble. Fourth, he had a degree of aptitude for the mechanics of clarinet playing which only occurs a few times in each generation. And, fifth, he was both astute and lucky.

But Goodman, when he first began to make an impression on

the jazz world, was still literally a boy. The technical devotion had not yet asserted itself, and his life was still virtually the jazz life. According to Goodman's own reflections, it was not till 1932 that he began to concentrate on perfecting his technique, and the reasons he gives are most revealing. He says that he realized that a musician who could read and execute any musical score would stand the best chance 'of riding out the worsening depression'. Goodman was twenty-two years old when he arrived at that conclusion, and it makes a quaint contrast with the attitude towards jazz and survival of some of his more picaresque contemporaries. The mere thought of somebody like Bix or Muggsy Spanier sitting down to work out how best to 'ride out the worsening depression' is enough to stress the fundamental difference between Goodman and all the other Chicagoans of the period. It was no accident that it was Goodman and not Pee Wee Russell or Jack Teagarden or Eddie Condon who became a brand image and a national effigy a year or two later.

As the years passed, Goodman's technique loomed larger and larger, until by the time I became a young musician during the war, he was our trump card in all arguments concerning the illiteracy of the jazz musician. 'Look at Benny Goodman,' we would say, 'He plays Mozart, doesn't he?'; the speaker never having heard anything by Mozart in his life. And of course it was true. The retort was unanswerable. Goodman was a superlative musician even by the most rigorous conservatoire standards, a very convenient thing for those suffering from an inferiority complex as to the cultural bona fides of jazz music. Francis Newton has very perceptively written of generations of jazz lovers who have grown up 'to repeat the same rare crumbs of praise for jazz by classical musicians (first or second-rate) and to hail with touching gratitude the occasional recognition of jazz by the Third Programme of the BBC or similar established cultural institutions'. Goodman was the most effective bribe which jazz had to offer the musical Establishment.

It was inevitable. Technique, as it begins to amass, will demand problems to solve. It will fret at the absence of constant challenge, like a medieval knight steadily running out of opponents to vanquish. It was inconceivable that Goodman, as he moved relentlessly forward to complete mastery over the clarinet keyboard, should be satisfied with 'Royal Garden Blues' and 'I

Got Rhythm', which is how curiosities like 'Clarinet À La King' and 'Caprice Paganini' happened.

This progress of Goodman's towards complete technical domination was something more superficial than and quite divorced from Bix Beiderbecke's yearning to plumb the innermost depths of music. Goodman's infatuation was primarily an infatuation with the co-ordination of mind and fingers rather than the creative process itself. But before he emerged into middle age with his dreamed-of mastery, a million dollars and a jazz spirit that had run dry, he produced some classic jazz recordings, leaving the analysts with a far simpler task than they might otherwise have inherited. Goodman is one of the most convenient figures on the jazz landscape. He is a long addition sum, neatly and impeccably worked out pat.

The events of 1935 may be explained by many factors and endless permutations of those factors, but one fact that is quite indisputable is that there had to be a Benny Goodman. His name might have been any one of half a dozen of his contemporaries, Tommy Dorsey or Jack Teagarden, Jimmy Dorsey or Glenn Miller, Joe Venuti or Bud Freeman, but whoever it was, there had to be a symbolic figure, the materialization of the American Dream in the form of a bandleader, and the fact that it happened to be Benny Goodman is the most fascinating single thing about him.

By 1935 the pattern of jazz was changing. The repeal of Prohibition had speeded the end of the era which nurtured the Chicagoans and their brash music. It is at least a reasonable hypothesis that jazz might then have slowly curled up and died away. Either it would do something like that, now it was passé as the incidental music to the manufacture of bootleg liquor, or else it had to make the giant step and become respectable, commercial, accepted by the bourgeoisie. It had to find a new audience, a wider one, formed of those who respected the letter of the law rather more closely than any of its predecessors.

It is now, with the advent of a fresh prototype, the Famous Bandleader, that economics and art, profit and psychology, hot jazz and guilt motives become indivisible. Jazz was about to take its most significant stride away from the Storyville legend. It was about to capture the middle-class adolescent heart. And it did so through the agency of a musician who had, three years before, amended his practice routine to dovetail with the national unemployment figures. Goodman came along with his organized mind just at the time when the United States was poised on the brink of its recovery from the imbecilities of the Coolidge regime. At this distance of time it seems only natural that jazz, too, should have procured for itself a New Deal.

The large orchestra was by no means unknown to the jazz musician. It is often overlooked that when Goodman became the King of Swing he was not the first monarch of the realm. Long before him Paul Whiteman had waggled a fatuous baton in the faces of Bix and Teagarden and the rest of them. But Whiteman's way of selling jazz to the masses was to drain all the blood away first. Had it not been for Bix none of Whiteman's recordings would today be worth the wax it was pressed on. His was a big band, certainly, but it was more than that. It was a huge band, a vast band, a cumbersome band, a lumbering elephantine band whose leader was apparently never aware of the beautiful parody of the real thing he was creating. Besides, Whiteman was comfortably plump, reassuringly middle-aged. This was the new era of the Proletarian Ideal, and Whiteman looked too much like a stockbroker to be accepted by the New Youth. Whiteman was, in a word, passé, no less than bathtub gin and the Charleston.

There were other big bands, far better than Whiteman had ever dreamed of, but they consisted of musicians with the wrong pigmentation for national acceptance. The fact that they were always better than any orchestra Goodman ever led, that they included in their ranks musicians with whom most of Goodman's sidemen do not bear comparison, is a fact which must always be kept very firmly in the foreground of any history of the Swing Age. The Benny Goodman band was never at any time the best band in jazz. It is debatable whether it was ever one of the best three. It just happened to be the best of those that were exploitable on a national scale.

One assumes that Goodman was at the time far too shrewd an assessor of jazz quality not to have been aware of the fact, and his actions on one or two occasions seem to prove that he knew where the true inspiration lay. There is a certain admirable ruthlessness about those actions which typify Goodman's single-mindedness at the time. It must have required considerable courage to carry a coloured musician on tour with the orchestra, but once Goodman had played with Teddy Wilson there was never any doubt in his mind that Wilson would have to become part of the Goodman act. Even shrewder was the strategy he deployed when first forming his band.

Long before Goodman had ever thought of forming his own orchestra, back in the Ben Pollock days, the Fletcher Henderson band had been at its zenith. It was infinitely the most skilled large unit of its day, including in its ranks some of the most brilliant jazz musicians of all time. Henderson, a moderate pianist, happened to be an outstanding orchestrator, that is if he is measured against the prevailing environment of the late 1920s. He was one of the first men to conceive the idea of using sections of instruments instead of individuals to provide a background for soloists as well as to create an integrated orchestral effect. His writing was skilled but relatively simple in phraseology. Many of his written section figures were no more than a kind of individual riff which might occur in a more casual performance, except that Henderson was able to increase their power by using three or four voices in unison, or harmonizing the rhythmic phrase he had hit upon. As for the ensemble, the ideal was to get several men playing the melody with the same expression and inflections that a soloist might use.

The territory Henderson explored contains more bear-traps than any in the world of jazz. All the orchestral ingenuity in the world cannot justify the loss of rhythmic spirit in a jazz performance. Unfortunately the temptation to create sumptuous orchestral sounds within the jazz frame almost always results in the dissipation of the jazz itself. Henderson, keeping his effects fairly simple, was one of the very few jazz musicians who committed his choruses to manuscript without stabbing them to death with the end of his pen nib. Apart from Duke Ellington, who, for a thousand obvious reasons was unavailable to Goodman, Henderson was the natural choice for anyone who desired to form a band playing orchestrations without sounding too cumbersome, like Whiteman's, or too effete, like the spineless meanderings of bands like the Casa Loma.

Henderson's band had died of natural causes in 1934, when the entire personnel had handed in their notice en bloc, rather than see Henderson struggling desperately to hold together an organization for which there was not enough work to exist. Goodman's decision to form a large unit so shortly after the end of the great days of the Fletcher Henderson band was one of the happiest accidents in the entire Goodman story.

One fact about Goodman and his first band which is too easily overlooked is that in the beginning the whole episode was a huge accident, not some diabolical plot. Goodman had no more idea than anyone else that a wide public existed for jazz. In the beginning the musicians he gathered about him were concerned only with playing something fresh, something they might enjoy. It just happened that in indulging this whim, Goodman was the first man to stumble on to the gold mine destined to yield such rich profits for years to come.

The number of factors which might be reasonably listed in explanation of Goodman's frightening breakthrough at the Palomar Ballroom are endless and bafflingly varied, from the birth of Marconi to the teaming of Fred Astaire with Ginger Rogers. The truth Goodman half-discovered at the Palomar was that the entire continent was full of young people who enjoyed dancing to jazz enough to pay for the privilege. Even then the enormity of his discovery does not seem to have hit him hard enough to convince him fully. It was not till the second great day in history of his social-economic triumph (there were three altogether, the Palomar, the Paramount and Carnegie Hall) in March 1937 that it dawned upon him that the city gates were wide open and the treasury undefended.

It is impossible to say precisely when the Goodman band stopped being a select club for musicians to enjoy themselves and changed into a corporation producing a commodity for mass consumption, but the process of change was a very gradual one and only became really obvious after some years of popular triumph. Had the big band been all that came out of the Goodman Era, history might be inclined to dismiss it with an indulgent shrug of the shoulders. After all, nothing the Goodman band played ever had half the musical content of the Ellington band of the same period. Certainly the Basie band was superior to Goodman's in all departments except clarinet playing. A good case could be made out to prove the superiority of bands like those of Chick Webb and Jimmy Lunceford, and although the Goodman band recordings still possess an engaging bounce, their chief importance today is as the secondary musical result of an accidental economic process.

It is in one of Goodman's gimmicks that the true importance lies. The band-within-a-band idea has obvious attractions for the booker, the fan and the leader, all of whom believe they are getting two bands for the price of one. Indeed, in a few exceptional cases that is exactly what they are getting. Although there are instances of leaders before Goodman featuring smaller groups from time to time, nobody had actually made one of these splinter groups an added attraction to the full orchestra. It is clear today that the Benny Goodman Trio, and later the Quartet, were Goodman's artistic relief from the rigours of leading a large dance orchestra. The group-within-a-group conception was a safety valve for musicians subjecting themselves to a more rigorous professional discipline than they had ever known before and soon found to be excruciatingly boring.

Without any question the Goodman small groups are a milestone in jazz history because they were an acknowledgement of the further advance of that instrumental virtuosity which had been gathering ever since jazz started to advance north. In Goodman, jazz possessed for the first time a man with all the attributes needed for expressing this advance in popular terms. He was young enough and white enough and proletarian enough in his origins to appeal to a large enough mass of paying customers. And, vitally important, he possessed what was by now one of the most dazzling instrumental techniques in the history of jazz.

Its formula was as simple as its instrumentation. A piano introduction, a fairly faithful statement of the theme on clarinet, a series of improvised solos and a final ride-out chorus in the true Chicagoan tradition. Now and again they might tinker with the written chord sequence, as in 'Lady Be Good', when they uprooted the theme and transplanted it in the harmonic minor. Or they might play an original, like the wittily conceived 'Opus A Half' and 'Opus Three-Quarters'. But the whole point about the Goodman small-groups is that the bulk of their output adhered as strictly to the written harmonic pattern, and was markedly similar in the nature of its repertoire, as the Chicago ensembles had been a few years before. The result of this combination of circumstances was that Benny Goodman, with his jazz experience, his instrumental mastery and his nimble mind, produced a summation of the entire musical environment which had first nurtured him. In his small-group recordings he pursued the Chicago style to its absolute limits, stretched existing harmonic conventions to what seemed like their ultimate, snatched for the soloist a kind of concentrated attention he had never possessed before, and suggested for the first time that deliberate stylization might have charms to compensate for the aggressive carelessness of the jazz of a few years before.

This comprehensive grasp of Goodman's of what the clarinet had been doing in jazz for the past twenty years might be said in the long run to have killed the instrument stone dead. When Modernism finally swept away the relics of the 1930s, its practitioners very soon discovered that for their purposes there was something very seriously wrong with the clarinet. This peculiar fact has never been explained very satisfactorily. Certainly the inflexibility of pitch of the notes in the lower reaches of the clarinet's register was no encouragement. It is also true that the considerable complexities of modernism in its execution reach daunting proportions when allied to the tortuous fingerings of the clarinet keyboard. There was no doubt that the instrument sounded woefully incongruous in a Bebop setting.

The result has been an almost total eclipse of the instrument in Modern jazz. Nobody pretends that Buddy de Franco, for all his phenomenal technique, has a tithe of the significance of a Rollins or a Miles Davis, or even of a Getz or a Sims. Leaving aside the ineptitude, shocking in its arrogance of players like Tony Scott, there remain only the Goodman imitators, a few veterans like Edmund Hall and Pee Wee Russell, and Jimmy Hamilton, a curious case who shows the influence both of Goodman and his only serious rival in the Musical Matinee Idol Stakes during the heyday of Swing, Artie Shaw. No young musician today thinks of becoming a modern musician through the medium of the clarinet, and the reason may not altogether be one of tone or technique.

In the 1930s Goodman stamped upon the instrument he played a conception so irresistible and so absolute that it has conditioned jazz thought ever since. When people claim the clarinet is not suited to the movements of modernism, what many of them really mean is that these movements are antipathetic to the clarinet style which Goodman consummated and made worldwide. His success, both artistically and economically, was too overwhelming to be forgotten. The natural parry to this theoretical thrust is the one involving Louis Armstrong and Dizzy Gillespie. Nobody made his influence felt in jazz more than Louis Armstrong, and yet in time Gillespie came along to overthrow every one of the canons of style laid down in Armstrong's trumpet playing. The difference is this. Armstrong achieved his dominance on an actual, whole, independent musical instrument. Benny Goodman did not, for so far as jazz music is concerned, the clarinet is not really a separate independent instrument at all. It is a first cousin to the saxophone, although admittedly this relationship is a reversal of the historical facts.

No musician ever becomes technically very proficient on the clarinet without also becoming a reasonable saxophonist in the process. The reason for the spectacular role of the clarinet in the early days of jazz is that its tonal properties and the range of its upper register made it the ideal upper voice in the three-man ensembles of New Orleans. A saxophone would have been drowned in a sea of strident decibels, so the clarinet was literally indispensable. As soon as the ensemble conception was discarded, as it was in time through the virtuosity of Armstrong, then the clarinet was doomed to at least partial eclipse. Before that eclipse came, Goodman synthesized the whole process so completely that the eclipse itself became more marked than ever. And because the ensemble demand has vanished with the golden age of the improvised ensemble, and because also of the convenience of closed pads and the suitability of its tone, most men will prefer a saxophone when the choice has to be made. For these reasons it seems most unlikely that anybody else will ever leave a body of recorded clarinet jazz to challenge the coherence and comprehensiveness of the Goodman small-groups. There will be no clarinettist to play Parker to Goodman's Hodges, or Gillespie to his Armstrong. However well any future jazz clarinettist may play, we will always wonder why he didn't play a saxophone instead, especially if, like Jimmy Hamilton, he gets closer to the spirit of jazz on the heavier instrument.

When Goodman made those recordings, the rules of jazz were very clear cut. Harmonies always resolved in a certain way, which is why the cadences of the period are so instantly recognizable.

The chord of the seventh moved with a comforting inevitability on to the chord with its root an interval of a fourth away. The diminished chord was a pleasant little extravagance, a baroque gesture that apparently resolved nowhere at all in many cases, few soloists having appreciated at the time that the chord of the diminished seventh is really only the same old dominant seventh chord with a Minor ninth perched on its head and its root chopped away.

There was, in fact, a classically rigid framework within which men like Goodman had to work. To the musician bred on the subtleties of Parker and his generation, the diatonic laws of Goodman's day seem merely the result of a few hours study; the naturally endowed musician might even master them with no theoretical knowledge at all, relying on the sensibilites of a refined ear to guide him home. Goodman's supreme virtue was that despite the simplicity of the harmonic rules, he always displayed a delightful ingenuity in the way he threaded the harmonies together, an ingenuity which at certain peak moments became transmuted into real inspiration.

The session with the Venuti–Lang group is one example, and in the trios and quartets he rose to the occasion time and again. All the very greatest jazz solos are wrought so artistically that the harmonic frame on which they are suspended becomes camouflaged by the continuity and the relevance of the solo both to itself and the theme which inspired it. It is this sense of form, this cloaking of the skeleton of the harmonic frame with the flesh of artistic invention which is the rarest and most significant possession of any jazz musician, and it is the reason why the greatness of a solo never at any time depends merely on the degree of modernity or reaction of its harmonic foundation.

The best of the clarinet solos with the trio and quartet stand as homilies in the art of the jazz solo. In recordings like 'S'Wonderful', the first 'After You've Gone', 'I Cried For You', 'Sweet Georgia Brown', Goodman achieved the ultimate consummation of the style he had first begun to digest in the Ben Pollock days and earlier. Many of his phrases in these small-group recordings would not be out of place in a Chicago ensemble, except that now they are being executed with a confidence and urbanity that the Teschmakers and Russells had never dreamed of, and, let it be admitted, perhaps never really desired.

By now the classical influences Goodman had brought to bear on his style had merged exquisitely with his natural jazz flair. He could now play anything his mind conceived. The long succession of small-group recordings is remarkable for its technical intricacy and lack of any technical blemish. The same is true, of course, of the clarinet solos with the big band, but in the smaller unit Goodman had created the open spaces in which to move, sweeping aside all the distractions of orchestration and section figures which so often stand like clumsy signposts guiding the soloist towards the obvious. In the trio it was Goodman's inventive power and musical wit against the gods.

His integration of the diminished chord in the third and fourth bars of 'S'Wonderful' into the harmonic frame of the eight-bar phrase, the reshaping of the eight bars which open the second half of 'Sweet Sue', the fire and originality of the phrase based on the dominant seventh chord occurring at the juncture in 'I Cried For You' where the lyric says 'has a turning', all these remembered fragments from twenty years of listening suggest a jazz talent of the very highest class.

Running concurrently with this long succession of recordings with his own groups, the Goodman discography reveals another, completely independent series, likely to be forgotten, at least in the text of the Goodman story, because on the face of it they are not so appealing, by which I mean they do not present the cheapskate copywriter with the same happy clichés as the rags-to-riches success of the big band, which was after all one of those rare moments in social history when reality and outrageous romance come together and touch for a while, when the facts take on the amorphous aspect of a sentimental legend whose only excuse for existing at all is the fact that it really did happen. The Goodman success was another illustration of life imitating art, that is, if the Hollywood output of the period could by any stretch of the critical imagination be regarded as art.

The recordings Goodman made with Billie Holiday and Teddy Wilson marked the moment in his career when this astonishing duality of attitude began to be noticeable. The discography now starts to list items whose juxtaposition transforms Goodman's career into slapstick of the crudest kind. The discography tells us that the big band recorded 'When A Lady Meets A Gentleman Down South' within six weeks of the date on which Goodman played on 'Pennies From Heaven' with Billie Holiday, a session on which Lester Young created a twenty-four bar solo for which the only suitable adjective is marvellous; that he recorded 'Jingle Bells' with his own band on 1 July 1935, and 'I Wished On The Moon' with Wilson and Holiday on 2 July 1935; that on successive sessions he made 'After You've Gone' with the trio and 'Santa Claus Comes In The Spring' with the orchestra; that in one four-week period in 1938 he cut some reasonable sides with the orchestra, four superlative tracks with a Wilson–Holiday pick-up group, including 'He Ain't Got Rhythm' and 'I Must Have That Man'; and a quartet session which produced an outstanding interpretation of 'Tea For Two'.

The dichotomy became more marked as time went on. Indeed, once the big band had captured the mass imagination, it could not have been avoided. By the time Goodman became the undisputed King of Swing, his orchestra, his commercial potential, his economic significance, had taken control of him. There was little he could do now but sit in the driver's seat and wait for the whole clanking machinery of the Big Band Touring Age to grind to a halt, as inevitably it had to in time. But before it did Goodman had been granted all the wishes implicit in that statement of his about riding out the worsening depression of 1932.

The trios and quartets were the product of a natural jazz talent allied to fanatical technical ambition. Gradually the jazz talent shrank as Goodman grew older, while the technical aspirations remained undimmed. Slowly the perfect imbalance between the two was destroyed, and the official date of the abandonment of the perfect four-man formula Goodman had evolved for himself was 2 October 1939. On this day he made a recording which in two very different but equally vital ways heralded the end of Goodman's Golden Age. For the first time he resorted to the sextet formula, although in effect the first sextet was still just a rhythm section plus the clarinet. The second profound change was the presence in this rhythm section of a remarkable guitarist symbolic of a new younger generation whose playing now began to make Goodman's appear flabby in contrast.

Charlie Christian had virtually no recording career apart from the Goodman sides, but in his brief life he created the only music for which the Goodman sextets are likely to be remembered. Christian is the musician usually cited as the symbolic figure caught flat-footed between the old jazz and the new, a generalization which is more convenient than accurate, being one of those half-truths which tempt people to think no further after they have digested them. In his phrasing and his inflexions Christian was an archetype of the Swing Age. The riffs he concocted, of which 'Flying Home' may be taken as typical, have about them not a glimmering of a suggestion that a harmonic revolution was now imminent. Some of Christian's riffs sound so essentially children of the middle 1930s that they can strike the ear as excruciating. But they do so because of the incongruity between them and the musical content of some of the solos rising out of them. It is here that Christian's playing suggests at odd moments that the frame that has served jazz for so long may soon be rejected as too restrictive by younger musicians.

Here and there in Christian's solos occur those same leaps, apparently quite irrational, later to be one of the most disconcerting of Charlie Parker's new tactics. The irrationality in both cases was quite imaginary, being due to the rigid conception of how a jazz phrase should move to which the jazz world was so thoroughly attuned in the 1930s. To this extent only was Christian an apocalyptic figure. Rhythmically he was as addicted as all the rest to the chug-chug-chug of the rhythm section, which is not to belittle his wonderful gift. So far from being the revolutionary, Christian was the final consummation of the diatonic approach, standing head and shoulders above almost everybody he played with. His presence in the Goodman Sextet, allied to the almost comic formalism of many of the group's themes, like 'Shivers' and 'Seven Come Eleven', misled many people into the suspicion that this sextet, with its bright, ingenious little arrangements and its suave riffs, might be the beginning of a new era in jazz. Every time Christian took a solo the suspicion was strengthened because certainly there was something fresh about him. It is ironic indeed that Benny Goodman of all people, the musician who was soon to slang all the modernists, should have given Christian such lavish solo time.

So far from being the start of something, the Goodman Sextet was the ending of something very old. It was an attempt to bring to the small-group the kind of premeditated precision of a large one. But the premeditated precision had only been created at all because the big band demanded it. The amusing thing is that for all their tailored impeccability and their tortuous commonplaces, Goodman can find for them no climaxes to match the careful stylization of the rest of the performance. Time and again Goodman returns to that Chicagoan tear-up last chorus, as though looking nostalgically over his shoulder at the good old days.

Count Basie

When Count Basie's orchestra came to Britain in 1969, Benny compiled this overview of Basie's life and career.

Born in Red Bank, New Jersey, in August 1904, Bill Basie is one of the few jazz musicians of his generation to have had the questionable benefit of formal education in childhood, although details of this education are so sparse as to be almost non-existent. His first lessons were delivered by his mother, who later gave way to a Mrs Holloway, who charged twenty-five cents a lesson. Reading between the lines, it seems that the child Basie was not totally committed to these piano lessons, because the records also inform us that his first musical ambition was to play the drums, and that this idea was only abandoned after Basie realized that his own drumming was eclipsed by that of a neighbouring friend, who later became the Sonny Greer of the Duke Ellington band.

In the early 1920s Basie made the obligatory move to Harlem, at a time when that remarkable musical centre was being dominated by the dynasty of Stride pianists headed by James P. Johnson and Willie 'The Lion' Smith. Basie was by no means the only young man who was influenced by towering personalities like Johnson and Smith. The two star pupils in that particular school were Duke Ellington and Thomas 'Fats' Waller, who in turn became mentors to the next wave of young pianists. To this day the Stride influence is rampant in Basie's piano playing, although this aspect of his work is usually neglected in favour of the other side of his musical style, the extraordinary clipped, aphoristic manner for which he has become recognized as an original.

At the time Basie arrived in Harlem there seems to have been unlimited work for musicians. Clubs, saloons, cabarets and bars sprang up like mushrooms, and most of them could find room for a young pianist with a good rudimentary grasp. Basie has always been explicit about influences on his style at this crucial point in his life. The name he always quotes in this connection is that of Thomas 'Fats' Waller, who Basie first heard playing the organ in the pit of the Lincoln Theatre. Once encountered, Waller was not a man to be forgotten, and Basie became a daily visitor, watching Waller's technique as an organist. Soon Waller was inviting Basie to sit alongside him at the keyboard, thus establishing the rudiments of that organ style which Basie has demonstrated from time to time on record albums over the years.

For a time Basie went into vaudeville, with interludes as an accompanist to blues singers Clara Smith and Maggie Jones. It was while he was barnstorming through the South-West with a troupe called Gonzel White's, that he arrived at two prime points in his life, one geographical, the other musical. The White troupe found itself stranded in Kansas City, and around this time the troupe crossed paths, in Tulsa, Oklahoma, with a group called Walter Page's Blue Devils. It is from these twin points that the apotheosis of Basie was first to begin. James Rushing, who was singing with Page's band, remembers this first encounter, and recalls that in addition to playing piano in White's quartet, Basie also doubled as the villain in one of the comedy sketches.

Soon Basie was a member of the Blue Devils, a group which he later described as 'the happiest band I've ever been in'. The group lasted until the early 1930s, when it broke up and the nucleus of its personnel was absorbed into the band of Benny Moten, a well-established Midwestern leader. In the Moten band Basie was very much a back number. Not only did Moten himself play piano, but his brother Buster played piano-accordion, which meant that Basie was really third-choice pianist. Moten died in 1935, Buster took over and gave up after six months, at which point Basie returned to Kansas City, which he remembers as 'a cracker town, but a happy town'.

In the autumn of 1935, Basie and several of the old Moten band moved into the Reno Club where, according to John Hammond, 'the musicians got fifteen dollars a week, and the hours were eight to four, except on Saturday, when it was twelve solid hours, from eight to eight. It was a seven day week, and nobody got rich, least of all the club owner.' In December 1935, Hammond picked up a Basie broadcast being transmitted from a Kansas City experimental radio station, and immediately began evangelizing on its behalf. In 1936, four more musicians were added to the group, a booking agency was found, and by October of that year the first authentic Count Basie Orchestra was ready to make its entry into jazz history.

In view of the fact that this original band was one of the best that jazz was ever to know, it is interesting to take a more detailed look at its methods, particularly in view of the fact that those methods are at the heart of the Basie band today, and that they differ so diametrically from those of his greatest contemporary, Duke Ellington. No more profound difference could be discovered anywhere in jazz than that between Count and Duke. Whereas the Ellington band is a group whose effectiveness radiates outwards from the orchestral genius of its leader, the Basie band is essentially a band of jazz soloists whose freedom is cluttered as little as possible by orchestral parts. In fact, many of the pieces which we are inclined to think of as 'orchestrations' or 'arrangements' were really nothing of the kind. Several of them were never written down at all, but were organic growths emanating from inside the heads of the players who evolved them. This is, of course, one of the greatest ironies of jazz history, that some of the most successful big band orchestrations of all time, the ones that have often been cited as a justification for scored jazz, were in fact an argument against what they appeared to represent. I can still recall my astonishment when playing in the Kenton band some years ago, to be informed by Lennie Neihaus, that the number we were about to play, 'The Peanut Vendor', had no written parts at all.

There is no question that much of the vitality of the Basie band of the late 1930s stemmed from this fact that much of the section work was really the improvised riff of an accompanying player stylized into a harmonized version of itself. There are, of course, disadvantages in this system, and so far as the original Basie band is concerned, the group's drummer, Jo Jones, once described them very graphically:

We didn't have any idea at all that we would record 'One O'Clock Jump' and that it would be our first big record.

> *We had twenty-five or thirty tunes we could have played, tunes we felt better in. In fact, we didn't want to record 'One O'Clock Jump' at all. I remember in the recording studio when it was decided we record that one, we wanted to go back to Kansas City. People should have had the privilege of hearing those other twenty-five pieces we had. They were all head arrangements. I'm afraid they're lost though, because they were never written down.*

Today that band is virtually a myth in jazz history, although unlike so many myths, one which can be substantiated by the evidence. The Basie recordings of the period indicate two things, first the wonderful animation of the band, and second the profound gifts of its more important soloists. There was the eccentric trombonist Dicky Wells, the frank, clean playing of the trumpeter Buck Clayton, the mutual understanding between Basie, Jo Jones, Walter Page and Freddie Greene that made them into one of the finest rhythm sections ever heard and, above all, the genius of Lester Young on tenor. It was the flair of these men that time and again lifted a fine orchestration into the realms of greatness.

Basie has often confessed a partiality for tenor saxophonists in particular, and when one glances at the succession, one can believe him. After Lester had gone and Herschel Evans had died, Don Byas, Buddy Tate, Eddie 'Lockjaw' Davis, Paul Gonsalves, Frank Foster are just some of the men Basie used in the section. And although he has not said so, Basie has also shown a taste for the melodic rather than the complicated soloist. The logical extension from Buck Clayton in more recent years was the very rich melodiousness of Joe Newman, and in the current era, of Al Aarons.

That first Basie band thrived in the heyday of the big bands, when Benny Goodman was being called the King of Swing and Duke Ellington, Basie, Chick Webb, Jimmy Lunceford and others were producing the kind of music which really justified such a title. But the war years cut into the high profits and eventually caused a big band slump which slowly and sadly developed into almost total annihilation of the form. By the early 1950s, Basie, who symbolized the big band ethos, was reduced to a septet which, although it was a very good septet, was alien to our conception of him. Modernism had now taken hold, and it seemed reasonable to assume that the great days of the Basie big band were over.

But in 1952 occurred what must rank as one of the most brilliant comebacks ever seen in the jazz world. Basie re-formed, used the same instrumentation, and proved that the direct approach could still be as effective as it ever had been in the past. From that day in 1952 when he returned to the big band arena, he has never looked back. The personnel has changed constantly, but never suddenly or radically enough for it to affect the overall sound of the band, so that the orchestra we get this evening is a direct descendant, not only of the 1952 group, but also of the pre-war band which made such brilliant history.

Basie himself became set in his musical ways many years ago, and a study of his piano playing reveals the same two sides of his playing which were so apparent when he first emerged as a force more than thirty-five years ago. On the surface, he is the most economical of all the outstanding jazz pianists of history, a player who can very cunningly get the silences and the empty spaces to do the work for him. Some of his pecked aphorisms with his own group and with the Benny Goodman Sextets of around 1939–42 are classics in the art of rigid economy, and it is remarkable how broad a range of effects he can achieve with this sparse material.

But Basie also remains a child of the friendships with Waller, Johnson and the rest of the Stride players of his youth. Today the signs can be found quite easily, especially in those delightful, relaxed introductions he uses to bring in the next number of a concert. For a moment, as the great powerful machine of the orchestra awaits its cue, we are transported back to the 1920s as Basie uses the rolling rhythms of the old Stride style to convey both to his men and to us the mood and tempo of the next piece. And the strangest thing of all is that this throwback in style sounds not in the slightest incongruous. For some obscure reason, Basie can give us the super-streamlined music of the 1960s prefaced with the comparative innocence of the playing of the 1920s, and the effect is an entirely happy one.

One last point which I have not yet mentioned about the current Basie band, and that is its sheer professionalism. Recently Basie brought the band to this country for *Jazz Expo '68*, in the course of which he, in company with most of the other attractions on that mammoth series of concerts, appeared on TV for the *Jazz at The Maltings* series. The groups had a long way to travel and two shows to rehearse and film when they arrived. Time was at a very high premium. Often the groups involved were unable to squeeze all their rehearsing into the allotted period. A few of the smaller and more efficient groups just about managed to cram everything in. But the Basie band, all sixteen of them, plus a singer, arrived on time, went through the rehearsals of both shows to everybody's satisfaction, and came out the other end with twenty-five minutes to spare. That was not all. When they came back from their tea break to film their two shows, they performed so brilliantly that the BBC realized that to present such expertise in two instalments would be sacrilege, and so spliced the two shows together. It has taken Basie forty years of doing this kind of thing to reach this degree of confidence and sophistication. Nobody would dream of arguing with the proposition that we are seeing tonight one of the greatest big bandleaders jazz has ever known, or is likely to know.

*In the 1970s, Basie, by now the grandest of jazz's old men, recorded a series of interesting albums for Pablo. Instead of the power of his big band, they showcased his gnomic piano style. A pianist who had begun as a florid, ten-fingered Stride player matured into one of the great jazz epigrammatists. Pablo recorded Basie in three novel situations: in a quartet with tenorist Zoot Sims (*Basie and Zoot*); as one half of a piano duet with Oscar Peterson (the* Satch and Josh *albums); and as the leader of a trio (*For The First Time*), an album which featured two versions of 'Lady Be Good', both of which Benny considers here.*

There are some works of art where all the relevant action took place a long time ago, the most notorious examples of this probably being the plays of Ibsen, where what we see happening on the stage is no more than the final inevitable working-out of what once took place deep in the unfathomable past before the curtain went up. So it is with some jazz performances – the most rewarding ones of all, as it happens – and in the case of the 1974 Basie trio there are so many points of historical departure that it becomes difficult to know which road to take, which allusions to pick up first. Perhaps it does not matter which route we settle for, because in the end they all lead to Rome, to the source of James P. and Willie the Lion and Thomas 'Fats', although those three weighty musketeers are by no means the only heroic archetypes we will meet on the way.

On first acquaintance, Basie as a child of the old Stride school really is a most misleading character, for it would be easy to believe, on first being introduced to those deft little exercises in right-hand economy, that he had never made the pilgrimage to the full-blooded, two-fisted, ten-fingered world of one-man bands like James P. But then you listen to those casual introductions of Basie's which define the mood as well as the tempo of the performance to come and the signs start to show through. At no time was this clearer than when, more than thirty years ago, Basie made some sides with a group modestly billed as the All-American Rhythm Section, in which the aphoristic brevity of the usual Basie right-hand figures was occasionally broken up by rhetoric that was unmistakably part of the Stride tradition.

Of course that All-American Rhythm Section consisted of four musicians, while the performances on this album were created by only three. This time there is no guitar plonking out the four beats to each bar with the studied exactitude of a Victorian bandmaster. This time, instead of four musicians, what we get is three creating the pleasurable illusion of four. At only one juncture in the proceedings, during one of the bridges in the faster of the two 'Lady Be Good's, did I suddenly become conscious of the guitar's absence, and experienced the desire to plug the interstices between bass and piano with a bit of old-time strumming. But the moment passed even before the bridge was over.

In the context of Basie's career, no reference to 'Lady Be Good' may be made lightly, for even so much as a mention of its title is to evoke recollections of one of the great days of jazz history, 9 October 1936, when Lester Young, the cat who walked alone so far as jazz saxophone of the 1930s was concerned, made his first recording and introduced the jazz world to the refined joys of what Bertrand Russell once defined as 'the obliquity of the elliptic'. In that classic recording the tune was first laid down by the Basie rhythm section playing as though no other musician were on the premises, so that Lester's entry had the piquancy of surprise as well as the grandeur of genius. Listening to Basie play the same song today, I can see more clearly than ever before what a thoughtful stimulus such playing must have been for Lester, and how perfectly Basie's tact as an accompanist suited Lester's inscrutable purposes.

It is interesting that the ghost of Lester does not hover over the slower version of 'Lady Be Good' as it undeniably does over the faster one. Sometimes the character of a song can be amended so drastically merely by slowing down or speeding up its tempo that it literally becomes a different tune. (The most startling example of this is certainly 'After You've Gone', which, as the leisurely twenty-bar ramble of the youthful Jack Teagarden was a sentimental journey, but transformed into the frantic forty-bar version of Benny Goodman in one of his pedagogic moods or Sonny Stitt with all the stops out, was a musical experience not unlike being fired out of a cannon.) Basie's two 'Lady Be Good's are in fact two quite independent exercises, and may well be quoted one day as proof that Basie had the gift, not only of finding a song's perfect tempo, but of finding two perfect tempos, either of which worked equally well.

The allusions now begin to fly thick and fast. Lester was also the moving spirit behind that song whose presence in a jazz context so often surprises people, 'Song Of The Islands'. Both 'Royal Garden Blues' and 'As Long As I Live' were once recorded by Basie in those sessions with the Benny Goodman Sextet at around the time the 1930s were turning into the 1940s. The Basie–Goodman 'As Long As I Live' was very much slower than this new version, with Goodman using a sustained tremolo to fill all the spaces while Basie pecked away at the melody. This time the rhythmic spine is much suppler, and reminds us that this is almost the only song that Harold Arlen composed which at no time borrows from the mood and structure of the Blues for inspiration.

The Blues had to come up in the end, Basie being one of the greatest living masters of that form. To play the Blues as Basie does on this album requires no more than fifty or sixty years constant attention to the problem, which brings us to the longest of all the byways signposted by this album, the one leading back to the day in the 1920s when Basie first met Willie the Lion's star pupil, Thomas 'Fats' Waller:

The first time I saw Fats, I had dropped into the old Lincoln Theatre in Harlem and heard a young fellow beating it out on the organ. From that time on, I was a daily customer, hanging on to his every note, sitting behind him all the time, fascinated by the ease with which his hands pounded the keys and manipulated the pedals. He got used to seeing me, as though I were part of the show. One day he asked me whether I played the organ. 'No,' I said, 'but I'd give my right arm to learn.' The next day he invited me to sit in the pit and start working the pedals. I sat on the floor watching his feet and using my hands to imitate them. Then I sat beside him and he taught me.

It is one of the greatest grievances of my listening life that on those rare occasions when great jazzmen master a second instrument, they so often become coy about proving it. How many memorable performances, for instance, have we missed through the decision of Johnny Hodges to play no more soprano saxophone after the mid-1940s? Basie has been almost as bashful with his organ playing, and its reappearance now would make this album outstanding even if there were no other music on it. To a lesser extent, the same bashfulness has been evident in Basie the pianist, who has performed the function of greatness in the arts by taking an accepted style – in his case Stride piano – and utterly altering its nature by passing the light of its spirit through the prism of his own personality. One thing only remains to be said, and that is that while in jazz some things have got worse and some things have got better since the days of the All-American Rhythm Section, there is no doubt that neither in the days of his youth in Kansas City nor in the days of his maturity in New York City did Basie have the benefit of two musicians as superlative as Ray Brown and Louis Bellson. Their kind of eclectic mastery did not exist in those days, and it is reassuring to think that not all the good things reside in the past where we can no longer get at them.

1974's Satch and Josh *and the follow-up,* Satch and Josh . . . Again *(1977) paired Basie with Oscar Peterson. In his notes, producer Norman Granz explained the records' titles, inspired by Basie's cry of 'Satch!' in response to one of Oscar's unanswerable double-handed and double-time flurries. 'Satch' was Satchel Paige, and*

'Josh' was Josh Gibson, who were, respectively, among the greatest pitchers and hitters in the history of baseball, a pairing that came to Basie's mind when he found himself at close quarters with Oscar. As Basie explained to Granz, Satchel Paige, then at his peak, was about to pitch against a team featuring Josh Gibson:

> *Gibson saw Paige a few days before the game and said, 'Look, Satch, next Sunday my mother's going to be in the stands, and I'd really like to hit one good one for her, so why don't you ease up and give me one good pitch as a kind of a favour?' Satch replied, 'Don't worry about a thing, buddy, just leave it to me.'*
>
> *Well, the game began and Josh came to bat against Satch. Satch fired the first one right past Josh. Strike one. Josh cried out, 'Hey, Satch, remember what you promised me!' Satch didn't say a word; burned the second one right past Josh. Strike two. Josh in anguish cried, 'Hey, come on Satch, my mother's in the stands, give me a good one, remember what you promised me.'*
>
> *Now here comes the difficult part, because at this point Basie, imitating Satch, closes his eyes, shakes his head, saying, 'No way, no way,' as he fired the third strike.*

The point that Basie was making is that in this album, he replaces Satch for Oscar Peterson and himself, modestly, for Josh Gibson, but the truth of it is that in this album Oscar not only achieves his strike outs, but at the same time Basie hits his home runs.

When it comes to art, people generally, and jazz fanciers in particular, are able to concentrate on only one thing at a time, and very often not even that. This explains among other things why Bill Basie's piano playing is less highly regarded than it deserves to be. If the virtue of a jazz performance is to be measured by the degree of exhilaration it conveys to the listener, then Basie is one of the major pianists in jazz, a claim so unfashionable that I would not think of making it were it not borne out by the contents of this album. But having led one of the most important orchestras in jazz history, Basie's ability as an executant has been shuttled into the background just as Duke Ellington's was, and for the same reasons. In Basie's case the neglect has been compounded by the accident that his style happens to sound very much simpler than it really is; men of few words are sometimes great speakers, and because Basie's piano style has tended to make a fetish out of economy and understatement, some people have been misled into thinking anyone could do it, although the fact that no other pianist in jazz history sounds remotely like Basie should have given food for thought.

In the mutual admiration society which Basie and Oscar Peterson form between them, we get the juxtaposition of two styles which could hardly be more contrasted even if contrast had been the sole aim of the exercise. Peterson's technique is prolific and flawless. Basie's sparse and flawless. The fundamental difference is seen whenever the two men state a melodic theme; under Oscar's fingers tiny little turns and arabesques, fluttering appoggiaturas and grace notes embellish the written line: when Basie states a theme he gives us the bare bones of the matter, telling the composer's tale in clipped notes, so that the daylight of silence streams through the interstices of the music.

Further parallels may be drawn. Harmonically too Oscar will embellish the original by enriching the changes on the song copy, while Basie, in performance after performance, remains true to the tenets of his own youth by going consistently for the third of the chord, the note which defines that chord's tonality by telling us whether it is Major or Minor: this mannerism crops up all over the place in this album, and is especially effective in 'These Foolish Things' and 'Exactly Like You'.

If such basic differences exist between the two men, how do they achieve the wonderful synthesis they do? The answer is that syntheses are achieved, not despite differences but because of similarities, and that the one area where the two pianists make common cause is the most vital area in jazz, the sense of Time. There are an infinite number of ways in which the time of a performance can be conceived. These vary from the sublime to the ridiculous, and when the contrast between individual concepts is too great, no satisfactory blend can ever occur, which is why the mind boggles at the thought that Lester Young once worked for King Oliver. Basie's phrasing, which in an altogether remarkable way appears to be ageless and dateless and is therefore more or less contemporaneous with Oscar's, creates the more indolent effect of the two, especially in those passages at medium tempos when he reverts to his Stride origins and dots his quarter-notes (or crotchets, as the crotchety English persist in calling them) so markedly as to appear on the verge of falling behind the beat. At such junctures in Basie's solos, the music strolls along with such a charming air of leisurely relaxation that discord seems to reach its destined appointment with resolution almost by accident.

All this is legerdemain. There is no accident about it. Basie is an old fox of jazz piano who knows the full implications of every breath he takes at the keyboard. On this album one of the most expressive of those breaths comes when he suddenly blurts out an exclamation at the sheer felicity of something Oscar has just played. The moment brings home to the listener the true nature of the spirit in which the collaboration has been approached, of two masters willing to explore possibilities, never quite sure what might turn up, but too fascinated by the situation to be anything but sanguine about the prospects. When Oscar leaps into his solo in 'Jumpin' At The Woodside', or when Basie slips into the lower register for that simple last bridge in 'These Foolish Things', we sense that the experiment has been an unqualified success and that both men realize it. Not the least important factor in this success is the accompanying group, for the two pianists have the benefit of a highly experienced rhythm section which is the last word in tact and foresight. Ray Brown and Louie Bellson have long been familiar with every small-group contingency which could ever occur, and besides, they know Peterson's playing almost as well as he does himself. Freddie Greene has been sitting at Basie's elbow for so long now that his status is very nearly that of doppelganger to the leader who first hired him way back in 1937.

The reader will have noticed that I have made no mention of the various blues tracks on the album, which may appear strange, as it is the blues sequences which dominate the programme. But then what is there to say about a series of perfectly executed blues, except that they are perfectly executed? The accepted liner-note technique is to listen to each track and take notes which are later worked up into a coherent text. But I find that when it came to the blues tracks I began humming and striding around the room in a rhythmic pattern and my notes were forgotten. At the time I worried about this, but I realize now that I could make no more eloquent observation than that about the way Basie and Peterson play. As the performance is essentially one of collective improvisation, some listeners might feel that guidance is required as to where Basie ends and Peterson begins. I am disinclined to provide this guidance, largely because I have a sneaking suspicion that those in need of it have no business to be listening in the first place.

But apart from the spectacle of the generations riding in tandem, what is the point of putting Satch and Josh together? The two albums prove that the alliance of Basie and Peterson and the dramatic confrontation of styles it brings about, is very much more than a stroke of attractive programming, because to place the distilled essence of one alongside the magnificent baroque elaborations of the other, is to propound one of the vital truths about jazz: There are more ways than one of building a performance, and often methods which are starkly contrasting can be seen also to be complementary. I will resist the temptation to list all the points at which it seems to me the contrasts become especially enlightening; half the fun of listening to these albums resides in finding one's own points for oneself. But I must mention the fact that when the pianists take to the electric piano, Oscar in 'Li'l Darlin'', Basie in 'Lady Fitz', the divergence of the sound into two tonal colours exemplifies the best in both men's playing. And for one moment to sum up all the others, there is the first middle eight of 'Cherry' where the two personalities, the fundamental and the decorative, fling a bridge of mutual sympathy across the great divide. That the gamble should have come off so well twice in succession seems a wonder to me, so I will snatch at the chance to quote the metaphysics of Wonderland to explain *why* I think it has succeeded. It is to do with Time, keeping Time, making Time, having a sense of Time, or whichever phrase you prefer to describe the jazz musician's conception of where the beat is. As the Mad Hatter once explained to Alice, 'If you only kept on good terms with Time, he'd do almost anything you liked.' Basie and Peterson have always kept on good terms with Time. That is why they can do almost anything they like with him.

∾

Basie and Zoot *in 1975 saw Basie diverging from his customary blues for a set of standards from his youth.*

These days Basie likes indulging the whim that he can't remember any tunes and wouldn't be inclined to bother with them even if he could. A few weeks after the music on this album was recorded, Basie passed through London to perform some tunes in duet with Oscar Peterson for a BBC television show, it being my nebulous duty to intercede between musicians and producer in matters of repertoire and small talk. When I asked Basie what numbers he thought he might like to play, he fixed me with what the old Victorian novelists used to call a basilisk eye and said quizzically, 'Numbers?' There then followed an interminable pause, during which I had ample time to wish I was dead, after which Basie completed his speech by saying 'Number'. Never has the letter 's' at the end of a word been more pugnacious in its absence. In the event Basie played the blues on the programme, of which venerable sequences turn up again on this album. But the harmless fiction that he can't remember anything else is put aside by Basie on all the other tracks, and as the themes for which a man retains an affinity are as infallible a guide to his sensibilities as the women for whom he retains an affection, we could do worse than analyse the origins of the standard pieces which make up the rest of this recorded programme.

All were first published in the decade between 1925 and 1934, which means that their harmonic construction is ideally suited to the kind of improvising conventions which obtained in the days of pre-modernism. Every one of them has survived precisely because musicians like Basie have survived, carrying with them into another epoch the musical baggage of their youth. When songs like 'I Never Knew' and 'Mean To Me' were first making their mark, Basie was making his with the old Benny Moten band, and by the time of 'Paper Moon' was just beginning to gather his orchestra for the great days of the mid and later 1930s. It was a period when songwriters were not afraid of sentimental connotations in their chord sequences, and a song like 'I Surrender Dear' whose constant shift from dominant to Minor tonic chord is like a series of palpitating sighs, is a perfect example of this. Of course the unsung lyrics may have something to do with this, just as 'Mean To Me' conjures up recollections of the Billie

Holiday recording, and 'Honeysuckle Rose' of 'Fats' Waller's outrageous insistence on chortling self-parody.

As a matter of fact the ghost of Thomas 'Fats' stalks every groove. He was of course Basie's hero as well as his friend, and is really directly responsible for what we hear in 'I Surrender Dear', because it was he who first showed Basie how the organ worked, and who first gave Basie the confidence to play that intractable instrument in public. These days, when he is not pretending to have forgotten songs like 'I Surrender Dear', Basie likes to pose as a man who has forgotten how to play the organ, but the evidence of this album contradicts him. Without straying too far from the original written line of the song, he contrives to create an atmosphere of pensive syncopated preoccupation with his art, playing the chords with a self-absorption conveying itself to the listener from the very first bars. What he is thinking of at such moments is impossible to guess, but I could not help wondering whether, when after the bass solo the tenor saxophone enters for the bridge with a series of catacoustic honks, Basie's thoughts did not stray to a one-time employee of his called Lester Young who once effected a one-man revolution in saxophone tone. The presence of Zoot is a pure delight. Not being a player with a particularly gladiatorial outlook on life, Zoot I think excels in the kind of musical environment in which he finds himself on this album, just a rhythm section with an old-time piano player, and a few old songs whose sequences read like sequences and not the formula for quadratic equations. The Reluctant-Dragon aspect of Zoot's musical psychology is a fascinating thing, for very often in competition with other players he will perform as if there was no competition at all, and yet when the competition falls away he will usually play as though his very life depended on it. Anyone who knows about Zoot's career will be aware of his abiding affection for the chord sequence of 'I Never Knew', and on turning to that track, will discover Zoot playing with a marvellous freedom and gusto. In 'Mean To Me' also the tenor saxophone displays a kind of blissful ease in the face of the raw material.

However, the mind, and the ear, keep straying back to the old fox at the piano. Prompted by John Heard's walking bass and the whispering tact of Louie Bellson's drumming, Basie goes through the whole session with a manifestation of creative energy which is amazing, and doubly so because of this pretence of his that the time has come for him to put aside the childish exuberance of jazzmaking. It is a very elaborate joke, in fact, I think perhaps it is the best one I know, this pose of an old master as a harmless old gentleman.

Benny also wrote liner notes for two big band albums: I Told You So *(1976) and* Fancy Pants, *released after the master's death in 1984.*

There exist a handful of jazz recordings whose significance transcends the music to be found on them. For a variety of historical reasons, performances like the duet between Louis Armstrong and Earl Hines in 'Weather Bird', the Bix Beiderbecke sides with the Wolverines, Artie Shaw with Strings, Lester Young on the Kansas City Five recording of 'Lady Be Good', all these are, in addition to exercises in musicmaking, moments in history when a door turned, either opening on a wondrous career or closing on a broken life. This album too falls into the category of a musical performance marking a moment of history. There had been a Basie band for more than half a century, and although there were times when this extraordinary group, or succession of groups, appeared to have gone away for the last time, back it came, always exciting, always with a smattering of outstanding soloists and, in some mysterious way, always sounding like Basie.

How could this possibly be? How can a band in 1935 have such intimate relations with a band fifty years later? The answer has to be that its leader had certain very strong ideas about what it was that generated energy in a band, and an infallible way of producing that mysterious X factor. The result is that although Basie's output has varied over his career from goodish to utterly brilliant, it is not possible to find any recorded performance by any of his groups which does not swing. And as the only musician who was present on all Basie recording sessions over the years was Basie himself it would be wise to look to him for an explanation. The fact that Basie himself never put his ideas into words and, I suspect, was amused by musicians who did, ought not to mislead anyone in thinking that the whole thing was an accident. Basie was some sort of a genius, one of the very few players whose wit at the keyboard could actually make you laugh.

One of the most striking passages in the entire anthology of American criticism of the popular arts was achieved some years ago by the drama critic Walter Kerr. As it happened, he was reviewing an old Broadway comedy, but there is a sense in which he might quite easily have been writing about the Basie band instead; certainly he stole a march on every jazz writer who has ever tried to come up with a definition precise enough yet fanciful enough to do justice to the unique compromise between outrageous romance and stern realism that the Basie big band represents. Kerr went one night to see a revival of the old Ben Hecht–Charles MacArthur newspaper farce *The Front Page,* and in looking back at the decade which produced it, wrote: 'A play was held to be something of a machine in those days. It was a machine for surprising and delighting the audience, regularly, logically, insanely, but accountably. A play was like a watch that laughed.'

A watch that laughs. No more appropriate definition of Basie's band has ever been coined, so long as we slip in the qualifying clause that no denigratory comment is intended by the use of a word like machine. In a sense all the outstanding big bands in jazz history have had about them a certain mechanistic element; they had to, otherwise they would have collapsed in a heap of self-indulgence. The spiritual redemption of the big band stems from the wit of the individuals who comprise it and write for it, but the discipline and control and precision required, that is what makes Kerr's marvellous metaphor so apt in Basie's context.

Basie's band is built on a concept of stylization; that is to say, all the effects are very slightly larger than life, so that the swell from diminuendo to crescendo is more marked than in some bands, the extent of the wide open spaces between phrases microscopically larger, the singlemindedness of the ensemble so impeccable as sometimes to be funny; everybody knows that notorious moment in the Basie chart of 'All Of Me' where the stabbing ensemble note, intruding on a rhythm-section interlude, and vanishing as abruptly as it arrived, actually induces audiences to chuckle . . . the watch that laughs.

It follows that it is always of vital importance that Basie hires for the production of his orchestrations men who understand the nature of the orchestra, men who know precisely where to peg down the limits of harmonic advance, where to draw the line in linear complexities, where to put the wide open spaces into which they know Basie will be inserting his aphorisms. Over the years there has been a succession of these men, every one of them accomplished instrumentalists in their own right, and orchestrators with an instinctive feeling for the gleaming machinery of the big band at its best.

Over the years the musicians came and went in his band, and one day historians will make something of the fact that he hired a succession of tenor saxophonists whose names comprise a comprehensive history of the instrument. What Basie and his arrangers eventually arrived at was a stylization of phrasing which made the band instantly identifiable. By toying with the time values as though they shared a single mind, the sixteen men in the ensemble were able to create the illusion of an improvised solo played simultaneously by all present. And through the interstices of their wittily eccentric phrasing could be discerned that piano, pecking away, keeping things rolling, the very soul of humility and yet somehow dominating the performance. For this sort of show, there were certain tempos which suited better than others, and although at very fast speeds the band swung just as easily, and although in ultra-slow exhibitions like 'Li'l Darlin'', it gave amazing disclosures of complete mastery of phrasing, it was in the middle tempos that the band was most typically the Basie band. 'Putting It Right Here', 'By My Side' and 'Hi-Five' are examples, and if 'Time Stream' is much faster, it still hints at that deceptive indolence which is at the heart of all rhythmic well-being.

Why are these sides significant in a way quite different from any other Basie recordings? Because they mark the end of the long road. These were the last studio sides ever cut by the Basie band featuring Bill Basie. 'Samantha', a sentimental ballad, and 'Strike Up The Band' one of the Gershwin brothers' great standards, belong to an earlier session, but the rest of this music stands as the last contribution of the Count Basie Orchestra. When last I saw him, Basie, swathed like an old-time fighter in a white towelling dressing gown, sat there clenching and unclenching an exercise ball in an attempt to stave off the advance of arthritis in his hands. Yet listen to the piano playing on this album, and try to reconcile it with the maunderings of an invalid. Basie sounds as resilient, as relaxed, as confident as ever. In a sense, all great jazz styles are enigmatic in that nobody can explain how they happened or why. The mystery of Basie's evolution, from Stride pupil to aphorist of few notes, is unaccountable. All anyone can be sure of about him is that there will never be another remotely like him. A man of infinite jest, insatiable appetite for music, and especially for the Blues, which lay at the core of all he did, a musician gifted with regard to the control and expression of Time, almost more than anyone else in the field, Basie was one of those geniuses who laugh at exposition, explanation, analysis. May the earth rest lightly on him, and may his legacy, the thousands of recordings, continue to enlighten generations still unborn who will one day want to know what a big band could sound like.

Lester Young

Now we are not to consider that every new and personal beauty in art abrogates past achievements as an Act of Parliament does preceding ones. You are to consider these beauties, these innovations, as additions to an existing family. How barbarous you would seem if you were unable to bestow admiration and affection on a fascinating child in the nursery without at once finding yourselves compelled to rush downstairs and cut its mother's throat and stifle its grandmother. These ladies may still have their uses.

WALTER SICKERT

Ever since I first encountered it in my apprentice days, the paradox of Lester Young has never ceased to amaze me. For me there has been no other musical experience quite like it, not even the disconcerting afternoon in the summer of 1947 when a clinical friend played me a record called 'Anthropology' and by so doing brought the entire superstructure of my musical thought crashing down about my ears.

What was so singular about Lester Young? There had been jazz musicians before him as great as he, although far fewer than conventional criticism has allowed. His reign as a leader of thought in the jazz world was relatively short-lived, for within a year or two of the final parting with Basie, from which time the gradual decline of Young's powers may be charted, Charlie Parker was already conducting a revolution of his own. It could even be fairly claimed that Lester never dominated his field, which is where the paradox finally overwhelms. The acknowledgement of Lester's superiority over all his rivals was so belated that by the time he came to be recognized as a historically significant figure, he was already ceasing to play the kind of jazz that earned him such recognition. It is in its context of time and place that the emergence of Lester Young is so startling, for he confronts the critical mind with the problem of genuine originality only tenuously connected with anything that had gone before. Lester, it seems, owes nothing to any of his predecessors.

Jazz is the reluctant art which lacks a classical tradition. Its critics, committed, by their limitations to a policy of chasing their own tails, have quite failed to establish more than the crudest canons of judgement. Most jazz critique has been based with a kind of hapless desperation on the theory of cross-influence. Henry Allen Jr is said to have been 'heavily influenced' by Louis Armstrong. Ben Webster is supposed to play 'in the Hawkins tradition'. It is understood one is supposed to detect the influence of Frank Trumbauer in the tonal quality of Lee Konitz. No doubt there is a certain limited pleasure to be derived from this kind of approach. Certainly the device has proved a godsend to commentators on an art form who possess scant knowledge of its technicalities. But it is quite useless telling the student of jazz that Ben Webster plays in the Hawkins tradition unless you tell him also what the Hawkins tradition comprises. It is with its great originals that jazz criticism, technically inept and musically uneducated, has done woefully badly. Its exponents took long enough to realize that Lester Young was an original at all, for years rejecting his originality as an aberration and his artistic courage as mere perversity. Whenever confronted with true originality, the ill-equipped critic has instinctively retired in disorder, trailing his abstruse jargon behind him.

With Lester Young, whose list of idolators and imitators is now longer than that of any other man or school in the entire genealogy of jazz music, the problem is more subtly complicated, because Lester was not just original but quite isolated by the schools of action around him. It comes as no real surprise for the neophyte to discover that Hawkins recorded with Bessie Smith, or that Jimmy Dorsey played in the same jazz ensemble as Bix Beiderbecke. But it comes as a sudden unreasonable shock to be told for the first time that Lester Young actually aspired towards the Hawkins chair in the Fletcher Henderson band, and even filled it for a short time, to the evident exasperation of almost everyone involved, including Lester, or that, even more incredible, that Lester once worked with King Oliver, surely the most incongruous relationship to be found anywhere in the history of jazz. The point about Lester Young is that one is continually surprised to hear that he ever had anything to do with anybody at all.

Young represents a regenesis, a second chance as it were, for the tenor saxophone in jazz. It was all too unfortunate for his reputation that he emerged at a time when a traditional school of tenor saxophone playing was firmly established and flourishing. He was obliged to fight bitterly for some years before his revolutionary statagems acquired respectability, which is precisely why his reputation as a giant began to grow after his stature as a creative musician had begun to shrink. The story of his experiences in the Fletcher Henderson band in 1934 is one of the most ironic in jazz history, with Henderson's wife plying Lester with Coleman Hawkins records, while the saxophone section, Edgar Sampson, Russell Procope and Buster Bailey, expressed horror at what Lester was doing. As John Hammond has euphemistically put it, 'Fletcher bowed to the will of the majority, hired Chu Berry and sent Lester back to Kansas City.' Lester himself gives a subtle twist to the story when he says he asked Henderson for a release note certifying he had not been fired on the usual grounds, and then left voluntarily rather than ape the mannerisms of another. It is not difficult to picture the general scene during Lester's stay with Henderson, the first occasion on which the revolutionary came into open conflict with the Establishment.

We can excuse Henderson and his saxophonists for their reaction to Lester, for he was in effect rejecting the accepted canons of phrase-making more uncompromisingly than any other musician had before him or was to do again till Charlie Parker. In even the early Lester the very principles of saxophone playing have been drastically amended. For this reason a judgement of him is not to be arrived at merely through the possession of a recondite vocabulary and a working knowledge of the theory of matrix numbers. To an uneducated critic, Lester Young's was the most disconcerting arrival of all before the Parker–Gillespie dynasty.

Lester, being an anachronistic freak, seems to be out of context wherever he is placed. Seen against the post-Minton background, of which he is often wrongly assumed to be a part, he is a languorous misfit. Yet, considered in the context of the time when he actually did emerge, his style seems to be a startling error of fifteen years misplacement. To cast around in search of any established saxophonist who sounded even remotely like him is a futile pursuit. There are none. Even among his young contemporaries there is only Dick Wilson who had some idea of what Lester was up to.

The situation was remarkable. There stood Hawkins, the acknowledged master, bestriding the era like the colossus he was, a passionate rhapsode of great romantic power. The only variations on his style were minor ones like the dry charm of Bud Freeman. And then, with no warning in the form of gradual amendment of tone or approach, takes place the most dramatic single entry in the history of jazz up to that time, the emergence of a new and already perfected style (for Lester never got very much better than that first recording of 'Lady Be Good'), a fresh style related to nothing that had gone before, mature from its conception and so revolutionary that there is literally nobody to keep it musical company. Even on some of the memorable Basie recordings of the late 1930s, involving more than one member of the avant garde of the day, can be detected the occasional slight uncertainty of the rhythm section quite how to follow Lester.

Either through innate modesty or an impish sense of humour Lester himself has told how his evolving style was influenced by Frank Trumbauer and Bud Freeman. This confession would seem to be no more than a conversational device, like Hawkins's insistence that everyone is very good, or Illinois Jacquet's, that they are very bad. Trumbauer's drastic reduction of vibrato and Freeman's dilution of the customary wrath and passion of the pre-Lester saxophonists may both certainly be seen in relation to

Lester's style, but these influences are merely tonal and are quite divorced from the revolution in the shaping of the aural patterns of jazz music which was aesthetically too startling a feature of the new style. Whether or not Lester was the first to amend the tenor saxophone tone, or to employ false fingerings for tonal contrast at the same pitch, or consistently to augment the chord of the dominant seventh, is not really relevant to the issue of his originality. It is Lester Young's achievement that he synthesized these scattered mannerisms into a coherent and intensely personal style. The most interesting fact which does emerge from Lester's mention of Trumbauer and Freeman is that both these men were white. It seems that in Lester the process becomes apparent for the first time of the customary racial handing down of jazz being reversed. Lester represented a generation of urbanized Negroes whose attitude to life as well as jazz was profoundly different from men who had travelled afield with the music of New Orleans. In Lester the racial lines of jazz style began to get blurred over. Twenty years after 'Lady Be Good' it would no longer be possible to tell a man's colour from the tone he produced on a musical instrument. Most of the saxophonists who modelled their style on Lester happened to be white.

Before a musician can produce a tone, he must first possess some kind of mental conception of that tone. His instrument will re-echo his inner ear, and the inclinations of that inner ear will be influenced profoundly by the prevailing musical environment. There are fashions in instrumental tone in jazz, just as surely as there are fashions in any other kind of art form. The intriguing question about Lester Young is how he contrived, in a Hawkins-saturated climate, to hear the tenor in an entirely original manner, keeping in mind the fact that Trumbauer, Freeman and others may unwittingly have pointed the way. Young's own explanations for this phenomenon are whimsical but unenlightening. One feels more bewildered than ever after reading them.

The problem of whether Lester's original sound influenced the shaping of his aural patterns, or whether the originality of the patterns instinctively produced a new tone (for such an unconscious evolution is very possible), is a *pons asinorum* for the jazz theorist. There is no doubt that the two were twin facets of the same process. With Lester it is hopeless attempting to differentiate between the form and the content, or between technical cause and effect, for they are one and the same. Ever since its confrontation with the unfamiliarity of Lester's approach, criticism has tended to wriggle out of an awkward corner by tacking on to Lester the word 'cerebral', implying as it does so that Hawkins was just a country boy with his heart in the right place, or that there is more evidence of intellectual activity in Lester Young's 'Twelfth Street Rag' than there is in Coleman Hawkins's 'Body And Soul', all of which sadly begs the question.

Young's style may create the illusion of greater cerebral activity because of its sophistication in comparison with anything that had gone before. It is the obviousness of his perfect equipoise which can mislead even the perceptive listener into the delusion that Hawkins is a mere clodhopper by comparison. That equipoise was achieved by the deployment of new devices, and the delusion created by the spectral strangeness of those devices to those whose musical experience went no further afield than jazz music. The Young tone sounded more refined and his phraseology subtler. Indeed there is a sense in which Lester's approach to a chord progression is more ingenious than that of any of his predecessors. Where Hawkins would exploit every note in the chord, racing breathlessly up and down the arpeggios, Young would pass along the same harmonic path by the devious means of omission, implication and suggestion, endowing familiar progressions with a strange orientation by the use of neglected intervals, economy of notes and great pungency of wit in selecting them.

But there is nothing less cerebral about Hawkins's impeccable melodic sense in tracing a complex chord progression, the sequential beauty of his climbing phrases, or the rich romanticism of his melodic lines, which stamp him unmistakably as a creative artist of resource and culture. Where Hawkins is profuse Lester is pithy, where Hawkins is passionate Lester is reflective. In such a technical connotation a word like 'cerebral' has no meaning at all and has simply been employed for critical convenience.

Now this is an issue vital to the understanding of Lester's place in the history of jazz development. Failure to arrive at this understanding means a failure to appreciate fully the fascinating innovations Lester was responsible for, and which comprise the basis of one of the most delightful, witty and original personal styles in jazz history. It was not Lester Young who brought cerebral powers to bear on a chaotic scene to produce order. Hawkins had done that years before. What Lester achieved was the creation of an alternative kind of order to the one Hawkins had offered the jazz world.

A great deal of lip-service is paid today to the Lester Young Legend, for it is understood in some vague, undefined and perhaps indefinable way that Lester Young changed the expression for good and all on the face of the goddess Jazz. If his contribution to the music is to be fully divined, it is vital that the apparent inscrutability of his genius is intelligently broken down into its component parts and correctly interpreted in relation to the contributions of, say, Goodman, Bix and Parker. Whatever we do, we have all had enough of the maundering gibberish about Les the Pres.

The Young style of the halcyon days is a highly mannered one, constantly avoiding by a hairsbreadth the pitfall of affection. To an ear educated only by what had gone before in jazz, his playing always contained the element of surprise. The piquant deviations from conventional patterns were quite original, often anticipating amendments that became clichés in the Bebop era. On many Lester solos of the middle 1930s may be detected the instinctive groping towards the chromatic progressions of descending Minor sevenths which became such an overworked device in Modern jazz ten or fifteen years later, although it is doubtful, from the context of those phrases, whether Lester was actually thinking in terms of Minor seventh progressions at the time.

His resource during this period seems to have been unlimited and he to have exulted in it so much as to have extended deliberately his own powers to the utmost. His gambit of usurping the pianist's introductory role was something quite different in character from Louis Armstrong's incredible exhibition of virtuosity in his curtain-raiser to 'West End Blues' or Benny Goodman's occasional static solo introductions with the trios and quartets of the period. In his four-bar introduction to the Wilson–Holiday 'I Can't Get Started', Lester shows a remarkable sense of harmonic mood, improvising on what seems today a commonplace harmonic sequence, but weaving what was for the times a brilliantly original melodic line subtly related to the line of the melody to come. Later in the same recording Lester improvises for sixteen bars, and it is difficult to believe that this is 1937, two years before Hawkins finally wrapped up 'Body And Soul' for posterity. In Lester's solo, passion has been replaced by deliberation, as he threads a new strange path through the intricacies of the harmonies with a dexterous evasion of the obvious sorely tempting one to the use of the most abused and overworked noun in jazz criticism – genius.

There has been much talk of that genius, most of it inept and misleading. Lester has been accorded a kind of honorary position among modernists, placed in juxtaposition to Charlie Parker for services rendered, as it were, although nobody seems to have taken very much trouble to discover exactly what those services were. They are surprisingly simple, at least in conception if not execution, and are so remote from the orbit of Parker's world that to think of these two great originals as twin revolutionaries is to commit an error of aesthetic judgment of the grossest kind. Parker said once, 'I was crazy about Lester. He played so clean and beautiful. But I wasn't influenced by Lester. Our ideas ran on differently.'

Lester's tonal devices are simple to the point of being glaringly obvious. Hundreds of resourceful saxophonists have since contrived to produce recognizably accurate facsimiles. Instinctively Lester distilled the tonal qualities of his instrument almost beyond recognition, to produce what misguided critics have since referred to with some naiveté and much shamelessness as the 'hard-reed' sound, which is something like explaining away the virtues of *Macbeth* by describing the shape of the stage at the Globe Theatre. It is not even obligatory to use a metal mouthpiece to produce Lester's tone, even though that tone in its heyday undeniably sounded metallic. But the metallic impression is an aesthetic one and has nothing to do with the material realities of Lester Young's equipment.

Having cast aside the traditions of twenty years of jazz saxophone playing, Lester actually extended the very limits of the instrument, introducing fingerings of his own that would no doubt have scandalized the late Adolphe Sax. That is why Young's playing has always given the impression that its executant was intrigued by the mechanisms of his instrument more so than any of his predecessors. Unlike Hawkins, who seems to have snatched up a saxophone as a means of bridging the gulf between his ideas and the outside world, Lester seems to have lingered with an exploratory curiosity, seeking new devices. It must have required endless patience to have discovered all the alternative fingerings which formed so important a part of Lester's style. The significant point is that his technical innovations and eccentricities have an intrinsic musical value which is lacking in, say, the supersonic variations of a Ted Nash. Although Lester's playing incorporates these points technically intriguing to other saxophonists, inducing in them the question, 'How does he do it?', these devices are always rigidly subservient to the style, never being allowed to dominate and even become the style itself, as in the case of poor Illinois Jacquet.

And yet in Lester's playing, so intensely personal, so easily identifiable, there are moments when all human agency seems to have evaporated. From an executive viewpoint there seems to be not a man but a spirit behind the solos, as if Lester had tiptoed away under his pork-pie hat and left the instrument to manipulate itself. No breath seems to be drawn and no embouchure to be controlling the mouthpiece. Others might occasionally close the gap between reed and mouthpiece to produce a squeak or a moment of unintended silence, but never Lester. Where the saxophone seems to have become absorbed within the massive frame of Hawkins, Lester seems to have disappeared inside his and become a diabolic extension of the keys. In the greatest work of Lester Young there is something uncanny.

The few harmonic devices Lester may be said to have introduced are interesting but, perhaps surprisingly, not particularly revolutionary. It could never be claimed that he drastically amended the harmonic structure of jazz improvisation. Lester's miracle was not the Charlie Parker miracle which brushed aside the old harmonic limitations with a flourish of impatient genius to grant the soloist so much greater freedom of movement. Lester's achievement was to accept the limitations of traditional harmonies and, remaining confined by them, nevertheless contrive to coin a new jazz vocabulary.

It is especially to the point that Lester apparently always preferred tunes which moved in the conventional cycles of resolving sevenths. His very greatness lies in the fact that restricted by these narrow boundaries he imbued commonplace structures with new and beautiful shapes sounding at times perversely complex, but which in fact bore the simplicity of true greatness.

Only a man with remarkable fecundity of musical invention could have achieved what Lester did with such comparatively slender harmonic resources.

On many of his finest recorded solos he is restricted to the most limited harmonic material. On some of the Wilson–Holiday pick-up sessions, the commercial song copy was the only music visible in the studio. Sometimes the sheer inadequacy of these melodic trifles crippled lesser lights, but Lester always moved benignly along, making the most futile commercial jingles sound poignant or exuberant. There are no apparent tricks of technique, no exhibitionism, but an unbending catholicity of taste lending grace and dignity to vehicles of the slenderest musical content. Ronnie Scott once described one of these vintage solos to me in awe and perplexity as 'just notes', which is what Charlie Parker meant when he said that Lester always played so clean and beautiful.

In bars seventeen to twenty in his solo on the Wilson–Holiday recording of 'When You're Smiling' – and what more skeletal chord progression could anyone select? – Lester's choice of notes, their duration, the intervals between them and the shape he gives the whole are staggeringly original. There was at the time no other mind in the whole of jazz that would ever have dreamed of tracing such patterns at such a time. In the face of such impudent grace and felicitous execution, many efforts of Lester's disciples twenty-five years after sound hollow and bloodless, no more than a faint echo of a faint echo.

The mannerisms of the Lester Young style actually seem commonplace today, which is the most eloquent testimony of all to the fact that they have long since become a normal part of the jazz vocabulary, like Dizzy Gillespie's double-tempo runs and Charlie Parker's Minor sevenths. The original thought of one generation becomes the commonplace of the next. It is the forgotten revolutionaries who are the truly successful ones.

An early mannerism of Lester Young's style, illustrated perfectly in the entrance to the tenor solo in the Basie version of 'Twelfth Street Rag', is the curiously suggestive effect of the deftly punched crotchets, soft and yet penetrative, involving the use of the tongue in a way that suggests a fine degree of relaxation and deliberation, a mental awareness of the precise musical situation, as though Lester knew perfectly well what was coming four bars later. It is this innate sense of form of Lester's that is aesthetically the most impressive quality of his playing. A transcribed solo from his great days with the Basie band, despite the eccentric aural shapes, stands as an entity, a perfect model of improvisation, balanced without being obvious, logical yet unpredictable, possessing a kind of warped symmetry of its own.

The most plagiarized instrumental mannerism of all, the one most closely associated with Lester, one which has long since become part of the jazz saxophonists' normal equipment, was the use, always with impeccable taste, of false fingerings to obtain an effect of two, or sometimes even three different densities of sound on the same note. It is sometimes difficult for us to grasp the fact that Lester literally invented these now hackneyed effects, and always used them with a sense of form too often lacking in his imitators. The false fingering effects were, to him, extra weapons in the soloist's armoury, devices which could miraculously transform a succession of notes at the same pitch, and therefore without movement, into a set of notes having little in common with each other except that the pitch itself was the same. Nine successive lower A's punched out by Lester sounded not like a tattoo with merely rhythmic significance, but a rounded, mature phrase, in which the varying densities of sound ingeniously suggested the chord changes they were to lead to.

It is when we come to examine the harmonic devices of Lester as distinct from the instrumental that we are for the moment profoundly shocked. For years it has been regarded as a truism that Lester Young was a great innovator. So he was. He is understood to have been a precursor of the moderns. So he was, in a way. But for all that, his harmonic devices are not in themselves very remarkable. Probably none of them are entirely original, in the sense that many players used them before Lester. But he was the first to blend them into a personal style, making his mannerisms among the most distinctive in all jazz. The augmenting of the fifth in the dominant seventh chord, resolving on the tonic, usually at the end of a middle eight, was an effect admirably suited to the melodic whimsicality of Lester's conception, but certainly others before him had used it. Benny Goodman employed the very effect while Lester sat next to him in the same recording studio. On the Wilson–Holiday track of 'I Must Have That Man', Goodman, following Lester in the solo order, illustrates the use of the augmented chord of the dominant seventh resolving on the tonic chord as it emerges at the end of the middle eight, returning to the first theme. There is nothing bad about Goodman's phrase, but when it is compared to Lester's use of the same device, one realizes more clearly than ever how profoundly Lester changed the aural shapes of improvisation. Time and again by augmenting the fifth of the dominant seventh chord Lester imbues an otherwise stock phrase with the spice of the unexpected. Once the effect has been achieved it seems all to have been so simple that anybody might have thought of it.

In his clarinet solo on the Billie Holiday recording of 'The Very Thought Of You', Lester's demonstration of the happy use of this device sounds a childishly simple affair, mocking in its casual ease and yet thrusting the short solo, whose climax it is, far beyond any other instrumental fragment on the record. Since Parker and Gillespie the augmented fifth of the dominant seventh chord, inclined somewhat towards sentimentality, has fallen from grace, forgotten in the triumphal march of the chord of the flattened ninth used in its stead, underlining once again that the Lester Young revolution was a shortlived one, harmonically at least remoter from the upheavals of the Bebop age than criticism has perceived.

Lester seems also to have been the first of the jazz improvisers to have appreciated the dramatic possibilities of the use of the Major sixth in the Minor triad, or the chord of the Minor sixth as it is known in jazz club parlance. Since Lester's zenith, the Minor sixth has gone the way of the augmented dominant chord, almost totally eclipsed by its modernist cousin the Minor seventh, so much more easily adapted to the chromatic movements of Modern jazz. But the slight incongruity of the Major sixth against the Minor third in the Minor triad was ideally suited to the element of uncanniness in Lester's melodic conception.

Recognition of originality in jazz sometimes takes a long time. In Lester's case the critics were only about fifteen years too late, not bad at all for the critics. When they did finally wake up they showered all the adjectives over him and brought him the acclaim he deserved. Only by now he was an older man no longer distinguished for the quicksilver felicities of his technique. Sometimes when I suggest that the later Lester was inferior to the earlier Lester I am misconstrued. I am accused of being a Lesterphobe. I am told I do not understand the beauty of what Lester was doing, and that I seek for perversity for its own sake, just as people used to say Lester was doing in the 1930s. If anything I am a Lesterphile, not a Lesterphobe. And when I talk of decline I do not mean that a once great player was reduced by the years to gibbering incoherence. Lester always remained a fine saxophonist, as Benny Goodman might have said. The style of the later years was just as original as that of the Basie days. It too had its felicities and its beauties. But the difference was that by now it was no longer the most adventurous or the most exciting saxophone playing to be heard. And its motif was no longer bland virtuosity but weary sentiment. It was eminently listenable but it was already a backwater now. The difficulty is that in order to recapture the thrill of the first discovery of Lester the student has to have a sense of the historic about jazz, by which I mean he must have an adjustable ear. He must be able to sit down before his turntable and wear his 1936 ears.

When a man is a revolutionary the implication is that he is attempting to overthrow a status quo. The feel of the era in which Lester sprang up can easily be acquired by a study of Hawkins, the Goodman Quartet, Benny Carter and the Hodges small-groups. Then, and only then, does the sublimity of 'Twelfth Street Rag', the first 'Lester Leaps In' and 'Taxi War Dance' become clear. The first recording Lester ever made was 'Lady Be Good', in 1936. A comparison between that recording and, say, Goodman's 'Avalon' or Hawkins's 'Crazy Rhythm' reveals how fresh and daring the early Lester could be.

Just as surely, the Lester recording with 'King' Cole and Buddy Rich some years later reveal a gradual slowing down of the creative pace. From then on, the decline is gradual but unmistakable, until with the reunion with Teddy Wilson in 1956, Lester is revealed as a tired man whose vocabulary has shrunk in inverse proportion to his gathering deification. It is natural enough for people to assume that a musician's prowess is at its peak at the moment when his reputation stands at its highest, because the time lag in the workings of the cumbersome machinery of recognition is not a factor that automatically occurs to mind. In Britain to this very day, the recordings of the era of the LP are usually taken to be those that show the best Lester Young. Even in the *Memorial Volumes* issued by Philips after Lester's death, there is a track or two included where Lester does not take any solo at all, the compilers having confused him with Buddy Tate, an error so alarming that it suggests that even those who sincerely attempt to revive his vintage work cannot really recognize it when they see it. It is rather as though a student of Edwardian literature were to avow a deep respect for the novels of H.G. Wells without ever having read *Kipps* or *The History of Mr Polly*.

That is the paradox. A great musician is revered for music that is rather less than great. It takes his best music twenty years to win intelligent acclaim, by which time all the praises are lavished on later work that is very good without being epochal. By 1950 or 1960, the ear of the jazz lover had already been corrupted by the innovations of the Bebop revolution, so that even the most thrilling originality of Lester stood in danger of sounding old hat. After all, Zoot Sims, Al Cohn, Stan Getz and the rest of them did it all with rather more panache, if rather less originality, so why get excited about Lester? The answer is that no musician can be fairly judged and fully appreciated without careful consideration of the time element. Jazz moves so fast that even a misplacement of five years, or three or one, can disturb the balance of the evidence. The catacoustic tone with which Lester honked his way through the 1930s is one of the happiest sounds in jazz history. The detachment of the aphorist can be sensed in every phrase. The rhythmic buoyancy never flags. Above all, the stream of phrases somehow shaped ever so slightly differently from anybody else's, never seems in danger of drying up. The diatonic approach to jazz is usually within the grasp of those who know nothing of the mumbo-jumbo of musical terminology, but in Lester they encountered a player who brought to bear on this diatonic conception a mind devious and subtle, so that the most mundane of progressions might emerge in strange uncanny garb. Lester was the first of the soloists to put paid to the Good-Time theory of jazz appreciation. His music was not the kind you could be bibulous about. It demanded full attention, developed sensibilities, some standard of musical intelligence. That is why musicians were so much quicker than anybody else to recognize his power. Unpalatable as the truth may be, musicians know more about the art of playing jazz than anybody else.

∾

Billie Holiday

Mom and Pop were just a couple of kids when they got married. He was eighteen, she was sixteen, and I was three.

BILLIE HOLIDAY

The primary fact about the career of Billie Holiday is its purity. This is a truth so obvious and so unconditional that it often tends to be overlooked, or worse, taken for granted. It is an astonishing truth when considered in the context of the musical world in which Billie Holiday lived and worked. For a woman to sing for nearly thirty years without once bowing to the demands of the world of commercial music surrounding her sounds literally impossible when we remember that most of her material was borrowed from that very world, a world that has never regarded jazz as anything much more than an undefended treasure house to be pillaged at leisure, with vast sums of money to be made out of sickly, bowdlerized versions.

It may, on the face of it, appear unpardonable to claim as a virtue in the jazz art an integrity taken for granted in most others. After all, to claim respect for a singer merely because she refused to commit artistic suicide seems like a very negative compliment. But it must be remembered that Billie Holiday's position was unique in that she had either to borrow the songs written for the popular market or elect not to sing anything at all. Because she had to use these songs, it was remarkable that she never succumbed to the stylistic outrages to which many of them so obligingly lend themselves. Billie Holiday was chained by circumstance to the jingles of Tin Pan Alley, explaining the perception of Charles Fox's remark that while Bessie Smith drew on the poetry of the Blues, Billie Holiday had largely to create her own. It raises a vital point, this dubious material. It was the price that people like Billie Holiday had to pay for the handicap of not being household words, like Shirley Temple, Kate Smith and Rudy Vallee. The companies for which Billie Holiday recorded required some bait to catch the unenlightened eye of the record-buying public, for Billie was never issued in the Race series of recordings that followed a prescribed racial pattern. Her work was thrown into the open market, yet another musical result of a sociological phenomenon, the urbanization of the American Negro as he moved into the industrialized areas and fought for the same fruits of city life as his white counterpart. Billie was cut off from the rich poetic imagery of the Blues on two counts, the lack of demand for it among the audiences on which companies like Vocalion had their eye, and her own environment. There were no cotton fields in Baltimore, but there were plenty of clubs and dance halls.

That was how Billie Holiday came to record tunes like 'If You Were Mine' and 'Me, Myself And I', which, left to the kind of performers for whom they were probably intended, would have been forgotten long ago. But Billie rose far above these limitations, making the instinctive adjustment between the triviality of the material and the grandeur of her own conception. It so happens that 'Me, Myself And I' is one of the great vocal masterpieces of jazz.

The first Billie Holiday recording sessions may be described as a false start. They typify the levity of approach that riddles jazz history in all its phases. Of the countless songs she might have sung, Billie works over one dismal little piece called 'Riffin' The Scotch', whose only virtue is its limitation to three minutes duration. Consider the situation. A young girl appears who possesses the rarest of all jazz gifts, the ability of a singer to hold her own with outstanding instrumentalists. She gets the chance to record, with musicians as distinguished as Benny Goodman and the Teagarden brothers. The result is a lyrical outrage like 'Riffin' The Scotch'. It was Goodman's tune and Goodman's invitation to record, but it is depressing to think that the same man who could appreciate Billie's gifts well enough to ask her to the studio should then saddle her with some inane concoction of his own. Another instance of Goodman looking for the main chance, another phase in the campaign to 'ride out the worsening depression'.

The session is interesting in another way, for it was the only time Billie ever got mixed up with the older generation in a recording studio. Not that Goodman or the Teagarden brothers were old men, but they favoured a style that was already in the process of being superseded. Billie was essentially a child of the Swing Age, a purveyor of art music rather than the folk poetry of Bessie Smith. Her aura was essentially that of witty stylists like Teddy Wilson. In 'Riffin' the Scotch', the accompanying group represents the tail-end of a dying era rather than the early flourishes on an emergent one. The jolly extroversion of the whole accompaniment made quite the wrong setting. Jazz was passing out of the brash stage. Billie required the poise of a group more sophisticated than a Chicago ensemble with a few scored passages thrown in. It is a depressing reminder of the realities of the jazz life that the greatest singer of her generation should make her recording debut with a cheapjack lyric whose final cadence is the excruciating jocosity of a cork being pulled out of a bottle.

This episode occurred in December 1933, and it was not for another eighteen months that the first masterpieces began to appear. In the summer of 1935 she recorded four sides much closer in spirit to the work she was to produce over the next ten years. Indeed these tracks are already typical of the vintage Billie Holiday. Not all of them were pitched in quite the same stylistic key, because one of them was virtually by the Benny Goodman Trio with a few extras thrown in. 'Miss Brown To You' opens with brilliant interplay between Goodman and Teddy Wilson, typical of the small-group series beginning to appear about this time. The rest of the session was rather different and established a pattern for all the successful Holiday recordings of the next few years. 'What A Little Moonlight Can Do' and 'I Wished On The Moon' allowed great freedom of movement to the front line of Goodman, Roy Eldridge and Ben Webster, and the result was vastly different from the background Goodman and the two Teagardens had provided for 'Riffin' The Scotch'. And in at least one of the four songs, 'I Wished On The Moon', there was that kind of melodic literacy and lyrical imagination that the singer's talent merited.

Now the formula for this session, being typical of all those that followed in the next three or four years, is worth examining in some detail. The first important point is that usually the songs were not those one would normally expect to find in the repertoire of the jazzman of the period, due, of course, to the insistence by the business interests involved that at least the titles should mean something to a public which had never heard of Billie Holiday or Teddy Wilson. So that songs like 'I Wished On The Moon' would have to be mugged up in the studio, there being no orchestration to hand upon which either the musicians or the singer cared to waste any breath.

In her autobiography, *Lady Sings the Blues*, Billie gives her own description of how these sessions were conducted. There are few more revealing passages in any book on jazz. The musicians arrived at the studio, sometimes not entirely sure who else was going to be there, but confident there would be no passengers. The selected song copy would be handed round, the chord sequence digested and the solos meted out. There was no music and very little plan. In other words, the recordings were quite plainly jazz performances which differed from the normal live session only in that they had to be restricted to three minutes playing time. In a most touching paragraph, Billie bemoans the passing of the madcap days without seeming to realize why they were gone forever:

> *On a recent date I tried to do it like the old days. I'd never seen the band or the arrangements, and I didn't know the songs they had picked for me, and they wanted me to do eight sides in three hours. We were doing all standards but nobody could read the stuff; the drummer did nothing but sit there grinning; the music had wrong chords; everybody was squawking. We pushed out about nine sides like they wanted. But not a damn one of them was any good.*

The clue to the difference, not only between the early Billie sessions and the later albums, but between the entire jazz scene of, say, 1937 and 1957, is contained in that remarkable phrase of Billie's, 'the music had wrong chords'. In the sense in which Billie evidently meant it, there is literally no such thing as a wrong chord. I am not talking now of obvious solecisms like a Major third in a Minor triad, or the inclusion of the Major seventh in a dominant seventh chord, but of altered chords, amended chords, substituted chords and the rest of the chromatic virtuosity which coloured the whole of jazz from the moment Parker and Gillespie forced themselves on to a world whose ear at first was too bigoted to listen.

The reason why the session Billie refers to was a failure had nothing to do with the ineptitude of the arrangers or indeed the grin of the drummer. It was linked to the fact that the kind of recordings for which Billie Holiday is now revered, required for their creation an implicit assumption on the part of the musicians taking part that no prearrangement was necessary because the harmonic conventions to which they were adhering were sufficiently limited to preclude any possibility of clash or confusion. The men who supported Billie in the early days were the most talented jazz musicians of their era. In such a situation, written arrangements would have been folly. The Swing Age was the last time in jazz history that the music was still free enough not to require the stratagems of prearrangement. Ten years later Sarah Vaughan could not do the same thing because by now the music had lost its innocence and demanded planning of the most detailed nature.

After the 'I Wished On The Moon' session, the recordings occurred regularly. A glance at the titles reveals that in theory both the singer and the instrumentalists should have been hamstrung by the mediocre quality of many of the songs. 'If You Were Mine' has a chord sequence well enough suited to the diatonic days of jazz, but the lyric is only passable. 'One, Two, Button Your Shoe' is a similar case, a reasonable harmonic structure but a lyric that is no more than an excuse for the counting house gimmick. 'Me, Myself And I', 'If Dreams Come True', 'How Could You', were none of them bad tunes, but hardly the kind of material to inspire a great artist to great performances.

Sometimes her luck was better. 'These Foolish Things', 'Body And Soul', 'More Than You Know', 'You Go To My Head' and 'Easy Living' represent the higher musical reaches of the Holiday discography. But when one listens to all these recordings indiscriminately, the skilful songs and the average jingles, the peculiar truth emerges that for some reason they were all more or less as good as each other, that apparently Billie Holiday was independent of the material she used. Songs came to her as competent minor products of the popular music machine of the day went through the treatment, and emerged as the touching expression of thoughts and emotions their composers had never dreamed of. 'Me, Myself And I' sung by anyone else would be no more than the slightly cretinous but not objectionable expression of the infatuation of one person for another. The Billie Holiday recording is positively joyous. It abounds with the expression of a happy, helpless love, so that the triteness of the lyric disappears to be replaced by a wit of expression whose incongruity with the original tune is almost comical.

The process is even more impressive when it takes place in a worthier song. Billie Holiday's 'Summertime', recorded with an Artie Shaw struggling desperately and not quite successfully to be a big bad jazzman, possesses a quality of worldliness which no other recording of the song remotely approaches. The poesy of Ira Gershwin is transmuted into the realist expression of something more resilient. 'Your daddy's rich and your ma is good lookin'', has a mature felicity about it that somehow enhances the phrase beyond all measure, reducing the conventional pseudo-operatic interpretation of the song to mere pap.

The same is true of 'Body And Soul' which, although it departs from the small jazz group formula of the other records, is identical in its vocal freedom. When Billie sings the words, she invests them with an intensity achieved by the childishly simple device of singing them as though she meant them. The fact that she chooses to sing the lesser-known alternate lyrics on the last middle eight, the lines that begin, 'What lies before me, a future that's stormy?' suggests that she must have given close thought to the meaning of the words before singing them.

The woman herself was inclined to be a little disingenuous about this autobiographical facet of her art. 'I've been told that nobody sings the word "hunger" like I do. Or the word "love". Maybe I remember what those words are all about.' What she means is that she knows very well that the overtones of a tragic personal life obtrude into every performance, but the curious thing is that these are not the only overtones. In some way suggestions of sweetness and light also become noticeable whenever she approaches a certain phrase or cadence.

There are two recordings from this period alive with optimism and bravery of spirit. Neither 'Without Your Love' nor 'Laughing At Life' sounds like the kind of song to defy the years. The lyrics in each case are competently constructed, and 'Without Your Love' has a few couplets easier to criticize than they are to compose. However, anyone who looked through the song copy would expect no more than a passable vocal performance. Billie Holiday invests it with an astonishing vitality that cannot be explained away by technical analysis. Her first chorus is comparatively subdued, and gives way to solos by Teddy Wilson and Buck Clayton. But when Billie returns for the last middle eight, the performance builds to an emotional climax in which the voice transforms the melody into an exultant cry. 'I'm like a plane without wings,' sings Billie, and the written melody is almost abandoned. 'A violin with no strings,' she continues, and the performance becomes a triumphal statement.

'Laughing At Life' is a valuable performance for rather different reasons. It demonstrates the nebulous process whereby an unplanned recording magically grows out of itself, so that in the end it does indeed have a form no less firm because apparently accidental. During the first vocal chorus Lester Young complements the vocal line with a certain phrase which later appears in the last chorus as a formal riff behind the voice. When it first appears, in Lester's first-chorus accompaniment to Billie, it appears to exist for a fleeting moment before subsiding. But the idea evidently stayed inside the head of Lester, because at the end he repeats the phrase after trimming it down. The other members of the band join in and the effect lifts the vocal up on its shoulders, so to speak. Had an orchestrator attempted something similar, the phrase would have lacked the light spontaneity of the version of 'Laughing At Life' we actually do possess. A successful jazz performance of this kind always lives on a knife-edge of failure until the very last cadence has been struck. The riff effect fitting so happily behind the vocal is one of those thousand-to-one shots which come off more than once with Billie Holiday because of the superlative quality of the men supporting her.

Some of these recordings from Billie's early days rank as the best jazz of their era. If the lay world, so readily fobbed off with imbecile corruptions of the term 'jam session', really wants to discover something true about jazz, it has only to give a few hours of its time to the Wilson–Holiday recording of 'I Must Have That Man', a side which contains the very quintessence of the jazz of the period. The sentiment of Dorothy Fields's lyric is ideally suited to the tender disillusion of Billie's delivery, so constrained as she opens the first chorus. The vocal is followed by solos from Benny Goodman, Lester Young and Buck Clayton, which brings us to the most remarkable fact of all about this remarkable recording. Billie completes the first chorus, then retires in favour of the soloists. Despite the greatness of the musicians involved, the listener finds himself awaiting the return of the voice, a return that on this recording never comes. It is one of the most impressive tributes to her ability that Billie Holiday was able to form a link in a chain comprised of the most gifted musicians of the period without ever allowing the tension of the performance to sag. The essence of this whole group of recordings is that the voice, besides being preoccupied with second-class light verse, is also elevated to the status of featured instrumentalist. As soon as Billie changed the formula, as in time she did, something of the integrated purity of performance was lost.

Why was the formula ever changed at all? Presumably because the professional status of the artist herself was changing. The 'Summertime' session was the first to appear under the name Billie Holiday and Her Orchestra – a studio fiction no doubt, but still some slight indication of the rising tide of recognition. That was in the summer of 1936, and by the spring of the following year, another session under the same official heading is beginning to show signs of an evolution away from the small informal jam session of earlier days. On 'Where Is The Sun' and 'I Don't Know If I'm Coming Or Going', the instrumentation is almost identical but the musicians are cast in a far more subservient role. There is little solo time for any of them, for the performance begins and ends with the vocal, now the chief attraction.

But the change was gradual and did not become the rule for some time yet. Indeed, the greatest triumphs of the informal sessions were still to come. The twenty-fifth of January 1937, was a key date in jazz history because it was the first time that Billie Holiday and Lester Young recorded together. So monumental were the achievements of this partnership that we are now half-inclined to regard this whole pre-war era as one in which Billie and Lester were perpetually working together in the studios. In fact, it was not till Billie had been recording for three years that Lester made his appearance in her discography, by which time the formula for the unrehearsed method had already been evolved. Lester was not always available, possibly because of the touring commitments of the Basie band, but from now on, whenever it was possible, he appeared on every Wilson–Holiday recording date. It is worth remembering that recognition of Lester's talent was still rare in those days, another hint as to the instinctive musical acumen of a woman with no formal training or instrumental experience.

On the very first session they shared, the results were outstanding. Apart from 'I Must Have That Man', so typical of the best jazz of the day, there was 'He Ain't Got Rhythm', a little-known song of Irving Berlin's, on which Lester played one of the most cunningly wrought solos of his life. The lyric happened to possess just that degree of piquancy that Billie's voice could express so naturally. The time values she gives to the word 'equator' and her slightly unusual pronunciation of 'aviator' with which it rhymes, makes the whole phrase sound far wittier than it really is. Billie's insistence that her phrasing was strongly influenced by Lester's instrumental mannerisms is borne out by another track from the same session, 'This Year's Kisses', where Lester states the melody with that bland elegance reflected later when Billie starts to sing.

From then on, the Billie–Lester antiphonies flowed from the studios with astonishing consistency. 'I'll Never Be The Same' is one of the most skilful of all because it demonstrates a facet of the Holiday style that may have been born of either of two factors, or perhaps a combination of both. Instead of singing the written melody over the first two bars of the second half of the first chorus, Billie dispenses with the phrase, which is unexpectedly chromatic, employing instead a simple device of her own. The whole impact of the first phrase is changed. In the original the line 'I'll never be the same' contains a furious activity, but Billie amends it to a single note repeated to accommodate the syllables of the phrase. It was a similar gambit to the one she used in 'I'll Get By', recorded earlier the same year, although the latter was so drastically amended that for a bar or two one is not quite sure she is not singing a different song from the one named on the label.

Now this paraphrasing of the written melody in an instrumental manner was sometimes due to the limitations of her range. 'I'll Get By', for instance, has unusually generous intervals spanning its opening few bars, and it is very possible that Billie Holiday, always very much a middle-of-the-register singer, felt more comfortable compressing the range of the song rather than impose upon herself the slightest element of the wrong kind of strain, or have the musicians fishing around for appropriate keys. On the other hand, I believe that the kind of paraphrase to be found in 'I'll Never Be The Same', which typifies all her work, has artistic rather than technical origins. Billie Holiday was removing the odium of a slightly precocious phrase, replacing it with one that is alive with all the candour and apparent simplicity of much of the best jazz.

There is one recording from this period where the considerations of range really did cause her some hard thinking, so that on 'I Cried For You', encompassing a jump of a Major ninth in its first three bars, the group plays jazz first. Johnny Hodges gives a masterly statement of the theme which departs from the written line without ever ceasing to pay it deference, before Teddy Wilson plays an impeccable four-bar modulation taking the key down a Minor third for the convenience of the singer. Somebody like Sarah Vaughan would never have to resort to such tactics, which is why she is able to sing a tune like 'Poor Butterfly', again with a demanding range, without resorting to the anticlimactic device of dropping down an octave to avoid a crisis of pitch. But what handicap is a restricted range when the act of compression can achieve such felicities as the remoulding of the first phrase of 'I'll Never Be The Same' or the complete recasting of the melodic line of 'I'll Get By'?

Much later in her career, when the ravages of a desperately unhappy life were beginning to tell, her range shrank much more seriously, so that in singing old stand-bys like 'Body And Soul' and 'These Foolish Things', she dropped her key by a tone or sometimes more. But by then her voice had changed so profoundly in character that she was a different kind of artist altogether. The great virtue of the recordings from the first period was their heart-lifting optimism, a certain buoyancy of spirit which made the listener feel an affinity for a disembodied sound whose owner he might never have heard of before. I am convinced that for much of the time Billie was not consciously aware of what she was doing while she was doing it. To her, singing was not so much the exercise of an artistic function as the natural means of expression towards the world. This relationship involving the mechanics of making music is common enough among the best instrumentalists, but certainly no singer since Bessie Smith could be said to need to sing as desperately as Billie Holiday. The casual effects she threw off would be psychological masterstrokes had they been thought out and planned ahead. As it was, they remained emphatic triumphs of intuition.

One of the most affecting examples occurs in the Holiday recording of 'What Shall I Say?', a deceptively simple-sounding little melody with one of those invisible dynamos built into it so that one has only to play it as written with a modicum of rhythmic understanding to produce a reasonable jazz performance. In the lyric the following lines occur:

> *What shall I say when the phone rings*
> *and somebody asks for you?*
> *They don't know I ask for you too.*
> *What shall I say?*

The vowel sounds at the end of the second and third lines could be awkward to sing. The word 'you' is included twice, but with obviously different stresses, and at very different points in the line. Moreover, the second 'you' occurs immediately before the word rhyming with the first 'you'. It is not a clumsily written lyric, but it might have been constructed with rather more consideration for the singer than the writer has shown. There are a dozen ways round the problem. Billie Holiday's is the best, as well as the simplest of all. She pronounces the first 'you' in the normal way, doing the same with the word 'too' which rhymes with it. The second 'you' she simply changes to 'ya', thus eliminating any danger of idiotically echoing vowel sounds.

But the mere technical process is not what is important. Probably Billie never even considered it. She must have come to the amendment of the second 'you' by an entirely different path, and when we listen to the recording it is very obvious where that path lay. When that second 'you' occurs, changed to a 'ya', the whole performance suddenly stops being a formal musical exercise and instead confronts the listener with a human statement, directed specifically at whoever happens to be present. There is an amazing colloquial candour about that second 'you', born of the ability of the woman singing it to make the tritest lyric a valid statement of emotional experience. When 'ya' appears, one suddenly realizes with a disturbed shock of surprise, that Billie is experiencing the lyric dramatically as well as musically, so that the finished product has a depth of sensitivity unknown to other women singers since Bessie Smith.

Sometimes the ability to make a certain phrase, or word, or

perhaps just a syllable, shine with a fresh lustre, seems to be a lucky shot in the dark, but it is really part of a system no less comprehensive because it happens to be subconscious. Billie Holiday, who never suggested she might know of factors in a poetic performance like mantic overtones, had an infallible instinct for evoking these overtones every time she stepped up to a microphone. In 'Blame It On The Weather', an obscure pop song recorded in January 1939, with Wilson, Benny Carter and Roy Eldridge, she sings the phrase, 'they'll see through me like glass', delivering the last word in such a way as to rehabilitate it, investing it with all its translucent qualities. The word flashes and shimmers with a crystalline brilliance, transmuting a commonplace simile into a shaft of genuine poetry. This ability to restore to tired words the vitality they once had, abounds throughout her work and is the key to several truths about her style, especially its inimicability.

There are surprisingly few instances where she actually creates a specific melodic phrase of the kind one used to find in the quaint old series, *Fifty Hot Licks*. Her improvisations can hardly ever be torn out of context because they are rather affairs of stresses of syllables, subtleties of phrasing, regrouping of notes. None of her inventions are as elaborate or as ambitious as, say, Sarah Vaughan's celebrated version of 'Body And Soul', which is better compared with instrumental versions like those of Hawkins and Red Allen than it is with Billie Holiday's. The Sarah Vaughan 'Body And Soul' is highly ingenious rather than inspired. It accepts the challenge of modern harmony with brilliant resource, but it reeks of the midnight oil in a way that none of Billie Holiday's performances ever did. The difference between them is the difference between a perfect abstraction and a slice of humanism.

Now and then a whole phrase does leap out of its context into the memory purely as a fragment of musical invention, like the rephrasing of the notes of 'a telephone that rings' in the 1952 version of 'These Foolish Things', recorded with one of the JATP concert parties. More typical is the way she remoulds an entire song, flattening a phrase here, stretching a time value there, reducing the arpeggio phrases to the very bone, slipping in a grace note which just so happens to be one of the most important harmonies of the chord.

In 'One Two, Button Your Shoe', made in the vintage days

with Bunny Berigan and Irving Fazola, she virtually abandons the written line completely, using the harmonies whose names she did not know, to build a new, sleeker melodic line which reduced the number of pitches by more than half, until a phrase like 'tell me you get a thrill', originally linked syllable by syllable to the arpeggio of the Major seventh with the Major sixth thrown in to make up the number, emerges through the voice simply as the actual note of the Major seventh and not its arpeggio, repeated four times, exactly as Lester Young might have played it, or any competent jazzman of experience. The next phrase is identical except that the Major seventh chord now becomes the dominant seventh, whereupon Billie promptly performs the same trick a semitone lower, giving form to her variations just as though she had swotted up the harmonies from the textbooks the night before, when really she is trusting to her ear and her taste.

No jazz musician, whether he uses his vocal chords or an instrumental keyboard, can be taught this kind of invention. It is the fruit of instinct wedded to experience, and therefore remains exclusively the possession of the man who spends most of his life weaving instrumental patterns round chord sequences. From people with no instrumental training it is unfair even to expect it, which is why Billie Holiday is unique in all the annals of jazz.

Because of the apparently nebulous nature of this art of making jazz, a process impossible to convey by teaching or by writing down in congruous terms, or even recognizable without a certain sympathy in the mind and heart of the observer, there are very few technicalities by which the theorists can blind us with their science when discussing Billie Holiday's singing. M. Hodeir may potter about indefinitely preaching to the converted and terrifying everybody else by the diabolonian cunning with which he computes the mathematical processes which go into the making of a jazz record, but his method founders in the face of a performance by Billie Holiday. There is nothing to compute, no inversions to detect, no daring passing chords to recognize by name, none of the contents of the usual box of vocal tricks which may easily be defined according to the rules of discord and resolution. There are a few Holiday mannerisms reducible to academic terms, but far less than in the case of the two contemporaries whom most people mistakenly regard as her closest rivals, Ella Fitzgerald and Sarah Vaughan.

One habit in particular of Billie's has a wry relevance to her art because many people who know of it misconstrue it as a serious deficiency and even a source of embarrassment. On recordings spanning her entire career, Billie has a habit of falling away from the pitch of a note soon after she arrives at it. I have heard this device cited as proof of her inability to hold a note long enough to establish its pitch. But the musician who listens carefully to these falls soon notices that far from being technical solecisms, they are musically correct effects enhancing the dramatic impact of the lyric. It is not by accident that every time Billie falls away from these notes, she allows the fall to continue just so far and then arrests it – at the next note down in the arpeggio of the relevant chord. She was especially partial to this effect when the chord in question was a diminished seventh, probably because her instinct told her that the intervals between the notes of that chord, all Minor thirds, were not so broad that they might sound too protracted. This fall is one of her devices in the transmutation of 'I'll Never Be The Same', on the phrase, 'a lot that a smile may hide'.

However, this description of what is after all an elementary trick of improvisation does not do justice to the artist, because once again the device was a means to an end, the end being the expression of a kind of fatality in the world she sang about. The fall would express a wry sense of philosophic despair, as though even the happy songs were wise in the knowledge of sadder lyrics and sadder lives. There is a profound difference between this kind of stylistic sophistication and the harmonic dexterity of Ella Fitzgerald which, being an end in itself, finally reduces the art of singing to the decadence of gibberish. Instead of aspiring to establish the voice as a second-class instrumental keyboard, the singer should attempt to raise it to the highest jazz level because of its potential value in expressing specific ideas and emotions rather than the impressionistic gestures of most instrumental jazz. The gibberish vocal makes a mockery of communication instead of exalting it. The thought of Billie Holiday indulging in such antics is too far from reality to be considered for more than a moment. It is useless your analysts telling you that Ella Fitzgerald or Sarah Vaughan can follow the most intricate chord sequence through to the ultimate flattened fifth in the final tonic chord, hitting resolution after resolution with the same correctitude as any suburban music teacher. When the emotional content is nil, all the correctitude in the world will not save the performance from artistic damnation, an observation that applies more than ever in the world of Modern jazz, with its daunting harmonic complexities and its pathetic pursuit of legitimate acceptance.

In the early 1940s Billie Holiday's career entered on the second of its three phases. Gradually the small-group formula was cast aside, being replaced by an accompanying orchestra playing decorous arrangements, neatly rehearsed and carefully tailored to meet the demands of the singer. The implication was quite clear. Billie Holiday was now the star. No longer was she one of a group of jazzmen creating variations on written themes. The voice was now the focal point, apart from a few fragments thrown the way of the soloist, like Roy Eldridge's masterly eight bars in 'Body And Soul', used as a buffer between the end of the first chorus and the introduction into the performance of the alternate lyrics to the middle eight. From the purist point of view these recordings have nothing like the value of the earlier masterpieces, which had Billie to offer and half a dozen others besides. But judged strictly as vocal performances they show no noticeable decline from the sessions of the middle 1930s.

'Mandy Is Two' bears forcible testimony to Billie's talent for endowing any old jingle with the grace of art. The lyric is a piece of sentimentality of the worst kind, difficult to endure without resort to Rabelaisian noises. Its conquest by Billie Holiday is symbolic of her whole career. By showing she could make such songs valid in the jazz context, she was demonstrating in the most dramatic way that there is no material that cannot be used as jazz material if the artist involved is gifted enough, and that triteness itself, pitifully inferior to the realist beauty of the words Bessie Smith sang, may be invested with an emotional depth to move the most hardened of cynics.

Billie, was, in fact, annexing a huge area of musical experience on behalf of jazz. She was reclaiming all the land of the popular song. Of course she was not the first to attempt this. Musicians had been borrowing silly jingles and making great jazz out of them for two generations. She was not even the first singer to do this. Louis Armstrong had actually made 'Song Of The Islands' sound something like the real thing. But Billie was the first figure in jazz whose entire career was concerned with this type of performance of this type of material. She was dealing in the medium of words all the time, so that no matter how prejudiced you might be towards jazz, no matter how indifferent you were to the pathos of its cadences, you could at least understand what it was this woman was singing about.

Usually she was singing about love, one of the two subjects in the world about which everybody in the world professes to be an expert. (The other is music.) She took these songs far more seriously than anyone else dreamed of doing. To other singers they were the excuse for standing up and simulating a few emotional platitudes. To audiences they bore no relationship to reality at all, being the incidental music of a dream world where unrequited love wept crocodile tears, all expressed in mediocre verse. To the men who wrote the songs, they were factory products, designed to live for a few moments and then be cast aside, so that their component parts might be broken down and redesigned in fresh permutations. When Billie Holiday hit upon songs like 'I've Got A Date With A Dream' or 'Please Keep Me In Your Dreams' the tunesmiths of Tin Pan Alley got more than they had ever bargained for and certainly more than they deserved.

The use of more formal musical settings for her recordings raises a point about Billie Holiday which may never effectively be answered. In 1941, Lester Young made his last recordings with her. Many factors must have contributed towards this split. It was the period when Lester was severing his connections with the Basie band. It was also the time when Billie was sufficiently established, at least with a small coterie audience, to record under her own name. And possibly more important than either of these factors, the Swing Age was slowly grinding to a halt. In retrospect, we can see quite clearly that during the early 1940s the Wilson–Young–Eldridge axis was gradually being replaced as the advance guard of jazz. The arrivistes Parker and Gillespie were soon to make the work of the Wilson generation, so quaint in its comparative innocence that its eventual appeal was destined to be the elusive charm of a period piece. The era of the small jazz group, busking away in the recording studio without much of a plan to guide the musicians, was slowly becoming no more than a glorious chapter of the past.

However, the assessment of these factors soon becomes impossible, because the most dominant fact of all is one which by its very nature cannot be measured with any accuracy. The romance between Billie and Lester is one of those rare exquisite moments when melodrama and prosaic reality reach out and touch for a while. It is a truism of jazz history that the partnership with Lester Young, personal as well as professional, was the most vital association of Billie Holiday's career. It proved to be a working romance which was unusually fruitful, as connoisseurs well know. Were its two central figures artists of the same magnitude in any other sphere, then the task of the biographer would be eased considerably. But the mature approach to this kind of situation is consistently lacking in the jazz world, almost as though in the final reckoning the musicians were too self-conscious about the artistic possibilities of what they were doing to accept their own place with complete savoir-faire. It is understandable enough that nobody will ever read *The Collected Letters of Billie Holiday* or *The Private Correspondence of Lester Young*, so it is left for the curious to wonder about the possible clues to the nature of the close friendship of the period's most remarkable singer and instrumentalist.

It is too tempting to draw the obvious conclusions, to say that the two careers became one and were therefore never the same after the parting. Or that Lester's uncanny knack of complementing Billie's vocal phrases with his own aphorisms was the result not just of musical instinct, but of musical instinct enhanced by the passion of a love affair. There is a remarkable parallelism in both the rate and nature of their artistic declines that might be more than coincidence. But, then, Lester's oblique instrumental comments on a vocal performance may just as easily be found behind Jimmy Rushing as Billie Holiday, and nobody has suggested that Lester ever felt unduly romantic about Jimmy Rushing. What failure there was in the careers of each of them seems to have been a failure of temperament, not the failure to meet a romantic crisis.

Neither Lester nor Billie said anything very substantial about the effect of their relationship on their work together. Each one bore for the rest of his professional career the nickname the other concocted, and Billie did say, several times, that she always felt happier about a session when she knew Lester would be present. In her own words:

> *For my money Lester was the world's greatest. I loved his music, and some of my favourite recordings are the ones with Lester's pretty solos. . . . Lester sings with his horn; you listen to him and can almost hear the words. People think he's so cocky and secure, but you can hurt his feelings in two seconds. I know, because I found out once that I had. We've been hungry together, and I'll always love him and his horn.*

Her reference to the vocal overtones of Lester's style establishes beyond reasonable doubt that there was some artistic as well as emotional interdependence. Lester's whimsy about always thinking of the lyrics to a song when you were improvising on it, is worth considering also. It is fair to assume that on recordings like 'Laughing At Life', 'Without Your Love', 'Me, Myself And I', 'Mean To Me' and 'Time On My Hands', on all of which Lester displays an instinct for what Billie is going to sing that is almost psychic, there were moments where the warmth of a private liaison spilled over on to the grooves of the record. Whatever anyone cares to imagine, the antiphony they created remains unmatched in all jazz, ranking among the rarest delights the music has to offer.

The tragic decline of Billie Holiday's fortunes in the last years of her life is another of those commonplaces of jazz criticism about which nothing new of any relevance to the music can be said. The same element of self-destruction that shadowed the life of Charlie Parker is evident in Billie's career. Nobody has any illusions about the terrifying inroads on her talent made by the way she chose to live.

Because her recognition, like Lester's, was a belated one, there is a tendency to revere anything she did in the last years of her life, to ignore conveniently the fact that by the middle 1950s she had hardly any voice left at all. This decay may be charted in every detail throughout the recordings she has left us, but before it began to be serious, and after the break with Lester, she cut several more outstanding tracks, in some of which can be noted a brave attempt to behave as though time were not racing ahead at all. The sessions with Eddie Heywood are a case in point. 'How Am I To Know?' shows her amending arpeggio phrases once again into a flatter line while still suggesting the framework of the original tune by stressing the more prominent of the harmonies. 'I'll Be Seeing You' shows how she could take a popular ballad, admittedly of a superior kind, and transform it into something so touching that nobody who knows the recording can take anyone else's version very seriously.

'On The Sunny Side Of The Street', recorded with a rhythm section led by Heywood in April 1944, demonstrates the instrumental nature of her thought. The opening phrases of the first theme, containing the words, 'Take your coat and take your hat', and 'Can't you hear that pitter pat?', make use of only three notes in the diatonic scale, and are reminiscent of the remarkable phrase Lester played in his Aladdin recording of the same song a little later, when he makes a fall of an octave in the most unexpected place.

Throughout the 1940s Billie continued to make records which although they were distinct in character from the pre-war hit-or-miss classics, were unmatched in their field, then and now. The more commercial nature of the orchestral backing may have won them a slightly wider fringe audience that she usually commanded, but the songs themselves compromise not a single crotchet in their suitability to her style. 'Good Morning, Heartache', with its rise from Minor to Major in its first eight bars, is typical Holiday material. But the side I usually associate with this period and this type of recording is 'Crazy He Calls Me', which, besides having an amusing lyric and an unusual melodic line, happens to possess a certain relevance to Billie's attitude towards her lovers in private life. In *Lady Sings The Blues*, there is more than one echo of the futile devotion of this song.

The divine spark died very hard. Almost to the end she was capable of producing the kind of vocal vitality that can carry an entire accompanying group, as she did in a heroic version of 'All Of Me', recorded with one of the earliest JATP groups. As late as 1955 in 'Please Don't Talk About Me When I'm Gone', she eclipses Benny Carter, Harry Edison and Barney Kessell in the buoyancy of her delivery, producing another colloquial effect that lends an unexpected edge to the words. At the opening of the second eight she sings 'listen', dropping the second syllable an octave in a manner so casual that for a moment the performance ceases to be vocal and becomes speech instead. Both these tracks revive to some extent the glories of earlier times, with their rough insistence that jazz is a down-to-earth affair, making a strange contrast with the tonal felicities of Sarah Vaughan's commercial output and Ella Fitzgerald's faithful deadpan transcriptions of the *Songbooks*.

In the last two or three years of her life the songs she chose to record were usually sad ballads whose lyrics time and again forced even the most objective of listeners to see the parallels with her private life, for by now her technique was so ravaged by physical decline that she was by all the normal rules, no longer qualified to sing any song demanding sustained notes and skilled control. But the normal rules applied to her no more at the end of her life than they had in the beginning. Whatever shortcomings there might now be in her breathing, her range and her pronunciation, she had retained, because it was a very real part of her personality, this unfailing ability to wrest out of every lyric the last drop of significance, and even to insert her own where the lyricist had failed to include it. As this was the very core of her art, the last recordings overcame their own technical limitations in a miraculous way.

THE ART TATUM *SOLO MASTERPIECES*

Originally released on the Clef and Verve labels, the Solo Masterpieces *(1953–4), were a self-explanatory dissection of 121 popular songs spread over twenty-six sides. That Tatum had been honing his (re)arrangements of his material is evinced by the ease with which he dispensed no less than sixty-nine solo tracks over the course of 28 and 29 December 1953, and all but three of them in one take. The* Masterpieces *caught one of jazz's greatest artists at the peak of his abilities. They were re-released as a boxset on Pablo Records in 1974 with extensive notes by Benny, which were subsequently nominated for a Grammy.*

* * *

In Feather's *Encyclopaedia of Jazz*, out of 126 pianists asked to name their prime influence, seventy-eight nominate Art Tatum. Elsewhere in the same volume the editor tells us that in a poll conducted among one hundred of the most famous jazz musicians, sixty-eight placed Tatum first in their list of preferences. In an art form where tastes have always been bafflingly fragmented and judgements bewilderingly contradictory, such comparative unanimity is stupefying. It is as though seventy-eight out of the world's 126 most distinguished novelists were to plump for Proust, or sixty-eight out of the world's one hundred most gifted painters were to agree on Velasquez. Such events could never conceivably happen, and yet in so notoriously fissiparous an area as jazz music, an area renowned for its schools and schisms and cults and pigeonholes, it appears that one man has so dominated his instrument that roughly two out of every three of his professional rivals prefer his mastery to anyone else's, including their own. Of course it might be said that all such manifestations of the democratic process are meaningless when applied to relative merits in the arts, but it is as well to remember that while most jazz polls are conducted either among members of the public, who know little about comparative judgements, or among critics, who know even less, the Tatum polls were held among men who earned their livelihood by the same methods as Tatum did, that is, making music, and that therefore their unanimity is not to be taken lightly.

Who was Art Tatum? He was born on 13 October 1910 in Toledo, Ohio, the son of a mechanic who had migrated north from North Carolina. He was born totally blind in one eye and with only slight vision in the other (it is said that he could distinguish some colours and, by holding the cards close to his face, play an efficient game of pinochle), so that of the myriad things he was never able to see, the most significant was a note of music printed on a sheet of paper. The importance of this fact in arriving at some understanding of his style is obviously paramount. It is a truism that many of the great baroque recorded masterpieces in jazz are of a technical complexity which would be quite beyond the ability of their creators to play them were they faced with the notes written out as a composition. But the very essence of jazz, the one element in the mechanics of making it which separates it from all other forms, is the fact that the improviser, by exploiting the art of impromptu composition, or extemporization as it used to be called, has short-circuited the creative process in music. The notes go from mind to keyboard without the intervening stage of manuscript, so that by an irony too deep to plumb, the blind musician finds in jazz a world where his handicap is of relatively no consequence and sometimes even an advantage, for to be uncorrupted, as it were, by the sight of music that has congealed into composition, the pianist can evolve an essentially pianistic style based on intimacies of the tactile sense.

And this is where Tatum's style becomes so problematic for the jazz world. He seems to have done all the unorthodox things so far as style and development are concerned. He matured at an absurdly precocious age, for instance, long before other jazz musicians have even found their way around the main roads of the harmonic map. A bass player called June Cole, who once worked with McKinney's Cotton Pickers, claimed to have heard Tatum for the first time at a gambling joint, and said that already the Tatum style was fully formed, the Tatum technique fully controlled. The year of this reminiscence is 1925, which puts Tatum in midteens at the very most. Another rare fact about Tatum is that once he arrived he stayed. There was no trial period, no quibbling about his status as a master, no haggling about his acceptance. There were one or two dips in his popularity, but these were only comparative; and must have concerned Tatum as little as they now concern posterity. Then again, the Tatum style, once it appeared, never changed very much. There were no 'periods' in his career for analysts to argue about, although the embellishments became slightly more lavish towards the end. So what we wind up with is a career packed with lack of incident, leaving the frustrated commentator only the actual music to talk about.

At which point the situation changes from difficult to impossible. There is no way of analysing the content of Tatum's playing which is not in the end self-defeating. Every sentence ever written about Tatum's music, every evaluation of one of his solos, every puff for one of his albums, is nothing more than proof of the old proposition that if it were really possible to describe the sound of music in words, then there would be no need to listen to it. The best anyone can do is to make a few points about those aspects of Tatum's jazz which have caused him sometimes to be neglected, or underrated, or even on occasions to be dismissed altogether; and to try to find out of what component parts Tatum's style is composed.

In approaching this area, we have to remember that for the most part jazz criticism has been conducted by those whose passionate love of the music was never quite passionate enough for them to learn the rudiments of jazzmaking, which means that when a player like Tatum puts his genius and his vast experience into a thirty-two bar chorus, it would be foolhardy to expect the average commentator to have the remotest idea what is going on. This explains why for many years there was a sizeable body of jazz critical opinion which dismissed Tatum as a jazz pianist altogether, and refused to admit his qualifications to be counted among such rivals as, say, Jess Stacy or Bob Zurke. (I am casting no aspersions on the playing of either Stacy or Zurke, but merely making the point that to a critic who can only count up to four, the piano playing he will find the most appealing will be the type of piano playing mastered by players like Stacy and Zurke, and that the inevitable result of this preference will be the mistaken impression that unless you play that way, you are not playing jazz. Absurd, certainly, but it is exactly what happened to Tatum's reputation.)

The problem always was Tatum's frightening mastery of Time, and his ability to subdivide it into the most deceptive segments. In the recordings to which this essay is a hopeful introduction, the listener will no doubt find time and time again that there comes a moment when he loses his grasp on the pulse of what Tatum is doing, that in tapping his foot, either mentally or physically, the beat seems to have evaporated. At such moments, the disorientated listener, having lost all sense of polarity as it were, can only sit there and await the return of the familiar pulse he knows, and almost every time that pulse comes back to him, it is either a split second later or a split second earlier than he expected. The explanation is quite simple. Tatum has been sliding imperceptibly from triplets to semiquavers, or from semiquavers to grace notes, which are of course not part of the complement of the bar in which they occur, but embellishments of that complement. When these moments occur the situation is crystal clear. The beat has gone, and that means that somebody has made a mistake. Either Tatum or the listener has lost his way, and it is a tribute to the enormity of the old-time jazz critic's pretensions to omniscience that he always insisted that it was Tatum who was wrong. Thus there grew up the canard that Tatum was not able to hold a tempo.

There was always a way out of this dilemma, and you may ask why the confused critic did not take it. The answer is that the solution lay in recourse to that invaluable invention, the metronome, a tiny machine which sets and maintains any one tempo with a rigidity that only some mad scientist could ever have achieved. However, the chances are that when a man is so ignorant as to assume that he knows more about the pulse of a musical performance than Art Tatum does, then he will also be too ignorant ever to have heard of such a machine as a metronome. The interesting thing is that when the so-called ramblings of Tatum at his most rococo are tested by the metronome, Tatum is found right every time. The rumour that Tatum couldn't maintain a tempo was a piece of imbecility which may safely be discounted in any serious discussion of his art.

What of his style in terms of jazz history? Whose influences flicker across the landscape of a Tatum solo? Who played Bechet to his Hodges, Oliver to his Armstrong, Hawkins to his Webster? The answer to these questions is, embarrassingly, everyone and no one. Tatum has been the only soloist in jazz history to date who has made an attempt to conceive a style based on all styles, to master the mannerisms of all schools and then synthesize them into something personal. Obviously such a heroic concept requires miraculous technical mastery, which Tatum has. It also requires a complete understanding of what other players have been trying to do, which Tatum has. It requires an aesthetic morality compounded of courage and imagination, which Tatum has. Above all, it requires the ability to see the whole of jazz piano development in a single all-embracing context, an ability which Tatum has. (The exact parallel to this kind of eclecticism is James Joyce's *Ulysses* where, in the chapter entitled 'The Oxen of the Sun', the writer offers perfect facsimiles of succeeding styles in English literature, going from Anglo-Saxon infelicities, through Malory, Sir Thomas Browne, Bunyan, Pepys, Swift, Addison, Sterne and so on.)

In a desperate attempt to follow Tatum through the labyrinth of his own reflections on style in jazz, let us concentrate for a moment on three of Tatum's greatest contemporaries at various stages of his journey, three men whose piano playing unquestionably changed the face of jazz, and whose originality is beyond reasonable argument, let us say James P. Johnson, Earl Hines and Bud Powell. James P. was the founding father of a school of jazz piano known as 'Stride' because of the broad span required of a player's hands, which created the illusion when you watched them instead of listening, of a man striding along a road. The Stride style remains interesting long after the world which nurtured it has faded away, because of the striking imbalance achieved by players like Johnson, between the three component parts of music, Melody, Harmony and Rhythm. In the Stride school, melody is to some extent sacrificed at the altar of harmonic and rhythmic expediency. The Stride school was composed of men like Johnson who spent a great part of their lives playing unaccompanied in environments where nobody could afford a large band, or even a rhythm section, so that the Stride pianist had to have a left hand like a built-in rhythm section, and a right hand which would not only play the tune but also define the harmonic texture of that tune. The result was an intriguing musical style in which the melody was always there but never quite defined, like a fish constantly threatening to come to the surface but always remaining just under the curl of the wave. (Paradoxically, both the elder statesman of Stride piano James P., and his two most gifted pupils, Duke Ellington and Thomas 'Fats' Waller, were past masters at the elusive art of writing commercial tunes. The prowess of Duke and Fats in this regard is too well known to need any amplification here, but it is sometimes forgotten that Johnson, too, wrote some of the best standard songs of his era, including 'Running Wild' and 'If I Could Be With You'.)

The player who invented a new style to supersede Stride, or at least the man who evangelized on behalf of the new style, was Earl Hines. (The extent to which he invented the new style or borrowed it from Teddy Weatherford is problematic and of no vital importance in this context.) Hines conceived the idea of using the right hand to play single note improvisations based upon the chords, in contrast to the Stride pianists who were using their right hands to define the chords themselves. To clarify this distinction, let us say that a saxophonist faced with the challenge of playing on his instrument what James P. or Thomas 'Fats' was playing in the right hand, would admit defeat as quickly as an octopus faced with the prospect of a pair of spectacles, and for the same reason. The saxophone, or the trumpet or the clarinet or any other instrument which is able to produce only one note at a time, cannot, by the very nature of its mechanics, play what a Stride pianist plays because the Stride pianist is playing ten notes at any one time. Hines introduced the antithesis to Stride playing, and it came to be called 'Trumpet-style' piano, because the right hand of the pianist played single note lines which might easily have been transcribed from a Louis Armstrong solo. (The interplay between Hines and Armstrong on their famous recording of 'Weather Bird' marks one of the great moments of stylistic departure in jazz history.)

When a new age of Modernism arrived in the 1940s it was clear that of the two piano styles, it was Trumpet-style which was to dominate. In any case through the 1930s the Hines school had come into its own, for while the school of James P. was slowly petering out in imitations of imitations (James P. taught Waller who taught Joe Sullivan who influenced Jess Stacy, etc.), the Hines approach carried all before it, and even produced players influenced by Hines who were thought by many to have become better than their master. (Hines inspired Teddy Wilson, who invented Mel Powell, and so on.) The modern style rejoiced in a soloist like Bud Powell who, like Hines before him, was creating right-hand figures which echoed the solos of the great horn players, except of course that where Hines had followed Armstrong, Powell was calling to mind Charlie Parker. But Powell was different in kind from Hines for another reason. He was thinking in a harmonic dimension quite different from the world through which Hines had moved with such insolent ease. Powell was a child of the generation that discovered the delights of chromatic thinking, that took hold of the genial sequences of the Swing Age and altered them almost beyond recognition. Powell and his contempories were deploying the methods of Hines to express the ideas of Parker, and the result was a style of piano playing aeons removed from Hines, both for its harmonic intricacy and for the subtle amendments in rhythmic stress.

The reader may be pardoned for wondering at this stage what Johnson, Hines and Powell have to do with Art Tatum. The answer is that in Tatum's playing are incorporated the very essence of the Stride school's great thumping tirades, the very essence of the incandescence of Hines's right hand, the very essence of Powell's harmonic sophistication. To put it another way, Johnson, Hines and Powell were three men who each achieved the colossal feat of amending the aesthetic of jazz piano; Tatum achieved the even more colossal feat of demonstrating that it was possible to master all three styles, to flit from one to another within the space of a few bars, and to blend these disparate elements into a coherent, codified style by imposing on those elements the mark of his own personality.

In Tatum's piano playing jazz finds its ultimate pianistic expression, a piano style incorporating mastery of all piano styles, just as in literature the English language found its ultimate verbal expression in James Joyce, whose prose style was composed of the elements of all prose styles. What is utterly fascinating about Tatum is that once having mastered the various ways of playing jazz piano, he then showed how, by switching from one to another in midthought, he could express a style of his own. So many examples of this exist that there is neither time nor space or purpose in listing them, but a single example will surely be sufficient to make the point. In 'Lover Come Back To Me' Tatum repeatedly returns to a leisurely, Johnsonian statement of Romberg's melody after flirting with more baroque thoughts; the effect of this switch from the ingenious to the ingenuous and back again to the ingenious may be taken as an identifying feature of Tatum's art. It is for this reason that his technique enabled him, not just to confuse listeners looking for a too-obvious statement of tempo, but also to define the elements of those styles which might have been thought to be antipathetic to him that even his most gifted contemporaries were flabbergasted by his jazz. One of his closest musical friends, Roy Eldridge, has described how, the first time Tatum appeared in a club where nobody was aware of this ability, 'everybody stop playing'. Such testaments proliferate through jazz history. Tatum shattered everyone; Tatum caused all the other musicians to lose confidence; Tatum terrified those who thought they knew how far jazz could be taken; and so on. It all reads like a first draft for a B-picture, and we would be inclined to reject it on those grounds were it not for the fact that the irrefutable evidence, the actual music, bears out everything the idolaters have ever said about Tatum.

Why, then, has there been so little analytical discussion of Tatum's music? After all, Coleman Hawkins's great solos have been transcribed; Bix Beiderbecke's fingerings have been written about with a solemnity that would have fractured Bix; you can buy a book of Earl Hines's fifty best hot licks; Louis Armstrong's solos have been put together and then taken apart again by every quack and every hack who ever enjoyed a Bunk Johnson performance; even the beautiful butterfly of Duke Ellington's orchestral technique has many times been broken on the wheel of textual investigation. Why, then, virtually nothing about the way Tatum goes about his business? The answer incorporates one of the best jokes in jazz history. The reason why nobody has tackled Tatum on this level is that nobody has been able to. Tatum is so good that he has daunted everybody. The jazz world has been too idle or too dumb to tackle so vast a project. Indeed, it is one of the great scandals of jazz history that while almost every major style has been given detailed attention, Tatum's remains an enigma, and for as long as this remains true, then jazz criticism will not be in a state of grace.

But Excalibur with nothing to cleave is a mere encumbrance. Having developed the greatest technique and the subtlest improvising mind in jazz, what is there on which the virtuoso may express it? Some creative artists of genius who find themselves delivered by circumstance into a world incapable of providing them with work to do commensurate with their abilities, provide their own, creating form as well as content. Liszt concocted keyboard problems worthy of his own technical mastery; Aeschylus, no doubt distracted by the voices he heard in his imagination, invented dialogue. Bernard Shaw not only perfected the discussion-drama but actually created performers to act it and audiences to applaud it. But Tatum could only have done something comparable by being a composer of appropriate themes at least fifty times as prolific as Gershwin, Porter, Berlin, Kern and Rodgers put together. For the jazz pianist might easily run through the entire life's work of a gifted songwriter in the course of single night's work, so how could he be expected to create a repertoire of his own songs vast enough to contain his own muse? Even Duke Ellington, who was the nearest thing to a bottomless pit of compositional melodic resource, was occasionally obliged to draw on the resources of other composers. Tatum found his own way round this problem, and it was a way which reveals one of the basic facts of the jazz life, a fact so obvious that we never even notice it, any more than we notice the taste of saliva in our own mouths.

And yet this one simple fact, which we take so much for granted that its implications are lost to us, is so extraordinary that there is surely no other kind of creative artist in any other line of business who would consider its restrictive effects compatible with the production of the highest quality work. It is as though a ballet company were required to please its audiences without benefit of Chopin or Tchaikovsky or Ravel or Stravinsky, or if Joe Louis had been asked to prove his mastery without the convenience of boxing rings, or Shakespeare expected to produce the plays without the existence of any English history. For the truth is that the jazz musician alone among the creative artists of our epoch has no repertoire which has been manufactured with his art in mind. So far as the jazz improviser is concerned, no repertoire of his own has ever existed, so that a player like Tatum is placed in the situation of, say, a great concert piano virtuoso abroad in a world which has not yet evolved the delights of the concerto. Of course there is always the Blues, but a man cannot improvise on the same chord sequence all his life. So what is the jazz soloist to do? The answer is provided the moment we nominate the other favourite chord sequence of the jazz musician, the one usually named as being second only to the Blues in its general usefulness to the improviser. That sequence is 'I Got Rhythm', at which point we are witnesses to the most spectacular collision of two autonomous musical cultures.

We know, for example, that the Blues is genuine American folk music in the sense that it arose and evolved through the vital needs of a social group. (When Ferdinand 'Jelly Roll' Morton confessed 'I did not invent the Blues,' it was one of the very rare occasions on which he was telling the plain, unvarnished truth. Nobody invented the Blues because everybody invented them.) But when we turn to 'I Got Rhythm', we are flung into a world that is highly artificial in the sense that the creative minds which adorn it are ultra-sophisticated, highly trained, commercially obligated, technically refined. And most important of all, for the most part unconcerned with and sometimes totally ignorant of jazz, at times even violently antipathetic towards it, witness the attempts from time to time of distinguished popular composers to ban the issue of jazz recordings which distort the written melody. And yet it is this world which, inadvertently perhaps, provided jazz with its raw material, its thematic resources.

The comical incongruity of all this is demonstrated by the bare facts about 'I Got Rhythm', which was first introduced to American audiences on 14 October 1930 at the Alvin Theatre, when a Miss Ethel Merman sang the words and music provided for her by George and Ira Gershwin. The show was called *Girl Crazy*, and its plot, a rambling farrago involving a dude ranch and lots of chorus girls, need not concern us here, except to make the point that the sheer irrelevance of these facts is an impressive testimony to the watchfulness of the jazz musician when it comes to finding suitable songs to play. (*Girl Crazy* was perhaps a special case in this regard, for its pit orchestra was not uncharacteristically packed with jazz musicians like Benny Goodman, Gene Krupa and Charlie Teagarden, who no doubt spread the word regarding the suitability of 'I Got Rhythm' for jazz improvisation.)

It so happens that the American musical theatre enjoyed a golden age so far as melodic invention was concerned, and that this golden age coincided roughly with the professional lifespan of an artist like Tatum. Specific dates must always be arbitrary, but it is not altogether misleading to suggest that this great period began with the publication of Jerome Kern's 'They Didn't Believe Me' in 1914 and ended after Irving Berlin shot his bolt, most brilliantly, by the way, with *Call Me Madam* in 1950. Why such golden ages occur is difficult, perhaps impossible to say, but certainly one of the more potent factors was the imbecility of the Romanov dynasty, which obligingly flung into the arms of American culture the families of George Gershwin and Irving Berlin. Another factor must have been the comparative lowness of Broadway production costs, which made the gambling with untried talent a less terrifying affair than it later became. Undoubtedly a third factor was the pervading influence of jazz music on American culture generally, even though many of the songwriters who benefited remained all their lives in total ignorance of what had happened to them. Of course, not all the great composers of Broadway were unaware of what the jazz musician could do with their raw material, and it is perhaps aesthetic justice that the greatest of all these composers should have acknowledged the mastery of the greatest of these jazz musicians. In Oscar Levant's *A Smattering of Ignorance* we read:

> *Despite his increasing interest in formal music and its background, Gershwin never lost his love for dance music. The emergence of the swing phenomenon interested but did not surprise him, for such eminent performers as Benny Goodman, Gene Krupa, Red Nichols, Jack Teagarden, Jimmy Dorsey, Babe Rusin and Glenn Miller had contributed to the gaiety of* Strike Up the Band *and* Girl Crazy *as members of the pit orchestra. The Goodman Trio's record of 'Lady Be Good' delighted him, and he listened with rapture to Art Tatum (the great blind Negro pianist), especially to his playing of 'Liza' and 'I Got Rhythm'. He was so enthused with Tatum's playing that he had an evening for him at his 72nd Street apartment before leaving for Hollywood. Among George's invited guests was Leopold Godowsky, who listened with amazement for twenty minutes to Tatum's remarkable runs, embroideries, counter-figures and passage playing. The succeeding hour and a half of the same thing bored him, however. Some time after he arrived in California Gershwin discovered that Tatum was playing at a local nightclub, and we went together to hear him. It was a small, dingy, badly lighted room – an intimate version of the too-intimate Onyx Club. We joined the group of enthusiasts clustered around the piano where the blind virtuoso was in full swing. To George's great joy, Tatum played virtually the equivalent of Beethoven's thirty-two variations on his tune 'Liza'. Then George asked for more.*

Why should a musician like Art Tatum have found a song like 'Liza' so intriguing? After all, it had been written as part of an indifferent backstage musical none of whose protagonists (apart from Gershwin himself) knew or cared a fig for musicians of Tatum's stamp. The answer to that question – indeed the answer to the question, Why the intimate relationship between the commercial theatre and an art-for-art's-sake music like jazz? – consists of a single word; that word is harmony.

To explain; what is jazz music, just how is it made? The improviser takes a theme, states its melody briefly, and then creates fresh melodic lines based on the harmonies of the original melody. It becomes obvious that the lifeblood of the jazz musician is harmony; or rather combinations and sequences of harmony which engage his creative attention, those sequences which suggest to him certain new melodic patterns, sequences which mysteriously possess their own rhythmic dynamic, sequences whose ingenious convolutions help the improviser not to repeat himself. And Tatum's whole generation stumbled on the truth that whether or not the tunesmiths of Broadway cared, they were turning out sequence after sequence of this kind, so that when the other circumstances of the successful musical had fallen away and been forgotten, when all the tinsel had gone back in the wardrobe and the crows' feet were treading all over the faces of once-beautiful leading ladies, when the jokes in the dialogue had long been left for dead and the thunderous hoofbeats of the chorus girls no longer reverberated to the back of the gallery, a residue was left behind, a residue of pure gold – the songs.

It is yet another irony of the history of twentieth-century music that it should have been the songs, which were at the time considered the least important items in the musical theatre, less vital than the drawing power of the star, less commercial than the style of the costumes, less respected than the libretto, should eventually have given the American musical comedy its only lasting element. Perhaps no more need be said about the interaction of the debt between the jazz soloist and the musical comedy writer than that out of the 179 sides which Art Tatum cut for Norman Granz, no fewer than forty-four of them involved the work of the five major songwriters of the Golden Age – Gershwin, Berlin, Porter, Rodgers, and Kern – and that if we extend the list to include five other masters almost as accomplished, Walter Donaldson, Vincent Youmans, Harold Arlen, Duke Ellington, and Kurt Weill, the total goes up to seventy. (These figures become even more impressive when we remember that most of the other themes come from Tin Pan Alley, whose songwriting methods were identical to those of Broadway, at least in the sense that qualitatively, there is little to choose between, say, 'Dancing In The Dark' which comes from the musical stage, 'Too Marvellous For Words' which comes from the musical cinema, and 'Cherokee', which is just a song; the Golden Age was all-pervading.)

It is a piquant experience, this savouring of the accidental meeting of two cultures, this unpredictable romance between the contrivance of musical theatre and the tough, uncompromising, proudly uncommercial world of the jazz soloist. But mere piquancy would not be enough, I think, to justify any lengthy analysis. The most important thing of all to be said, not only about Tatum's jazz on these amazing sides, but also about the nature of his repertoire, is that, unbelievably, all these songs achieved their apotheosis, not at the hands of those artists for whom they were originally designed, but through the gifts of men like Tatum, who perhaps never sat through a musical comedy in his life. If 'Liza' survives as a fragment of twentieth-century musical art, who will Gershwin have to thank, Ruby Keeler or Art Tatum? If 'There'll Never Be Another You' survives long enough to commend its neat harmonic structure to the musicologists of the twenty-first century, who can Harry Warren thank for that, Sonja Henie or the generation of jazzmen who explored its potential? One sometimes wonders if George Gershwin ever knew that the most affecting vocal version of 'Summertime', and perhaps the most original in concept, was Billie Holiday's.

Now it so happens that this whole area generally covered by the generic phrase, 'show-tunes', has been shockingly badly documented, almost never annotated, never anthologized. The student who thinks that sheer artistic merit is enough to guarantee the survival of a song is advised to try buying the sheet music of 'Stay As Sweet As You Are' or 'That Old Feeling' and see how far he gets. It seems to me unarguable that the survival of such items is important, because a great deal of what is best in twentieth-century popular music is contained in items of that kind. A great many of the men who composed them were artistically feckless, some of them were shameless money-grubbers, a few were pretentious popinjays, and some of them were so blinkered musically that they actually hated jazz. None of this has any relevance; all that matters is that this body of men produced a repertoire of songs so witty, so skilfully wrought, so finely finished, that it demands the talent of an Art Tatum to do it justice.

Such arrangements never come about. When has a great jazz virtuoso ever been invited into a studio and asked to play nearly two hundred songs of his choice the way he wants, sometimes even playing the same item twice if he believes, as is often the case, that a different tempo will reveal a different song? That is why the Art Tatum marathon is unique as well as vitally important for our understanding of two cultures, that of Broadway and that of the jazz musician. What Tatum did smacks of real genius. He sat at the piano and, drawing on a lifetime's experience in the smoky club rooms of his youth, the days as a solo attraction and a trio leader, as a concert artist and a legend, he drew out from the stockroom of his recollection the songs that America had sung and danced to for the last thirty years. Of course he had no such intention in mind. But posterity must draw its conclusions from what the artist did, not what he thought he was doing, or meant to do, or felt he ought to do. Time and again in this remarkable collection of the finest piano solos ever made, the listener is pulled up short and his attention distracted for a moment by the sheer loveliness of the theme. Sometimes the tempo may surprise him, sometimes the drastic restructuring of the harmonic base may disconcert him; occasionally even the choice of theme will catch him unawares. But never will he find himself wondering why Tatum should have allowed into his pantheon an inferior theme, for in this collection there are no inferior themes.

A final reflection on how to listen to so vast an oeuvre of improvised music from a single voice. I remember back in the 1950s a friend of mine, a professional musician, acquired four of the Tatum solo albums, and finally came to the same conclusion that Mr Godowsky does in Oscar Levant's memoir, namely that twenty minutes of Tatum is enough for any man. Mr Godowsky was quite wrong and so was my friend, who would certainly have reached a similar conclusion had he attempted to read ten Shakespeare plays in a day, or tried to mug up on all four Brahms symphonies at once. (I am not suggesting that Tatum is to be measured against Shakespeare or Brahms, but merely trying to point out that whatever the level of aesthetic power, there is such a thing as indigestion of the appreciative faculty.) Anyone who attempts to digest hours and hours of Tatum solo piano at a sitting is not only living his life the wrong way, but is also spoiling a great many pleasures which belong to tomorrow. Personal habits vary enormously, of course, and I can only report my own experiences with Tatum, without suggesting for a moment that they will be the same as anyone else's. (If anything

I am unusually slow in building a close acquaintanceship with a great jazz performance.) After two months I found I could remember my way around some of the solo sides. After three months I was beginning to prefer some to others, always a good sign that understanding is flowering. After four months, I began to be able to name the titles even when switching on the middle of a moment of inspired fantasia on Tatum's part. After six months I sat down to compose these few reflections of one of the great recording events in the musical history of our time.

I would have liked longer, say another six months, but I suspect that even then I would still have wanted more time. For Tatum's art reveals more and more as one's study of it continues. My experience has been that first it discloses the nature of the instrument, then the nature of the material, then the nature of the musician. And then, ultimately, the nature of the listener. I know now, after living with Tatum's music for a time, that it was foolhardy of me ever to have become an instrumentalist myself.

Charlie Parker

> *. . . the technical history of modern harmony is a history of growth of toleration by the human ear of chords that at first sounded discordant and senseless to the main body of contemporary professional musicians.*
>
> BERNARD SHAW

The advent of Charlie Parker caused more violent irruptions, more bitterness, more sheer apoplectic rage than that of any jazz musician before him. Before he happened, there was no serious split down the middle of the jazz ranks. After he arrived, it was no longer sufficient to claim you were a jazz fan. The term no longer had a precise or narrow meaning. It was now necessary to qualify the claim, to explain what kind of jazz fan you were, to commit yourself either to the music that was pre-Charlie Parker or the music he was playing. From now on there were to be two quite distinct jazz worlds, the ancient and the modern, and in the cut-and-thrust of the war which followed it escaped the notice of most people, musicians included, that it was by no means obligatory to choose one side or the other. Even in later years, when Parker's neologisms became standard jazz practice, the jazz lover of catholicity who made no secret of his admiration both of Armstrong and Parker was aware he was admiring two very different kinds of music.

There were two main reasons for an event like the arrival of Charlie Parker, apart of course from the truism that it is always in the nature of the young artist to extend his boundaries to the limits of his ability. First, jazz had been stuck long enough in the same diatonic groove for its men to have become hampered by restrictions of harmonic thought. A bright fellow could digest all the laws of the time in a few weeks, although it might take him the rest of his life to make practical instrumental use of his knowledge. G7 still resolved on to C Major or C Minor, no matter whether you were Coleman Hawkins or the second tenor saxophone at the local palais. The path was so well-beaten that it had slowly degenerated into a rut. The other reason was just as understandable. The young rising musician looked around him and was daunted by the stature of the giants of the Swing Age. He was shrewd enough to know there was no sense in attempting an improvement on the styles of Hodges, Carter, Eldridge, Hawkins, for the good reason that these men had invented their own styles. The choice before the apprentice of 1940 was either to become a minor imitator or a revolutionary.

The difficulty is that the revolutionary, if he has no alternative of his own to the status quo he is challenging, becomes a mere roughneck. Vital though it was for jazz to find a new approach if it were not to curl up and die from sheer lack of inspiration, at the time, nobody had the faintest glimmering of an idea what the new approach was likely to be, whether it would be instrumental, as Artie Shaw evidently hoped when he toyed with strings and harpsichords, overlooking the fact that a platitude on the piano remains a platitude when it is played on a harpsichord or a spinet or a celeste; or whether the new direction might take the form of a more intense stylization of older conventions, as the Benny Goodman Sextet attempted.

The breakthrough had to come from a young man not yet set

in his musical ways. And whoever this young man was to be, he would have to have an ear instinctively attuned to harmonic movement of the most complex kind. He would also have to possess a melodic gift and a sense of form at least as great as any other jazz musician who ever lived, and perhaps greater, for reasons which we will see.

The most daunting condition for this new approach to improvisation was that tradition had apparently to be ignored; I say apparently because in actual fact Charlie Parker's jazz went closer to the roots of the matter than any musician since Louis Armstrong, but for many years the strangeness of the world he created obscured this fact. All kinds of conventions would have to be ignored, not only those of discord and resolution. The old idea of a musicianly tone might have to be ditched, and so might the old idea about the finished performance being immaculate and unblemished, as Hodges and Carter were. The element of gambling would re-enter the process of making jazz, because the artist would once more be casting himself on an unknown tide.

The peculiar properties of the human ear now enter the argument to cause hopeless confusion. It is one of the physiological features of our species that the most outrageous cacophony might well come to sound perfectly innocuous if only we give it time. Amazing but true, that what sounds like an outrageous gaffe to one generation will be accepted with a yawn by the next. At the time Charlie Parker made his recording debut, all but a few musicians and one or two shrewd aficionados dismissed him as a buffoon, because to them the progressions he was using seemed grammatically incorrect. And so they were if you judged them according to the method of Johnny Hodges.

The surprising thing is that only a knife-edge separated the one from the other, a fact most conveniently demonstrated by one of the earliest Parker recordings. On the first, subsequently rejected take of 'Red Cross', Parker, coping with the harmonies of 'I Got Rhythm', makes an almost staid start, perhaps because he was on the horns of the same dilemma as the guitarist Tiny Grimes had been when he composed the piece. The first four bars of 'Red Cross' consist of a two-bar repeated phrase suffering from all the ennui of the period. It might have been lifted straight out of one of Benny Goodman's prim little pieces for the sextet. There is not the slightest sign that this is the dawn of a new era in jazz. But then, without any preparation, occurs in the fifth and sixth bars a new-minted phrase which has nothing to do with the phrase that went before. The two fragments belong to different stages of jazz development, and the impact on first hearing is most disturbing. The strange beauty of the new shape is then accented even further by the fact that the two-bar cadence following is as conventional as the opening four bars. It is a Bebop sandwich, with the Swing Age playing the part of the bread.

When Parker enters after the theme statement on the first take, his phrase pays such deference to the jazz tradition that it might literally be Johnny Hodges playing something like 'Squatty Roo'. The phrase consists of four notes based harmonically on the tonic Major chord. No revolution here, although after this opening the solo careers off on its own strange path. This take was rejected and another immediately cut, and it is now that an apparently minute alteration occurs in the shaping of the first alto phrase, an alteration symbolic of much of the fuss which arose about Parker and what he was about to do to jazz over the next few years.

The first three notes of the four-note entry phrase are identical, almost as though the soloist had made a mental note to play them no matter how many takes there might be. But the last quaver of the phrase flies off in a completely unexpected direction. The listener hearing it for the first time is caught flat-footed and can only tell himself that the man is mad, that he is playing wrong notes in the most shameless manner, that jazz is nothing like as trustworthy as it used to be in the good old days. At the time 'Red Cross' was made, in September 1944, people could get really nasty with each other over the legitimacy of that fourth note. They might develop an enmity expressing itself in physical assault, or if they were musicians, ripen into a vendetta whose bitterness would remain undiluted for ten or fifteen years.

For all that, there was nothing blasphemous or technically incorrect about that note, or many others like it that Parker scattered all over his recordings. It was perfectly permissible. The only point was that from now on the world of sound embodied by the term 'jazz' became irrevocably divided into two factions, those who could accept that note and those who could not. The question was perhaps a little more complicated than that for many people. There were those willing, not only to accept that note, but to accept that note and nothing else, and even to construct around it a philosophy of social insurrection. They were the crackpots and the professional hipsters who seemed to think that now Charlie Parker had arrived, everything played before him was placed out of court. Every extraneous factor about him, from his dress to his private habits, became an essential part of the wooing of the new muse.

Acceptance or rejection of that note, and the nature and degree of the acceptance and rejection of that note, was a kind of litmus test for the sensitivity of the ear of the judge. Whatever anyone may have felt personally about Charlie Parker in those days, it was certainly true that very many people who had regarded themselves, quite sincerely, as jazz lovers, now found themselves jazz haters. Some of them were too bewildered about the upheaval to do very much about it, so they retired in a state of bitterness and complete bewilderment. Some of them, the more spirited ones, tried to concoct the most comical sophistries to retain their position. M. Pannassie made an inspired attempt at defending the castle by claiming that anything he didn't like wasn't jazz at all. Of course he did not say this in so many words, but what he did say was that Charlie Parker's music, or Bebop as it was known in those quaintly onomatopoeic days, was not jazz at all, but some ghastly hybrid which M. Pannassie was very careful not to define.

In other words, a few uses of that note from 'Red Cross' and Charlie Parker had lopped away a huge percentage of jazz followers from the body of the music itself. All the romantics of the 'Red light district of Storyville and Louis in the Reformatory' school were out. All the followers of the New Orleans legend abandoned their position with indecent haste and became self-confessed nostalgia-mongers with no real interest in the present or the future of jazz. All the adulators of the Big Band ethos, with its attendant imbecilities of screaming solos and half-witted novelty, disappeared from view. The trouble was that none of those who objected to that note were really sure of themselves. Not knowing what the note was, or what its syntactical justification might be, or whether it was a joke in poor taste, the anti-Parkerites, or if you like the ante-Parkerites, either gnashed their teeth in ineffectual rage, thus becoming a constant source of amusement to younger musicians, or took the bit between their teeth and entered the lists with the most astonishing theories.

The delicious thing is that the diehards included many musicians who had themselves once been adventurers. Benny Goodman, who evidently believed that now he had stopped evolving himself, everyone else ought to stop evolving too, mumbled something about 'wrong notes'. Louis Armstrong felt so strongly about it that he actually was moved to make a definite statement about music. The Beboppers, he remarked, were killing the business. Of course such asperities became diluted with the passing years. Goodman even went so far as to hire Wardell Gray, and Louis Armstrong, perhaps reassured by the fact that business, despite the Beboppers, had never been better, was rumoured to be on friendly terms with Dizzy Gillespie of all people. But it is the immediate impact of the new jazz and the lunacies of bigotry and partisanship it caused that is symptomatic of the heresy of Charlie Parker's music.

After reflecting on the magnitude of the dialectical war which raged over the birth of Modern jazz, it is ironic to note how innocuous those outrageous notes really were. To slide for a moment into the degeneracy of technicalities once more, the Hodges-like phrase in the first take of 'Red Cross' ended on C, the root of the tonic Major chord, whereas in the second take the phrase ended on a movement from F sharp to F natural, and the F sharp was none other than that dreaded scourge of the reactionaries, the terror of the sentimentalists, the bane of the professional fans, the pretenders and the usurpers, the Flattened Fifth.

Now the flattened fifth of the common chord is not right and it is not wrong, in the same way that when a man accepts as silence what a dog will bark at as a piercing scream, neither the man nor the dog is right or wrong. It is simply a question of the relative sensitivity of their ears. To a man whose musical experience is limited to listening to jazz, and jazz of the past at that, the flattened fifth will indeed sound like a mocking insult. On the other hand, the musician who has heard even a few bars of the Impressionist composers, the same ones who captivated the young Bix Beiderbecke, cannot honestly see what all the fuss is about. With Charlie Parker jazz was simply trying to catch up with the movement of formal music into the realms of chromaticism which had swept across the entire world of music during the nineteenth century. It is no coincidence that the composers whom adventurous jazzmen always prefer are Debussy, Ravel, Stravinsky and Bartok, and that they, who too have their bigoted moments, cannot often tolerate more than a few bars of a composer like Handel, who probably represents to them the classical counterpart of a mouldy fig.

What the Modern movement was doing was to broaden the harmonic territory available to the improvising musician, which brings us to the Olympian achievement of Charlie Parker. The more complex the harmony, the more difficult becomes the soloist's task of retaining the relaxed spirit of a good jazz performance. Once a tune begins, the harmonic changes rush by like telegraph poles on a railway line, and the more poles there are the harder it becomes to pay full attention to them all, until in the end so preoccupied with them will the traveller become that he is in real danger of failing to observe the unity of the surrounding landscape. Parker was so richly endowed a musician that he was not only able to introduce into the jazz context shades of harmonic subtlety never before heard in jazz, but he was able at the same time to restore to jazz an emotional sincerity it had forgotten about in the preceding era of sophisticated techniques, ambitious orchestrations, and compromise with the tastes of the dance hall.

The two effects are apparently contradictory. How can a man complicate an art form technically and at the same time simplify it emotionally? He can only achieve this if his emotional depth is so profound that not only can it cleanse the existing form with its attendant rules and conventions, but can accept further complexities and still manage to retain the effect of simplicity. That is why Charlie Parker might be said to have possessed a melodic gift greater than any other jazz musician before him. The mere fact of his success proves the point. Had he not possessed a prodigious instinct for the moulding of a clean and beautiful phrase, his work would have been doomed to the same arid precosity of many of his contemporaries and followers, who were too often guilty of a kind of instrumental chicane, by which the passion of inspiration is usurped by an impressive but fundamentally pointless manual dexterity.

At first Parker was not able to produce the thoroughly integrated performance in the new idiom, because jazz happens to be a communal effort. No matter how great he may have been, Parker was not able to conjure up rhythm sections to complement his own playing. In recordings like 'Red Cross' can be found the intriguing and slightly comic spectacle of the new jazz presented against the old familiar background of four chunks to a bar. Only in time did a comprehensive world of modernism come into being.

What must have surprised the old guard of the jazz world, players and spectators alike, was Parker's repeated insistence on the twelve-bar Blues, a form which although it had not gone into complete decline, had not been too happily used by the outstanding musicians of the Swing Age. The reason is not hard to find. Players like Hawkins and Carter required for the fulfilment of their styles, sophisticated and ornate, material whose harmonies were far more complex than the Blues, with its three indispensable harmonic changes. As it never occurred to these players to take the Blues form and amend it, the only alternative was to borrow themes like 'Body And Soul' or 'Out Of Nowhere' from the popular song idiom, because these tunes had ever-moving harmonies designed by trained musicians in original patterns.

But Parker had superior endowment to his predecessors, talented as they were. He was more conversant than they with unusual harmonic shapes, and in addition, had a creative spark which was not quite the same as that which enables the soloist to play a succession of good jazz choruses. Parker's ear instinctively heard harmonies implied in a melody which most musicians never thought about. He was therefore tempted to insert into his harmonic sequences chords that were not wrong, but different from those originally written into the song. These new harmonies, or 'substitutions', as some musicians refer to them, are the key to his whole aesthetic. If the jazz soloist is an artist who creates his effect by weaving designs in the harmonies of a theme, then it is quite obvious that when those harmonies are strangely fresh, then the patterns comprising his solos will themselves be strangely fresh, although only if the instrumentalist involved is a gifted jazz musician will the patterns be more than just unusual. There were dozens of early Modernists who produced strange patterns, but Parker's strangeness was profound and beautiful. In using the Blues form, he was making it most embarrassing for the diehards whose ears were unable to guide them through the labyrinth of Parker's musical thought.

Some of the most superlative Parker recordings are those of the Blues, and now that the captains and the kings have departed, nobody, not even the most crackpotted bigot, denies their virtues, for he knows that time has reversed the situation, that it is now he, not the recordings, that are on trial. Even so, allowing for all the belated wisdom of hindsight, it is hard to accept the fact that bloody critical battles raged about such recordings as 'Now's The Time', which in retrospect is seen to be one of the classic blues recordings in the entire jazz repertoire.

Parker plays three choruses on the issued master of 'Now's The Time', and although there are some dazzling innovations, it is very simple to chart the parallel between this interpretation of the Blues and any of a thousand from earlier stages in jazz development. Parker's entrance, for instance. There is nothing at all revolutionary about this beautifully conceived, perfectly executed and meticulously defined phrase. It was original certainly, but there was nothing revolutionary about it. It happens to have been played by a revolutionary, but that is not the same thing. Its strangeness was due, not to its harmonic inspiration, of which there is virtually none, but to the breathtaking freshness of the player's style, as though he had heard about the common chord of the Major triad for the first time a few minutes before the recording began. These simple, passionate phrases were to remain one of the staples of Parker's style, an antidote he employed instinctively to balance the complexity of some of his bewildering flights into double tempo.

After the first four bars, moving into the Minor tonality, the phrase is once again quite simple, although not so stark as the opening. In this second section of the first chorus, there occur at least two intimations of a very important truth about jazz, which is that each new style demands its own technique, because each new style is only new at all because it moves through the harmonies over a path not previously exploited. Parker's phrase is built around the device of a fall from the keynote to the Minor third, but not as Hodges might have executed it. There is no suggestion of a glissando. Instead, the intervening notes are lightly touched, no more than suggested, in the descent. The device is executed so casually that it might go unnoticed. However, for the saxophonist with aspirations to master the new idiom, here was a new problem to be solved. When Parker repeats the phrase another characteristic of what was then called Bebop rears its head. After the second descent the phrase climbs upwards again, but instead of a continuous sweep, there is a quaver followed by a triplet, executed as fast as light, but with every detail perfectly defined. Because it was one of the few tangibles of Parker's personal keyboard style, this triplet device came to be one of the most maddening clichés of Modern jazz for several years, reducing more than one individual style to the dimensions of a prolonged and ugly hiccup. To Parker it was only one of many personal quirks of style never allowed to shatter the whole. The third and last four-bar section of his first chorus is conventional, except for the fact that infinitesimal adjustments of the time values of the notes hints at an independence of the four-in-a-bar cage which had hitherto been sedulously avoided in jazz.

The second chorus opens with a modest elaboration of the start of the previous chorus, except that at the end of the second bar the appearance, brief but significant, of the augmented second of the key implies one of the substituted chords which gave Parker's playing a new dimension of beauty. It is important to appreciate that this note was the augmented second and not the Minor third. In their actual pitch the two notes are the same, but the enharmonic distinction must be made to underline the nature of the harmony in whose terms Parker was thinking. The first real shock to the Establishment comes in the second section, where the melody makes a sudden astonishing leap upwards to create an interval so perplexing to the jazz ear of the time that some people assumed that the high note in the phrase was a slip of the fingers not intended by the soloist at all.

Having flown off at a tangent in this way, Parker then proceeds to another convention of the new jazz, the deployment of an extended passage in double time. It should be made clear that playing sixteen notes in a bar was nothing new. What made these phrases sound like a lunatic scramble to the ear too sluggish to follow them was not the mere presence of the sixteen notes in one bar, but the arrangement of the inflections and time values to suggest that for a moment or two the tempo of the performance had actually doubled. The effect of this on the listener of the time was catastrophic, for he now had not only to digest new modes of expression, but to digest them at exactly twice the speed for which his mind had been prepared at the start of the performance. No wonder so many people gave up in disgust, overlooking the fact that the melodic content of a phrase like the one which ended the second of Parker's choruses in 'Now's The Time' was ravishing.

The third chorus begins with yet another variation of the phrase that opened the alto solo, only now there are to be found sprinkled about the phrases certain grace notes embellishing the melodic line and seem to complicate it without actually doing so. These grace notes were another Parker mannerism that broke out in an unsightly rash of affectation right across the face of Modern jazz, but here again Parker himself kept this kind of virtuosity strictly in check, subordinating its effect to the overall welfare of the solo.

As he approaches the third and final cadence of this last chorus, the soloist breaks out again in a passionate outburst of double-tempo phrasing. It is when he arrives at one of the key junctures of the blues sequence, the eighth bar, that he coins an epigram as beautifully rounded as any that jazz had heard. The eighth bar of the Blues is vital because it is one of the moments of resolution at which the soloist arrives on his way round the harmonic cycle, back to the starting tonality, the point where the mood recedes to the quietism of the opening. The harmonic change he uses at the end of the eighth bar is the one that will lead him back to the dominant chord linked to the tonic on which he must end. In Modern jazz the ear of many of its pioneers, instead of settling for a normal diatonic change, substituted a tiny progression of descending Minor seventh chords. It must not be thought that players like Charlie Parker suddenly discovered a new musical effect. The chord of the Minor seventh is as old as music itself. Ravel's *Allegro for Harp*, written before Parker was born, opens with an elaborate exposition of the use of the progression, but the descending Minor seventh was not the kind of discord on which the mind of a musician might settle unless he were quite free of the conventions of diatonic harmony.

In effect, Parker, in using these descending Minor sevenths, was in the enviable position of having at his disposal a musical device virtually unknown to the idiom in which he was working. Suggestions of the movement may be found in jazz of an earlier period. There is one moment on 'Billie's Blues', recorded in 1937, when Bunny Berigan of all people, seems about to stumble on the sequence. But with Parker it is clear that the effect is designed, intended, thoroughly digested and integrated into the framework of the most traditional of all jazz forms. The phrase Parker coins is romantically overwhelming. Its technical originality is secondary. It is the emerging melodic shape that is vital, and it is at such moments that Parker demonstrates this astonishing gift for bequeathing to future generations of jazz musicians a new harmonic scope at the same time as he cuts away all the fripperies and false sophistications, leaving a residue which, for all its technical ingenuity, is emotionally simple and frank. It is in its complete candour that Parker's style is something new in jazz music. With phrases like his entrance in 'Now's The Time', and the Minor seventh device later in the same recording, he bridges the vast gulf between audience and performer through the alchemy of an almost desperate sincerity.

In the sense that he was a sublimely gifted jazz musician, Parker was something of a freak. Never at any time could the listener, no matter how well acquainted with Parker's playing he might be, feel confident that Parker would not play something unexpected. Of course he had his private clichés. All musicians do. They are the means by which we identify them. There were times when Parker might jog along, putting a solo together with no more than a high degree of professionalism without venturing beyond the familiar limits of his own more casual performances. But he was always able suddenly to rise above himself to produce yet another solo unique in form and scope.

Instrumental virtuosity reached a new climax with Charlie Parker. All previous laws were invalid. Collective improvisation in the light of a Parker performance like 'Embraceable You' was now clearly seen to be a compensatory device to cloak the limitations of the musicians who resorted to it. With a musician of Parker's genius, the solo voice was the only conceivable approach, because it was the only way he would be able to suggest to the listener more than a tithe of his potential. The string background was still no more than a background and had no bearing on the actual content of the saxophone solos. Had Parker been distressed or thrown out of his stride by the experiment then the decriers would have been justified. In fact, both on his own testimony and that of the records, Parker thoroughly enjoyed the whole affair.

The *Parker with Strings* tracks are another demonstration of the soloist's refusal to be disconcerted and therefore inhibited by the intensity of his own passion. Performances like 'Just Friends' and 'If I Should Lose You' are towering examples of musical romanticism. They are unashamedly sentimental without ever degenerating into mere sentimentality, and they also exhibit one facet of Parker's sublimity which was accepted for many years, and is indeed often challenged today. He had one of the most inexpressively beautiful instrumental tones any jazzman ever produced. Because it was not the dandiacal, elegant tone of Benny Carter or the voluptuous cry of Johnny Hodges, it was dismissed as a fraud by critics who had never blown any instruments in their lives, apart possibly from their own trumpets. Bandleaders hated it, and still do in Britain, because it wrought havoc with the vibrato blend of the conventional saxophone section. And purists complained that more than one Parker recording was issued although blemished by the indiscretion of a squeak.

It was true that Parker sounded like neither Hodges nor Carter. It was also true that he sounded more inspired than either of them. The laws of saxophone section playing may be discounted, for they were formulated for the edification of dance hall patrons and have no musical significance. As for the squeaks, they were the occasional price Parker had to pay for the power he produced from an alto saxophone. Now and again he put into his embouchure more muscular pressure than any reed or mouthpiece could cope with, hence the squeak. Sometimes the squeaks caused a recording to be rejected, but in certain cases the solo was so outstanding that the master was released, squeak and all, just as a publishing firm might elect to release on to the market a great literary masterpiece with a small print smudge on every hundredth page.

What is more to the point is that when a saxophonist squeaks it is no reflection on his musicianship. It may imply a condemnation of his reed, his mouthpiece or his selection of these two appurtenances, but it has literally nothing to do with his technical ability. There are thousands of saxophonists who never squeaked in their lives, but this does not place them above Charlie Parker in the hierarchy of jazz. The modern revolution was a hectic affair. Its pioneers had no time for the niceties of public performance.

Parker was an experimenter, an explorer, forever poised on the brink of chaos, just as some of those he displaced as the preeminent jazz voice had been poised for ten years or more on the brink of latitude. He was attempting to hammer out a whole set of conventions new to jazz, and considering the complete originality of his playing, it is truly miraculous that he achieved as many perfect performances as he did.

With Parker, jazz was rising phoenix-like from the debris of its own ashes. It was being given another chance. Parker was bestowing upon it a mine of musical thought so rich in potential that his successors have been quarrying the mine ever since. Unlike Parker, most of these successors are not unlimited jazz soloists, finding it an indispensable aid to inspiration to lean on the teachings of Parker. They are also on occasions hamstrung by musical climates that Parker was able to take in his stride. Big band, small-band, strings or trumpet-alto front line, vocal groups, scat singers, nothing impeded the flow of his expression.

Some of the big band sides he made in the middle 1950s are thrilling matches between the orchestra on one hand and Parker on the other. The orchestrations are ordinary enough, and time has been particularly harsh on them, but Parker redeems all. Time and again he soars over the concerted voice of the accompaniment, painting dazzling resplendent pictures which take the breath away. The infinite grace of his variations on 'Stella By Starlight', the whimsical chromatic tricks he plays with the first phrase of 'What Is This Thing Called Love?', that hair-raising moment when he soars over the written melody by a mere semitone in 'Almost Like Being In Love' so that the ear is almost too terrified to follow, all these manifestations of the soloist's genius make otherwise indifferent recordings historic.

When a man towers over the whole realm of his artistic exploits, it is certain that for some time after he has gone, critical standards will be all awry, like a trusty compass fallen inside the field of a mighty magnet. Parker's recognition, like Lester's, was belated, with the difference that while Lester lived to see the vindication of his methods, Parker did not. The pathos of the situation is increased by the fact that Parker missed out only by a year or two. Had he lived into the 1960s he would have been lionized as Gillespie was lionized, he would have become at forty the Grand Old Man of a glorious artistic triumphal upheaval.

He would even have made large sums of money, something always pleasing to jazz musicians, no matter what any of them may say to the contrary. But he did not live. He actively strove to die, for personal reasons which nobody can adequately explain. It is too glib to say he became a drug addict for the same reason Alice ate the cake marked 'Eat Me', to gain entry into the enchanted garden. And no less glib to say he behaved as he did because of his confrontation by the long line of blank uncomprehending faces which for years showed no reaction to the music he was conjuring up out of his own head. What terrifying private visions might have dogged him, what oppression might have fell upon him through his inescapable artistic loneliness, what disgust he might have succumbed to when the imbecile denigrations poured in, we do not know. His life was a turbulent enigma and the only coherence to emerge from it was the music.

During a career short even by jazz standards, he wrecked the canons of criticism and severed the music for ever from the dilettante followers to whom an affection of jazz enthusiasm was a social asset or a personal vanity. After Parker you had to be something of a musician to follow the best jazz of the day. If you were sentimental about the good old days, if you clutched at fading recollections of your own adolescence, if you thought your opinions were valid just because you possessed the recordings, Parker exposed you for a charlatan. There was nothing left for you to do but feign wisdom of his art, like the professional hipsters and the beat writers, or run screaming from the arena, like the revivalists and those who collected matrix numbers as a schoolboy collects train numbers, without wit or selectivity.

Even if you were conversant with the grammar and syntax of the language Parker was using, it was improbable that you would be able to grasp the full import of what he was pioneering. It is a sad reflection of jazz development since Parker that what we call modernism is already twenty years old, that what Charlie Parker played in the early 1940s still has about it a contemporary ring carrying a damning implied criticism of those who have followed him. Any of a hundred Parker recordings prove the point, for all of them contain the raw material for a thousand solos recorded by others in later years. The phrases still sound fresh today, yet they were routine to Parker years ago, thrown off by him in the course of his life as a working musician as casually as another musician might race through a few warming-up exercises.

The extent to which he was passed over by professed experts is truly extraordinary. What of the earless ones who said he was playing wrong notes? What of those brilliant analysts who announced the whole thing was a practical joke? What of those who denied his music the descriptive adjective 'jazz'? There was one priceless philistine who took his tape recorder to the Minton's sessions and switched off whenever Parker started to play, because his jazz was not as decorous as that of Herbie Fields, a musician whom the owner of the machine worshipped to such an insane degree that he compiled tape after tape.

Early in 1950, Parker fulfilled a ballroom date which was taped and later issued as an authentic album: *The Bird at St Nick's*. For reasons of economy the tracks were trimmed up into excerpts that spotlight Parker at the expense of everyone else, but despite this, the *St Nick's* album has about it an element of truth which many studio recordings do not.

It was one of the first examples we ever had of the Modern jazz musician out in the world selling his music to the customers of a dance hall. It is instantly clear what Parker was up against. The broken rhythms and cascades of notes which might seem, to the uneducated ear, to wreak havoc with the tempo, the splendour of the saxophonist's whole conception, none of these things are ever likely to commend themselves to patrons raised on and looking for the conventional dance hall pap. In fact, there is a schism here that no amount of striving on the artist's part can ever hope to resolve. This is the fundamental difference between Parker's music and the jazz of all the preceding generations. With Parker jazz had evolved to the stage where it was too complex to be accepted merely as a background for that Saturday night social round of the dancer. It was now ceasing to be a functional music in so far as the only way to arrive at any depth of understanding was not to dance to it, or eat with it in the distant background, or discuss abstruse philosophy to the promptings of its rhythms, but to listen to it, intently, respectfully, with all the sensitivity one can muster, because it was a maturing art form demanding full attention or none at all.

In the *St Nick's* album are all the elements in the life of a jazz musician which create the exquisite irony of his situation. The dancers shuffle round on their treadmill, the extraneous noises of the patrons drift in over the music, the acoustics are distorted by the accidental echo chamber effect of most indoor arenas. And Parker tries to cut across these factors, playing the most amazing music, jazz fresh-minted, somehow implying a relationship with the early jazz that the Pannassies of this world doggedly refused to see, and yet carrying with it the implications of the era in which it flowered, as unmistakably as the Bix records re-echo the Roaring Twenties and Goodman's soporifics with the big band are characteristic of the college tastes of the New Deal.

What does a musician do in this unfortunate situation? Does he fret at the thought of his art being misused? Does he attempt to make converts? At first he might possibly attempt to do both these things, but as he slowly becomes worldlywise, he does the only thing left to him. He ignores all the extraneous factors as completely as possible. He shuts his mind off from the imbecilities of his audiences. He throws his music at the heads of whoever happens to be within earshot. As far as he is concerned, the audience happens to be there by accident. It is he, and not they, who is the focal point of the event. The fact that their admission fee is paying his wage for the night would only have some bearing on the artist-and-audience relationship if with their admission fee they contributed a guarantee of sensitivity, of willingness to understand, of awareness. But most audiences do not, especially in dance halls, and it is perfectly clear that in *The Bird at St Nick's* album Parker and the rest of them are just going through the motions of earning a living. Somebody has booked them for a gig. They have accepted it gracefully. The creation of a work of art is so alien to their thoughts and attitudes that the suggestion of it would only inspire them to ribaldry. But they have created art, for all their avowed indifference to such a grandiose conception. Parker at St Nick's is earning a living for a single night of his life, but in doing so he is also minting a few gems which may fly over the heads of the shuffling dancers but remain on the record for connoisseurs to prize out of the content if they feel so inclined.

This forsaking of his audience by the Modern musician is the most vital and tragic fact in all the evolution of jazz. It was inevitable, because the moment musicians began to explore the possibilities of the world of harmony, instead of accepting without question the narrow conventions of the early days, sounds were imminent which required for their appreciation a comparatively trained ear, the very thing that audiences have never been able to give the jazz musician. There is no solution. Parker was right to dream of subtleties like 'Confirmation' instead of attempting to cut his way through the jungle of ignorance and prejudice to a popular acclaim. When an artist is able to conjure up work of the sublime beauty of the best Parker, it is the duty, not of the artist to reach down to the outside world, but of the outside world to aspire to the heights of the artist, wherein is contained all the elements of Charlie Parker's tragedy.

For it was indeed a tragedy in the classic sense. The end was ordained before the beginning. He was haunted by the incubus of a consummate musical gift all his life. He was no dance band musician, no happy member of the ensemble. He was a lone musical spirit to whom compromise was an alien and uncomprehended thing. The playing speaks without compromise. There is no fooling when Parker plays. He puts into it everything he knows and feels. The best he can hope for is that somehow the emotional force of the performance will convey itself to ears unversed in the laws of harmonic exploration.

Parker's jazz is built on irrevocable harmonic logic, none the less irrevocable because it happens to be beyond the scope of many people who profess to understand it. The younger Modern experimenters, in courting some nebulous lunacy called Free Form, which is really no form at all, are applying the direct negation of Parker's methods. They are abandoning the very harmonic discipline which gave strength and grace to Parker's eloquence. One thing it is safe to say. Parker himself would not be surprised. His career was the final link in the chain of jazz evolution which rendered it an art form. Once any activity becomes an art form, however reluctantly it may have achieved the status, good and bad will disappear. In their place will be substituted critical theories. In the meantime, all the innovations in the world cannot alter the truth that the greatest jazz is that which has melodic grace, harmonic courage and the sense of form which can miraculously render abstract musical improvisation into genuine artistic expression. Jazz today awaits the coming of another Charlie Parker. When he arrives, it will no doubt cast at his head the same brickbats it heaved at Bix Beiderbecke, Lester Young and Charlie Parker. Critical brickbats are apparently just as durable as great jazz records.

THE ELLA FITZGERALD *SONGBOOKS*

Between 1955 and 1965, Ella Fitzgerald recorded a series of Songbook *albums for Verve Records, bookended by* The Cole Porter Songbook, *and* The Johnny Mercer Songbook. *The work of ten songwriters was covered with a careful selection of 240 songs, a priceless body of work that collectively forms the definitive account of the American popular song. Benny wrote his first Ella liner note for the* Harold Arlen Songbook *in 1961, and also provided notes for the* Jerome Kern *(1963) and* Johnny Mercer *(1965) albums. The following essay is from the 1997 reissue of the entire* Songbooks *in a ten-CD boxset.*

The American popular song is, with the possible exception of its sister-art, jazz music, the most extraordinary cultural phenomenon of our deplorable century. It has been created by the schooled and the unschooled, by millionaires and by beggars, by the immigrant and by the native American. There exists for it no formal training. The great songwriters started out as everything from qualified attorneys to piano salesmen, from newspaper columnists to failed actors, from politicians to academics, from generals to U-boat sailors. No wonder it has defied the attempts of musicologists and social historians to explain it. The only valid generalization about it is that you must never make generalizations about it. Persistently ignored by the culture vultures of the Fine Arts, it is now set fair to become timeless. 'All The Things You Are' and 'The Man I Love' are no more antiquated than *The Pickwick Papers* or *The Cherry Orchard.*

It was nurtured by a multiplicity of causes, historical, social and technological. (If the popular song has a patron saint, it would have to be Thomas Edison, for without his invention of the phonograph . . .) An over-simplification would be that it came about through the collision between the emancipated migrants streaming north after the Civil War, and the immigrant tide drummed up by that prodigious imbecile, Alexander III, Tsar of All the Russias and master of none. Yet even that broad claim is not quite accurate. Vernon Duke and the Gershwins were both Russian refugees. But the Gershwins fled from the Romanovs, Duke from the commissars. The ultimate irony is that Duke and Ira Gershwin eventually collaborated to produce an American classic in 'I Can't Get Started'. It is revealing that of the ten writers honoured by inclusion in the *Songbooks*, only three, Cole Porter, Johnny Mercer and Duke Ellington, could be defined as American, ancestrally speaking.

The oldest of the ten is Jerome Kern (1885–1945), the youngest Johnny Mercer (1909–76). Yet the span of the popular song has been so brief that the oldest collaborated with the youngest (see the *Kern Songbook* below). As to the precise moment of birth of the American standard song, it would be foolish to select this or that incident. But there are a few possible starting lines. Some jazz musicians (and they are the ultimate arbiters) might be inclined to think that the process began with Raymond Hubbell's 'Poor Butterfly' (1916). But Arthur Schwartz, himself a prodigious contributor to the maturing process, has nominated Kern's 'They Didn't Believe Me' (1914) as the first modern popular song. But jazz musicians may well look back to Sheldon Brooks's dazzlingly original contrivance of 1910, 'Some Of These Days'. And there may even be a case for 'Shine On, Harvest Moon', part-written by the ogress Nora Bayes in 1907. But whichever song and whichever year, it is clear that as the new century got under way, so did the popular song in America. In this collection, the oldest item, by a wide margin, is Irving Berlin's 'Alexander's Ragtime Band' (1911), which would seem to suggest that the golden age of the American standard song lasted about fifty years, and that its span has been roughly from the second to the seventh decade of the century.

The institutions which propagated the gospel of popular song were, in ascending order of importance, Tin Pan Alley, Hollywood, and Broadway. Of the 240 items in the *Songbook* series, fifty-six were commissioned by the moguls of Beverley Hills, and exactly twice that number by the impresarios of

Broadway. And just as there were three main sources of income for songwriters, so were there three dominant influences which shaped the product. The first was the Austro-Hungarian Empire, whose operettas poured across the Atlantic and were rendered passé only by the advent of the Great War. Well do we remember the reaction of the English partner of Kern, P. G. Wodehouse, invited for the umpteenth time to Americanize the latest Austrian import. The producer, eager to persuade Wodehouse, said, 'It was a big hit in Vienna,' to which Wodehouse, jaded with the Wiener schnitzel school of composition, replied, 'What wouldn't be?' But the Viennese effect, for all its flummery, was a prime source of Broadway material, and the influence of its composers on the American school may be discerned all too clearly in the operettas of Victor Herbert and, to a lesser extent in the chromatic exfloriations of Jerome Kern.

The second influence came from London, from the comic operas of Gilbert and Sullivan. Sullivan's style has disappeared without trace from the world of popular song, but Gilbert is altogether another matter. Porter, Ira Gershwin, Lorenz Hart and Wodehouse are among those who have testified to the inspiration of Gilbert's deft verbal gymnastics. As late as 1941, Porter was plagiarising Gilbert in a song called 'Let's Not Talk About Love', and even his famous rhyming of 'a glimpse of stocking' with 'shocking' was anticipated in the Savoy operas. And it was Wodehouse, the disciple of Gilbert, who taught the lyricists of the great age of American song how to shed the blowzy euphemisms of the Habsburgs and write colloquially, conversationally. As Alan Lerner writes in *The Street Where I Live*, the early Kern–Wodehouse shows 'inaugurated the American musical'.

The third influence on the evolution of popular song was American to the core. In vaudeville, where there were no plots and no characterizations, the songs had to be either deeply sentimental or rhythmically robust to survive. The giant leap on to the musical stage was made by George M. Cohan, who, around the turn of the century, was the most successful writer of musical comedy in America. Yet in even Cohan's best work, in *Give My Regards to Broadway* and his belated flirtations with ragtime, there is something which smacks of John L. Sullivan, horsedrawn traffic and the formidable ramparts of Lillian Russell's corsage.

It soon becomes obvious that after Cohan, some kind of revolution in musical style had taken place, a revolution which speedily rendered the harmonic vocabulary of the popular song more sophisticated, the melodic line more imaginative and the rhythmic interpretation more relaxed, less arthritic. A new generation of songwriters now began to fashion an American art form, limitless in its possibilities, with a potential audience of tens of millions, eager to digest the songs in dance halls and at concerts, on the newfangled phonograph and radio, even on the parlour piano.

The underlying intent of the *Songbooks* begins to emerge. What might happen to a song once it had been published? More or less anything. It might become the big hit of a long running success, like dozens of items in this collection. But what of the outstanding song which went unnoticed at the time? Or a song dropped from the show during the out-of-town tryout, either because the producer's brother-in-law didn't care for it, or the artist assigned it was incapable of doing it justice, or simply because the show was running too long and something had to go. And what of the great song stuck in a turkey? Suppose the production closed down in a few weeks? Could even the greatest item in the world surmount such an obstacle? A song is like a book. Once it is published, it has a life of its own which nobody can control. A song can lie dormant for half a lifetime and then suddenly come into its own through circumstances entirely unconnected with the degree of its excellence. All these possibilities and many others have conspired from time to time to render a song's future problematic.

In the Gershwin set may be found one of the greatest of all American ballads, 'The Man I Love', which three times was included in a Broadway score, three times was rejected, and finally established its immortality beyond the theatre walls, in the hotels and dance halls. Another contender for the title of Best American Ballad, 'All The Things You Are', was written for Kern's last Broadway show, a fiasco of 1939 called *Very Warm for May*, a show which was very cold by July. Yet despite the disaster, and despite Kern's fear that the song was 'too difficult for them', the song stands today as a masterpiece of the genre, not even the enharmonic change at the end of the release confusing listeners who have never heard about enharmonic changes but know beauty when they hear it. There have been several cases of songs getting off to a false start because the lyric was wrong for the tune, which explains why there have been two published versions of 'Easter Parade', two of 'Sometimes I'm Happy', two of 'Something To Remember You By'. All these cases fade into insignificance when measured against the bizarre case history of 'Blue Moon'. Sometimes great songs have failed to surface until after the composer's death. Others have languished in cupboards for as long as half a century, awaiting the healing touch of some sensitive researcher. We will never know how many hundreds, perhaps thousands, of modern songs were fated to be stillborn. The most that anyone can do about it is, first, to conduct rigorous sorties into the dusty corners of the songwriters' estates, and, second, to record any gems they might unearth under near-faultless conditions, so that as much of the heritage as we know about is saved for posterity.

But what are near-faultless conditions? First, a singer whose range is so wide and whose style is so protean that it can handle all sorts of songs written originally for all sorts of characters in all sorts of situations. Second, somebody possessing the resources to undertake a mammoth operation, and the overview which understands the importance of these shimmering musical miniatures flung up by the great writers of the golden age. And at this stage posterity and the popular song can count themselves prodigiously lucky that the producer and the singer turned up at the same time. Ella Fitzgerald had begun singing with the Chick Webb band in the mid-1930s, when she was little more than a child. She had enjoyed hit records and passing fame. She could sing anything, had an ear for harmony better than a great many jazz musicians, and combined a sweet purity of tone with diction to please even the most neurotic lyricist.

In 1945, she began a working relationship with Norman Granz which has endured ever since. The contract took the form of a handshake. At the time he first recruited Ella for his barnstorming show *Jazz at the Philharmonic*, Granz would dearly have liked to include her in the series of albums he released on his own label, and which consisted of music recorded live at his concerts. But Ella was bound by a virtually self-perpetuating contract with another company, signed in her teens, and all attempts to break the deadlock failed. At last, in 1955 Grant finally acquired control of Ella's recording career, which instantly became transformed in the most dramatic way. For twenty years she had dutifully recorded what she was told to record, and though some of her releases over the period were successful, there was no discernable direction to her career, no logic in the selection of songs, no strategy behind the day-to-day policy. With Granz everything changed.

A concept as remarkable as the *Songbooks* required for its planning and execution a remarkable man. Granz is a connoisseur of not just music but of all the fine arts, and he saw, as nobody else in the industry saw, that the ravishing arabesques of popular song held much more than their commercial potential. They were authentic works of art, miniatures which had never been treated as they deserved, never shown to be incidents in the development of their writers. It has to be remembered that in 1955, when the grand strategy was first set in motion, most of the men whose work was to be featured in the series were still alive. George Gershwin had died in 1937, Hart in 1943, Kern two years later. The other seven were still active, and Granz was on personal terms with more than one of them. This was to prove a huge asset, as became apparent as the series began to unfold. For Ella, who all her life had been trying to make a song sound, not like itself but like herself, the discipline of the *Songbooks*, where the writer, not the singer, is the star must have seemed very odd.

There had been a few vestigial signs in the past that one day the *Songbooks* would become an accepted form. In 1939, Lee Wiley had recorded eight Gershwin songs on 78s which made a sort of fragmented songbook. And in 1952, Ella herself had made an album with piano accompaniment containing ten Gershwin songs. But the new campaign was to be fought on a far wider front, not ten songs but 240, not piano accompaniment but full orchestral trappings. Some of these beautiful old songs Ella had literally never heard of, particularly with regard to the verses, which have usually been neglected by singers eager to state a famous chorus. But on Broadway the verse was an integral part of the songwriter's art, a causeway across which the performers might blithely flit in making the awkward transition from speech to song. This time the job was to be done properly, once and for all time. Ella picked up the material and sang it magnificently.

The rest is a priceless fragment of history which the reader now holds in his hand.

The Cole Porter Songbook

This opening salvo was heard in February 1956, thirty-two songs ranging from 1928 ('Let's Do It') to 1955 ('All Of Me'). The effect was devastating. Nobody had ever sat down before to listen to thirty-two successive songs by one composer, sung by one artist. There were several effects on the listener, educational as well as pleasurable. To hear the romantic fervour of 'Night And Day' followed by the worldly cynicism of 'Ace In The Hole', or the depths of emotion of 'I Concentrate On You' preceding the sagebrush slapstick of 'Don't Fence Me In', is to begin to understand the resource of the great writers. Able to conjure up expressive pieces for any character in any story, Porter applied his style with a sort of indolent vigour, so that for all the switches of setting, character, mood and tempo, he was remaining true to his own muse.

Among the outstanding features of the Porter collection are the dazzling displays of the catalogue song, or the laundry list as it is sometimes defined by lyricists. 'You're The Top', 'Anything Goes' and 'Let's Do It', are three of the most erudite and inspired list songs of the musical theatre. All three bear Porter's sardonic stamp, yet each is quite different from the other two. There were also four selections from Porter's ultimate masterwork, *Kiss Me Kate (*1948), and four classic Hollywood songs, including one, 'Easy To Love', which somehow contrived to impress itself on the world in spite of the alarming fact that it was introduced by one of the great non-singers of movie history, James Stewart, in a comedy of 1936 called *Born to Dance.*

The world and his wife, who of course knew all about 'Night And Day' and 'In The Still Of The Night', were less well acquainted with items like 'I Am In Love', 'Ace In The Hole', and the seductive gravity of that magnificent shadowed hymn, 'All Through The Night'. There was that most contentious song of the 1930s, 'Love For Sale', whose stagey candour was too much for the delicate sensibilities of the radio industry, in Britain as well as America. The banning of the song only added to its notoriety, although today its daring has dissolved into something comically innocuous. Among other noteworthy items was the oddity 'Miss Otis Regrets', which began its life as a party piece for Porter's intimate friend Monty Woolley. This story, like all the stories propagated by Porter regarding the genesis of his songs, must be taken with a large pinch of salt. Porter, despairing of ever educating the masses into the subtleties of his art, whipped up widespread publicity for the songs by attaching to them anecdotes, usually involving exotic foreign parts. But the passing of time has proved that his work can stand on its own sublime merits. More than any other production anywhere, before or since, Ella's thirty-two sides revealed Porter as an artist of true stature. Whether Porter would have agreed remains unknown. When Granz went to call on him, armed with the acetates of the albums, Porter's only comment was 'My, what diction!', which puts me in mind of the merchant who praised Boudin's *Jetty at Trouville* for the sturdiness of its frame.

The Rodgers and Hart Songbook

The appearance of the second instalment in the series only six months after the first confirmed the fond hope that the Porter albums, so far from being a shot in the dark, were the opening salvo of a breathtaking campaign. This time there were thirty-four songs covering the period between 1922 ('Manhattan') and 1943 ('To Keep My Love Alive'). If there lingers about these songs, even the sad ballads, a faint bouquet of innocent optimism, it is because Rodgers and Hart when their partnership was first formed, were little more than overgrown schoolboys. Hart in 1919 was twenty-four years old but still immersed in the world of the campus and amateur charity nights. Rodgers was sixteen years old when he first had the pleasure of setting Hart's verses to music, and although their collaboration endured to the frontiers of middle age, neither of them ever lost the exuberance of youth so far as their music was concerned.

As with Porter, catalogue songs play a prominent part in the work of the partnership. 'Manhattan', written for a stillborn show of 1922, *Winkle Town*, did not appear in public until 1925 and *The Garrick Gaieties*, a Sunday night fundraiser which went on to play over 200 performances. A year later, having sung the glories of the city, Hart showed the obverse side of the medal with that famous hymn to the rustic life, 'Mountain Greenery'. Hart revelled in compiling rhymed lists; later came 'I've Got Five Dollars' (1931), 'I Wish I Were In Love Again' (1937), 'Give It Back To The Indians' (1939), and 'Everything I've Got' (1942). But by far the subtlest of the list songs is 'The Lady Is A Tramp', which inverts the meaning of its own title. 'The Lady Is A Tramp' came from that brilliant score of 1937, *Babes in Arms*. No fewer than five items from that show are included in this collection, including the gossamer delicacy of Hart's wonderful description of the sense of deja vu, 'Where Or When'.

There is something else about the Rodgers and Hart selections which is of prime importance. Every musician likes to dream that one day he will find a great song previously unknown to him. As he grows older and wiser, the inexorable law of diminishing returns tells him that the chances of this ever happening are very remote. But in 1956 the world was still young in this regard, and I shall never forget my sense of stumbling on to riches previously unsuspected when, on the first side of the *Songbook*, I heard 'A Ship Without A Sail'. This is a remarkable ballad in more ways than one, not least for the resolution of a discord at the end of the middle section as it arrives back at the main theme. The structure is revolutionary, a twelve-bar theme, a middle of eight bars, then another twelve. Why had it remained totally unknown to me? The show for which it was written, *Me for You* (1929), closed in Detroit. Within weeks it had been transferred to a new show called *Heads Up*, which survived a few months. Ella's delivery is nothing short of perfect, and I could not help feeling at the time that this was why the *Songbooks* were not only intensely pleasurable, but also indispensable to anyone with an interest in the popular song.

Rodgers and Hart were essentially writers for Broadway and Hollywood, men who worked only from a script with characters. The only exception in their career and ironically a huge hit, was 'Blue Moon', and thereby hangs a tale. In 1934 the partners were commissioned to write songs for a movie called *Hollywood Party*. Most of what they wrote was rejected, including an item called 'Prayer', in which Jean Harlow was to sing a request to the Creator of the Universe for a break in show business. Later that year the song was slipped into *Manhattan Melodrama*, rewritten as 'The Bad In Every Man', and sung by Shirley Ross disguised by a facial consisting of black shoe polish. The same melody was used as the film's theme song, under yet another title 'It's That Kind Of A Play'. Finally, at the suggestion of a friendly publisher, Hart tried again, and at his fourth attempt, achieved a lyric acceptable to the masses.

But the most significant point of all about the *Rodgers and Hart Songbook*, was that its contents were compiled to the exclusion of Rodger's latest career with Oscar Hammerstein, a preference shared by every working musician. The enigma of the two composers, the vivacious swinger of the Hart days, and the sedate purveyor of passion for the bourgeoisie of the Hammerstein years, is usually taken as proof that the brio and sophisticated tenderness of the earlier years were rooted in Hart's wry metropolitan wit, and that these qualities were squashed by the rhythmic hand of Hammerstein. This may well be so, but there is another possible interpretation. With Hart it was the music which came first, with Hammerstein it was the lyrics. So it just might be that it was not Hart who inspired Rodgers' lightness of touch but Hammerstein who flattened it.

The Irving Berlin Songbook

Nothing could be more indicative of the growing prestige of the *Songbooks* than the circumstances in which the third instalment came into being. Irving Berlin, at this time a mere sprite of seventy, became increasingly irked by the way his grandchildren went about the house singing extracts from Rodgers and Hart. Berlin's standing as a grandfather was clearly under threat and so, in an attempt to show the kids that he too had been in the same racket, he asked Granz if Ella would record some of his songs. There was even talk of a preferential royalty arrangement, which was hardly necessary; it would never have occurred to Granz not to include Berlin in the series. While Jerome Kern's claim that Berlin was American music was just a little exaggerated, Berlin's part in the germination of popular song was a vital one.

Berlin had been writing songs far longer than anyone else in the pantheon. His range seemed to be limitless. He wrote songs for all occasions, sometimes producing items hardly worthy of him. But his best work was sublime. Even had he written nothing but waltzes, his place in history would be secure. Between 1924 and 1925 he wrote at least five songs in three-quarter time which have remained popular ever since. Two of them are included in the *Songbook*, 'Remember' and the composer's wedding gift to his second wife, 'Always'. The publication of 'Alexander's Ragtime Band' created a furore unequalled by any song this century. Overnight it made Berlin into a world figure. Its durability has been so extraordinary that at last Congress changed the law of copyright so that Berlin could continue to draw his royalties. No wonder the profession went in awe of him. When some interviewer asked him what type of songs he enjoyed writing most, he replied 'Hits'.

Berlin was a refugee from Tsarist Russia. He arrived with his impoverished family in New York when he was four years old and for the rest of his life never tired of asserting his patriotism to his new home. He even wrote a popular song which was overtly political; the waltz 'Russian Lullaby', sung by Ella with great tenderness and contains the passage:

Rockabye my baby,
Somewhere there may be
a land that's free for you and me . . .

And if anyone happened to miss the anti-Tsarist intent, Berlin was always ready to point it out.

His greatest songs have enjoyed such acclaim that we take their originality for granted. Yet his *Songbook* is awash with heresy. 'Let's Face The Music And Dance' breaks down into four sections comprising twelve, fourteen, eight and eighteen bars, an unheard-of contrivance. 'Cheek To Cheek' has two middle sections. The middle of 'Top Hat, White Tie And Tails' consists of two five-bar sections instead of the obligatory four. Yet the point about this persistent unorthodoxy is not that it sounds unorthodox, but creates an impression of a model of formal rectitude. People who know that Berlin never received an education and ask how he could have achieved such miracles miss the point. It was because of his indifference to the rules that he could break them with such divine impunity.

The poverty of his early years left Berlin with an attitude to the rich which never left him even when he became one of them. In his long career he wrote several pieces which reflect this derisive attitude to the monied classes. Two of them may be found in this collection, 'Puttin' On The Ritz' (1931) and 'Slumming On Park Avenue' (1937). This sense of having tramped the streets is never very far away from Berlin's muse, just as the comfort of a fabulous inheritance coloured everything Cole Porter ever wrote.

His feistiness remained with him through his life and is best exemplified by one of the most outrageous episodes in Broadway history. In 1926, Rodgers and Hart found themselves writing two shows at once, *Peggy-Ann* for Lew Fields, *Betsy* for Flo Ziegfeld. An irony of circumstance dictated that the two openings should happen on successive nights. Rodgers and Hart naturally attended the opening of *Peggy-Ann*, which meant they were absent from the final dress rehearsal of *Betsy*. The star of that show, the busty vaudevillian, Belle Baker, decided that night that Rodgers and Hart had put all the good stuff into *Peggy-Ann* and left her nothing worth singing. So she paid a midnight call on Berlin, an old friend and one-time collaborator of her husband's. She explained her problem and asked him if he had anything in the bottom drawer. Berlin told her of half a song which he might be able to finish. So Belle sat there in the small hours while Berlin searched with his uneducated fingers for the missing bridge. When finally he found it, the enraptured Belle snatched the song and left in search of Ziegfeld, whom she awoke at seven in the morning. This was a bad time for the impresario, who was just going to bed. When Belle told him what she wanted, he became fully awake. Belle demanded that Berlin's song be inserted in the opening that night. Ziegfeld was thunderstruck. 'You can't do that. It's unethical. It's outrageous. What key do you want it in?' So that night Belle sang a Berlin song in the second act of a Rodgers and Hart opening. Naturally it stopped the show. She did twenty-four encores, and when at last she forgot the words, there was Berlin standing up in the stalls prompting her. In his autobiography Rodgers writes that it took him twelve years to forgive Belle. He says nothing about how long it took him to forgive Berlin. The song was 'Blue Skies'.

When Granz went by appointment to Berlin's home with the first pressing, it was to find the old man sitting up in bed flanked by a pair of business managers. And each time one of the less famous songs came up, newly enriched by the platonic perfection of Ella's interpretation, Berlin would turn to his two punchbags and snarl, 'I told you that one should have been a hit. What were you doing?' But all in all he was a happy man. Now he had something to come back at his grandchildren with.

The Duke Ellington Songbook

The next recordings in the series came as a great surprise to everybody. Though he was one of America's greatest songwriters, Duke Ellington was, and still is, generally regarded as a pianist who led the world's finest big band. This was indeed true, but there were frequent sublime moments when his peerless instrumental features for the assorted virtuosi who made up the orchestra sounded as if somewhere there was a set of words which belonged to them. Several of the thirty-eight tracks in the Ellington collection fall into this category. 'Don't Get Around Much Any More' started out in life as an instrumental called 'Never No Lament'. 'Just Squeeze Me' evolved out of 'Subtle Slough', 'Lost In Meditation' out of 'Have A Heart', 'I Didn't Know About You' out of 'Sentimental Lady', 'Do Nothing Till You Hear From Me' out of 'Concerto For Cootie'. A second category was that group of songs which retained their original title even though they later acquired words, for example 'Sophisticated Lady' and 'Satin Doll'. In addition, Duke sometimes started from scratch with the idea of writing a popular song, or even a musical. His 1941 score for *Jump for Joy* included one of the loveliest ballads he ever wrote, 'I Got It Bad And That Ain't Good', with a lyric by Paul Francis Webster. Other pieces which were songs from the start were 'Drop Me Off In Harlem', 'I Ain't Got Nothing But The Blues' and 'I Let A Song Go Out Of My Heart' among others.

It used to be assumed that Ellington's work as a writer of popular songs ran parallel with his career as a bandleader. In fact the two careers were part of the same equation. Duke's band was an expensive one to run. It was his luxury, his way of having instant access to the aural effect of what he had just written. The band was, in fact, not cost-effective, and it was the huge royalties from the songs which helped to bridge the gap between solvency and collapse. Certainly by including Ellington in his series, Granz was ensuring that aesthetic justice was being done. There were periods when the relationship between the two men became amended to promoter and artist, and one only had to watch Granz standing in the wings of some theatre watching the Ellington band go through its paces to know that nobody could have loved that band more than Granz did.

The original plan had been for Ellington and his other half, Billy Strayhorn, to produce a set of orchestrations to suit the occasion. The result would have been pure sorcery as only Ellington could produce. But it seems that with a feckless mood upon him, Duke arrived at the studio with much less manuscript than had been hoped for. Some of the tracks were indeed fully orchestrated. Others were old orchestrations which happened to fit Ella's range. Still others were loosely organized head arrangements. In addition – and this was to prove an enormous asset to the finished *Songbook* – there were sides featuring a small-group whose especial glories included Duke's one-time tenor saxophone star Ben Webster, and Hezekish Leroy Gordon 'Stuff' Smith, a dazzling rogue elephant of a violinist who combined in his playing a complete mastery of the jazz art and a whimsical sense of humour. At the time there was a general feeling that this *Songbook* was neither fish nor fowl, neither jazz nor song. In fact it was both, and more. As the years have passed, the virtues of the *Ellington Songbook* seem to have shone through in great triumph. Nobody ever wrote more rapturous ballads than 'Solitude' or 'Sophisticated Lady'. And what of those flawless pearls which are hardly ever heard, for instance 'I Didn't Know About You' and 'All Too Soon'. Once again the songbook formulae had saved from oblivion immeasurable musical wealth.

The George and Ira Gershwin Songbook

By 1959, in numerical terms the *Songbooks* had reached their halfway stage. Now came the moment when the project was to surpass itself. In the context of popular song in this century, nobody stands higher than George Gershwin. Doomed to the tragedy of premature death at the age of thirty-eight, Gershwin is still the most prolific of all the writers of unforgettable songs. It has been said that writing songs came easily to him. In the words of his most idolatrous fan, Oscar Levant, 'There was no gap between his dream and his doing, no uncertainty. The music was there and it came out, naturally, easily.' And it is certainly true that his songs embody a sweet paradox. They are unpredictable, as genius must be, yet they possess an easeful inevitability, the phrases following each other as surely as night follows day. George represents the perfect middle ground between the meticulous academicism of Kern and the purely intuitive gift of Berlin. He was akin to both and like neither. More than any other songwriter before or since, he was his own man, and there is every reason to suppose that songs like 'I Got Rhythm', 'Embraceable You', 'They Can't Take That Away From Me', 'Our Love Is Here To Stay', in fact all fifty-three items in this collection, will join the Gershwin concert works in the pantheon of enduring works of art.

The songs also commemorate a most remarkable family alliance, between George and his older brother Ira. For a few years when he first started, George worked with several other lyricists but by 1924 had made one of the sweetest discoveries of his life, which was that his ideal partner was his own beloved brother. Ira, the studious, bookish, modest connoisseur of literature, was the diametric opposite in terms of temperament of his extrovert, self-confident, irresistibly charming George. Together they would create a repertoire of civilized delights in their work for Broadway and Hollywood from the early 1920s until George's untimely death in 1937.

If George was long gone by the time the *Songbooks* appeared, his partner was very much alive and well and eager to collaborate in any way which might enhance the finished product. His longstanding friendship with Granz was a further asset, and through 1958 the pair of them collaborated with the orchestrator Nelson Riddle and beavered towards their final selection. By practising rigid self-denial, they managed to restrict themselves to fifty-three songs which were recorded in three stages in January, March and July 1959. The result was an unblemished masterpiece, inspired in design, flawless in execution. Ira rewrote a verse here, a line there, in an attempt to render the recordings as near perfect as possible. It was due to his diligence and elephantine memory that two items were included that nobody had heard before. 'Just Another Rhumba', with its playfully perverse rhyming of 'number' with 'Septumber', had been intended for Astaire, but ended up in *Goldwyn Follies*. It was rehearsed but never shot, and had been slumbering in the cupboard ever since. It was due to Ira again that 'The Real American Folk Song' was dug out of the file for 1918 and given a new lease of life. Ira had written the words to while away empty days working at his father's many speculative enterprises, a Turkish Baths to which nobody came. Later George set the verses to music. Ira tells in *Lyrics on Several Occasions* how the song made a brief appearance in a Nora Bayes revue called *Ladies First*, was dropped after a few weeks and earned him royalties totalling nil.

In contrast many of the other items have long since woven themselves into the tapestry of the century. The songs for Fred and Ginger which heralded the end of George's life, the prolific brilliance of the score for *Girl Crazy*, the charm of whimsical items like 'Strike Up The Band' and 'By Strauss', which were intended as friendly lampoons, 'Stiff Upper Lip', whose choice of words was a tribute from Ira to his old friend P. G. Wodehouse, 'Isn't It A Pity?', a priceless pearl from the flop of 1933, *Pardon My English*, and whose selection for the *Songbook* was the beginning of an active life as a standard. And most priceless of all, the songs from the only posthumous Hollywood musical ever made, *The Shocking Miss Pilgrim* (1946), especially 'For You, For Me, Forever More', one of the most hypnotic ballads in the popular catalogue, to hear just once the spectral beauty of Ella's rendering of the verse, is to be in love with the song for all time.

There remains perhaps the greatest popular song ever written. 'The Man I Love' was part of the score of the 1924 show, *Lady Be Good*, but was dropped. Three years later the brothers tried again with it in the first version of *Strike Up the Band*, which closed out of town. In 1928 they tried a third time by slipping it into *Rosalie*, but for reasons which have been forgotten, the song slipped out again. Eventually it became a world classic through hotel bands, nightclub chantoosies and dance hall hirelings. Outraged by the scurvy treatment dished out to this wonderful song, I asked Ira why George hadn't insisted on its inclusion in *Lady Be Good*. After all, George was a world figure by this time. How big did a composer have to be to insist? Ira's reply was part of my real education. He wrote, 'George always used to say it was easier to write a new song than to argue with the money.'

The Harold Arlen Songbook

Harold Arlen was a child of the same immigrant tide which swept up the Gershwins and the Berlins and dumped them on the eastern seaboard of the United States. Arlen was to become a close friend of the Gershwins and, at last, a partner of Ira's. But there was one stark contrast between Arlen's beginnings and George Gershwin's. No doubt ever crept into Gershwin's mind as to what he was. He knew before he was into his teens that he would compose music. Arlen had no such self-awareness and frittered away much time as an actor-singer. Any doubts that he was misled are dispelled by the evidence, an ancient recording of 'Little Girl' in which the dapper skills of the Joe Venuti–Eddie Lang small-group are desecrated by Arlen's vocal, which may best be described as eccentric. But it was his acting career, such as it was, which opened the gates through which he soon passed into the songwriting brotherhood.

In 1929 Arlen was given the acting-singing role in Vincent Youmans's ill-fated musical, *Great Day*, which had the misfortune to open a few days before Wall Street closed. One day the rehearsal pianist failed to show, and Arlen, known to be a useful pianist, was drafted in his place. The chores soon became tedious, especially the endless repetitions of the title song. To alleviate the boredom, Arlen began introducing small amendments to what Youmans had written. Soon these tiny alterations became so dominant that Arlen realized he had written his own song. A passing songwriter, by name Harry Warren, heard the new tune and advised Arlen to find a lyricist. Warren recommended Ted Koehler, and from these accidental beginnings emerged Arlen's first song, 'Get Happy'. The new partnership went on to one success after another, and became the resident writers at the Cotton Club. Ten of the twenty-six items which comprise the *Arlen Songbook* have words by Koehler. Some of these remain famous, 'Stormy Weather', 'I've Got The World On A String', 'I Gotta Right To Sing The Blues', 'Between The Devil And The Deep Blue Sea' and 'Ill Wind'.

Intermittently Arlen wrote for Hollywood with E. Y. 'Yip' Harburg; the alliance was culminated with 'Over The Rainbow'. But as the 1940s began, so did a brilliant phase in Arlen's career when he worked with Johnny Mercer. Mercer's name appears in credits of eight items in the *Songbook*, including two of the biggest successes of their day, 'That Old Black Magic' and 'Blues In The Night'. Among their other achievements was an extraordinary scenario put to music called 'One For My Baby', which Frank Sinatra was to establish as one of the most famous songs in the world. Four of the items have words by Harburg, and two by Leo Robin. Which of these partners Arlen preferred is unknown, but it is revealing that Mercer once told me that he believed that if he and Arlen had stayed together, they might have achieved something of the order of *My Fair Lady*.

Arlen has often been described by journalists, but not by musicians, as a 'jazz' composer, which is about as logical a premise as talk of a furniture tree. The mannerism in Arlen's style which led to this misapprehension was his fondness for the note of the Minor third and dominant seventh in his melodic line. An example would be the note which fits the monosyllable 'a' in 'I Got The World On A String', or the 'ger' in 'Got the string around my finger'. But Arlen also wrote successful songs where this trademark is conspicuous only by its absence, as in 'Over The Rainbow' and 'Let's Fall In Love'. His career effectively ended in 1954 when he and Ira Gershwin worked on Judy Garland's last screen triumph, *A Star is Born*. Their big song, 'The Man That Got Away', proved to be the last popular success for Ira as well as for Arlen. Proof of the song's quality is provided by the fact that it did not win an Academy Award, being ousted by the notorious 'Three Coins In The Fountain'.

The Arlen Songbook provides a clue as to how thoughtfully Granz had proceeded with the series. In deference to Arlen's high element of jazz-tinged phrasing, he recruited as orchestrator Billy May, who produced vintage work for the project. Ellington apart, the prime interest of the *Songbooks* is the songs. But the Arlen sides contain the bonus of brilliant instrumental interludes and the presence of gifted soloists like the saxophonists Benny Carter and Ted Nash. For me the peak arrives in the instrumental chorus of 'As Long As I Live', where the muted trumpet solo of Don Fagerquist is cushioned by some luscious orchestral paraphrases of Arlen's melody. Several of the songs come from shows or films long since assigned to the junkyard. The enduring quality of the music underlines one of the basic truths on which the series is founded: After all the dross has faded away, the residue of high quality always turns out to be the songs.

The Jerome Kern Songbook

The *Kern Songbook* followed in 1963, giving signals that the service was coming to a close by the limitation of the songs to twelve on a single album. Kern was the great scholar of popular song, a man whose erudition was so overpowering that there were moments when even he wondered if he had gone too far. 'All The Things You Are' is a case in point, but generally Kern, who was a wise old fox, knew that the public will digest any sort of technical refinement provided only that the melody is palatable. He summed up his own case with some wit when asked for advice from a British writer who had been told that his tunes were too complex for public consumption. 'Go on being uncommercial, young man', Kern replied, 'there's a lot of money in it.' And so there was. Kern wrote some of the best-selling as well as finely crafted songs of the century, and although his career stretched from 1904 to 1945, he never surrendered the knack of engaging public interest at the same time as he inspired the awe of his fellow-professionals.

His life can be divided up among the four lyricists who worked with him. From 1905 for about twenty years, with interruptions, with the English public schoolboy P. G. Wodehouse, whose mild-mannered temperament made the perfect foil to Kern's acerbic nature. It is sad that their best song 'Bill', is not included in the collection. For Kern, whose work occasionally betrayed lingering signs of the Habsburg influence of his youth, Otto Harbach and Oscar Hammerstein were ideal for the fashioning of beautiful melodramas like 'Yesterdays' and the towering grandeur of 'All The Things You Are'. But the best of Kern's regular partners was Dorothy Fields, who gave his scholarly products a contemporary snap. Miss Fields, daughter of the vaudeville-turned-producer Lew Fields, shocked her father when she told him of her intention to become a lyricist. 'You can't,' stormed the old boy, 'you're a lady.' 'No, I'm not,' replied Miss Fields, 'I'm your daughter,' and went on to become one of America's major versifiers. It is her collaborations with Kern, the rising crescendo of a 'Fine Romance' and the classic fervour of 'The Way You Look Tonight', which lend the recordings some of their finest moments. And for Kernesque complexity there is nothing to match the dizzying convolutions of 'Remind Me', written for of all things an Abbott and Costello movie.

There also attaches to this collection a mystery which remains unresolved. One of the songs written for the show *Roberta*, a witty romp called 'I'll Be Hard To Handle', has a lyric credited to somebody called Bernard Dougall. His name appears neither in reference books nor as part of the credits for any other song. After some years it was disclosed in a biography that he was a nephew of Otto Harbach's who 'wished to try his hand at lyric writing'. Instead of showing the young man the door, Kern gave him the tune of 'I'll Be Hard To Handle', and the boy made such a polished job of it that one cannot help wondering whatever became of him.

The writer of the twelfth lyric in the collection was Johnny Mercer, who worked with Kern on the Astaire–Hayworth picture of 1942, *You Were Never Lovelier*. Mercer was twenty-four years Kern's junior, yet the two men became the most relaxed and affable of partners. Mercer once told me, 'I think the old boy liked me because I could make him laugh.' It is likely that Kern also liked him for his work. Their one picture together produced two standards, 'Dearly Beloved' and 'I'm Old-Fashioned'. Which brings us to the last chapter in the story of the series, the one entitled . . .

The Johnny Mercer Songbook

This final episode was the biggest surprise of all, because Mercer was not a composer at all, but a lyricist. Indeed, he appears in two of the earlier *Songbooks*, in Kern's fleetingly, in Arlen's substantially. It had to be said that no compilation of American song would be complete without the inclusion of Mercer, who had the versatility to work with whoever could offer him a halfway decent melody. The breadth of his experience is shown by the remarkable fact that the thirteen songs represent twelve different composers; the one man to appear twice is Mercer himself who on occasion could turn out a good tune. Once when I complimented him on 'Dream' he thanked me and said, 'It's really "Whispering" sort of sideways.'

He worked at such dazzling speed that some of the details sound too far-fetched to be true – except that everyone corroborates his stories. 'Autumn Leaves' was the work of about twenty minutes; even faster was 'I Remember You', one of the greatest of all declarations of love. Mercer said it took him ten minutes, and that the last section, from 'When my life is through' to the end, was his favourite among his own works. On the rare occasions when a tune did give him problems, he would consign it to his subconscious. He was a firm believer that the mind will work for you even when you are engaged on something else. He told me that when Hoagy Carmichael gave him the tune of 'Skylark', he left it for several months, until, in his memorable phrase, 'I woke up one morning to find the lyric sitting there on the end of the bed.' His best work has genuine poetic overtones, for instance the opening lines of 'Early Autumn' and the wonderful series of impressionistic flashes which make up the words to 'Laura'. I discussed these and other songs with him endlessly. He was a mine of information because unlike most writers, he had never stayed too long with one partner, but had worked with almost everybody. When I asked him how important in the scheme of things the American popular song was, this was his reply. I have never forgotten it; 'One day, maybe in a hundred years, all this work, Porter's, the Gershwins', Kern's, Berlin's, maybe mine, will be collected, studied, annotated, published. And then forgotten. Like everything.'

What in the end did the *Songbooks* achieve? They rescued 240 songs from the terrible prospect of oblivion. They have become a measuring rod by which all subsequent attempts at the century's heritage will be assessed. The songs can now be seen, as they certainly were not when they were written, to represent a precious, priceless segment of social history. One snatch of 'I Concentrate On You', or 'Where Or When', or 'Let's Face The Music And Dance', or 'Laura', and we know the essence of romanticism in the pre-war world. The songs provided my generation with the conversational small change of day-to-day romance, raising the ordinary to something unique and often beautiful. And they have bequeathed to posterity a legacy of boundless wit, dapper technical command, melodic grace, literary sprightliness, perhaps too a touch of poetry. This was popular music's finest hour, and it was over in fifty years. But, in the words of an old Crosby song, it was great while it lasted, and it was not at all a bad thing to have achieved.

FRANK SINATRA

In 1967, while lying in bed one afternoon looking for work, I wrote a novel and had much trouble thinking of a title. At length, after several weeks of desperation and a lot of sleepless nights, I decided on burglary. It is one of the mixed blessings of this life that there is no copyright on titles, which explains why in the popular catalogue there are two songs called 'I Never Knew', two more called 'Long Ago And Far Away', two more called 'Day By Day', and so on. This rule extends to novels, and for a while I considered calling mine *War and Peace* or *The Pickwick Papers.* I finally decided against it because that sort of thing might have invited comparisons I wasn't ready for. Then I remembered something. In the summer of 1962 I had sat one night in a West London studio and watched Frank Sinatra recording 'A Nightingale Sang In Berkeley Square', which is one of those songs rendered unforgettable by its striking title. (Others include 'Fido Is A Hot-Dog Now', 'They Needed A Songbird In Heaven So God Took Caruso Away' and 'Daddy, You've Been A Mother To Me'.) The man credited with its invention is a long-gone lyric writer called Eric Maschwitz, who got the inspiration for it on the day he found out that someone else had already thought of it. So he lifted it, as he was legally entitled to do. It had originally been the title of a short story published by the Armenian novelist Michael Arlen around 1924, a generation before the song came out, and was by no means the only example of a successful song calling itself after a book. 'I Cover The Waterfront' was the name of the autobiography of a San Diego newspaper reporter; 'The Days Of Wine And Roses' comes from a very gifted, very hungry Victorian poet called Ernest Dowson, and in my playing days I worked one time with a trumpeter who told me that 'Yes Sir, That's My Baby' was a verbatim quote from the table-talk of William Wordsworth in the wake of a particularly muddy paternity suit.

But had there ever been an instance of anyone reversing the situation and naming a book after a song? At first I hesitated, but once I had come across a John O'Hara short story called *Body and Soul* I was encouraged to try the same trick. Those very few readers conversant with my published works will know that in the end I called my novel *Blame It On My Youth*, which is the title of a popular song written by Oscar Levant and Ed Heyman. What is revealing is how I came to know of the existence of this fairly obscure item. In a phrase, I had heard Sinatra sing it. Before that, I had never heard of it. In twenty years of playing with hundreds of musical groups and also the Dundee Scottish Country Dancing Ensemble, nobody to my knowledge had ever so much as mentioned it in my presence. And apart from the Sinatra recording, nobody to my knowledge ever has since. (There is a footnote to this glum tale of literary felony; Ed Heyman spent most of his old age in of all places Brighton, and when I told him I had absconded with his title, he said that anyone crazy enough to want it could have it.) One day, years after my book had been published, I acted on a whim and looked up the original song and discovered that it had been written in 1934. Now Sinatra was born in 1915, which makes him practically a schoolboy when the song came out. The song could hardly have been a part of his professional background, because by the time he emerged the song had long since been forgotten. As for the actual date when he recorded the song, that was in 1956, which means that he was deliberately choosing to revive an item which was now utterly erased from public memory. There was only one very tenuous link between the singer and the song. 'Blame It On My Youth' was recorded by the Dorsey Brothers Orchestra in the year of publication, and it is just feasible that the Dorsey Brother who was the last bandleader ever to employ Sinatra may have introduced him to it.

But it seemed a long shot. Then I remembered something else. In 1950, I was keeping body and soul apart by playing on Saturday nights at a municipal ballroom in Tottenham, doing everything I could to keep friends and relatives from walking into the place and catching me at such a low ebb. The band's repertoire was a parody of itself. Some of the band parts were so old that graffiti obscured the notation, and I recall that the tenor saxophone part of 'Opus One' had been defaced by some previous incumbent who had inked in the letters 'Oct' before the first word and a 'B' before the second, and then scribbled underneath the message, 'Help. They are holding me prisoner here', and signed it 'Edmond Dantes'. And among all this musical refuse was one song which I actually enjoyed playing. Again, I had no previous experience of it and no idea where it came from. It was called 'Why Should I Cry Over You?', and the only clue to its origins were the letters MCMXXII in the bottom left-hand corner, which left me with the uneasy suspicion that the song dated back to Ancient Rome. Anyway, after twenty or thirty of these purgatorial Saturday nights, I managed to escape back into the ranks of the unemployed and soon forgot all about the municipal dance hall and its decrepit repertoire . . .

. . . until one night, sitting in a tiny club frequented by large musicians, somebody put a record on the player. It was this ancient Roman song. (By now, having passed through the purifying fires of night-school, I knew that MCMXXII was a code indicating the date 1922.) The recording was Sinatra's, and it instantly recalled to mind the wit of the melody, especially the uplifting little key change in the twelfth bar, when things shift from B Flat to D minor. But Sinatra was barely three years old when Ned Miller and Chester Conn wrote it, and could hardly have been impressed at so tender an age by the recordings which launched the song. (There were two, one by a mysterious conspiracy called The Virginians, who subsequently suffered an endearing excess of humility and obligingly wiped themselves off the face of the earth, the other by a girl called Aileen Stanley, who, apart from being famous for having an old lady who couldn't spell 'Eileen', worked in a few Broadway shows, did a bit of radio work and then drifted over to England, at which point her tracks grow ever fainter and finally disappear in the mists of mediocrity.) Presumably Sinatra must have remembered the song from somewhere and been beguiled enough to dredge it up out of oblivion. To this day I have never heard anyone else sing it or play it, any more than I have ever heard a live performance of 'Blame It On My Youth'.

Now these two insignificant case histories, when placed together, begin to assume much more importance than the casual listener might think. Taken singly, they are mildly interesting. Placed alongside each other, they hint at the very essence of Sinatra's achievement as a musician, for there is nothing more revealing in any artist's life than the repertoire with which he is associated, especially if, as in Sinatra's case, he has been in a position for most of his career to do what he wants and not what some crumb in Front Office wants. In a sense, the repertoire *is* the man, because it defines his likes and dislikes, his prejudices and his preferences. Make a list of any musician's fifty favourite themes and you begin to see quite clearly which way he has been leaning all his life. And as Sinatra is the most gifted of all interpreters of popular music, his repertoire is bound to shed light on his professional procedures. Being a musician, I had always been a more or less uncritical admirer of his singing before the 'Blame It On My Youth' and 'Why Should I Cry Over You?' episodes, but after those two songs had inched into my consciousness, I began to look at the whole business in a different way.

The first thing to take note of is that there are certain songs to which Sinatra has come back again and again. What, for instance, have the following works in common: 'I Concentrate On You', 'Dream', 'Fools Rush In', 'It All Depends On You', 'I've Got You Under My Skin', 'One For My Baby', 'Always'? The answer is that Sinatra has recorded each of them three times, often over a twenty or thirty year time span. Nor are these tactics anything unusual for him. 'Have Yourself A Merry Little Christmas', 'I'll Be Seeing You' and 'The Moon Was Yellow' he has recorded four times, 'I'll Never Smile Again' and 'Imagination' at least five times. There is no parallel for this anywhere in the popular repertoire, but the repetition itself is not the only interesting thing here. There are other common denominators. All these oft-recorded tunes are quality songs, what the trade calls Standards, that is, songs which have survived the incidence of their own birth and have passed into the common stockpot of musical experience. But there is a third truth about them which is the most revealing of all, and it is this: that at the time Sinatra recorded them, hardly a one was a 'commercial' proposition, by which is meant a new song of the moment being pushed by the rickety engines of the music-publishing business. Indeed, some of Sinatra's selections must have struck conventional thinkers inside the profession as downright perverse. You don't record an esoteric item like 'The Moon Was Yellow' four times unless there is something about it that appeals to you very strongly. Nor is it likely to be a mere passing fancy. Sinatra first recorded it in August 1945, did it again in December 1958, again in November 1961, again in November 1965. Suddenly there is more than facetiousness behind the joke he has often cracked about having sung a certain song before and his intention to go on singing it till he gets it right. In terms of social history, it is not difficult to nail the origins of his affection for this particular old-time item. Crosby recorded it in the year of publication, 1934, by which time Sinatra had become the embryonic apprentice crooner wisely taking due note of what the head of his profession was up to. But there is the vital difference that Crosby was recording one of that season's new songs, whereas by the time Sinatra arrived at his fourth version, it was already more than thirty years old, its writers dead and gone, its publishers long since removed to more appropriate surroundings.

As to what it is about these old songs which attracts Sinatra to them, it is instructive to turn to another of his favourites, 'All Of Me'. The identical historical pattern emerges. Written in 1931, recorded by Sinatra in November 1946, October 1947, August 1954, February 1967. Why? The answer is that the song deserves that kind of deferential treatment, and when someone takes such strenuous measures to preserve it, what we are watching is the spectacle of virtue rewarded, a fact which is central to any true understanding of popular music, as we shall see. But if 'All Of Me' demands this special treatment of constant revivification, why Sinatra? Why not any of the hundreds of other performers who have come and gone over the years? There are two answers to that. Some of the popular singers had, and still have, insufficient grey matter to perceive that 'All Of Me', being a thing of beauty, deserves to be a joy forever; and some of the others, understanding it well enough, have tiptoed tactfully away in the self-knowledge that it was too good for them to cope with. If I were to start analysing the nature of 'All Of Me', I would soon have us all up to the neck in the kind of technical arcana that has no place here, and perhaps not anywhere. But 'All Of Me' is constructed in such a way that provided you pick the right tempo and a cultured rhythm section, you are going to move beautifully, like a man astride a thoroughbred racehorse. But you have to be a certain type of musician to recognize the racehorse for what it is, and not to fling yourself on to a camel by mistake, thereby becoming the last straw that broke its poor back.

We begin to see what has been going on. Instead of featuring new songs as they appear, Sinatra has been ranging back into his own past in search of material, a truth so glaringly obvious that there has been a danger of nobody noticing. The supreme mastery of *Songs for Swingin' Lovers*, to take one example among many, distracted from the fact that, in Tin Pan Alley terms, the album was an item of historical research as well as a topical production destined to be timeless. Of the fifteen songs featured, not one came out of the decade in which the album was conceived and executed; only four items were as recent as the 1940s; more than half were products of the 1930s; two, 'Swingin' Down The Lane' and 'Making Whoopee', were from the 1920s. We are now in the realms of morality, for if Sinatra had not taken hold of, say, an ancient battleaxe like 'Swingin' Down The Lane', or a scandalously neglected pearl of his young manhood like 'I Thought About You', what would the odds be against either of those outstanding publications being popular today? Evidence of this espousal of lost musical causes is scattered all over the place in that fascinating document, Sinatra's discography.

And it is especially fascinating to me as a musician. Never having been too madly in love with the gargling that has always gone on in the name of popular singing, I am constantly being surprised by the items in that discography. I glance at random and I see 'Just Friends', 'If I Had You', 'Melancholy Baby', 'Poor Butterfly', 'I Can't Believe That You're In Love With Me', 'Night and Day', 'Please Don't Talk About Me When I'm Gone', 'Ain't She Sweet', 'Wrap Your Troubles in Dreams'. The list goes on, and what is striking about it is that it has the look at times of being the repertoire, not of a singer at all, but of a working jazz musician who carries inside his head hundreds of harmonic sequences and melodic lines which he enjoys playing because of some flash of wit and originality in their structure. As a general rule, musicians do not work with singers, they suffer them, which is only to be expected when two frankly antipathetic arts collide.

From 12 June to 14 June, 1962, I spent three successive evenings in a recording studio in Bayswater, London, watching Frank Sinatra cutting the ten sides which comprise his album of British ballads. From the first moment, with the musicians in the accompanying orchestra rising in a burst of spontaneous applause as Sinatra made his first entry, to the last, when he cut three sides in just under the hour, the episode was most extraordinary. It

was obvious after only a few minutes that Sinatra was virtually A & R man for his own session. He spotted a wrong note among the second violins, amended tempos, explained the crescendos and diminuendos he thought should be made, and even gave the bar number on one occasion where he thought the tape might have to be spliced. He was the complete professional, thinking of a dozen things at once, and producing a vocal performance of superlative quality.

During the three evenings, half of British Show Business sat in the studio looking agape at the exhibition of virtuosity before them. Many of them, like myself, were seeing Sinatra for the first time, and the fact that he really had turned out to be as large as life seemed to delight them almost as much as his singing. The remarkable thing was his blend of ruthless concentration and gay self-mockery, which was demonstrated by his reaction to one of the songs.

Apparently the range of the song was causing him some deep thought. Halfway through the first take, he broke off on the climactic line and emerged from the voice box waving his arms for the orchestra to stop, remarking to the studio in general, 'I can't even talk in that key.' Then he drank a cup of coffee and tried again. This time he did a perfect take, and came out of the box smiling, remarking to the audience, 'See what you get when you keep good hours and live a clean life?'

The contrast to this surface flippancy came during the take and during the play-back which followed. While he was singing, Sinatra, eyes closed, body swaying, lived with the sentiments of the lyric and the rich undulations of the melody, oblivious of those around him. And soon after, when the take was fed back through the loudspeakers, he stood alone in the middle of the studio floor, listening like a musicologist for the slightest deviation from the standards he sets himself. It was now that he looked like the isolated figure people sometimes imagine him to be.

This pattern of all-out concentration on the work in hand, alternating with the humour which arises out of extreme candour about one's own professional ability, ran through all three evenings. When he heard the cascading sound of the brass section in 'Garden In The Rain' for the first time, he laughed in appreciation. Once, when an unusually witty phrase came out of the celeste, he caught my eye across the studio and smiled broadly, as if to say, 'How about that?' When there was a doubt about which of two takes to accept for 'A Nightingale Sang In Berkeley Square', he said, 'Keep the second one, because the trombone solo was excellent.'

Sinatra was well read, was clearly very interested in politics, and seemed to take a genuine interest in a wide variety of subjects which never seem to get mentioned in the published profiles.

One night he took a party of about sixteen of us to supper in Soho. The seating arrangements were revealing. He commandeered three places, sat himself in the centre, myself on his left and the late Ken Allsop on his right. He had surrounded himself with the only two writers in the room. I knew that I was there because I knew about music and I soon realized that Allsop was there because of a brilliant book he had written about the bootleggers of the Capone era. But that did not mean that the talk was restricted to music and gangsters. Two of the subjects I remember very vividly were boxing and novels.

Sinatra felt very strongly that boxers, being their own worst enemies, ought to be protected from poverty by having one third of their purses withheld by a benevolent nation, which would then return the money in the form of a retirement pension. He cited the case of a once-famous heavyweight, I think it was Tami Mauriello, who, thanks to Sinatra, was now working at one of the big film studios. At that point Sinatra showed us his credentials, a finger slightly misshapen after being broken in a teenage amateur fight.

Even more vividly do I recall a long discussion about contemporary American novels. Sinatra said he wasn't a good sleeper, and used to while away the insomniac hours by reading. There had recently been a big novel about the sculptor Michelangelo, and we kicked this around for about twenty minutes. Or rather, Sinatra and Allsop kicked it around as I hadn't read it. I think our only conclusion at the end of it all was that Michelangelo's statue of David didn't look Jewish enough. Another book which had evidently made a great impression on Sinatra was an old tract by Sinclair Lewis called *It Can't Happen Here.*

This one I had read, and recalled it as a lurid piece about a right-wing takeover in America at some vague point in the future. That anyone could consider this as a feasible proposition, even in a novel, seemed to disturb Sinatra. I remember he let his spaghetti go cold.

I don't wish to suggest from all this that Sinatra is a man who never uses a four-letter word, who never drinks alcohol, who never shows an interest in the difference between boys and girls. All I am doing is describing what went on when I was in his company.

The only anecdote to do with the opposite sex which I remember was again involving a musician, a well-known blind pianist (not George Shearing, by the way). Sinatra said that this pianist must have been born with radar, because whenever he was introduced to an attractive girl, he would reach out to shake hands, miss, and hit the left breast every time.

During that 1962 visit, one afternoon Sinatra showed me a huge pile of sheet music, with the air of a man displaying the latest albatross to land on his neck. The music was the raw material from which he was trying to sift the content of the *Great Songs of Great Britain* album. I took a quick look at some of the items in the pile and shuddered at the recollection of all those municipal halls of my past, upon whose french-chalked timbered boards the corpses of so many well-intentioned British songs had been left for dead. And yet the album in its ultimate form was a flattering synthesis of British songwriting at its very best, leaving only the congenital misanthropes to grumble at the omission of a song like 'I Hadn't Anyone Till You'. (But later I looked it up and saw that Sinatra had recorded that very song only six months earlier. In any case, he may well have been holding it back for the second of his *Great Britain* albums, the up-tempo selection which sadly never came about, and which would, I have no doubt, have included definitive versions of 'Limehouse Blues', 'Cherokee', 'Let There Be Love' and 'Poor Little Rich Girl'.)

All this would seem to suggest that for the last forty years Sinatra has been ploughing a lonely furrow in the field of popular music, or, to switch the metaphor, is a singing Autolycus snapping up those unconsidered trifles which ought never to have been unconsidered in the first place, hoping to restore to their youthful glory hundreds of good songs which, through no fault of their own, have fallen out of favour. Among other things, this would have endeared him to those composers and lyricists whose royalty statements have burgeoned as a result. But I sometimes doubt if this is so. An example is 'Stardust', one of the most extraordinary popular vocal performances ever recorded, in that it concentrates on the verse and leaves out the chorus altogether, a heresy unmatched since the days, a hundred years ago, when W. S. Gilbert wrote a Faust play and left out the Devil. There were some people who felt that Sinatra, in recording the verse at the expense of the chorus, was mistreating a popular classic. But then there is no pleasing some people, who will look even a gift-verse in the mouth. 'Stardust' was for many years the most frequently recorded song in the world. There could have been nobody left in the West, except perhaps for the occasional song publisher or movie producer, who could not whistle the chorus in recognizable form. But who knew the verse? And who realized that this verse embodies the most important clue to the enigma of Hoagy Carmichael's muse, in that when played at twice the normal tempo it discloses itself to be, of all things, a model of the improvising style of the 1920s cornettist Bix Beiderbecke, in whose revered memory Carmichael named his son.

Another example springs to mind, Sinatra's recording of 'Falling In Love With Love', an item more usually associated with the pulsating glottis and pained facial expression of the Palm Court tenor. Originally written by Rodgers and Hart for a mock-Ancient Greek romp called *The Boys From Syracuse*, 'Falling In Love With Love' is supposed to be sung by a bunch of Attic maidens weaving a tapestry in a paroxysm of virginity. Sinatra, with the connivance of Billy May, alters the piece profoundly but not beyond recognition, making the point that, virginal tapestries notwithstanding, the song may well be endowed with quite a different personality. The whole thing is over in less than two minutes, but after hearing it you know somehow that Thucydides will never be the same again. I would give much to learn Richard Rodgers's private feelings about that recording. He was not a man much given to humorous asides when it came to his own work, and I doubt if either Sinatra or Billy May would take very warmly to the opinion expressed in his autobiography that the improvisations of jazz musicians are nothing more than a collection of wrong notes. In their way, 'Falling In Love With Love' and 'Stardust' prove just as important a point as 'Blame It On My Youth' and 'Why Should I Cry Over You?' where the latter pair show that a good song need have no effective date of publication, the other two reveal that what Sinatra has been striving after is not just the preservation of good songs, but their preservation in a specific form, a form which he, and we, conceive to be the form best suited to them, even though in many cases not the form intended by their creators.

If there were any last lingering doubt of the truth of this, it is dispelled by another remarkable recording departure, the creation of something called the *Reprise Musical Repertory Theatre*. This series of recordings embodies another deep truth about popular music which, yet again, is so undeniable that most people never stop to consider it. The American musical theatre has contributed more than any group to the residue of outstanding songs. Without Gershwin, Kern, Porter, Rodgers and the rest of them, not only would the standard repertoire be decimated, but even the residue would be the poorer, because it was the work of the theatre composers which set standards and gave inspiration to the lesser writers of melody. And yet musical comedy is a kind of contradiction, because by its very nature it has to be not-so-musical comedy. Those artists who are privileged to introduce the great standard songs in a musical are never chosen for their vocal ability alone. They must also be able to act a little, dance quite a lot, be reasonably, conventionally pretty or handsome, have a stage 'presence' and be outgoing, none of which attributes has anything to do with being able to sing properly. The contradiction is compounded by the fact that very often the composers who write their beautiful songs for the stage do not like to see anything 'done' to these songs, that is to say, they wish the songs to be sung, in perpetuity, as they are sung in the drama of which they are a part. We have heard what Richard Rodgers thought of improvisation. Jerome Kern agreed with him. As for Porter, there is the priceless true story of the MGM staff arranger sent to talk to the great man about the scoring for the movies of one of his last Broadway successes. Porter told the young man that he did not intend to give him any instructions, but what he would do was play him a recording which typified everything he did *not* wish to see done to his music. He then proceeded to play a recording of the Woody Herman band's 'From This Moment On'.

The studio arranger listened politely, took the point, and left, never having had the nerve to tell Porter that he himself had been the orchestrator responsible for the Herman recording. The anecdote is risible, but it is also very serious, because it shows the gulf which often needs to be bridged between the aesthetic standards of the musical theatre and those of the very best interpreters. Apart from George Gershwin, who was great enough, and humble enough also, to feel flattered when Art Tatum improvised on 'Liza' for twenty minutes at a time, the world of the Broadway theatre has shown very little understanding of this aspect of popular music.

Where, for example, is the definitive version of 'Always True To You In My Fashion'? Not in the cast recording of *Kiss Me Kate*. And where the perfect evocation of the spirit of Damon Runyon in the recording of 'Fugue For Tinhorns'? Certainly not in any cast recording of *Guys and Dolls*. Where do we look for a version of 'The Begat' which brings out all the corruscating satire that Yip Harburg and Burton Lane put into it? Least of all in any cast recordings of *Finian's Rainbow*. This is not to denigrate anybody's cast recordings, which are made under differing conditions and with differing aims. All the same, the best music deserves the best singers, and it is one of the quaint truths of modern popular music that not once in this century has any great show song ever received its definitive treatment in the production which brought it into being. 'Manhattan' had to wait more than thirty years for the consecrating touch of Ella Fitzgerald; 'Bill' more than forty before Margaret Whiting wrapped it up; 'My Funny Valentine' more than twenty before Sinatra completed the creative process. Some great theatre songs have never received their consummation to this day, but still await the final stage in the progression. Of course there is a solution, but it costs money and requires the dedicated attention of a fanatic. The *Reprise Repertory Theatre* had both. Sinatra's idea was simplicity itself, to take the great American musicals, and deliver the songs as they might be treated in an ideal vocal world rather than in the theatre's world of necessary compromise. The results were so spectacular that I count it a major tragedy of modern popular music that the series only extended to four shows, *Kiss Me Kate*, *Guys and Dolls*, *South Pacific* and *Finian's Rainbow*.

'Fugue For Tinhorns' is an example of what can be done with unlimited funds and unlimited talent. The three horseplayers of Frank Loesser's dreams are Sinatra, Crosby and Dean Martin, and no finer version has ever been made, or ever will. The same applies to 'We Open In Venice', in which our three thespians are Sinatra, Martin and Sammy Davis. In the same series, 'Always True To You In My Fashion' arrives at the ultimate apotheosis in Keely Smith's wonderful version. 'The Begat' bursts out of its own limitations to become Harburg's most derisory rejection of the piffling moral standards imposed by the Daughters of the American Revolution. What Sinatra is doing, yet again, is to take the best songs and put them in their best setting, in the hope of achieving a platonic ideal, as for instance in his duet with Keely Smith in 'So In Love', his reading of 'When I'm Not Near The Girl I Love', and all the rest of the items which might otherwise have continued to languish inside the essentially dramatic settings for which they had been conceived.

And there rests the case for Sinatra as the champion of outstanding songs and the revivifier of forgotten ones, the one singer who takes care in all his public performances to give a credit to the men who wrote the song. But that tells only half the story. It is what Sinatra has done. But what has been its effect on people? It is one thing to gratify a bunch of jazz musicians, but quite another to reach the millions. As Charley Johnson observes in *The Tender Trap*, 'Let's get some musicians; they're more interesting than Earth-people.' But Johnson's earth-people have been just as gratified as the most sophisticated musician, and this has been Sinatra's greatest achievement of all, that his art stands as a representation of all their lives, that their youth is *Higher and Higher*, their young manhood *From Here to Eternity*, their maturity *Pal Joey* and their full ripeness in this auditorium this evening. I know men of my own generation who cannot listen to the Alex Stordahl sessions at all, so vividly do those sessions evoke a lost time. For a great many whose hairlines are receding even faster than their waistlines are advancing, those recordings represent their youth, are a reminder that that youth has gone forever. They would rather it had not, and find in the wax of those recordings so faithful an impression of their own young selves that they cannot bring themselves to look, and listen. No other artist has imposed himself on the consciousness, and the subconsciousness, of his audiences as utterly as Sinatra has. By insinuating himself into the biography of the world since 1940 he has transcended singing and acting and music to become a totemic figure. In the real world people tend to measure out their lives, not in coffee-spoons, as T. S. Eliot suggested, but in popular song. My own generation can recapture the emotions, ambitions, sensations of its teens not by referring to diaries or old newspapers, but by hearing a few bars of 'I Didn't Sleep A Wink Last Night'. The impression has endured because the performance was not quite like anything that had gone before, even though in those early days we had no suspicion that Sinatra's march to originality had only just begun. Even in those days he was trying to sound like himself:

> *When I started singing in the mid-1930s, everybody was trying to copy the Crosby style – the casual kind of raspy sound in the throat. Bing was on top, and a bunch of us – Dick Todd, Bob Eberly, Perry Como and Dean Martin – were trying to break in. It occurred to me that maybe the world didn't need* another *Crosby. I decided to experiment a little and come up with something different. What I finally hit on was more the* bel canto *Italian school of singing, without making a point of it. That meant I had to stay in better shape because I had to sing more. It was more difficult than Crosby's style, much more difficult.*

Already by 1941 he was an historical figure as well as a working musician, someone by whom to mark and to measure the passing of the years. There is a touching proof of this in John O'Hara's novel *From the Terrace* (1958), in a scene between a middle-class mother and her precocious young daughter, set in 1941:

> *'Mummy.'*
> *'What, dear?'*
> *'Do you like Frank Sinatra?'*
> *'I don't know Frank Sinatra.'*
> *'But do you like his singing?'*
> *'Not very much.'*
> *'Oh, you're as bad as Alex. He says he sounds like a lost calf, and he does not.'*

'But he does to Alex. What does he sound like to you?'
'Nothing. He sounds like Frank Sinatra.'

Out of the mouths of babes. Later in the conversation, the mother plumps for Jolson, her husband votes for Crosby, and the pair of them console the daughter by saying, 'Your day will come, my dear. In 1951.' But the daughter's day had already come. The songs that first register upon us remain with us for the rest of our lives. As Sinatra's early recordings are to the daughter, so 'Makin' Whoopee' and 'My Baby Just Cares For Me' are to Sinatra, the key to childhood. What O'Hara is depicting in that exchange is the handing over of the succession from one generation to the next; the youngsters who once thrilled to Crosby's 'Can't We Talk It Over' are beginning to move over to make way for those who thrill in the identical way to Sinatra's 'I Didn't Sleep A Wink Last Night'. What nobody, including O'Hara, bargained for was that more than forty years after that domestic scene was supposed to have occurred, the same performer would still be at it, lending to musical life a thread of continuity which is so uncommon as to be very nearly unique.

Perhaps the most appropriate way to end these reflections is to keep the context as impeccably British as possible. Among the odd corners in which Sinatra has rummaged from time to time in his search for melodies and sets of lyrics which might be turned to his purpose, none has been odder than the collected prose and poetry of Rudyard Kipling (1865–1936), from which vast body of work he extracted a well-known song called 'On The Road To Mandalay' and recorded it – at which point the most astonishing trench warfare broke out. Kipling's descendents, not being conversant with developments in Tin Pan Alley, or indeed anywhere, took bitter exception to Sinatra's version of the song, a reaction which, in the light of the frankly ridiculous antics of the administrators of the estate in the days following the old boy's death, was something in the way of an accolade. The time for Sinatra to have worried was when the estate approved of what he was singing. At all events, Kipling's descendents, striking a mighty blow for that freedom of expression in which they had always believed so passionately, had Sinatra's recording banned in Britain, even though they countenanced with smiling faces all those vile plum-toned renderings of the same song perpetrated by generations of concert singers who delivered the words with the air of men who have never been to Mandalay in their lives and had no intention of ever going any nearer to it than the local club bar. Even as I write these words, the British ban on Sinatra's 'On The Road To Mandalay' is about to be lifted. It will be interesting to see if, once this happens, the ghost of Kipling rises up in posthumous wrath and Perfidious Albion slides into the sea. Probably not.

But there is a priceless farcical footnote to all this. The Kipling estate, which took such pains to stop Sinatra using the old boy's works, might just as well not have bothered, because he already had, and only their blanket ignorance of the affairs of the modern musical world prevented them from realizing it. After all, what do they know of Kipling who only Kipling know? One of the nicest ironies available to the researcher is to turn to Kipling's finest novel, a British-in-India yarn called *Kim*, one of those tales whose every chapter is headed by a short poem penned by the author. The reader is invited to turn to the fourth chapter of *Kim*, where he will find a brief verse entitled *The Wishing Caps*:

> *Good Luck, she is never a lady,*
> *But the cursedest queen alive.*
> *Tricksy, wincing, and jady –*
> *Kittle to lead or drive.*
> *Greet her – she's hailing a stranger!*
> *Meet her – she's busking to leave!*
> *Let her alone for a shrew to the bone*
> *And the hussy comes plucking your sleeve.*

I need draw no relief maps to show the way from Kipling's hussy to that marvellous moment in the *Reprise Repertory Theatre* album of *Guys and Dolls* where Sinatra sings Sky Masterson's 'Luck Be A Lady', need not annotate the links between the one set of verses and the other, need not speculate on how Frank Loesser came by those lines of Kipling's and transmuted them so brilliantly into the stuff of Runyonese. But if it is any belated consolation to the Kipling estate, they need not fret themselves too much about 'Luck Be A Lady', because nobody is ever going to sing it again half as well as Sinatra did. Nobody except Sinatra, that is.

∾

In 1972, I was invited by the editors of a world-famous reference book which shall remain nameless, called the *Encyclopaedia Britannica*, to contribute on one hundred biographical entries to their new edition. Among the entries requested of me was that of Frank Sinatra. I was particularly happy to perform this chore because as a musician, it seemed to me then, and still does now, that appreciation of Sinatra's art has for at least thirty years been bedevilled by considerations which, however fascinating they may be to people who happen to have been born with cloth ears, have not the slightest bearing on how Sinatra has performed. I thought in my innocence that perhaps an entry in a reputable work of reference might do a tiny bit to redress the balance, and in composing my biographical sketch tried to imagine some student in a hundred years time, always assuming that there is anything left to study, and anyone left to study it, in a hundred years' time, who was curious to know who Sinatra was, and what sort of social-artistic conditions had produced his singing. But the entry I composed must have been either too long or too technical for the purposes of the *Encyclopaedia*, because although most of my other entries appeared in a form I could recognize, the one on Sinatra had been rewritten by someone else, and was, as it happens, composed of facts and thoughts which are going to help that hypothetical student of the twenty-first century hardly at all.

I was extremely disappointed about this, not for financial reasons (the editors paid up like gentlemen), but because if popular music and the artists who produce it are ever to receive the critical attention they deserve, if the genre is to be understood on any level higher than that of moronic sycophancy or gossip-column tittle-tattle, then serious works of reference must lead the way. I knew perfectly well that Sinatra was the best singer of popular songs of modern times, by which I mean the times which began when Thomas Edison first recorded sound. I knew perfectly well that technically and emotionally Sinatra was rich ground indeed for the musicologist to explore; and I knew perfectly well that his performances of popular songs were so deeply ingrained into the consciousness of his period as to have become social documents, historical evidence, as well as musical performances. Possibly my professional musical background has left me with a certain lack of worldliness but whatever the reason I am not really very interested in how many executive jet planes Sinatra has owned, or what his private life is all about, or what his morality is, or who he has or has not loved. The thing about him which is hypnotic is the thing he does better than anyone else, singing songs, and it is that aspect of his life which posterity will want to know about.

Our first meeting was reminiscent of a Le Carré melodrama, with me instructed to stand in a doorway of the Savoy Hotel and jump into the first brown limousine that drew up. As I have said, being rewarded for my faith by having several conversations with Sinatra over the next few days whose contents I have never forgotten, partly because I have a remarkable memory, but mainly because I wrote them all down and sold them to a magazine. (When I asked Sinatra if he minded my selling the piece he replied 'If you can make some bread out of it, go ahead.' When I asked him if he wanted to read it first he declined. So much for the anti-journalist stories.)

Since then I have seen some of his concerts, and met him once more, very briefly, but for the most part my relationship with him has been the invisible one which exists between performer and audience. By around 1956 it had become quite clear to me that no other popular singer had ever come within a mile of him, and since then I have seen no reason to amend my opinion. This is the thumbnail sketch which I had hoped would make the reference libraries but which got left behind:

SINATRA, Francis Albert, 'Frank'. Singer, Actor, b. Hoboken, N. J. 12 December 1915. The best loved popular singer of the twentieth century, and certainly the most technically and stylistically accomplished, he has enjoyed a career whose bewildering multiplicity of facets has tended to obscure the musical excellence of his vocal art. He began by entering an amateur talent contest in 1933, later joining a semi-professional group, the Hoboken Four. In 1939 he was discovered working in a roadhouse by the bandleader Harry James, who immediately recruited him. His recording debut with the James band, 'From The Bottom Of My Heart', was on 13 July 1939. From 1940–2 he sang in the Tommy Dorsey Orchestra, and on 31 December 1942 made his solo debut in New York City. World fame followed. His first starring movie was *Higher and Higher* (1943) and in 1945 he won an Academy Award for a film on racial intolerance, *The House I Live In*. In 1953, with his career in apparent decline he played the non-singing role of Angelo Maggio in *From Here to Eternity*, winning another Academy Award and beginning a come-back which has raised him to an eminence unprecedented in any branch of entertainment. His outstanding films include *Guys and Dolls* (1955); *Man with the Golden Arm* (1956); *The Manchurian Candidate* (1962). Outstanding albums include *Songs for Young Lovers* (1954); *Songs for Swingin' Lovers* (1956), one of the most successful vocal albums of all time; *Only the Lonely* (1958); *Sinatra's Sinatra* (1963). In 1960 he formed his own recording company, Reprise Records, merging with Warner Brothers three years later. In 1962 he embarked on a series of world charity concerts for underprivileged children, and until his retirement in 1971 continued to raise funds for his favourite causes.

A much-imitated but inimitable vocal stylist, he has an instinct for phrasing which is part inborn, part picked up from the jazz musicians of his early professional years, also a unique diction which renders vowel sounds and glottal effects more succulent than any other singer, and a joy in rhythmic animation which he has never failed to convey to audiences. It is often overlooked that throughout his career, and particularly in periods when musical standards in the popular field were being debased, he has consistently campaigned for quality, acquainting millions with outstanding but neglected songs which might otherwise have continued to lie dormant. Posterity will judge him to have been so superior to all his professional rivals as to have rendered himself not so much better than they as different in kind.

The Trumpet Kings

In 1974, another of Norman Granz's many good ideas came to fruition. As their collective name suggests, The Trumpet Kings *were a colloquy of that instrument's masters: Dizzy Gillespie,*

Roy Eldridge, Harry 'Sweets' Edison, and Clark Terry, augmented by the young pretender to their company, Jon Faddis. Pablo recorded them in a variety of situations: jamming the blues with Joe Turner, live in concert, in the studio with quartets, and, most intriguingly, in a series of duets with Pablo's resident piano colossus, Oscar Peterson.

Like the music they describe, the sleevenotes for these albums offer a rare study in comparative jazz. The Trumpet Kings *series, and the solo albums that accompanied it, allow us to hear the interaction of a group of instrumentalists who represent little less than a potted history of post-Louis Armstrong trumpet playing.*

The Trumpet Kings Meet Joe Turner

A useful working definition of a living language is one which is constantly being amended by usage. Vocabulary ebbs and flows, conventions of grammar and syntax are adapted, the very speech patterns of day-to-day exchange and arrange themselves. It is not only a vital process but an incomprehensible one; I think it was P. G. Wodehouse's Jeeves who once explained to Bertie Wooster that 'eft' and 'newt' are the same word developed down parallel courses of linguistic history. Music too is a language, a living one, whose vocabulary, grammar, speech patterns, change with the times. Combinations of notes that would have bewildered Bach and mortified Mendelssohn sounded like positive clichés to Debussy, and as it happens there is an interesting trail of evidence to show how a particular chord can advance into the public consciousness. As early as 1859, one of Turgenev's characters is found 'pausing entranced over Minor sevenths'. By 1907, with *Introduction and Allegro*, a work deftly combining the melodic and the modernistic, Maurice Ravel had provided a brilliant exposition of the use of the chord; by the 1940s that sound was common currency among the new generation of jazz musicians led by Charlie Parker and Dizzy Gillespie. There is nothing new about all this, except that the freakish situation of jazz in this regard is too often overlooked. Elizabethan English could never be coeval with, say, the English of the Romantic poets, any more than Goya could take a cool look at Picasso. But this is precisely the position in jazz, where the astonishing pace at which the music has evolved makes it possible for ages and eras to jostle each other in the recording studio. Now there is no more fascinating spectacle in all art than the meeting of epochs, which is why the contents of *The Trumpet Kings Meet Joe Turner* are food and drink to the student of jazz history.

There are four trumpeters present on this album, four originals, four contemporaries who are not quite contemporaries after all, for in jazz the displacement of even a year or two can sometimes make all the harmonic difference. In this connection it is worth taking a very close look at the approach to the final cadence in the fourth and seventh choruses of 'I Know You Loves Me, Baby', where two different improvisers take two different paths towards their final resolution. That difference is one of personal style, of temperament, of mannerism. But it is also one of environment and background. The names of the two players are Roy Eldridge and Dizzy Gillespie. The identical complementary relationship is evident throughout the album. In 'Mornin', Noon And Night' the broad aggressive tones of Eldridge are succeeded by the muted wit of a quite different style. This time the instrument approximates often to the inflections of the human voice, and the technical mastery is almost insolent in its ease, witness the execution of the sustained triplet figure dominating the second muted chorus. The name of the trumpeter is Clark Terry. Again, in that apparent blues which is not really a blues at all, 'Ain't Nobody's Business', Gillespie is followed by perhaps the sparsest of all the four trumpet voices. The muted phrases have been pared down to the minimum; later this same voice appears without the mute, and once again the simplest figures achieve the most profound emotional effects; soon the simplicity of structure (although not of conception) is contrasted by the bubbling vivacity of Clark Terry, echoing at the start of his third eight-bar section the eccentric swoop which some listeners will remember from his remarkable performance as Puck in Duke Ellington's 'Lord, What Fools'. The name of the trumpeter who preceeds Terry is Harry 'Sweets' Edison.

Eldridge, Edison, Terry, Gillespie, four men in whose styles reside all the revelations that jazz trumpet has to offer. Eldridge, born 1911, an improviser of heroic stature, and one of the first to venture further afield than dominant-to-tonic; Edison, born 1915, a great aphorist who never played a bar of mere verbiage in his life; Terry, born 1920, the great Ellingtonian, a player of extraordinary impish originality and one of the few capable of injecting humour into his solos; and Gillespie, born 1917, erudite and brilliant, one of the half dozen most important musicians in jazz history, a trail-blazer whose surface levity should deceive nobody as to the beauty and serene logic of his music. Over the years all four men have reacted on each other as well as on every other trumpeter, and to trace all the cross-references of their influence on each other would be literally impossible. Only in an art form as swiftly evolving as jazz could their kind of collaboration have occurred.

Dizzy Gillespie

Gosfield Street, a narrow, nondescript London alley lost in the welter of streets just north of Oxford Street, is a more likely place for performing artistic deeds than it looks. James Boswell used to live in the next street; Dickens wrote *David Copperfield* five minutes walk to the west, and Bernard Shaw made himself the best dramatic critic of the nineteenth century only two minutes to the east. And in the next street but two lay the imaginary studio where Thackeray installed Becky Sharp's dissolute artist-father. But on 28 and 29 November 1974, when Oscar Peterson and Dizzy Gillespie entered the recording studios which now prosper in Gosfield Street, they were raising historical issues of a rather different kind. To make history, which is what Oscar and Dizzy were doing, is always interesting; to repeat it never fails to be utterly fascinating, which brings us to a set of events parallel to those involving Oscar and Dizzy.

In jazz, the challenge of the duologue has generally been rejected for the most practical of reasons, that it is a form difficult very nearly to the point of being impossible. Lonnie Johnson and Eddie Lang conducted a few enlightening exchanges, but these, featuring two guitars, were less duologues than duets. Venuti and Lang strictly speaking achieved duologues, but the resemblance in timbre between two stringed instruments virtually reduced the nature of the exercise to a duet. Trumbauer and Beiderbecke, abetted by Lang, very nearly committed themselves to duologue once or twice, while the Duke Ellington–Jimmy Blanton sides were certainly authentic duologues of the most revelatory kind, perhaps the most brilliant of that whole genre which began in 1927 when Louis Armstrong and Earl Hines, in recording 'Weather Bird', left posterity the most profound of clues, to the effect that instrumental differentiation is less decisive than we think, provided the players are examining the landscape through the same window.

But if the Armstrong–Hines partnership was the most influential in the symbolic sense, being the first of any aesthetic importance, and if the Ellington–Blanton sides were the most profound in that they signalled that the course of history was about to be changed on behalf of one of the two instruments involved, there is no question that the most comprehensive examination of the art of the jazz duologue to date was the one embarked upon by Oscar Peterson in 1974–5, in which he recorded works with five contemporary trumpeters. The albums which emerged from these sessions were all memorable, offering a fascinating example of how, within the rigid constraints of the form, both parties to the duologue can extend the limits of their own self-expression, the pianist by drifting in and out of the role of accompanist, either to himself or his partner, and the trumpeter by varying the tone of his voice by recourse to mutes.

What is even more important is that the Peterson trumpet series produced five albums which were not simply memorable, but memorable in five quite distinct ways. The point about jazz which can never be made too often is its exaltation of the individual voice; in effect it is the musical manifestation of the cult of personality. Peterson performed his duologues with five very different men, and no student of the five linked but independent events could fail to be struck by the element of enlightenment contained by the contrasts between the five. To hear the differences scattered across a series of albums was, and still is, a musical education in itself. To hear them as we now do on this one album, to hear five intimate conversations compressed, as it were, within the walls of a single room, is in a way even more stimulating, because the concentrated essence of the exercise gives the differences a heightened immediacy. What we find is Peterson exchanging musical views with five men committed to five distinct lifestyles.

I think it is well known by now that neither Oscar nor Dizzy are the sort of artists who look for the easiest way. When no rhythm section exists, the obvious course is to go for the middle-of-the-road medium pace tempo which establishes itself in the first four bars and gives no further trouble, and in, say, 'Autumn Leaves', that is what happens. But what can we make of 'Caravan', which careers off at a frightening pace? Or 'Dizzy Atmosphere', that old warhorse from Bebop days whose whole purpose was to prove that impossible tempi are possible after all? In 'Caravan' Oscar uses the piano behind Dizzy to lay down the kind of thumping syncopated arabesques that Duke Ellington associated so closely with the song that he never played one without the other. The eastern connotations of 'Caravan' are, of course, food and drink to Dizzy, who has always loved sporting in the harmonic Minor key. Talk of Minor keys raises a point which may or may not be a coincidence. An unusually high proportion of the themes are those which flit from Major to Minor and back again. Both 'Close Your Eyes' and 'Alone Together' achieve their tensions by slipping in Major thirds in a Minor melody, while 'Autumn Leaves' is on a seesaw between the two tonalities. The degree to which the piano and trumpet playing fuse in these tracks varies. Ideally a trumpet-piano duet of this kind should consist in its entirety of collective improvisation: in fact that would be impossible, if only because a trumpet cannot vamp chords. But when the fusion does occur the music is positively uplifting. If anyone wanted to know the purpose of such a session, then 'Autumn Leaves' can serve as the justification, because as that performance proceeds to its climax, the twin voices stop deferring to each other and become an orchestra in miniature, more thoroughly than Armstrong and Hines ever did, or ever dreamed of doing.

The same process takes place in the blues, particularly the slow blues, a track dedicated to Charlie Parker, which demonstrates one of the great glories of Oscar's piano playing. Possessing as he does the most comprehensive piano technique since Tatum, Oscar, like any player who devotes his life to achieving coherence and sophistication, would seem to be exposing himself to the danger which has crippled a great deal of jazz over the last thirty years, the sacrifice of emotional candour for technical fireworks. With that thought in mind, listen to the piano playing on the slow blues, and savour Oscar's apparently effortless knack of synthesizing two antipathetic streams, his own modernistic environment and the fervent, almost naive passion of the old down-home blues players. The cadences come rolling off the keys, sweet with memories and yet fiercely contemporary in their pulse and vocabulary.

The extra-musical problems of pulling off the difficult trick of the jazz duet involve, of course, individual personalities, the irony being that it is much easier to get a synthesis of sorts between two run-of-the-mill musicians. But great players, by the very nature of their greatness, are always different from each other; the challenge is to find where the differences are complementary. There are hundreds of answers to this question, but 'Caravan' can stand for all the others. At one point in the proceedings the two players exchange four-bar phrases. Because of the shifting juxtaposition of the two voices, the portraits of the two players are sketched in, most dramatically, and we realize what the session is all about. The divisive elements of individual style have melted away in the heat of creation, and the two players are performing a non-existent work of contrapuntal brilliance by benefit of force of personality, of length of experience, of pure instinct.

Roy Eldridge

The listener does not get very far into the music on *Oscar Peterson and Roy Eldridge* before realizing that it is so different from Oscar's other duets with trumpeters as to fall into a separate category. The dominant factor in all the trumpet collaborations is the technical infallibility and creative aplomb of the piano playing. We know that whatever contingencies might arise in the course of the performance, Oscar will prove to be more than equal to them. And of course this confidence is justified. The track on this album where Oscar and Roy Eldridge tear into Jerome Kern's award-winning song 'The Way You Look Tonight' is proof, if proof were still needed. The piano playing on this track is so exhilarating as to be overwhelming at first hearing; indeed the only person not to be overwhelmed by it is Roy, who performs just as prodigiously as Oscar does.

But 'The Way You Look Tonight' is untypical of the album, which is for the most part not a piano-trumpet exhibition at all but an organ-trumpet duet. The effect this has on the end product is enormous. For obvious reasons the degree of Oscar's control over his instrument, a degree we have all learned to take for granted, is reduced. The organ is something of a special case in jazz, even a kind of rogue elephant, for its keyboard has been built to respond in quite a different way from the notes on a piano. Runs which would fly off the piano have an awkward habit of refusing to fly anywhere on the organ. In effect a brand new technique has to be acquired, a technique which discovers which clusters and combinations of notes are practical propositions at which tempo, and what will now fall under the fingers and what will not.

Then there is the tonal aspect, at which point we find the performance moving into its own area. One of the prime challenges in these piano-trumpet albums is the absence of a rhythm section, which puts the two musicians into the position of trapeze artists working without a net. One slip and the whole thing disintegrates. But now study the effect which Oscar's organ playing has in, say, 'Between The Devil And The Deep Blue Sea'. The first impression is of the slightly spectral sound of Oscar's bass line behind Roy's improvisation. Tonally it is a highly pleasing effect, a dramatic contrast with the piano-accompaniment sound, and an interesting addition to the soloist's armoury. But as the performance proceeds, two much more important aspects emerge.

First, by concentrating for the most part on single-figure lines in the left hand, Oscar is performing the act of precis on the harmonies. Instead of rich combinations to express inversions and substitutions, we get the sparsest of harmonic formulae. The chords, no longer fleshed out by their component parts, are now mere skeletons, which all has the effect of clarifying what the musicians are up to. A much odder effect is the percussive one. The unique splatting sound of the organ notes, especially in the lower reaches of the instrument, are a compensation for the absence of the drums. This is more or less true of all the tracks on which Oscar plays organ, although of course he does indulge in rococo effects, double-tempo runs brilliantly conceived arpeggios at certain points. But still, it is a subtly amended Oscar, thinking his way through the kind of keyboard challenges which must have melted away for him as a pianist decades ago. The blues playing in particular makes the listener keep his fingers crossed that Oscar continues with his organ playing, one of the most neglected of all the jazz arts.

As for Roy, he remains constant as always to his own muse. To my knowledge nothing has ever really disturbed the classic lines of his style, which is rather well defined by the original he wrote half a lifetime ago, 'Little Jazz'. Soloists sometimes put more than they know of themselves into their compositions, and just as Benny Goodman produced an effect of glibness with 'Slipped Disc' and Lester Young one of suave assurance with 'Lester Leaps In', so Roy in 'Little Jazz' echoed the disarming emotional generosity of his playing, especially in that heavily accented E natural at the end of the fourth bar. Roy has always given everything in his jazz, and none of that has changed at all since he first recorded 'Little Jazz'. He still has his gladiatorial view of performance, the professional's fierce pride in his own ability which, for example, makes him insist on conquering the challenge of the high note which ends 'Devil And The Deep Blue Sea' even though the performance would have passed muster without it; and again sends him soaring up into the higher reaches of his instrument for the last chorus of 'She's Funny That Way'. The pugnacity comes through, as the expression of tremendous pent-up emotion. Roy is one of those players whose transcribed solos would never give more than half an indication of their effect, for they are built on the broad rich tone and the characteristic phrasing.

I think there is one track on this album where the music transcends even the challenge of performance, to become a perfectly natural expression of what the musicians want to say. That is the slow blues, where the curbed emotion of the start gradually builds to the ferocity of Roy's attack as he senses a climax. The whole track is beautifully poised and unselfconscious, not so much two virtuosi performing the desperately complex trick of making jazz without a rhythm section, as a couple of men making jazz together in a room. As the music flows pensively along, it becomes the very definition of what jazz is at its best. It cannot surely be coincidence that this kind of reaction occurs in the listener's mind and heart so often where Roy is involved.

Clark Terry

It is the repertoire of *Oscar Peterson and Clark Terry* which effectively defines its place in the cultural scheme of things. Of the eight themes five have their origins in that world of musical expression bounded on one side by the musical drama and on the other by the native shrewdness of the American songwriters of the golden age. Of the other three, two are devoted to the commendable cause of demonstrating how the traditional blues drastically changes personality merely by changing tempo; as for the third, 'Shaw Nuff', it belongs to those emergent days of Bebop when themes were often conceived as pretexts on which to demonstrate a freakishly fast tempo, although even 'Shaw Nuff' might be said to have its origins in musical comedy, at least with regard to its bridge, which is our old friend the bridge of 'I Got Rhythm', a song which the Gershwin brothers wrote for the 1930 Broadway show *Girl Crazy*.

But the rest of the themes belong to that body of songs which represent American popular musical culture at its very best, even if, like 'Satin Doll', they might have begun life as specialist jazz themes, or like 'Mack The Knife', been born a few thousand miles to the east. What are the virtues of such material, and why do jazz musicians repeatedly reveal affection for them, especially on occasions like this one, where the players are pitting themselves against frightful technical problems, in this case no rhythm section, no access to tonal variation, no recourse to anything remotely resembling orchestral blandishment? Perhaps the question may best be answered by taking a closer look at one of those themes, say that hit of the 1949 season, 'Slow Boat To China'.

This song was composed by a master of the form, Frank Loesser, who cunningly concealed behind the arras of a whimsically commercial lyric a harmonic structure of beautiful resilience, perfectly suited to jazz improvisation. The wit can be discerned in the second and fourth bars of a main theme composed in the key of B Flat. By resorting to the surprise tactic of a G7 chord in bar two and an A7 in bar four, Loesser sketches in the implications of a counter-melody rising chromatically from the key note through the first four bars, in the identical way that Gershwin built a chromatic line descending from the mediant of 'The Man I Love'. Such a structure stimulates the improviser in his constant search for those sequential patterns which can lend a solo its formal strength, and incidentally explains why, when Charlie Parker recorded the piece at a time long before people generally had understood the strength of the song, he was not going for the fleshpots, as some demented commentators suggested, but merely taking advantage of a theme tailor-made for sophisticated jazzmaking.

The same kind of cultural worldliness can be found in 'But Beautiful', one of the best popular ballads of the 1940s, a song which moves in almost academic patterns and displays its harmonies most subtly. Its composer, Jimmy Van Heusen, is especially adept at using a mundane occasion for the production of witty songs of this kind, witness 'Darn That Dream', 'Like Someone In Love' and 'It Could Happen To You', all of them part of larger works long since forgotten. Jazz musicians are always thankful for such items, a fact which is proved in a most interesting way by another album in this remarkable series of trumpet-piano duets, where Harry Edison chose 'Satin Doll' and 'Makin' Whoopee' just at Clark Terry has on this album – and it goes without saying that there has been no collusion.

Oscar and Clark know each other's styles so well by now that the listener tends to take their faultless understanding for granted. In fact, the absence of any other musicians makes this session different in kind from all the others. Oscar is here playing two roles, and the second of these roles, that of accompanist, he subdivides into the various component parts of the accompanist's art over the years that jazz has evolved, so that an introduction to a song might effervesce with the sparkle of a Nat Cole aphorism, while the sturdy rhythmic foundation of the performance is a tribute to what James P. Johnson and company once worked out. Some of the piano solo interludes echo the influence of the amazing Tatum, but there is no informed ear anywhere in the world which could mistake the touch of the piano playing for anyone but Oscar's. As for the musical personality of Clark Terry as revealed on this album and countless others, it is one of the most fascinating and unusual in all jazz. A puckish wit allied to a superlative technique has enabled Terry to come closer to the art of actually telling jazz jokes and recounting jazz anecdotes through his instrument than any other player who ever lived. The listener will find, for instance, that in the slow 'No Flugel Blues' the trumpet entry is very nearly a specific statement in the sweet gravity of its mood; also that in the trumpet theme statement of 'Mack The Knife' the wonderful technical facility transforms the playing into a kind of clever doggerel which appears on the surface to be nothing more than an exercise but whose actual content would reveal surprising beauties were the machine to be reduced to half-speed. Terry also has the useful knack of imparting to familiar patterns a not-quite-familiar shape, so that when the listener attempts to sing along with the last trumpet bridge in 'Makin' Whoopee' in an attempt to anticipate the line of the improvisation, all the accents and syncopations come out right but the choice of notes remains evasive. As a matter of fact, 'Makin' Whoopee' contains enough subtleties to fill an entire album by itself, from the casual strength of the walking left hand piano in the first sixteen and the way the last eight bars of that chorus define the harmonies as originally laid down by Walter Donaldson, to the way Terry, having baffled us with that unpredictable bridge, echoes the shapes of those cogitations in the coda, almost as though he has been planning the subterfuge all along. He hasn't of course, but the best jazz, achieving its sense of form through a kind of sublime instinct on the part of the improvisers, always creates this illusion.

Harry 'Sweets' Edison

In some respects this duet between Oscar Peterson and Harry Edison becomes a kind of mirror-image of the Peterson–Clark Terry duet in the same series. There is, of course, a very strong sense in which Oscar's entire sequence of piano-trumpet duets is integrated to form a single body of remarkable work, each collaboration a sensational incident in a prolonged episodic adventure. But the Edison and Terry sessions, besides having one or two overlaps in the way of repertoire, are related also in the very interesting way in which the two trumpeters constitute opposing poles of their chosen school. For while Terry will often deploy the calculated use of verbosity to create the effect of a bubbling spring, Edison has spent the last thirty years of a distinguished career carefully paring down the content of his solos until arriving finally at a style whose economy is unique among improvisers of his era.

For this reason Edison is one of the most easily recognizable of soloists, a player who favours certain little instrumental aphorisms which constitute his musical signature, so to speak. Of course all the great soloists have their pet phrases, otherwise we would never learn to distinguish them from each other, but Edison's seem doubly idiosyncratic because of the dramatic absence of any verbiage. For instance, his habit of playing a chromatic run of quavers from the Minor third of the home key, seeming to be headed for the fifth, actually leaves out the fifth altogether, stopping instead on the flattened fifth, almost as if by an afterthought; it is the simplest of devices which Edison infinitely complicates by dragging the tempo back while executing the run, in a way which would cause hopeless confusion in the mind of anyone trying to transcribe the solo: this trick is scattered all over the album. Then again in 'Mean To Me', we hear another of Edison's amiable eccentricities, his knack of beginning a new phrase with several repeated crotchets whose consistency of pitch and unwavering regularity of pulse, smack on the beat, never fail to create a tension rooted in our anticipation of the coming break-up of the pattern. In the past, Edison has thought nothing of filling two whole bars with eight crotchets in this way; in 'Mean To Me' he punches twelve crotchets over three bars, and in 'Willow Weep For Me' he actually plays fourteen on the trot. The effect is remarkable, of a player with immense powers of relaxation and the gift of epigram, showing us how easy a business the making of jazz can sometimes be.

'Makin' Whoopee' further illustrates the point, for the first jazz trumpet chorus after the theme statement is a marvellous demonstration of the art of concision in improvisation; not a note could be removed without damaging the structure, and yet not a note could be inserted without unbalancing what is there. The other interesting thing about the track is that Oscar's first improvised sixteen bars is so strong and formal a paraphrase of the original that a lyricist in the theatre might be forgiven for seizing on it as an interlude in the song and putting words to it. The only unorthodoxy of treatment comes in 'Days Of Wine And Roses', Johnny Mercer's two-sentence summary of the gloom of Ernest Dowson. (Dowson was an English poet in the Naughty Nineties whose work has proved a happy hunting ground for songwriters; 'Gone With The Wind' and 'Always True To You In My Fashion' are both his phrases.) The tempo here is strikingly fast, and works very well indeed, because liberated from the demands of the words, the melody can show how firm are the harmonies on which it is based.

Throughout the album the listener is impressed once more by the difficulties facing the pianist. The trumpeter's troubles are demanding enough, to generate heat without drums or bass. But at least he is not obliged also to play the part of accompanist. To take 'Easy Living' as an example, Oscar here is really two separate pianists, or rather one pianist performing two quite distinct functions. The first chorus, fine enough to evoke thoughts of Tatum without being derivative, is beyond criticism; so is the comparative simplicity and total effectiveness of the vamp behind Edison. But the gulf between the two roles is profound, and is a demonstration of an element in Oscar's playing not often remarked on, its great breadth of range, an aspect revealed in an altogether different way in the jazz piano in 'Mean To Me', which flashes a revealing light on the styles of players like Nat Cole and Tatum as well as Peterson himself.

In fact, the listener ought never to take any single bar for granted, because there is too much wit and inventiveness flying around for that. In 'You Go To My Head', when the trumpet returns to the main theme of the melody halfway through the chorus, Oscar insinuates the tune of 'Green Dolphin Street', a gesture which defines the chord change in the second bar more effectively than any text book or song sheet; in the blues track, things boil up to a really startling climax where the two instrumental voices achieve all the inspired ferocity of ensemble improvisation even though there is no ensemble; and in 'Willow Weep For Me', the two men show us how the most sophisticated of art-songs may be transmuted into earthy jazz without detracting from the beauty of the original.

But the most striking thing of all about this album is the clarity with which it lays down the precepts of jazzmaking. As a sometime player myself, I find that listening to Edison and Peterson creates the pleasurable illusion that really there is nothing very difficult about it. The improvised line moves on to the next chord change as if with an air of inevitability; the pulse never flags and the overall form is so confidently defined that it hints at blueprints and prearrangement. In fact, of course, making jazz can be a very tough and demanding business,

Peterson and Edison are merely showing how it all comes out when everything is right.

Jon Faddis

Tutelage is a sweet sight, in jazz as in the other creative arts. The history of the music is studded with examples of the benign influence of a great player on an emergent one, each of these relationships varying in the degree of personal as well as artistic affinity, and each one leading to conclusions as varied as they are fascinating. There was Bechet, for instance, whose swaggering panache was eventually refined through the sensibilities of his disciple Johnny Hodges; there was Hawkins, who caused a musician as brilliant as the young Ben Webster to desire only to be mistaken for the great man; there was Lester, in whose giant shadow were obscured the outlines of so many lesser men, from Allen Eager to Paul Quinichette; there was that unforgettable College of Two presided over by James P. Johnson and Willie the Lion, whose acolytes, being Duke Ellington and Thomas 'Fats', eventually turned out to be even more prolific than their masters; most inexplicable of all, there was the case of Rex Stewart, whose adoration for Louis Armstrong was so excessive that 'I tried to walk like him, talk like him, eat like him, sleep like him', and which somehow caused him to end up sounding rather like Bix Beiderbecke, which just goes to show how strange are the ways of tutelage.

Jon Faddis is a twenty-one-year-old trumpeter whose preoccupation with the collected works of Dizzy Gillespie is apparent the moment he starts to play. He is an unusually precocious musician, having been already known to discerning professionals while only eighteen. Thad Jones and Mel Lewis, who have used Faddis in their big band recordings, heard about him in connection with a Lionel Hampton session, and drafted him into the orchestra the moment there was a vacancy. But what is especially impressive is that Faddis's role in the Jones–Lewis band is not just a soloist but also leader of the trumpet section, a job whose responsibilities are usually met by far more experienced players.

Of course what will be vital to Faddis in the development of his own life is the degree to which he eventually differs from

Dizzy, not the degree to which he resembles him, for every player has in the end to discover his own style rather than somebody else's, and the listener will find himself arrested constantly by those moments in this album when Faddis plays things which Dizzy never did. As for the similarities, they are marked, particularly in the codas, where Dizzy's whimsical tricks are echoed almost to the life. In 'Blues For Birks' the short clipped notes surrounded by empty spaces which open the trumpet playing, then to be followed by a blistering high attack, are authentic Dizzy, as are the exaggerated sforzandos which are squeezed out of the instrument, falling away in pitch slightly at the end of the note. After the piano solo, when the two men exchange four-bar phrases, Faddis ends the first chorus of the exchanges with a verbatim quote from Dizzy's book, a quote which Oscar then echoes in the four-bar break which follows. Examples of this kind could be quoted from every track, ranging from the furious double-tempo runs to the sly quote in 'Summertime' from 'It Ain't Necessarily So' a theme stemming from the same operatic source as 'Summertime'.

As it happens there are a couple of booby traps for the inattentive listener, for although the two staple sequences of the jazz life, the Blues and 'I Got Rhythm' are both well in evidence, they are featured in unusual permutations of themselves. For example, in the fast blues, the form has been amended so that strictly speaking it is not a blues at all, or rather, is a blues with something added. What has been added is the famous bridge passage from 'I Got Rhythm', where Gershwin makes the chords dance the dance of resolution through four keys; the form of the track turns out to be 12–12–8–12, so that each complete chorus comprises three blues sets broken by an 'I Got Rhythm' middle section. And then, having cloaked the Blues in a Gershwinesque disguise, the two men then reverse the procedure in using the famous Lester Young riff, 'Lester Leaps In', not as a paraphrase of the main theme of 'I Got Rhythm' as Lester did, but as a four-bar phrase played three times to comprise a conventional blues. Then there is a blues with no disguise or amendment at all, 'Things Ain't What They Used To Be', which incorporates one of those interludes which appear from time to time in a jazz album, disarming all criticism and justifying the expense of the entire product. This interlude can be found in

Oscar's first twelve-bar chorus after Faddis has completed his solo. There is nothing to be said about such playing except that it is a great privilege as well as a great pleasure to listen to it.

Faddis's appearance in such exalted company at so early a stage of his career (the other trumpeters featured in Peterson duets are Dizzy Gillespie, Clark Terry, Harry Edison and Roy Eldridge) is a hopeful augury for jazz in general as well as for Faddis in particular, for one of the most depressing facts of life about jazz today is the lack of very young players possessing the hallmarks of confidence and imagination. Never before in its history has the music been so barren of players of stature under the age of thirty, which makes it even more welcome to hear how on this album two generations combine to form a concerted whole. I am thinking of two moments in particular. The pace of 'Autumn Leaves' is unusually fast, and it is highly instructive to observe the nature of Oscar's support to the trumpet solo. The left hand becomes an entire rhythm section, defining the tempo in the simplest as well as the most effective terms, underpinning the furious mood of the trumpet playing with an utterly reassuring aplomb. There is an identical moment, although a very different vamp, in 'Summertime', when Faddis, after building an entire chorus on his paraphrase of 'It Ain't Necessarily So', reverts to 'Summertime'. Here Oscar provides another left-hand support, a much more melodramatic one than we are used to hearing in these ultra-sophisticated days, but which works to perfection. If two-man bands are to justify themselves, then they ought to provide moments which neither the conventional small-group nor the solo performer can supply. The Peterson–Faddis collaboration provides such moments in abundance.

DIARY OF A FESTIVAL – *MONTREUX 1975*

Festivals are the curate's egg of the jazz world. What may appear on paper to be an invitation to musical gluttony on an Epicurean scale, can in reality produce little more than epic indigestion. The root of the problem is in the nature of the average festival: an unwieldy selection of often incompatible artists appearing on a programme dictated more by opportunity and opportunism than by artistic criteria. For European audiences, the word 'festival' summons images of the American legends who every summer stampede from event to event like a herd of senescent wildebeest. A chance to hear the greats it may be, but is it good jazz? Exceptional festivals are so rare that they swiftly become legendary, as in the case of the 1956 Newport Festival, remembered for Paul Gonsalves' exertions on 'Diminuendo and Crescendo in Blue' and the popular rehabilitation of Duke Ellington that they inspired.

The 1975 Montreux Festival was another such exception, this time for showcasing a stellar variety of musicians at a time in their lives and careers that now seems like an Indian summer. As Norman Granz observed afterwards, the chance to compile a programme from a Pablo roster that included Count Basie, Ella Fitzgerald, Dizzy Gillespie, Lockjaw Davis and Benny Carter was too good to miss.

Although I present many individual concerts yearly with my various tours, it's rare that I participate in a jazz festival in any way whatsoever. Almost twenty years ago (1956 or 1957) I recorded virtually the entire Newport Jazz Festival and in 1972 I helped to present a festival in Nice, but in both cases I had little to say about selection and use of the artists. This year, however, I was given by Claude Nobs, the director of the entire Montreux Music Festival, the opportunity to do three nights in which I could do anything I wanted. I could work with any musicians I wanted, make up any combinations I wanted, routing the concerts whichever way I wanted – in effect, I was given my own festival.

Fully realizing the importance of the occasion, Granz made arrangements to record every note of Montreux 1975, and flew Benny over from London, so that he would have some on-the-spot anecdotage to add to his sleevenotes on the nine albums that would follow. Benny spent three hot July nights backstage at the festival, mingling with the performers as monitors relayed sound and pictures of the onstage proceedings into the bandroom of the Montreux Casino. The resulting notes form a personal diary of an event that was unique even for artists habituated to big halls and all-star line-ups, such as Oscar Peterson, whose trio had doubled as the rhythm section for many of the performers.

> This is the greatest festival I've ever been to in my life! I've never played in a festival before where you could immediately feel in the air that everyone was looking forward to playing as much as they did at Montreux. From the moment I got there and began talking to musicians, at the press conference, in the hotel lobby, in the bandroom at the Casino, everywhere, you got the feeling of everyone anxiously awaiting the chance to start blowing. It was something!

Wednesday, 16 July 1975

I am not what you would call a very cosmopolitan type. I dislike travel so much that even for me to reach the far end of my garden requires a considerable psychological adjustment which I find arduous. Before I went to Montreux for the 1975 festival, I had a vague impression that it was somewhere in southern France. I can now disclose with a fair degree of confidence that Montreux is indeed in Switzerland and that, contrary to all appearances, there would seem to be something about its location which is mysteriously conducive to the playing of outstanding jazz.

Why Montreux? I am not sure and nor is anyone else. The Swiss national tendency to a kind of antiseptic conservatism is not quite the ambience which has come to be associated with the making of good jazz, and Montreux itself, nestling securely on the eastern rim of Lake Léman, seems more suited to one of those fruity Edwardian tales by Stefan Zweig or perhaps to a Graham Greene entertainment than to a jazz festival. As for the Swiss themselves, the last improvisers of any account to come out of the cantons were Jacob Burckhardt, a teller of tall stories masquerading as a historian, and Albert Einstein, a religious mystic masquerading as a mathematician. And yet, Montreux is not altogether incongruous in the jazz context. The nearby castle of Chillon, the one which so memorably gave Lord Byron the horrors, is on what Jimmy Lunceford would have called the outskirts of town, a Romantic approach to the bland prettiness of the district. And then there is the Casino itself, where the music was actually performed. It is an excellently appointed concert hall with good acoustics and that illusion of a low ceiling which never fails to have a benign effect on improvisers.

The Oscar Peterson Big 6 (Oscar Peterson – piano; Milt Jackson – vibes; Joe Pass – guitar; Toots Thielmans – harmonica; Niels Pedersen – bass; Louis Bellson – drums)

The three nights of marathon jazzmaking began in the early evening. The sun was still high in the sky when the musicians came on stage, and the light out in the streets was still good enough to read the latest market reports from Zurich by. In such balmy conditions, it is perhaps assuming too much poetic licence to describe this set as an icebreaker, but its accuracy as an indication of where the music was going to head for in the next ninety-six hours is unquestioned. From the first theme statement, the pitch at which the music was performed was one of extreme emotional intensity. There was a competitive element in all the sessions which raised the game of the musicians involved, and the interaction with a series of rapturous audiences further increased the pressure.

The night began, as a great many successful nights do, with the Blues, in this case Charlie Parker's 'Au Privave'. Musicians tend to start this way because then they can take the chord sequence for granted and get down to the business of finding out if this is going to be one of those nights. The tempo in this case was fast but not too fast for the purpose, and the instrumental permutation unusual enough to add a dash of comparative unfamiliarity to events. This unfamiliarity took the form of a man standing on stage with his hands over his mouth, linked to some wires which swooped away from his trousers in a fine parabola. This was the harmonica player Toots Thielemans, who was the first soloist off the mark, blowing a tremendous gale of quavers into the night air, seeming at times, because of the position of his cupped hands, not to be playing an instrument at all but miming to a record, as slightly looney jazz buffs sometimes will, before a mirror in the privacy of their own room. After twelve bars you could tell that Toots was playing like a man inspired by a great idea, and after twenty-four bars you realized what that great idea was – the rhythm section behind him.

By the time Joe Pass had completed his solo and Milt Jackson had taken over, the other musicians were starting to lay little riffs behind the solo line, which is always a good sign, and after Oscar Peterson had ended his solo with a little ten-fingered impromptu composition, he could hardly bring himself to stop playing, and so pecked hungrily away at the keyboard behind Niels Pedersen's bass solo. It all comprised what the Victorian journalists used to describe as an auspicious commencement to the proceedings, and knowing as I did, how much more music there was to come before the night was over, I wondered whether the capacity of appreciation might not be exhausted long before the ultimate resolution of the ultimate discord.

The air having been cleared with this opening performance, there then followed Milt Jackson's 'Here's That Rainy Day', which turned out to be a revelation in the art of stating and embellishing a melody prior to giving it a thorough working over. While he plays, Milt's face works constantly, his eyebrows arching whimsically in response to the climax of a phrase, his mouth twisting with the effort of squeezing into the context one last refinement of a passing note. The effect of the music he achieves is the opposite, of serenity and a kind of grave assurance. But perhaps serenity is the wrong word to use for so passionate a player; after two choruses, Louis Bellson, sensing the rise in temperature, changed to sticks to keep in tune with things. The other soloists then followed in sequence, before Milt restated the melody to end.

After those two openers, a fast one and a reflective one, the set was an assured success, with each player uplifted by the contributions of all the others. Some idea of the length and durability of the tradition which a session of this kind represents is symbolized by 'Poor Butterfly', a song with so freakish a gift for longevity that if you trace its origins you find yourself back in the America of Pershing and Dempsey, when Broadway shamelessly pillaged the genius of Puccini and came up with a show whose every detail has long since been forgotten – except for its hit song, which is distinguished by the unusually fervid leap of a sixth between its third and fourth notes. There is a passage in Oscar Peterson's solo, in his second chorus, where the art of the trill and tremolo is incorporated into the context of the improvisation so finely that it all deserves comparison with Milt's once again exquisite opening choruses.

At the risk of sounding like one of those glib Eastern mystics who drive Arthur Koestler to distraction, I am bound to say that there was a pleasing circular symmetry to this opening set of the night, which began and ended with the traditional twelve-bar blues. There was, of course, a difference between these two blues; the first was exploratory, the second, Milt Jackson's 'Reunion Blues', exultant. By the time the six players came to the end, a kind of creative turbulence had been injected into events which kept the music at fever pitch the whole time. Watching the rhythm section, it was obvious that none of its members had any idea of, or care for, the amounts of physical energy they were investing in the playing, for they were all by now operating on the pure oxygen of exhilaration, an impression confirmed by the broad smile on Louis Bellson's face, a smile which only disappeared when the time came for him to play a solo of his own. And by the time this last solo came up, all the musicians knew they had been involved in something very happy and very successful.

It is difficult to disentangle any one solo from the general context, but there is a point to be made about Joe Pass's guitar solo in the final track which once again links a fiercely contemporary performance with the long long ago. In Joe's second twelve-bar chorus, the lines of the late Charlie Christian's style begin to creep into the consciousness; all the hallmarks are there, the basic, earthy harmonic design, the simple (but very far from simple-minded) clarity of the riffish phrases, the impelling rhythmic nature of the execution, which made half of Christian's best riffs into little compositions on their own, as those who employed him were quick to appreciate. This resemblance to Christian continues in Joe's third and fourth choruses, but what is fascinating to listen to is the way in which this piece of improvisation, which is after all a single unified statement rather than the sum of those sections which analysts can never resist examining, gradually leaves the 1940s shore of Christian's wonderful architectonic confidence and sails off into the deeper waters of the 1970s and Pass's fiercely contemporaneous way of playing guitar. Which seems to me to represent the very best in a jazz occasion, the way it reconciles its dependence on tradition and its debt to the past, with its insistence on expressing its own time and place.

The Dizzy Gillespie Big 7 (Dizzy Gillespie – trumpet; Milt Jackson – vibes; Eddie 'Lockjaw' Davis – tenor sax; Johnny Griffin – tenor sax; Tommy Flanagan – piano; Niels Pedersen – bass; Mickey Roker – drums)

Although it never struck me at the time, I realized when I thought about it later, that the second set of the evening was an exposition in the art of playing and thinking jazz at very high speeds. Naturally there were slower interludes, but primarily the entry on stage for the first time that night of trumpet and saxophones was the signal for the tempos to start flying. The hint came with the choice of the first number. Dizzy had entered last, and the announcement of his name had been greeted with such frenzied uproar that the only way to end it was to start playing. This Dizzy did, quickly and matter-of-factly, and although he played the first thirty-two bars of 'Lover Come Back To Me' leisurely and out of tempo, everyone in the building knew perfectly well that this theme, so cunningly wrought by that old Hungarian fox Sigmund Romberg, has survived its origins as part of the terrifying libretto of *The New Moon* because it happens to be the perfect vehicle for improvising at fast tempos. Sure enough, as Dizzy arrives at the bridge, the one where Romberg pays his respects to Tchaikovsky by plagiarizing him, the tempo suddenly reveals itself and the mind's eye suddenly jumps across the stage to Mickey Roker, whose wrists and arms we now know will be working like pistons for the next few minutes. And our admiration for the inflexible regularity and precision of the drumming is tempered by solicitude for the drummer's welfare. Playing at such speeds does after all involve a musician's physical powers too.

The one player nobody ever worries about at these speeds is

Dizzy himself, who actually seems to prefer them, ever since the early Bebop days, when some of the pieces he wrote and performed were conceived at such a breakneck tempo that there were times in the listener's mind – though never in Dizzy's – when the pulse of the performance seemed to have deliquesced into a constant stream of sound. The problems presented by this type of playing naturally vary a little from instrument to instrument; whereas on the trumpet they are merely impossible, on the vibraphone they are quite unthinkable, which raises the awkward question of how Milt Jackson manages to cope so well. There must be an answer to this, but I don't know what it is. Having sat there on the night, watching his arms operating his sticks for a couple of choruses, it was patently obvious that Milt was riding the tempo as easily as any musician could; the red felt tips of his mallets were blurs across the retina, but the solo line was gathered, controlled, coherent, as the listener can hear for himself.

It is always an exhilarating experience to watch musicians tackling the acutest problems of their craft, and the ultra-fast tempo certainly falls into the category of an acute problem. But the pleasure is heightened when two players on the same session are playing the same instrument. Then we realize that acute as a problem might be, there usually exist several ways of solving it; when Eddie 'Lockjaw' Davis and Johnny Griffin work together, the text for the day is that there are more ways than one of swinging a cat. Lockjaw and Griffin are, of course, no strangers to each other. Some years ago, for example, they combined to produce a marvellous exhibition of complementary saxophone virtuosity, an album called *Tough Tenors*, in which incidentally, they gave the definitive treatment to Lester Young's ingenious exercise in Minor legerdemian, 'Tickle Toe'. Clearly, in the case of Lockjaw and Griffin there are aspects of each player's style which strike sparks in the other, and even though they are distinctly, even profoundly different types of saxophonists, they have two essentials in common, a magnificent instrumental command, and what you might call progressive musical sensibilities.

As to the contrasts between them, 'Lover Come Back' and 'Cherokee' both make it clear that on extra-fast tempos, Lockjaw plays in furious flurries which leap in and leap out of the sequence with miraculous precision, while Griffin plays longer lines, ripping off long sequences of quavers, each of them defined meticulously in defiance of the limitations of the speed of things. The visual contrast is even more striking, for while Griffin, like almost every soloist, appears to be wrestling with demons, Lockjaw has a really amazing and rather alarming demeanour of a man on a Sunday morning stroll. Waving the saxophone about like a peashooter, appearing for long passages to be playing with only one hand, keeping his eyes open, he achieves a relaxation which seems hardly possible. Harmonically Griffin tends to explore more possibilities if only because he was raised in a later school, but the two of them make an amazing pair, who bring enlightenment and great delight to all saxophone students.

The other soloist involved in this protracted exhibition of *allegro furioso* is Milt Jackson, who was here making his second appearance of the evening. Here again the witness could watch as a great player manipulated his own art under the most rigorously testing conditions. The structure of the vibes dictates that even the most feather-light passing grace note has to be executed with as firm a movement as a double *forte* effect, and as Milt playing is finely wrought with those grace notes which often tumble over into the time-space of the note which they introduce, the visual effect is a bewildering one of mallets flying about all over the place in apparent defiance of the rhythm section. Of course it is an illusion. Milt too, is a past master at playing at whizzing speeds, and he combined with Dizzy, Lockjaw and Griffin throughout the set to give an impression of each soloist outdoing the one that had gone before. When the set ended and the musicians departed from the stage, the crowd howled in mortification as though deprived of its birthright.

Jazz at the Philharmonic (Benny Carter – alto sax; Roy Eldridge – trumpet; Zoot Sims – tenor sax; Clark Terry – trumpet and flugelhorn; Joe Pass – guitar; Tommy Flanagan – piano; Keter Betts – bass; Bobby Durham – drums)

As the third set of the evening began at the Montreux Casino on the torrid night of Wednesday 16 July, there was bafflement among the professionals and their followers of a very unusual kind. At these jam sessions, the players on stage made no public announcements as to the identity of the songs they were about to perform, or had just performed, or who had composed them, or what their origins were. The instrumentalists just began a new piece as the applause for the previous one was fading to a diminuendo. None of this mattered very much. As Thomas 'Fats' Waller once remarked in a slightly different context, 'Lady, if you gotta ask, don't bother.' Normally the identity of a theme is never a very difficult business, for the likely jazz sequences are so familiar to musicians, and have commended themselves over so long a period, that their every contour became known to the pros a long time ago. And yet, on 16 July, after the third set had been proceeding for a couple of minutes, Mrs Benny Carter, sitting there watching her husband launch into the first solo, turned and said, 'What are they playing?'

I could not tell her and felt exceedingly useless. I also felt faintly angry with myself, for apart from anything else it was a lost opportunity to play one of the classic scenes in the repertoire of the compulsive show-off, the one where the mysterious English stranger in a room full of American experts, waits till everyone else has thrown up his hands in desperation, and then casually and quietly solves the problem. I have seen the trick done many times in many movies, and in one of E. M. Forster's most amusing essays there is a delightful description of how the poet Coleridge, playing the fool after the unhappy conclusion of a love affair by masquerading for a few months as a trooper in the British cavalry, happened to overhear two passing officers misquoting from the Greek. Modestly, and with the abject servility which his false position obliged him to adopt, Coleridge corrected the misquotation and supplied chapter and verse of the source, leaving the two gentlemen suitably open-mouthed. But now that the chance had been thrust upon me to emulate Coleridge, I found myself unable to take my cue.

The bandroom at the Casino is a large irregular-shaped room, provided with a colour TV set on which the room's occupants can watch and hear what is being played on the stage outside. Over the hubbub of the musicians relaxing with their friends and families, the strains of this unidentified tune began to insinuate themselves, and after Mrs Carter had drawn a blank from the mysterious Englishman, she turned to Eddie 'Lockjaw' Davis and asked him. Lockjaw thought it was something that might be in the Minor, but he didn't think that Roy had played the actual written melody to start with. I then suggested, in a weak imitation of Coleridge, that it sounded faintly like 'S'Wonderful', only with the diminished chords left out. But 'S'Wonderful' without the diminished chords is like *Hamlet* without the Prince, and it was a foolish suggestion. Not as foolish as my next contribution, which was that the middle passage sounded rather like the bridge of 'Rosetta', Lockjaw politely gave me a funny look, and Milt Jackson was called in. He listened to the sequence, claimed he knew what it was only he couldn't remember the title. We all cheered derisively at that, but a few minutes later, when the song was over, Milt came back in the room and said, 'For You'. And then, as always in these cases, we kicked ourselves for not having seen the obvious.

I tell the story because it is instructive. The best musicians preparing for the kind of relaxed and free-wheeling session whose outcome can be heard in this album, usually give more thought to the composition of their programme than the rest of us to the composition of our reactions to it, and the fact that the group had conspired to include what is after all a rather abstruse theme so far as jazz is concerned is very revealing. On stage they looked like a handful of men having a good time, and this to be sure is exactly what they were. But they were also professionals delivering the goods, and watching them go about their work, you could not help noticing how unselfconsciously they combined a casual manner and a fierce dedication.

On 'For You', Clark Terry uses the flugelhorn, an instrument whose slight solemnity of tone compared to that of the trumpet subtly heightens the scintillating effect of Terry's irrepressible sense of fun. In 'Autumn Leaves' Clark is back again on trumpet, and this alternating between the lighter and the larger horn characterized Clark's tactics for most of the night. It is in 'Autumn Leaves', by the way, that Clark plays a magnificent muted solo against the background of a lone walking bass, with the rest of the rhythm section cutting out. In contrast Roy's playing here is open, and at one point Joe Pass's wizardry prompts Tommy Flanagan, Keter Betts and Bobby Durham to spring for a while into double time. For the last two tracks Clark sticks to flugelhorn, and Roy, dispensing with his mute, performs his usual trick, which is to excite himself and then convey that excitement to everyone listening; a man would have to be made of stone to hear Roy in 'I Never Knew' and not warm to the man.

There remain the saxophonists, Benny Carter, gliding and swooping through the changes in a way that makes a joke of the fact that these days he spends more time writing than playing; he is one of those performers who can apparently acquire his touch without practising. Then there is Zoot, whose playing has grown more gusty and broad in the last few years without losing the classical lines of its foundations. Players of his attitude revel in the conditions obtaining on the stand for this session, and indeed everyone concerned contributed to the useful effect of letting people know that the jam session idea is not quite as dead as the obituarists say it is.

The Trumpet Kings (Dizzy Gillespie – trumpet; Roy Eldridge – trumpet; Clark Terry – trumpet; Oscar Peterson – piano; Niels Pedersen – bass; Louis Bellson – drums)

There can hardly be a jazz fan anywhere in the world who would need to be told that when the melodrama of a night's jamming moves into its denouement and Roy Eldridge, Dizzy Gillespie and Clark Terry make their appearance downstage, then the proceedings have begun to take on a certain gladiatorial aspect. The relationship between three such men is a positive maze of influence and cross-influence, of personal relationship, of historical allusion, of mutual respect, regard, affection – and egotistical rivalry. And at Montreux in the broiling summer heat, by the time they confronted each other, all three trumpeters had had copious opportunity to warm up, to taste triumph, to take the measure of the crowd, the acoustics, the rhythm section, the atmosphere of the occasion. When this fourth and final set of the night began, it was a signal that the decks, figuratively speaking, had been cleared for action, as much as to say that now that the fripperies of saxophones has been dispensed with, the three champions could get down to a tough match with no distractions.

This is not to say that Roy, Diz and Clark are anything remotely approaching sworn enemies or bitter rivals. They are not like champion tennis players who sprawl between games back-to-back at the umpire's chair like Tweedledum and Tweedledee, exchanging no word, no glance, no cognisance of the other's existence. On the contrary, Roy, Diz and Clark are much more like three profound specialists of an arcane science, Freud, Jung and Adler perhaps, who having studied each other's findings very closely, rejecting part and accepting part, then go their own sweet ways, having each acquired for the other two that fundamental respect which all professionals must feel for true professionalism.

There also lies between the three men something rather more than respect. In the session before this one, Roy had been playing, Dizzy resting, and there had arrived one moment when Roy, practically coming apart at the seams with aspiring ambition, went for some crystalline epigram of his youth far up in the higher reaches of his instrument, and getting close enough to it for the experienced listener to pick up the allusion – at which point Diz, who had been passing the TV monitor in the bandroom, and had been arrested in mid-saunter as it were, by the spectacle of his old hero continuing to be heroic, turned to all the other musicians watching, and smiled that peculiarly significant smile which professionals are inclined to use when they want to say something like 'How about that?'

And during the closing session which followed this tiny tell-tale incident, the session preserved on this album, you can follow the plot of a most unexpected interlude in the Blues which provided a predictably false ending to the night. (It should have been the true ending, but the crowd refused to accept the idea, and was rewarded for its persistence with the bonus of 'Indiana'.) In the blues, in the middle of all the ferocious trumpet jousting, with the faces of all three players grave with their preoccupation, Diz and Clark suddenly burst into facetious song, to be followed by Roy, who sings his confession that he had no idea any of this was going to happen. Even at the height of a joust's clangour, humour and affection repeatedly break through, as they had done earlier when Roy, having stated the theme of a melody and made as if to stand back for Oscar to take over, stepped up to the microphone and performed every movement required to start playing, except actually to blow his instrument, getting his laugh and then sweeping upstage of allow the piano solo to proceed.

As a matter of fact, the fourth and final session began with a bit of upstaging of all three trumpeters by Oscar, who, having been quickly reduced to laughing delight by the three muted horns, launched into a most stupefying solo on 'Montreux Blues', crammed with technical miracles, and lit with frequent lightning flashes of melodic beauty. Here was a performance so overwhelming that one of the bandroom witnesses remarked in the tones of a tennis umpire announcing Game, Set and Match, that Oscar was the greatest, and got so overcome by the vehemence of his superlatives that he had to be admonished, gently, by Johnny Griffin who patiently explained that as far as he was concerned, regarding the greatest, 'there ain't no such animal; it's all a question of taste', a point of view whose philosophic subtleties were immediately lost in the welter of fiercely competitive jazz flooding from the bandstand.

After that the programme was a long succession of climaxes. 'There Is No Greater Love', a literate ballad from the good old days composed by that odd fish among commercial bandleaders, Isham Jones, is often heard these days in Oscar Peterson recitals, but on the night it seemed to suit all three trumpeters just as well, especially Roy, whose broad lazy statements are the ideal way of treating that song at that tempo. And then comes, of all things, more of Isham Jones, whose 'On The Alamo' is an excellent jazz theme which has fallen into comparative neglect since the Swing Era. Clark Terry's muted playing here is further proof of how right Duke Ellington was when he cast Clark, in the Shakespearean sketches, as Puck. There then follows that sensational blues and the version of 'Indiana' without which nobody would have agreed to leave the premises. One of the prime functions of staging such a set is that each of the front line men should raise the game of the others; sometimes this does not quite work out, and the result is reminiscent of what happened to the matador who found himself confronted one day by the pacifist bull Ferdinand. But at Montreux the stratagem worked perfectly, with Roy the broad, aggressive attacker, Dizzy more feline, Clark indulging in instrumental chuckles. I won't dare to insult the intelligence of any listener to a tape of this set by telling him which trumpeter takes which solo.

Thursday, 17 July 1975

Joe Pass (guitar)

The unaccompanied guitarist must surely be the loneliest man in the world so far as jazz is concerned. He is also the rarest, and because the rarest, also the most exotic, if not to himself then at least to everyone else. There must be thousands of people who have put in a lifetime of listening to the music without ever watching a major guitarist playing by himself on the stage of a crowded auditorium. I saw Wes Montgomery once or twice playing an occasional number unaccompanied in a club in the small hours, and I am quite convinced that Django Reinhardt could have played great unaccompanied solos on his head, under water, or wearing boxing gloves, there being no extremity I could imagine which would have curbed his gift. Of course there were any number of guitarists in my youth who did little else but play unaccompanied, but I am afraid that their splendid isolation was due not to their virtuosity but to the fact that no other musicians could be induced to have anything to do with them. And so for me, Joe Pass has become the first major jazz guitarist to be seen sometimes in my imagination sitting playing to a large audience in a large theatre.

On the night of the 17th, the difficulties of this situation were compounded for him by the fact that before he began the recital on this album, Oscar Peterson had just given a one-hour piano solo exhibition of his own, an exhibition into which he had packed every variation available to the solo performer, leaving the crown in so rapturous a condition that when Joe Pass made his entry people must have wondered what he thought he was going to be able to do. He then showed them by quietly launching into one of the best ballads in the entire popular repertoire, playing it first in that charming, rambling way, ruminative and out of tempo which seems so natural to the instrument, and then, for the second chorus inserting into the performance the spine of a rhythmic pulse.

Broadly speaking, this remained the pattern throughout the recital, both in the way the pieces were routined and in the nature of the pieces themselves. Pass has an unusually wide repertoire of songs he can call on at any time, and one can soon deduce from the evidence of a few concerts by him, that he has spent many years studying the standard tunes, scrutinizing their harmonies, familiarizing himself with their possibilities at all tempos, adding to his collection whenever a new and worthy item comes along. His method of treatment in solo recitals is to state the theme without bothering much with jazz time, defining both the melodic line and its relationship to the harmonies, and then going into time and playing straightforward jazz improvisations.

But jazz improvisations of what? His programme at Montreux begins with the flourish of Vincent Youmans's 'More Than You Know' before moving on to the other themes which belong in the same tradition, songs originally written for very different situations than jazz concerts, but which have since come to be recognized as the staple diet of the jazz soloist. 'Glad There Is You', for instance, is a song with one or two rather unusual chromatic thoughts written into its structure, and which many people will associate with Ella Fitzgerald's interpretation of it, while 'Willow Weep For Me' is one of the most imaginative and courageous popular songs ever written, demanding of its audience ten times the musical sensitivity which the popular song usually evokes in people.

Although Pass's 'Alison' is a conventional twelve-bar blues, the influence of the popular song form imposes itself on the guitar-playing in a very interesting way. There is one small phrase which keeps recurring, brief but memorable. At one point Pass returns to it and plays it over and over again, building its frail outline into a passage of considerable length. The listener will have no trouble finding this phrase; it is an elementary exercise on the Major sixth of the tonic chord and lasts three beats, so that by repeating it three times the player achieves the effect of a cross-rhythm. It sounded familiar to me and vaguely redolent of musical comedy, but at the moment when Pass produced it I was unable to stick a label on it. Later I remembered it as the main theme of the forgotten verse which Richard Rodgers wrote back in the 1920s for 'Blue Room', and that way back in the days when I was gingerly introducing myself to jazz, I had heard an ancient recording of the song which most unusually included the verse. The group which recorded it was a quartet featuring a once-revered jazz guitarist called Eddie Lang, which leads me to wonder whether that tiny phrase had first crept into Joe Pass's subconscious while he listened to Lang thirty or forty years ago.

Songs like 'The Very Thought Of You' and 'How Long Has This Been Going On' belong to the same cultural stockpot into which musicians like Pass are constantly dipping, even though the two songs stem from such different sources, the first from an English bandleader of the 1930s called Ray Noble, the second from the Gershwin brothers a few years earlier on Broadway.

Jazz musicians have kept such tunes alive over the years because they find the harmonic structure stimulating for purposes of improvising, and because the melodies have a curious property of manufacturing their own rhythmic propulsion. There are, however, two other pieces that Joe Pass hit upon at Montreux which are not quite in the same tradition. 'Li'l Darlin'' is a theme specifically designed to show off the mastery of the Basie band in the art of ensemble relaxation; it is one of those themes whose essence resides as much in the rests between the notes as in the notes themselves, and it can fairly be described as a composition which arose essentially out of the demands of orchestral jazz.

There is one other item on this album which comes from the heartlands of jazz rather than from Broadway or Tin Pan Alley. At Montreux Joe chose one particularly beautiful impressionistic commentary by Django Reinhardt. When Django first wrote it, or rather when he and it first discovered each other, it was referred to as 'Nuages'; later it became one of the few purely jazz themes to survive the metamorphosis into popular song, under its more commercial title of 'Bluest Kind Of Blues'. Perhaps it is not exactly sensational news that a composition by Django Reinhardt should so perfectly suit the personality of the guitar, but I felt I had to draw attention to the track somehow, because 'Nuages' has always been one of my favourite pieces – for which reason Joe's version of it qualifies as one of my fondest recollections of the festival at which it was so finely played.

The Milt Jackson Big 4 (Milt Jackson – vibes; Oscar Peterson – piano; Niels Pedersen – bass; Mickey Roker – drums)

There is nothing like small-group playing in informal surroundings for revealing the quintessence of style. Perhaps on the face of it, it sounds like a contradiction to describe so carefully organised an affair as the Montreux Festival as informal surroundings, but if the administration of the festival was formal, the performers themselves managed to preserve the air of men enjoying themselves. And of all these men, the great revelation for me was Milt Jackson. Having only ever seen him previously on the concert stage, and only then as part of the outrageous flamboyance of the Modern Jazz Quartet, I had very little idea of the personality behind the music. In the flesh Jackson had the sprightliness of a trained dancer, or perhaps an athlete, and a delicious sense of humour which must have been a bit of nuisance to him years ago when the photographers were putting on record the studied gloom of the MJQ. He also looks far too young for a man who, according to the record books, was born in 1923; and finally, the physical hard work that goes into his playing only becomes apparent from close range.

One of the most impressive things about Jackson's playing is that hallmark of the jazz virtuoso, the ability apparently to loiter fractionally behind the beat without dragging the tempo back. The faint hint of indolence which this property gives to a solo, even on an up-tempo, is the secret of the player's ability to convey his assurance to the listener, for it is this infinitesimal time lag which endows music with the quality we have come to call relaxation. Jackson's improvisations are a remarkable, perhaps a unique, alliance between the main body of the solo and the embellishments and grace notes which weld the melodic parts into a whole. Very often in an extended passage, time-values are implied which do not in fact turn up at all, so that for instance, what the ear has anticipated as a crotchet-triplet emerges as four quavers, the last of them arriving breathlessly but just in time to attach itself to the other three.

The overall effect of this intensely sophisticated rhythmic conception is that very often in a Jackson performance the solo seems to be floating above the bar lines, its flow undisturbed by the rigid obstacles of time divisions. And yet, for all this fluidity, nobody ever heard a supine Jackson solo, or one which failed to set the foot tapping. The explanation is that his sense of time is so impeccable that no matter how intricate the variations of his melodic time, the rhythmic pulse remains incorruptible. It is this alliance between the controlled discipliness of form and the liberation of the spirit which gives Jackson his unquestioned greatness as a jazz musician, and it is also the property which makes him equally effective at any tempo. While perfectly happy to race along at any speed the other musicians suggest, he is also one of the most sumptuous ballad players in all jazz, an aspect of his art which gave me one of my best moments at Montreux, 'Everything Must Change'.

For sheer exquisite beauty of tone and sound combinations, I heard nothing at the festival that was finer than this performance. In a sense it incorporates all the classic elements of the Jackson style, the lingering bouquet of the last bar while the next one has begun, the erudition of the harmonic method, the endless melodic inventiveness, the rock-steady beat. There is a grave and sombre beauty about this kind of playing which always induces a hush in the congregation, not so much of awe, as from a fear of missing some semiquaver of unusually profound import. Jackson's face while this is all going on is what the English humorists used to call a proper study. He twists the right side of his mouth up in his efforts to squeeze the last grace note into the bar, then relaxes when the last fluttering tonality has been slipped into place. At frequent junctures in the execution of a phrase he will raise his eyebrows, less in surprise than in whimsical consideration of the validity of the idea which has just occurred to him. His improvisations seem to be a constant surprise to him.

His teaming-up with Oscar Peterson had the piquancy of novelty, and Oscar later told me how long it had been since he last had a chance to play with Milt, and how much he had enjoyed the experience. Between them, the two virtuosi selected a programme of great literacy, the kind which would still be effective even if the theme-statement was all that was offered. As a matter of fact, in 'Nature Boy', the brooding Minor melody is never far below the surface of the playing, and to a lesser extent the same is true of 'Like Someone In Love' and that brilliant piece of popular songwriting, 'Stella By Starlight'. The playing in 'Mack The Knife' is a complete contrast to this kind of introspective jazz; instead it is extremely powerful and absolutely bubbling with high spirits. Milt turned up for the session wearing a short-backed white jacket whose enormous black buttons reminded you vaguely of Harlequin, as he stood there swaying over the burnished gold of his keyboard, twisting his body into the positions commensurate with the accurate placement of the notes, his self-absorption made a pretty contrast with the frequently laughing face of Oscar, who in these situations, often reacts to someone else's epigram with a chuckle of appreciation. Niels Pedersen and Mickey Roker emerge into the foreground here and there, especially in Ahmad Jamal's 'Night Mist Blues', where the bass solo is followed by some drum breaks; there is also a beautiful bass solo in 'Stella By Starlight'. But my final recollection of this session is of Harlequin grimacing through his own brilliance.

Ella Fitzgerald (with Tommy Flanagan – piano; Keter Betts – bass; Bobby Durham – drums)

The last session of the night was the one which had aroused the most expectancy, which was natural enough, as it was the one featuring Ella Fitzgerald. Earlier that evening, and for most of the previous night, audiences had been sated with instrumental brilliance so comprehensive that the festival posters could hardly contain all the names involved. Ella's recital was slightly different from what had gone before, because the details of the performance were unknown to the audience before that performance actually began. Nobody was sure what kind of group would accompany Ella or what kind of programme she would favour. And not only did nobody know, but I should guess that nobody cared very much either. People realized years ago that Ella is sufficient unto herself, and that whether she uses a small-group or a large orchestra, she remains unique. As it turned out, the Montreux audience got its answers within the first two and a half minutes, which is roughly the length which 'Caravan' runs. They saw that it was to be a trio and that it was to be an out-and-out jazz night, whose details are a little more complex than the list of song titles suggest.

On the face of it, it would appear that Ella sang nine songs. But these who are at all familiar with Ella's approach to a concert of this kind will not be surprised to find that strewn about among the listed items are innumerable references to other works, some of them in the popular canon, others very far removed from it indeed. This is neither the Ella of the definitive orchestral recordings, providing meticulous readings from the master composers, nor the Ella of the more formally constituted concert hall, divided from the audience by the great gulf of the footlights and the orchestra pit. This is Ella backed by a jazz trio, performing before an audience which somehow manages to reconcile its size with the spirit of intimacy to be looked for in a club. There is a euphoric anticipation in the air, and the result is that Ella, completely relaxed, scatters through her programme more allusions than the mind can identify at first hearing. Without having made notes at the time, I seem to recall her having jogged my memory with regard to such items as 'Dardanella', 'Heat Wave', *Rhapsody in Blue*, 'The Surrey With The Fringe On Top', 'I'm Beginning To See The Light', 'Poinciana', 'Deep Purple', 'Rockin' In Rhythm', 'Chicago', 'Idaho', 'Anthropology', 'Matchmaker', 'Smoke Gets In Your Eyes', *Peter and the Wolf* and even a slight smattering of one or two Italian operatic arias.

What the reactions of the composers of these items would be to these fleeting references to their beloved brainchildren there is no way of knowing, but as Ella has at various times given more fulsome treatment to almost all of them, I don't suppose anyone would complain. Provided one enters into the right spirit to enjoy such an exhibition, the result is a kind of whimsical musical game in which references fly past and settle briefly on certain appropriate harmonic perches before disappearing again as the chords change once more. Ella's lightness of touch as she plays this game often conceals the art that lies behind it, but it is a form of improvisation requiring great confidence and experience. (Sometimes, when Ella sings these catalogues completely unaccompanied, the heart of the listening musician leaps into his mouth for fear of hearing Ella stumble; she never does.)

As in all of Ella's sets, there are moments in this one of positively instrumental ingenuity in the way in which the original melody has been amended. There are some especially vivid examples in 'It's Alright With Me' and also in 'Caravan', which she assuredly sets the pattern for the rest of the night's entertainment. But some of the other tracks represent a different kind of approach to singing. Of these none is more extraordinary than 'Wave', which never bothers with the lyric at all, goes straight into a scat chorus and gradually evolves into a kind of vocal doodling pad on which Ella scribbles the random thoughts of a devoted collector. The same element pops up in 'How High The Moon', in the anthology of musical themes with which the track ends, but the spirit of laughter which informs this catalogue once again, should not detract from the cleverness and correctitude of the improvisations, or from the naturalness with which they come out of Ella.

Like Milt Jackson, Ella makes you wonder how musicians

preserve their modernity over so long a period; her voice defies the passage of time in an identical way. That she paces herself like an instrumentalist is shown in track after track, where the decorous opening steadily builds into uninhibited jazzmaking. (A perfect barometer for measuring this process is Bobby Durham's drumming, which steps up its force and volume each time to match the buoyancy and authority of the singing.) All three accompanying musicians are integrated closely into the performance. In 'It's Alright With Me', the opening takes the form of a finely balanced duet between Ella and Keter Betts, not till the second sixteen does Tommy Flanagan enter, whereas in Cole Porter's 'Let's Do It', the duet is between voice and piano.

In a sense the session attains its most profound moments with the encore to the encore. 'T'ain't Nobody's Bizness', one of those not-quite-a-blues which, when it is done well, as it is here, represents a whole musical culture. In fact its opening, where Ella states the verse with Flanagan's piano in support, is like a musical definition of jazz, salty in its sentiments, wonderfully poignant in its melodic structure, and exquisitely performed. The number is very far removed from a Tin Pan Alley hit like 'Teach Me Tonight', but it so happens that it is in these two tracks that one can most conveniently study the deep understanding and musicality lying behind Tommy Flanagan's modest demeanour. As he fills in the interstices between the vocal phrases, his playing is so utterly right that there is even a danger of forgetting for a moment that Ella too contributes to the beauty of such moments by instinctively knowing where to leave the spaces in the first place. Without such command of mental telepathy the best jazz would never exist at all.

Saturday, 19 July 1975

The Count Basie Jam Session (Count Basie – piano; Milt Jackson – vibes; Johnny Griffin – tenor sax; Roy Eldridge – trumpet; Niels Pedersen – bass; Louis Bellson – drums)

By now, the friendly summer weather – that old-time lyricist Otto Harbach would inevitably have described it as 'halcyon' – had broken. On the 18th, the night before Basie arrived, the sky was rent by giant hands of forked lightning, so melodramatic that they reminded you of phoney lightning from some second-rate movie version of *Wuthering Heights*. The lake was lit with brilliant flashes and the rain came coursing down the mountains into the valley, washing the streets of Montreux even cleaner than the local municipal arrangements had managed to contrive, which is saying a great deal. The great hotels rolled up their marquees like ancient schooners hauling in sail, and the rumble of thunder hinted that perhaps Louis Bellson was toying with the idea of a third bass drum. And there had indeed been something thunderous about the music. Lightning shafts of inspiration had constantly lit the stage of the casino, and on the night of the 19th, while the climatic conditions did their best to make reality look like a Delacroix landscape, the music inside reached its apotheosis with the Buddha-figure of Basie seated at the piano, surveying the other musicians like a king smilingly reviewing the condition of his court.

The Basie Jam Session was probably the most highly charged moment of the whole festival. Most jazz fans have slowly come to the realisation by now that as the Grand Old Man of the music, Basie's willingness to endure the rough-and-tumble of a jam session, inevitably with much younger men, is likely to decrease as time goes on. However, the evidence of this blues performance offers nothing in the way of proof that Basie is beginning to find it difficult keeping up. His sense of Time remains as perfect as ever, and the deep wisdom of his deceptively simple-sounding solo figures is as impressive as it was in the days of the All-American Rhythm Section. His delight in the playing of Pedersen and Bellson manifested itself in repeated broad grins of pleased surprise, while Griffin, Jackson and Eldridge aspired, almost visibly, to the heights achieved by the great masters of the past with whom Basie once worked.

In the early stages of Proust's *Remembrance of Things Past* there appears one of his most affecting characters, an old lady who combats the advancing years by adjusting her frontiers. As she finds herself conserving more and more energy she gives up the village and confines her movements to the house and garden, then to the house, then to the upstairs, then to her bedroom and finally to her bed, where her great experience and a kind of instinctive mastery of the art of life enable her to keep abreast of everything that happens in the district. By drawing in the dimensions of her life she had contrived to retain mastery over it. Now look at the list of themes which sprang instinctively into

Basie's mind when he found himself projected into the middle of a jam session. The Blues, 'I Got Rhythm', and the Blues again. By drawing in the dimensions of his repertoire, Basie has contrived to retain mastery over it. The temptation to draw further Proustian analogies, for instance that the old lady's village is Jazz and that her bed is really the bedrock of Kansas City style, is perhaps too dangerous to indulge, but certainly in recent times Basie has enjoyed playing the part of a man disinclined to play jazz for long stretches any more.

Sometimes this affectation produces abject panic in the ranks of those backstage who are committed to the certainty of a Basie performance, including on one recent occasion myself; when I asked Basie what numbers he wanted to play, he fixed me with what the poets used to call a basilisk gaze and said 'Numbers? You mean number.' That all this really is an infinitely comic game he plays is made quite clear the moment you hear him strike a chord. When he and Niels Pedersen are duetting in 'Billie's Bounce', it is not only the music which is ageless but also the performers. When he rides the tiger of the twelve-bar blues, Basie demonstrates the secret of everlasting youth, which is after all quite a simple business; it is to go on doing something as well as you did it as a youth. Well, when he plays the blues Basie is the young gadabout of the carnival days of the 1920s; I have listened most critically, many times to the small-group jazz albums he has been making recently, and I cannot for the life of me find the slightest sign that Basie's playing has deteriorated.

He is the master of a truly marvellous style, deft and neat and witty and finely balanced, and the rest of the adjectives we have sprinkled over his reputation in the last forty years. At the heart of the style is his feeling for time; in the trio blues which opens the second track it was fascinating to watch his hands lying supine on the keys in between pecks as the vibraphone enters the performance. One would observe the pecks and glance round at the faces of the musicians watching; every one was smiling, and every smile is a greater tribute to Basie's achievement than any of those adjectives I listed. Basie injects an amazing sensation of sheer joy in the listener when he starts playing. You find yourself smiling and tapping your foot and slapping your thigh and wanting to emit undignified animal grunts at vital points, all of which are symptoms of what is supposed to happen to homo sapiens in the presence of classic jazz perfectly executed.

In the one deviation from the blues to which Basie agreed at Montreux, 'Lester Leaps In' (or to give it its harmonic label, 'I Got Rhythm'), he gives us the most magnificent exhibition of Stride piano playing as a living art, raising all the favourite ghosts of his past as he thumps into his work with the relish of a mere boy. I think we ought to be quite clear about what we are confronted by with this kind of playing. We are reaping the benefits of a freakish situation; because the development of jazz has taken place so fast, we are able to savour, concurrently with later styles, the living past in jazz. Sentimentalists who wonder what it must have been like fifty years ago when Kansas City was full of jazz virtuosity need not wonder at all; 'Lester Leaps In' will give them the exact sensations.

Basie presided over this jam session like the proud patriarch of the family throwing grins of benign approval at the younger generation. Perhaps in the furious tensions of Johnny Griffin's tenor playing he recognized a few honking echoes of Lester, and several times he smiled up at Milt Jackson as that ever-resourceful gentleman got a new riff going behind the soloist. It is more than coincidence that the soloist in question usually turned out to be Roy Eldridge, who would begin a solo quietly, modestly, like someone patiently building a fire, and then suddenly start generating the terrific heat of his own ambition, so that the supporting riffs, little phrases calculated to excite and goad the soloist to even more extravagant flights, seem to have come out of Roy's head rather than those of the men actually playing the phrases. The whole atmosphere becomes so infectious that in 'Lester Leaps' you can even hear Basie inserting his little pecks behind Louie Bellson's drum solo.

The bandroom was crammed with musicians on the night of this jam session; there seemed to be dozens of them watching the TV monitor, sitting gossiping and sipping mild beverages, warming up their instruments, chatting, laughing, bellowing. And so in a sense, the jam session psychology had extended from the stage to the waiting room; it was not hard to see what it was that stimulated everybody into such buoyant animation. It was not the beverages or the company or the sense of holiday occasion, or even the Byronic thunderstorm flashing and crashing across the churning waters of Lake Léman a few yards away. The stimulus was the music, and at the heart of the music was Basie, the old fox, the sublime comedian, the great man, showing us with an embarrassed modesty that perfection in the arts is not after all impossible to achieve, so long as you know what you are doing and are prepared to go on doing it for fifty or sixty years.

Appendix

JAZZ
BY BENNY GREEN
(*ENCYCLOPAEDIA BRITANNICA*), 1974

Jazz

Although nobody has ever satisfactorily defined it in technical terms, jazz diverges widely, even violently, from all previous canons of musical composition and performance and is immediately distinguishable. Certainly, it is the most enigmatic of musical forms, never respecting any of the received truths about itself. It is generally accepted, for instance, that all jazz is improvised, which is untrue; that jazz is synonymous with syncopation, which is even more untrue; that jazz owes its idiosyncratic nature to the ingenious subtleties of its rhythmic pulse, whereas for at least the first half of the twentieth century the precise opposite was true, its rhythmic conception being extremely rigid and formalized. As jazz is neither purely composed music nor purely extemporized music and as it cannot be accurately notated, a logical positivist would have no difficulty demonstrating that, like the beach of the German philosopher Hegel, which was neither sea nor land, jazz does not exist at all. As jazz is essentially the musical experience of a passing moment, which cannot be repeated in quite the same way, in a sense the most important figure in all its history was Thomas A. Edison, who invented the phonograph.

A loose definition that has served well enough for most of jazz history is that it is a music where the performer plays melodic variations on a given harmonic base against a regular rhythmic pulse; in the 1960s even this definition became unacceptable, because the Avant Garde movement dispensed with prearranged harmonic signals, indeed, with any kind of form. Difficulties of definition are aggravated by the fact that the terminology of jazz retains its validity only within the jazz context, so that to describe, say, the leading figures of the harmonic revolution of the 1940s as 'Modernists' is to beg the question of Modernism as a movement in the music world at large that has been flourishing throughout the present century. An example is the chord of the Minor seventh (for instance, C–E♭–G–B♭), which the standard-bearers of jazz modernism held aloft like a banner but which in a 'classical' music context had long become venerable through the French composer Claude Debussy and the school of musical Impressionists. Indeed, much earlier still, in 1858, the Russian author Ivan Turgenev could make one of his heroes sit at the piano 'entranced over Minor sevenths'. In the same way, other terms, such as traditional, progressive, and classical, have very specialized meanings within the jazz world.

Because of the oddly eccentric nature of its whole being, jazz has enjoyed the questionable benefits of definitions that are either tautological – 'Jazz music is any music played by jazz musicians' – or confusing to the layman – 'Jazz is a matter of lip-technique.' What can be said with confidence is that, whereas in more conventional musical areas the artist is fundamentally an executant expressing the findings of the creative mind of the composer, in jazz the performer is usually his own composer. Within the strict meaning of the term, there can be no such thing as a jazz theme, although of course some themes will lend themselves to the jazz idiom more readily than others. The customer unable to acquire the recording of Brahms's *Fourth Symphony* conducted by Herbert von Karajan would probably settle for someone else's recording of that work, but the buyer thwarted in his attempt to buy the jazz musician Duke Ellington's version of 'Caravan' might well accept as a substitute anything else played by Ellington. That is why, in jazz, there is at least one truism that has always applied: the performer playing a theme always tries to make it sound not like itself but like himself.

Origins

The birth pangs of jazz are perhaps of more concern to the musicologist, the social historian, and even the anthropologist than the musician. The multiracial origins of jazz are clear enough. Had it not been for the traffic in slaves from West Africa to the United States, jazz would never have evolved, either in the United States or Africa, for jazz is the expression in music of the African native who is isolated both socially and geographically from his natural environment.

Among the West African tribes supplying victims for the slave trade, music, and especially vocal and percussive music, had developed in a way quite unknown to the academic Western ear. Scales and harmony were purely intuitive, and music was deployed less as an abstract aesthetic gesture than as a specific language conveying subtle shades of meaning and emotion. By varying the pitch of a note or changing the inflection of the voice while uttering a musical sound, the performer could convey far more concrete messages than his sophisticated Western counterpart.

If his art was cruder, his function was more practicable. Although most of the prehistory of jazz is speculative, the flexibility of this musical language, unfettered either by conventional ideas of correctness or by precedent, resulted in the unwitting development of a scale utterly original so far as the West was concerned. This scale, in which the third (E in the key of C), or mediant, and the seventh (B in the key of C), or leading tone, were flattened and thereby turned into what are sometimes referred to as 'blue notes', became the basis of the language that eventually emerged as jazz. The transfer of these West African tribal traditions to the slave fields, railways, and rivers of the southern US states was of advantage to oppressed and oppressor alike, the slave obviously taking solace in the cultural memory of his own collective past, the slaveowner encouraging work songs in the same spirit as an infantry general might approve of military bands – for the stimulus they gave to work rate. Many of the early examples of primitive vocal jazz relate closely to the labours being performed, and the content of the lyrics is a reminder that not only the cotton plantations but also the levees and railroads of the Deep South were created and maintained by slave labour. Joe 'King' Oliver's 'Lift 'Em Up Joe' and many of the songs of Huddie Ledbetter (Leadbelly) are examples of the work-song convention surviving as art long after its original functional need had declined.

There was another major influence on the evolution of

Afro-American vocal style. If the slave could derive no comfort from the laissez-faire philosophy of his owners, at least he could draw spiritual consolation from their religion. Until the beginning of the nineteenth century, the established church, by performing a series of comically dishonest intellectual cartwheels, had managed to reconcile Christianity with the possession of slaves, the argument being that, although one Christian must not enslave another, it was acceptable for him to enslave a savage. This meant that the work of the missionary was actually rendered sacrilegious, and throughout the eighteenth century the absurdity of such an attitude became more and more exposed, until about 1790 the Methodist movement began to address itself to the redemption of the souls of men who until now had not been thought to have possessed any. This missionary campaign flourished for almost a hundred years and had one of the most astounding outcomes of any evangelizing crusade in history, one that the Christian Church could never have anticipated. By attempting to convert the slaves to Christianity, the missionaries achieved the Africanization of their own hymnbooks.

By adapting his own ritual music to the liturgy of the Christian Church, by contributing, as a member of a congregation, to the creation of new tunes, or by making his own variations on the existing ones, the slave and his emancipated descendants developed the spiritual to the point where, in the form of hymns, ring shouts, revival chants, camp songs, and funeral songs, it gradually merged into a semi-secular tradition. Significantly, ragtime, that coarse yet disarming bridge between the old songs of slavery and emergent jazz, figured unmistakably in the accompaniment of hymns such as 'Good Lord'll Help Me On My Way' several years before ragtime music was published officially under its own name. This vast influence of Africanized church music on the development of jazz underlines one more fallacy about the music, which is that it was always linked irrevocably to the low life. Its connections with the brothels of Louisiana and the saloons of Chicago tell only half the story, for jazz has been concerned with sanctity as well as with sin, has been a sacred music as well as a profane one. Its links with Christianity and particularly with the act of worship and the rituals of birth, marriage, and death have proved so durable that they remain unbroken to this day, not only in the person of gospel singers, such as the late Mahalia

Jackson and Sister Rosetta Tharpe, but also in more secular figures who insist on the church as their primary source of musical inspiration.

Not all of the early Africanized church music was vocal, although, naturally, any instrumental playing was bound to be crude in conception, execution, and instrumentation. The slave generations obviously had access to neither conventional musical education nor to legitimate orchestral instruments, and, even after the liberation that followed the war between the States, such things as education and conventional musical instruments remained, if not impossible, at least difficult to acquire. The New Orleans pioneer drummer Warren 'Baby' Dodds is said to have made his first pair of drumsticks from the legs of a kitchen chair, and the semi-legendary cornet player Charles 'Buddy' Bolden was seen at times to thrust half a coconut shell, a bathroom plunger, and an old derby hat into the bell of his instrument to do service as mutes. The early jazz artists, it would seem, improvised not only the music they played but also the instruments with which they played it.

A key figure, because he personifies the antipathetic traditions of religious piety and worldly musical wit and also the tensions created by the unorthodoxies of musical education of so many of the pioneer jazz figures, is the pianist-composer-singer Thomas 'Fats' Waller. Waller was born into a religious family the head of which was a minister of the Abyssinian Baptist Church and who regarded jazz, to quote his son, 'as music from the devil's workshop'. Waller, a brilliant natural musician (see below), taught himself the piano and soon developed an outstanding gift for composition. His commercial as well as artistic success was enormous, but it seems reasonable to conclude, both from Waller's own occasional remarks and from the evidence of his love for the organ and the presence in his repertory of Bach, Liszt, and Rimsky-Korsakov, that Waller was a formal musician manqué.

The generation of men such as Bolden created the earliest jazz traditions. Liberated but not freed, cast on to the open labour market for the first time, and endowed with a musical tradition self-formed but speedily secularized, the men of Bolden's time had two problems to face, no less daunting simply because they were mere subconscious anxieties. How were they to arrive at some code of artistic behaviour when making communal music and for whom were they to play the music? Clearly, if jazz were to shed its religious connotations, it must become a functional music, and, equally clearly, if formal music offered neither any precedents for procedure nor even a polite interest, then jazz would have to create its own.

The latter third of the nineteenth century was a crucial point in the prehistory of jazz – a time when jazz was interacting with church music, with the white commercial world of dances, soirées, drawing room ballads, and concerts, with opera, with the theatre, with vague occasional wisps from the European tradition, and a time when the Southern Negro was learning how to live with uneasy freedom; during this period the traditions of jazz were slowly forged. It is a period and a process impossible to document with any accuracy, for obvious reasons, and about which even the most basic terms have remained in contention. The institution of ragtime piano playing, for instance, is regarded by many as no more than a subdivision of emerging jazz piano styles, but, by many others, it is regarded as a distinct, separate form, marked out from jazz because its repertory consisted largely of formal, composed works rather than slight themes for improvisation. There also exist several abstruse theories about regional variations in jazz styles. Nobody has ever decided to the satisfaction of anyone else where the 'folk' music of, say, the itinerant guitarists of the South-West ends and jazz proper begins. But, indisputably, by the beginning of the twentieth century, a few jazz forms had begun to combine into a recognizable tradition, and the hub of this development was located at the Louisiana seaport of New Orleans, where the dominant form among jazz musicians was the Blues.

The Blues

Much of the confusion over the identity of the Blues has been caused by the word itself, which has had to perform a dual purpose. It has been used for at least 200 years by writers as a synonym for a depressed mood and, more strictly, as a specific musical term, so that misconceptions have been perpetuated that all blues music must by definition be concerned with depressed subjects and even that only depressed musicians play it.

Another belief about the Blues, that it is the acid test of a performer's improvising ability, is more accurate for reasons intimately connected with its harmonic structure.

In jazz, a blues sequence extends over twelve bars, containing three harmonic crisis points, and only these give the improviser hints as to where his melodic variations should go and what kind of musical mood they should imply. The paradox is that, sparse though these are, they have a vast emotional potential for the gifted player to discover, so that, ever since the beginnings of instrumental jazz, a player's ability with a blues sequence has been a guide to his true talent. Perhaps the most extraordinary thing about the Blues has been its durability; it has retained its attraction for soloists of all eras and schools, changing with new approaches and movements but remaining intrinsically itself. The Negro composer William Christopher ('W. C.') Handy was an important figure in the development of the Blues. He was fundamentally a kind of folklorist orchestrator who took his themes from the Blues performers he heard around him, wrote them down, and harmonized them. Some blues was published before Handy's, but, as a result of his disseminating work, jazz players by the late 1920s were freely improvising and spontaneously inventing melodies on blues chord sequences. His most important compositions were the 'Memphis Blues' (1911) and 'St Louis Blues' (1914).

Exploration and improvisation

A close textual analysis of the harmonies employed in the Blues since the beginnings of recorded jazz reveals the process of ceaseless embellishment of the original sequence, and this process may stand as a symbol for the whole of jazz history. In effect, the story of jazz has been a saga of harmonic exploration. Most of the jazz pioneers were men without musical schooling or formal knowledge who had to evolve a musical language and harmonic vocabulary by trial and error. They were artists intent on hammering out some formality of procedure, some kind of convention that would reconcile the individual freedom of each player to express himself with the adherence to the demands of the ensemble without which all performances would disintegrate. This is the crowning paradox of the art of jazz: it is at once the art of the individual musician and an almost exclusively communal exercise.

Although jazz criticism has divided the music into three equal categories – traditional, mainstream, and modern – harmonic exploration and the growth of melodic vocabulary have comprised a constant, continuing process in jazz history. New labels have been attached to new styles not when some dramatic advance has been made but when the cumulative weight of several years' findings has caused people to realize that the music has steadily been changing its personality. The three compartments are useful as an approximation, not an arbitrary judgment. As the harmonic vocabulary of the jazz musician has been extended and as the degree of technical sophistication has increased accordingly, so have new conventions been forged, although it is not true that, as one style established itself, others have been superseded. Uniquely and because of the very fast pace of its evolution (covering an advance from primitivism to neoclassicism in little more than half a century), several schools of jazz have existed concurrently.

* * *

Early Jazz Styles

THE NEW ORLEANS STYLE

The rigid convention of collective improvisation, based on a specific instrumentation, flourished in Louisiana in the early years of the twentieth century, and two powerful factors dictating the formulation of the convention were probably the social and the functional. In the social life of the Negro, community music played a more prominent part than perhaps can now be easily comprehended. There was almost no social activity in New Orleans then that did not imply a musical corollary. There was live music for births, weddings, christenings, funerals, picnics, parades, marches, and all kinds of celebrations. A great deal of this music was naturally played outdoors, which may explain the unchallenged dominance of the trumpet over all other instruments. All the early leaders of New Orleans jazz were trumpeters, with the line of succession passing from Bolden, through historically documented musicians such as Freddie Keppard and Joe 'King' Oliver, and down to Louis Armstrong. New Orleans also produced brilliant players on other instruments, particularly a school of musicians who effected a limpid, highly attractive clarinet style, but leadership was almost exclusively the preserve of trumpeters like Bolden and Oliver.

In the classic New Orleans style, the trumpet's duty is to state and embellish the melodic line of the theme. The trombone stresses the harmonic root notes, providing also a solidity of resonance on which the other performers may build. Above the trumpet soars the clarinet voice, weaving further variations on the same harmonies. Thus, the three voices, linked yet independent, are able to compile between them the simple triads (chords consisting of a root and the third and fifth tone above it) that were the basis of all jazz harmony at this period of its development. And, as all three were playing together throughout the performance, the band, though small, was able to maintain a surprising degree of volume.

There was a vital reason why the ensemble convention was adhered to so faithfully. In New Orleans or, indeed, anywhere else at that time, there were few musicians capable of playing an extended solo, even had the rules of their game permitted them to do so. Apart from a handful of virtuosos, the idea that a jazz performance should consist of a succession of solos would have been unthinkable for the simple reason that there was no such thing as a succession of soloists. But the musicians were developing at an astonishing rate, and, in retrospect, it can be seen that the classic New Orleans style, rigid as it had to be, was doomed by its very nature: there was no question that, in time, a player or group of players would emerge for whom the constriction of the ensemble was intolerable. When this player arrived, then the whole New Orleans conception of tightly integrated ensemble improvisation would become obsolete. Another reason why the frailty of the New Orleans tradition is more apparent now than in the heyday of that style is the fact that jazz as a musical lubricant to oil the social machine was restricted largely to the New Orleans low life. Although the myth-making process has drawn a picture of jazz limited strictly to the brothels and sporting houses of Storyville, the town's bordello district, there were, of course, many instances of the music splashing over into the life of the city at large. Nonetheless, jazz, linked to the Negro performer and the social events of Negro life in the city, retained a connotation of sin and dissipation for many years after the New Orleans pioneers were forgotten.

The saxophonist Sidney Bechet, one of the most gifted of all the New Orleans musicians, insisted in his autobiography that the word jazz in its original form of jass was local slang for sexual intercourse, and the evidence in favour of Bechet's assertion seems overwhelming.

These brothels were thus a link in the jazz musician's economic chain, for many employed bands or, at the very least, a house pianist whose job was to thump out ragtime rhythms against a background of red plush and gilt. The collapse of the Storyville economy was naturally disastrous for the working musician. In 1917 the United States secretary of the Navy decreed that, in view of the repeated fighting and violence involving seamen on leave in the city, the New Orleans red-light district must be closed down. The sense of outrage and the disarming worldliness of the city are reflected in the official statement by the then mayor, Martin Behrman:

Preterpermitting the pros and cons of legislative recognition of prostitution as a necessary evil in a seaport the size of New Orleans, our city government has believed that the situation could be administered more easily and satisfactorily by confining it within a prescribed area. Our experience has taught us that the reasons for this are unanswerable, but the Navy Department of the Federal Government has decided otherwise.

The theory that the closing of Storyville brought the heyday of New Orleans jazz to an abrupt end is one of those critical platitudes excused by the fact that it is largely true. Jazz did not, however, immediately stop in New Orleans, nor was the migration north of the musicians sudden or absolute, nor had jazz until then been unknown in the North. As early as 1917, the year of the Storyville edict, the Original Dixieland Jass Band, a group of white Southerners with a comically inflated sense of their own importance as musical innovators, had introduced jazz to the patrons of Reisenweber's restaurant in New York and recorded two compositions.

One potent evangelizing factor was the riverboat, which would ply up and down the Mississippi, often with a jazz band aboard. More than one white middle-class jazz pioneer has testified that the first jazz he ever heard came floating across the water from one of these boats as they approached the levee of some Southern port of call. The accessibility of Europe was also a factor at a surprisingly early point in the music's history.

In 1919 the Southern Syncopated Orchestra, with Sidney Bechet as its star performer, played in London, there attracting the notice of a Swiss conductor, Ernest Ansermet, who was the first distinguished figure of formal music to react favourably to jazz and to discern in it uniquely vital qualities.

The main force pushing the New Orleans musician north was his need to find employment, and perhaps the most significant sequence of events after the closing of Storyville was that involving Joe 'King' Oliver. Early in 1918 Oliver, acknowledged trumpet champion of New Orleans, migrated north to Chicago. By 1920 he had become a popular bandleader there, and two years later, wanting to increase the size of his band, he sent to New Orleans for the most brilliant of his disciples and, indeed, of all the jazz musicians who came out of the city, Louis Daniel Armstrong. From this point on, jazz evolved from a local musical dialect into an international language, proliferating in geographical range and in stylistic variation to a degree that astonished those of the New Orleans founding fathers who lived long enough to watch the process for themselves.

The Louis Armstrong style

Armstrong may partly stand as a representative symbol of the history of the music itself. A trumpeter of freakish gifts, he performed at least three feats – two aesthetic, one sociological – for which he will be remembered as the most influential jazz musician of all time. He took the classic style of his native city and split it at the seams through his limitless ability as an imaginative soloist. The moment his style began to mature, the convention of ensemble playing was outmoded, and he established the primacy of the improvising soloist. Then, having liberated the player from an exclusively team performance, he unwittingly codified the vocabulary of the soloist in a series of famous recordings between 1925 and 1928.

These recordings, featuring his groups the Hot Five and the Hot Seven, emphasize the enormous gulf between Armstrong and even the best of his contemporaries. They also show how he summarized all that had gone before and enriched the jazz tradition with a whole range of melodic effects relevant ever after.

Several of the performances of the Hot Five and Hot Seven are traditional blues, successively asserting the power of the idiom in a way not to be equalled for at least a generation, until the rise of Charlie Parker. Still more important was Armstrong's success as an evangelist for the jazz cause. By the late 1920s, quickly graduating from the strictly specialist environment of his formative years into being a Broadway and nightclub star, he was the first jazz personality to become a national and then an international figure. Many with no particular interest in jazz were utterly beguiled by his genius. His sense of comedy, his career in Hollywood, his spectacular physical appearance and mannerisms, and, above all, his extraordinary vocal style, all contributed to this process. By using his voice in the same way that other musicians used their instruments, Armstrong, usually dispensing with words and substituting for them an odd, wholly idiosyncratic language of sounds, popularized scat singing. Had he not drifted into the world of entertainment at large, jazz might never have won the widespread currency it did. Although from around 1930 to the end of his life he did not develop as a musician, he never really found himself outflanked by others, his vitality enabling him to retain a hold on his art almost to the end of his life in 1971.

In his failure to develop, Armstrong was typical of most jazz musicians, who have generally become reconciled to the style formulated at a comparatively early time of life. Although the music itself seems to evolve, individuals hardly ever do so. The recorded evidence to support this theory is there, but it is usually overlooked in the hunt for fresh effects and styles. Although Armstrong was to improve vastly in the years following his decision to join Oliver in Chicago, his classic style was already becoming permanent before he had ever left his home town.

Chicago style

Armstrong's arrival in Chicago, added to the burgeoning of the speakeasies of the Prohibition era (the illegal drinking establishment became the 1920s equivalent, so far as the jazz musician was concerned, of the Louisiana brothels of the previous decade), made that city the new centre of jazz.

By the mid-1920s it was becoming clear that young, white, imitative musicians were quickly learning the lessons taught by men such as Armstrong. One of the better derivative groups of white musicians was the New Orleans Rhythm Kings, but the real flowering of white talent began a little later, farther north, in time causing the rise of a new style of playing jazz, which was a compromise between the ensemble tradition of New Orleans and Armstrong's solo power. In Chicago style, the triumvirate of trumpet, trombone, and clarinet was retained, though the saxophone was becoming much more common by the end of the decade. Although performances usually began and ended with a rousing ensemble variation of the theme, the central part of the performance usually consisted of a string of solos.

Because the term Chicago style is neither strictly geographically accurate nor musicologically precise, its umbrella usually covers stylists of widely contrasting or even antipathetic talents. The leading player of the style was Leon Bismarck 'Bix' Beiderbecke, a self-taught cornettist and pianist whose pure tone and introspective curiosity about harmonic theory mark him as the exact opposite of Armstrong, whose intuitive style was rooted in a radically different racial background (Bix was middle class, the son of German immigrants).

Beiderbecke, whose recordings of 'I'm Coming Virginia', 'Way Down Yonder In New Orleans', and 'Singin' The Blues' have become classics of the genre, was also responsible for one of the most remarkable and apocalyptic of all jazz recordings, the piano solo of his own composition, 'In A Mist'. In this fragment are strangely fused the honky-tonk beginnings of Bix's early musical life and the subtler overtones of those modern classical composers whose recitals he attended and whose comparatively complex harmony caused him to ask the question: 'Why should the jazzman be limited to the simplest triads when his conservatory-trained fellow musician has recourse to so many more variegated effects?' Although this has remained the most vital of all the questions posed by jazz, Beiderbecke did not live long enough to see it answered. He died a young man, technically of pneumonia, actually of frustration, self-neglect, disenchantment – ailments that can destroy any creative artist whose sensibilities far outstrip his technical equipment. Beiderbecke, the first patron saint of jazz, has remained the archetypal figure of the playing fool, the instinctive creator who operated against the frenetic background of illicit stills and gang warfare.

Racial segregation was long the rule in the recording studios, so posterity has tended to have a false view of the mingling of musicians in the 1920s. These players were by no means unaware of each other, as a glance at the recording catalogues of the period might suggest. Armstrong and Beiderbecke, for instance, admired each other's playing. The traffic in ideas was generally one-way, from black to white, but the white musician was occasionally something more than a plagiarist. One of these was the Texan trombonist Jack Teagarden, a musician of remarkable fluency and assurance even at the start of his career in the middle 1920s. After being associated largely with the Chicago-style groups of his first years in the North, Teagarden often worked with Armstrong, to whose All-Stars he belonged during 1947–51. Like Armstrong, he used his voice as a useful second instrument, and, like Armstrong, he retained his creative ability throughout his life. In retrospect, the recordings he made with the young white musicians of the late 1920s and early 1930s show an amazing poise and maturity. The other white Chicagoan who affected the course of jazz history was the clarinettist Benny Goodman. Born in Chicago, he was a child prodigy, a master of Chicago idiom while still in his teens, and destined to lead jazz into new areas.

Strictly speaking, Goodman's clarinet style was hardly original, consisting as it did of a brilliantly executed synthesis of all that had gone before, with particular reference to the limpid fluency of the New Orleans player Jimmie Noone; but Goodman brought to the playing of jazz a technical expertise, an academic intelligence, a speed of thought not heard before. In time his classically based style became ossified, and Goodman himself came to turn more and more frequently to playing Brahms and Mozart; but he remained the most prolific, technically accomplished, and melodically resourceful of the white musicians generally designated as the Chicagoans, though he was later dismissed by some as a peripheral rather than a central figure in jazz history.

Later Developments

The Emergence of the Virtuoso

Throughout the 1920s, techniques were steadily becoming more efficient, thinking more sophisticated, harmonic exploration gradually more daring, so that many styles that were to flower during the soloist's golden age of the 1930s were already being shaped.

One of the most gifted of all the musicians in jazz history, Coleman Hawkins, a tenor saxophonist, virtually single-handedly raised the status of that instrument. His work was characterized by a deep, passionate tone, which may be taken as the working definition of 'hot' music, by sequences of ingeniously related arpeggios and, above all, by an indefinable sense of form that enabled him to transmute successions of fragmentary phrases into a corporate whole. This sense of form, unteachable but unmistakable when encountered, had already distinguished the truly gifted improviser from the merely talented, and Hawkins, particularly in slower ballads, possessed this gift to a remarkable degree. His outstanding recordings are scattered over five decades. Especially noteworthy are his version of 'One Hour', made in 1929, one of the very first recordings by a racially mixed group and one of the very first on which the tenor saxophone in jazz approaches maturity; his famous recording of 'Body And Soul' in 1939, a performance so finely constructed that it has long since come to acquire the standing of formal composition; and some sides he made with a cosmopolitan band in Paris in 1937, of which 'Out Of Nowhere' was a remarkable exposition of the art of romantic extemporization. From 1934 to 1939 Hawkins travelled in Europe, inspiring European musicians to attain fluency in what was at that time an essentially alien art.

THE DEVELOPMENT OF JAZZ PIANO

There have been deviations of style and approach on all instruments throughout jazz history, giving rise to rival 'schools' the differing precepts of which were sometimes the centre of bitter debate, but the case of the piano in jazz is unique in the way that two antipathetic styles emerged and, at least for a time, developed concurrently but independently. These two approaches, embodying contrasting philosophies, were Stride and Trumpet-style piano playing. The Stride style, whose roots in the early jazz past are obvious enough, is based on the premise that any instrument that makes it possible for the performer to play two or more notes simultaneously and therefore to create a harmonic as well as melodic effect ought to deploy those possibilities as far as is practicable. At their best, the Stride pianists have produced work teeming with an orchestral richness, yet they have rarely been the kind of players to produce a single melodic line that might conceivably be transposed to a different instrument. The best Stride exponents, pounding out ten-note chords, stressing the rhythmic pulse with great muscularity in the left hand, have been men whose music is full of harmonic possibilities and enchanting rhythmic variation.

Probably the most important Stride pianist was James P. Johnson, one of the most resourceful figures in jazz history and a rare personality among the pioneers in that his musical accomplishments enabled him to compose and orchestrate at a period when such abilities were rare. Apart from his purely jazz activities, Johnson wrote some early film music, a tone poem, and a ballet; he also enjoyed great success as a songwriter, producing the 'One Hour' that Hawkins (and also Louis Armstrong) recorded so finely and 'Runnin' Wild'.

Johnson presided over what came to be known as the Harlem group of pianists, whose Stride playing in the 1920s made them virtually one-man jazz bands. Johnson's great friend and rival was Willie 'The Lion' Smith, and their two unofficial pupils were Thomas 'Fats' Waller and Edward Kennedy 'Duke' Ellington. In both cases, the Stride style underwent the most astonishing changes. Waller is perhaps the only example in all jazz of the pupil outstripping his masters. Apart from the irresistible strength and wit of his piano playing and his gifts as a composer ('Honeysuckle Rose', 'Ain't Misbehavin'', 'Blue Turning Grey Over You', and literally hundreds of others), Waller, like Armstrong, was a natural buffoon and stage extrovert, capitalizing on these gifts to become a popular as well as a jazz figure. Ellington's subsequent career was even more remarkable, and both he and Waller acknowledged their stylistic debt to Johnson and Smith. Ironically, although the Stride school avoided the dogmatic melodic statement in favour of the implied harmonic one, at least three of its greatest practitioners – Johnson, Waller, and Ellington – were also successful songwriters.

Events eventually overtook the Stride school, and its eclipse may be dated from the moment in the late 1920s when Earl Hines, yet another outstanding jazz pianist, who augmented his income by working as a songwriter, saw that, in addition to stating the harmony in the left hand, the pianist might well emulate the single-note instruments, such as the trumpet, in creating with the right hand linear improvisation producing melodic single-note variations on the melody. Probably the two great influences on Hines that helped crystallize his style were the pianist Teddy Weatherford, to whom Hines acknowledged a debt of inspiration, and Louis Armstrong, with whom Hines worked during the Hot Five and Hot Seven period. Armstrong's apparently limitless powers of invention must have shown Hines how the same kind of melodic aphorisms could be produced by a pianist.

Hines, a pianist of amazing technical command and tireless energy, had a profound influence on the development of jazz piano. His findings eventually led to the eclipse of the Stride style, especially when in the early 1940s the new modernism preferred the pianist with the ability to create right-hand, single-note lines. In the 1930s the most accomplished follower of Hines was Teddy Wilson, after which time the work of pioneer modernists such as Bud Powell and, later, the Canadian Oscar Peterson showed at least to some degree a corroboration of Hines's methods.

Art Tatum, one of the greatest and most controversial of jazz musicians and pianists, had a style too personal to be categorized. For him, Stride and Trumpet-style were not so much approaches to piano playing as incidents in the course of a single casual chorus, just two of many effects that Tatum had at his fingertips. Almost totally blind, Tatum developed a technique as unorthodox as it was infallible, so that he became the despair of his fellow musicians. Because of the rococo flourish of his style, Tatum was hardly ever able to integrate his piano playing into the texture of a group and was therefore almost always heard either at the head of a trio or as a solo pianist. Although he began about the time Hines was formulating the principles of Trumpet-style piano and lived on to know the violent disputes of the post-war modernist movement and after, Tatum remained a constant. Towards the end of his life, his playing became, if anything, more florid than ever, but it hardly evolved at all, so complete and subjective was his music. Because of the technical problems presented by Tatum's all-embracing style, he has had virtually no imitators, with the notable exception of Peterson, whose work grew increasingly closer to Tatum's in spirit as the years went by.

THE ERA OF THE BIG BANDS AND SWING

In the first years of its history, jazz was confined almost exclusively to small-group collective improvisation, and such a conception as orchestral effect was a refinement that, for obvious reasons in a world populated by musicians illiterate at least in the conventional sense, had to come later. The first musician to make a serious attempt to organize a group of players who might keep, at least in part, to a plan was Ferdinand 'Jelly Roll' Morton.

Although his career has been more heavily documented and annotated than that of any other jazz musician, his recorded legacy was not large enough to decide whether he was a pioneer or a charlatan. Certainly, his announcement that he 'invented jazz in 1902' did nothing to help.

The first indisputable figure in the evolution of orchestral jazz was Fletcher Henderson, an unremarkable pianist whose contribution to jazz lies in his pioneering of methods later universally adopted. Henderson, far better educated than most Negro musicians of his day, formed his own orchestra in 1923, and it became the first to gain wide fame by playing jazz. For several years after, his band employed the best Negro jazz talents, among them, at various times, Louis Armstrong (this was the last time in his life Armstrong was ever hired by a bandleader) and Coleman Hawkins. Despite an embarrassment of riches in the solo department, the Henderson band is unique for the way in which its leader experimented with orchestral effects. According to many purists, orchestral jazz is a contradiction in terms, for, if it is true that jazz is improvised music, then it follows that a jazz orchestra cannot exist. Henderson was among the first to see that it is not necessarily improvisation that lends jazz its fierce vitality but the preservation of its spirit. If musicians could play written parts with the same sense of self-discovery as a solo, then the effects need not be anticlimactic, and their solo talents could shape an ensemble into the contours of a jazz performance.

Henderson also contributed the concept of sections of instruments, comprising three or four voices, playing responses to the solo voice in harmony. The soloist, used to the accompanying figures provided for him, could often space his own improvisation, shape it, and adjust its dynamics to this scored accompaniment. Henderson's harmonic vocabulary and orchestral technique, profound in the jazz context of their period, were naive in the broader musical sense, and, by an irony of fortune, his most revolutionary success happened in the end to somebody else.

Many other bands of merit more or less followed Henderson's example, notably Chick Webb's band from 1926, Jimmie Lunceford's from 1927, and Bennie Moten, whose move from Kansas City eastward in 1926 coincided with the increase in the size of his group. Although none of these orchestras won the national and, in a few cases, the international fame that attended the touring orchestras of the 1930s, they were at least as good, if not much better, than their more exalted contemporaries. One of the main barriers to their being heard on a truly national scale was their colour.

As bands such as Henderson's, Webb's, and Lunceford's moved into the 1930s, the growing complexity of their harmony and technique combined with a more general process of advancing musical curiosity to produce a golden age of solo virtuosity. Some of the virtuosos remained in an orchestral setting, others were in the proliferating small-groups. One of the greatest of these soloists was the tenor saxophonist Lester Young, who was associated for many years with one of the finest of all jazz orchestras, the Kansas City-based Count Basie band, which had evolved from Bennie Moten's group after the leader's death. Basie, a Stride pianist, amended his style from a flow of harmony to a great plain of silence dotted with exquisite melodic epigrams neatly executed and gathered together a large orchestra that preserved the buoyancy of an improvised act by literally improvising. Many of his most effective orchestrations, such as 'One O'Clock Jump', were, in effect, not orchestrations at all but 'head arrangements' – that is to say, fragments of improvised music put together by the musicians in a process of trial and error, conned by rote, then gradually becoming a predictable performance. The Basie band, stressing four beats to a bar and retaining, long after others had abandoned it, the four-man rhythm section of piano, double bass, drums and guitar, set unsurpassed standards of vigour and precision, and in this setting Young, a remarkable soloist, thrived.

Young's contribution to the solo art was twofold. First, he displayed and popularized a peculiar sensibility that paved the way for the modernists of the following generation. Young is often credited with being the first modernist, but, strictly speaking, he was a man of his era who did nothing to corrupt the harmonic innocence of his day. His tone, revolutionary in the 1930s in the way it distilled the hot breath of Hawkins's romanticism into something far more sinuous and oblique, set the style for saxophonists for a generation to come. In this way he contributed an alternative approach to the instrument: ever after, an apprentice could follow either Young or Hawkins, but not both. Jazz saxophone playing was thus immeasurably enriched. His other achievement was to demonstrate a new way of building an improvised solo, by using little-used chords, such as the Minor sixth, by showing how silence could help a solo, by breaking down an arpeggio so that unusual intervals could express conventional harmonies, and by perfecting an ingenious series of false fingerings so that the player could produce different densities of sound on the same note. While the modernists of a later age added to the jazz language by their increased harmonic scope, Young created a new vocabulary for the soloist within the conventional apparatus.

Many imponderables contributed to the astonishing upsurge of popularity of the big bands in the 1930s. The end of Prohibition in 1933 was a large factor; it altered the social habits of a nation and deprived jazz musicians of their biggest potential source of employment. By 1934 jazz had to find a new audience, and by a happy coincidence it reached a stage of sophistication that made the capture of a new audience possible. Benny Goodman formed his first organized orchestra in 1934, and, after an unsuccessful beginning touring the nation's dance halls, stumbled on the truth that others were soon quick to discover: that a new generation of young people was ready to patronize jazz-oriented dance bands. Jazz, though admittedly in a somewhat bowdlerized form, took to the ballrooms of the day.

In 1935 at the Palomar Ballroom in Hollywood, Goodman found all the factors of the Swing Age: massed audiences, fans clustered around the bandstand, enthusiasm for individual musicians, pressures changing bandleaders into brand names. Soon, Goodman was the 'King of Swing', a Hollywood film star, a millionaire, an international celebrity. Naturally, others followed, among them a rival clarinettist, Artie Shaw, also Tommy and Jimmy Dorsey. Goodman ensured his success by recruiting the semi-retired Fletcher Henderson as chief arranger and by incorporating within his large group a smaller one (at first, a trio, later, a quartet), comprising the first racially mixed group ever to tour nationally in the United States – Goodman and drummer Gene Krupa being white, pianist Teddy Wilson and vibraphonist Lionel Hampton being Negroes.

The Swing Age culminated in Goodman's 1938 concert at Carnegie Hall. Then, with orchestras hit by the wartime draft and running costs rising all the time, it petered out, losing its jazz connotations. By 1941, with the hysterical career of Glenn Miller, it ran into the quicksands of commercialism. Perhaps the jazz purist would commend Goodman's career as a bandleader for discovering a hitherto obscure Midwestern guitarist, Charlie Christian, the first guitar virtuoso to use electrically amplified equipment, although others had pioneered this method. He was one of the few stars of the Swing Era psychologically and musically equipped to make the leap into the Modernist era of the 1940s; his early death ended a brilliant career.

Until this time, jazz had been more or less diatonic (adhering to the natural scale), restricting itself, for the most part, to cycles of resolving dominant seventh chords. The modernist movement of the 1940s thrust it forward into unexplored realms of chromaticism (use of harmonies built on notes not in the key of the piece), which split players and devotees into for-or-against armies and caused the advanced spirits to forgo the allegiance of mass audiences, which was never recovered.

Modernism

The origins of the Modernism of the 1940s, or 'Bebop', as it was then onomatopoetically known, are confused. One of its leaders, John Birks 'Dizzy' Gillespie, said it was a device to shake off white plagiarists, but its most gifted practitioner, Charlie Parker (known to many as Bird), explained it in strictly technical terms. By evolving a system of substituted chords superimposed on the original ones and by playing in double the time of the tempo being asserted by the rhythm section, Parker, an alto saxophonist of extraordinary gifts, changed the face of jazz. His early death was symbolic of the tragic involvement of many jazz musicians of his generation with drug addiction. Although technically he made jazz more complex, emotionally he cleansed it, and his famous blues recordings looked back to Armstrong's achievements with the Hot Five, in spirit, if not in method. Parker could not have realized it, but he was making, on behalf of jazz, the last great appropriation of musical territory. To use an American pioneer analogy, after jazz had moved harmonically westward for a half a century, Parker took it to the sea. This caused heart-searching among those who inherited Parker's findings. Among his disciples was the trumpeter Miles Davis, who in 1956 made the first coherent attempt to escape from the cage of 'discord to resolution', a method so persistently explored that the men of Davis's generation felt its usefulness to be ended. In an album called *Kind of Blue*, Davis substituted modal (scales not based on the Major and Minor) patterns for the more conventional harmonic ones, the first step in a process that was to characterize jazz thereafter. The theories of men such as Davis seemed to be negatively proved by the tenor saxophonists John Coltrane and Sonny Rollins, for, in the playing of both these men, the number of harmonic changes being crammed into each theme was so big that the music was in danger of being choked to death. One possible solution came from the alto saxophonist Ornette Coleman, who abandoned all rules of discord and resolution, time signatures, and keys, in his formulation of 'Free Form', which in effect was no form at all. That jazz was not yet reduced to such extremes was suggested by a few of Ornette Coleman's contemporaries, who continued to raise the technical and inventive standards of jazz. These included the pianist Oscar Peterson, the drummer Buddy Rich, the tenor saxophonist Stan Getz, and the guitarist Wes Montgomery, all of whom attained high standards of performance.

Much avant garde jazz of the 1960s was committed art, in the sense that its creators insisted vigorously on their music as an artistic expression of racial protest, but all that their polemic suggested was that, in accusing society of anarchic tendencies, they had induced those tendencies in their own music and that art committed to a good cause is not necessarily good art.

Throughout its history jazz has been abstract, in the sense that, subconsciously informed though it may be by race memory, it has been guided less by concrete or living factors than by the mathematical precision of the march from discord to resolution, the soloist being like a man working out an algebraic equation. For this reason Duke Ellington is unique, in that he has moved towards that ideal where authentic jazz performances may reflect the nuances of personality of some outside object or person. Ellington has thus attempted to make his music measure up to a constant dual standard, for not only has he meant it to be fine jazz but also intelligible programme music.

Nothing comparable has been attempted in jazz by anyone

else, although the work of 'progressive' jazz musicians such as Thelonius Monk and the Modern Jazz Quartet in the 1950s and 1960s hinted at extramusical connotations through the relentless Europeanization of its theme titles; and the Dave Brubeck Quartet made occasional gestures of a similar nature. Ellington has attempted to make his jazz mirror the people and places that led him to the extreme sophistication of his old age. After his graduation from the Harlem group of pianists and his recruitment of a quintet, the Washingtonians, he moved steadily forward to orchestral mastery, increasing the size of his group as his palette became broader. In 1939 he recruited an orchestral assistant, Billy Strayhorn, but by this time he was already far along the road to a technique enabling him to embrace a far wider range of sound than jazz musicians normally aspire to.

By using his orchestra as an instrument on which to perform his feats of orchestrating brilliance and by assimilating the talents of each individual member of that organization as a saxophonist might acquaint himself with the workings of every key on his instrument, Ellington welded together a group inimitable by any standards. The rich impressionism of his early works, in the late 1920s, slowly evolved into the thumbnail sketches of the 1930s. In 1943 came *Black, Brown and Beige*, a musical history of the Negro in the United States, after which Ellington scarcely stopped pouring out fresh works – some whole, some mere fragments, all of them informed by the romanticism of his view of the world.

Among his most remarkable achievements are many popular songs, such as 'Sophisticated Lady' and 'Mood Indigo', whose instrumental structure has not prevented them from becoming world famous. Of his more ambitious projects, he has composed *Perfume Suite*, the soundtrack for the film *Anatomy of a Murder*, jazz versions of Tchaikovsky's *The Nutcracker* and Grieg's *Peer Gynt*, *Liberian Suite*, *The Far East Suite*, and, possibly his masterpiece, *Such Sweet Thunder* (1957), a series of twelve Shakespearean vignettes that demonstrate Ellington's working method. By settling on the stylistic idiosyncrasies of each soloist, Ellington attempts, in this work, to express his own idea of a dramatic character; thus, the elegiac fervour of his greatest soloist, the saxophonist Johnny Hodges, became the voice of Cleopatra, the stratospheric range of trumpeter William 'Cat' Anderson the dementia of

Hamlet, the cold academic hauteur of clarinettist Jimmy Hamilton's tone the patrician disdain of Caesar.

VOCAL JAZZ

Although the essence of jazz is instrumental, one or two artists have shown that the human voice can express the spirit of the music. Apart from instrumentalists such as Armstrong and Teagarden, whose singing was an adjunct to instrumental expression, there have been two main groups of jazz singers, one rooted firmly in the folk-oriented communal past of the Southern US Negro, the other committed to the world of commercial music and the fringes of show business.

The male blues singers of the South, often men who earned their livelihood at some menial task, sang of life close to the bone, in terms whose graphic candour reflected the earthiness of the life they had known. Outstanding were Huddie Ledbetter, Big Bill Broonzy, Blind Lemon Jefferson, Sleepy John Estes and Peetie Wheatstraw. Their female counterparts, much more closely linked to the professional world of vaudeville and cabaret, include Gertrude 'Ma' Rainey, her young protégé Bessie Smith, Mamie Smith, and Bertha 'Chippie' Hill. By far the greatest was Bessie Smith, whose vast recorded output has preserved a style outstanding for its integrity, honesty to life, and immense technical skill. Less traditional male singers have included Count Basie's robust blues shouter James Rushing and Joe Turner, whose 1938 recordings with pianist Pete Johnson coincided with Johnson's short-lived but freakishly popular boogie-woogie piano style, a variation of blues playing whose hypnotic reiterated rhythmic patterns won a world following and whose other notable exponents included Albert Ammons and Meade 'Lux' Lewis. The most important female singers of this later period include Mildred Bailey, Ella Fitzgerald and Sarah Vaughan, but by far the finest singer of modern times and, with the possible exception of Bessie Smith, the most gifted vocalist of either sex that jazz has so far produced is Billie Holiday. Whereas Bessie Smith was incomparable as an interpreter of the poetry of the Blues, Billie Holiday achieved the same intensity with the far less substantial repertory of Tin Pan Alley. Many of her small-group recordings from 1935 to 1942, prized classics of the art of impromptu composition, reflect in musical terms the close personal relationship between the singer and saxophonist Lester Young. An interesting departure of the 1950s was tried by the Dave Lambert–Jon Hendricks–Annie Ross Trio, which sang lyrics composed to transcribed instrumental jazz solos.

Jazz as a Social Force

The question of the extent to which jazz reflects the society that has nurtured it has seldom been asked. The 1960s saw a belated acknowledgment of its powerful ability to evoke the urban ambience. Duke Ellington's music for *Anatomy of a Murder* (1959) was the first movie score ever composed by a jazz writer. Since then, the jazz language has overrun all spheres of popular musical expression. One of the most intriguing things about its career has been the way in which advancing technique has run concurrently with social improvement, so that, while the crude emergent music of early New Orleans was brothel music and its more polished descendant in the 1920s the music of the ginmill, the suave orchestral felicities of the Swing Age became the wholly respectable background music for the innocent romances of its college audiences. Finally, with the advance to chromaticism, jazz invaded the concert hall and installed itself at festivals all over the world.

For the most part, jazz has remained the province of the urban US Negro, who has contributed almost every viable new idea that has helped jazz along its path to literacy and self-confidence. Although there have been astonishing advances by European musicians in the past thirty years, there remains only one non-US figure in the entire history of jazz who had something original and also valid to contribute. This was the Basque guitarist Django Reinhardt, whose best work was achieved in the 1930s, before he succumbed to the blandishments of amplification.

The source of the musician's repertory has also changed radically over the years. While the Blues has retained its primacy throughout jazz history, the players of the Swing Era, harmonically cultured, turned to the urbanities of the best musical comedy writers, so that names such as George Gershwin and Jerome Kern occur repeatedly on recordings of all kinds. Indeed, Gershwin, with 'I Got Rhythm', created a harmonic pattern whose popularity with improvisers stands second only to the Blues. In recent years, however, there has been a tendency among the younger, more revolutionary players to write their own material, which has made it more difficult than ever for the onlooker to distinguish genuine inventiveness from mere charlatanism.

Jazz, in watered-down form, has strongly influenced various other kinds of music, many of them commercially more viable, such as 'pop' songs, rock 'n' roll, skiffle, Rhythm & Blues, Broadway musicals. Some critics include these in the history of jazz; others consider that anything other than original Dixieland, which had a revival in the 1950s and 1960s, cannot be considered as pure jazz. Another form, Afro-Cuban music, which has some affinities with jazz, in fact had different ethnic roots, but some jazz musicians, such as Gillespie, incorporated its rhythms in their music making.

By and large, attempts to wed jazz with more formal methods of music making and composition have not been successful, although attempts to create a 'third stream', involving musician-composers such as William Russo and Gunther Schuller, have not been without virtues to commend them. The oddest work in this direction remains Igor Stravinsky's *Ebony Concerto*, composed in 1945 for Woody Herman's Orchestra. Although not in the specialist sense a jazz composition, it underlined the inherent contradictions in a marriage between the two forms of music. There appears to be a distinct possibility that jazz, faced at last with the challenge that its room to expand is finite, may eventually be merged into the world of music at large, to become an orchestral effect in a more general context. On the other hand, the tradition as represented by such artists as Armstrong, Ellington, Hawkins, Young, Tatum, Parker and Holiday seems almost too fiery ever to be extinguished altogether.

ACKNOWLEDGEMENTS

I would like to thank Benny's agent John Pawsey; my agent, Lizzy Kremer at Ed Victor Ltd.; Elvis Costello; Rochelle Venables, Martin Fletcher, Ben Ball and Tim Binding at Simon & Schuster; and my wife Maja Löfdahl.

The source material was collected and filed by Leo and Natasha Green. It was magnificent to behold the cataloguer's art at first hand, and I can only say how glad I am that I avoided most of the work. They passed carloads of crates and files to me. After endless filtration and reduction with scissors and tape, I asked two tenor saxophonists, Leo Green and Ray Gelato, to check the manuscript for errors. At this point, the professionals at Simon & Schuster took over. They turned a pile of clippings and Sellotape into a book. Enormous care went into this process, so any mistakes must be mine.

Apart from cataloguing the material and reading the manuscript, Leo Green devoted many hours to digging out interesting items from the files. He also checked facts for me with complete disregard for his physical safety. Leo has a floor-to-ceiling reference library. Whenever I rang with a query, I would hang onto the phone in suspense as I listened to him climbing up the shelves. I would hear a cry of 'Found it!', followed by the sound of man and encyclopaedia crashing back to earth. He would then crawl to the receiver and gasp the required date. If it were possible to dedicate a collection of somebody else's work, I would dedicate this book to Leo. As it isn't, I have bought him a stepladder instead.

INDEX

Permissions

Part I: 'Drums in My Ears' © *Observer* (1973); 'Louis Armstrong' © *Observer* (1963); *Dizzy Gillespie's Big 4* first printed by Pablo Records, 1975; 'Errol Garner' © *Observer* (1967); 'George Lewis' © *Observer* (1959); 'Oscar Peterson: *Night Train*' first printed by Verve Records, 1962; 'Thelonious Monk' © *Observer* (1969); 'Jazz Goes To College' first appeared as 'Bubbles' © *Observer* (1973); Dave Brubeck © *Observer* (1964); 'The MJQ' © *Observer* (1963); 'Duke Ellington: *Such Sweet Thunder*' © *Observer* (1967); 'Cult and Culture' © *Observer* (1973); 'Fletcher Henderson' © *Observer* (1964); 'Zoot Sims . . . *and the Gershwin Brothers*' first printed by Pablo Records, 1975; 'The Singer not the Song' © *Observer* (1973); 'Anita O'Day' © *Observer* (1960); 'Tony Bennett' extracted from Harold Davison concert programme, 1969; 'Avant Garde' © *Observer* (1973); 'Miles Davis' © *Observer* (1961); 'John Coltrane: *Afro-Blues Impressions*' first printed by Pablo Records, 1977; 'Joe Turner and the Blues' first printed by Pablo Records, 1975; 'Oscar Peterson and Joe Pass: *Live à Salle Pleyel*' first printed by Pablo Records, 1975; 'Last Rites' © *Observer* (1973); 'Pee Wee Russell' © *Observer* (1968); 'The Club Eleven Reunion' first printed in the *Radio Times* (1986); 'Coleman Hawkins' © *Observer* (1969); 'Is There Jazz After Death?' © *Observer* (1969); 'Father Figures' © *Observer* (1973); 'The Duke' first appeared as 'Duke Ellington' and 'Duke at Seventy' © *Observer* (1967, 1969); 'Louis Armstrong' first appeared as 'Louis at Seventy' © *Observer* (1970)

Part II: All material originally published in *London: Jazz Decade* by Benny Green, (King's Road Publishing, London, 1969)